Asia Inside Out: Itinerant People

ASIA INSIDE OUT

ITINERANT PEOPLE

Edited by

ERIC TAGLIACOZZO

HELEN F. SIU

PETER C. PERDUE

Harvard University Press

Cambridge, Massachusetts
London, England
2019

Printed in the United States of America

First printing

Library of Congress Cataloging-in-Publication Data

Names: Tagliacozzo, Eric, editor. | Siu, Helen F., editor. | Perdue, Peter C., 1949– editor.
Title: Asia inside out : Itinerant people / edited by Eric Tagliacozzo, Helen F. Siu, Peter C. Perdue.
Other titles: Itinerant people
Description: Cambridge, Massachusetts : Harvard University Press, 2019. | This book is volume 3 of a 3 volume set which began with Asia inside out : Changing times, and continued with Asia inside out : Connected places. | Includes index.
Identifiers: LCCN 2018039154 | ISBN 9780674987630 (alk. paper)
Subjects: LCSH: Asians—Migrations. | Human geography—Asia. | Transnationalism.
Classification: LCC JV8490 .A84 2019 | DDC 304.8095—dc23
LC record available at https://lccn.loc.gov/2018039154

Contents

Asia Inside Out: Itinerant People

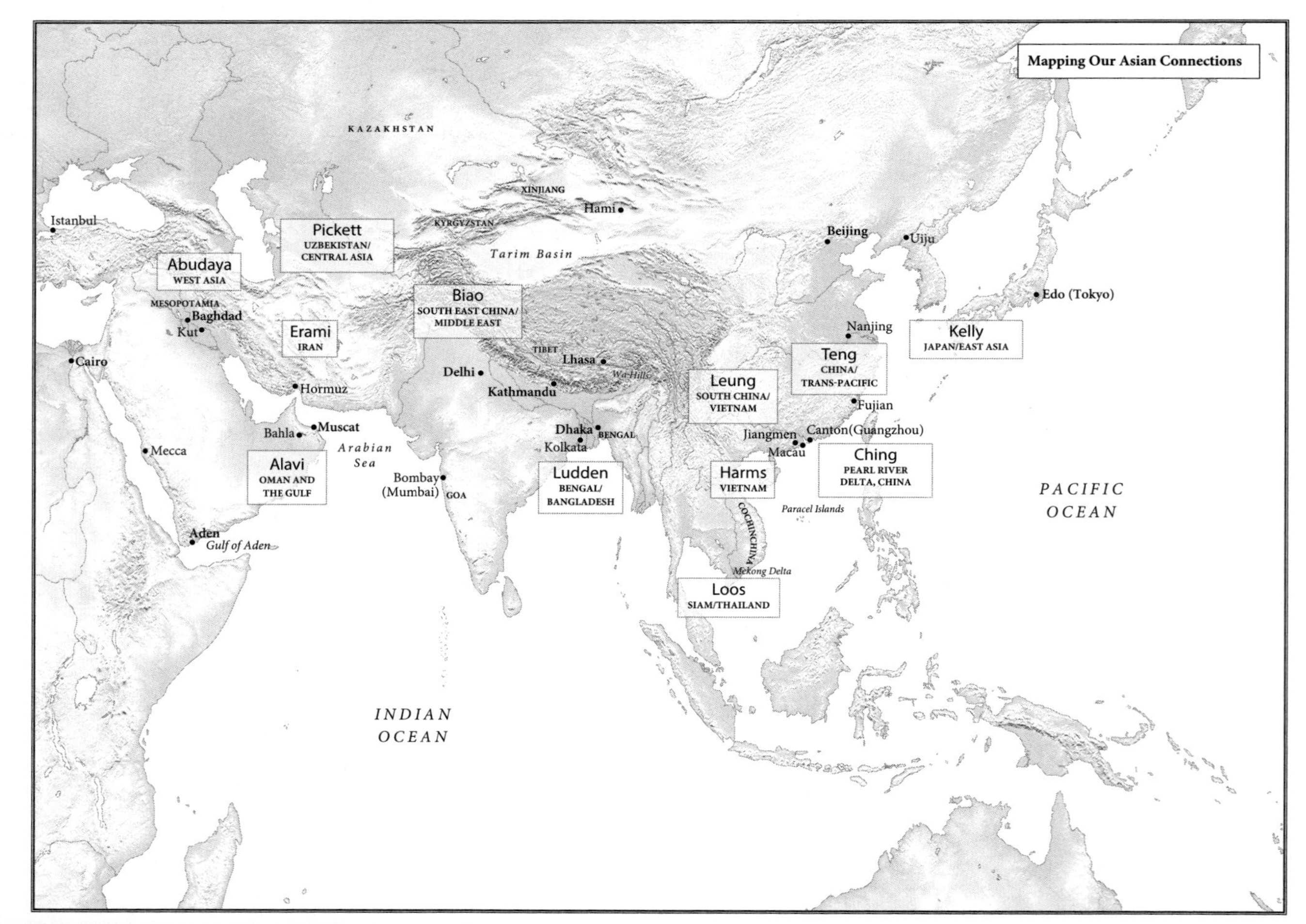
Mapping Our Asian Connections
KAZAKHSTAN
XINJIANG
Hami
KYRGYZSTAN
Tarim Basin
Istanbul
Pickett
UZBEKISTAN/
CENTRAL ASIA
Abudaya
WEST ASIA
MESOPOTAMIA
Baghdad
Kut
Biao
SOUTH EAST CHINA/
MIDDLE EAST
Erami
IRAN
Beijing
Uiju
Edo (Tokyo)
Nanjing
Kelly
JAPAN/EAST ASIA
Teng
CHINA/
TRANS-PACIFIC
Cairo
TIBET
Lhasa
Delhi
Kathmandu
Wa Hills
Hormuz
Leung
SOUTH CHINA/
VIETNAM
Fujian
Muscat
Bahla
Mecca
Arabian
Sea
Dhaka
BENGAL
Kolkata
Jiangmen
Canton(Guangzhou)
Macau
Alavi
OMAN AND
THE GULF
Bombay
(Mumbai)
GOA
Ludden
BENGAL/
BANGLADESH
Harms
VIETNAM
Ching
PEARL RIVER
DELTA, CHINA
PACIFIC
OCEAN
Paracel Islands
COCHINCHINA
Aden
Gulf of Aden
Mekong Delta
Loos
SIAM/THAILAND
INDIAN
OCEAN

Introduction

Seekers, Sojourners, and Meaningful Worlds in Motion

ERIC TAGLIACOZZO, HELEN F. SIU, and PETER C. PERDUE

In this third and final volume of *Asia Inside Out,* we continue the project of redefining Asian spaces by following people, objects, and processes that crossed national and cultural boundaries. The focus on humans and the objects they carried complements the central theme of time in the first volume and space in the second volume. By adding this dynamic component to the analysis we once again combine historical and ethnographic analysis to explore the multiple pathways that constructed contemporary Asia.

In *Asia Inside Out: Changing Times* (Tagliacozzo, Siu and Perdue 2015a), the notion of time was disassembled (and then reassembled) to show how Asia has come about in strange and unexpected ways. Instead of sticking to the usual "watershed" dates of Asian history that many of us know—1511 and the arrival of Europeans in Southeast Asia; 1644 and the end of the Ming Empire; 1868 and the Meiji Restoration in Japan, and so on—our assembled authors found new junctures and disjunctures where the notion of "Asia" was transformed via critical, connective processes. The purpose was to show that Asia does not have a fixed essence; instead, it is continually constructed over time. The moments chosen explore normative, linear narratives of development and unveil processes pregnant with agentive possibilities that have helped the region congeal into a web of interactions (Siu 2016, 2014). The temporal dimension has been important in this, because we see Asia as a diachronic reality. The Eurasian steppe, for example, fades in and out of "Asian" history; so too does the east coast of Africa, which has long been a part of the wider maritime orbit of Asia but for certain centuries does not figure at all (Siu and McGovern 2017). Oceania, the Philippines, and even Pacific Russia also fall into these categories (see Perdue 2005; Tagliacozzo 2005). What these spaces have in common is a temporal "phasing" into and out of a "shapeless" Asia, a kind of accordion-like flexibility that allows these landscapes to engage in the formation of Asia at some moments and not at others.[1]

Asia Inside Out: Connected Places (Tagliaozzo, Siu and Perdue 2015b) pushed these processual considerations further by focusing on "place" rather than "period" as our raison d'etre. It examined the questions What is Asia? and How is "place" made? What factors contribute to its construction, if place is (indeed) not a static category of geography but rather a fluid, dynamic process with embedded social relationships and contested meanings? The contributors came up with some novel considerations to help develop this paradigm. Perhaps the idea to highlight is that interconnectedness, in fact, *makes* place—Hong Kong might be a physical entity, but its radials of migration, trade, and cultural flows to the rich farmland of the Pearl River delta in Guangdong, to the Dan fisher-folk who moor along its coasts, to the Chinese seaboard where it forms a connective hub in shipping, and to the wider world of Asian and global commerce all constitute parts of its evolving reality. This would be the case for a number of other cities explored in the volume, and even many non-urban spaces, such as stretches of coast, rivers, and floodplains where settlements eventually "happen." Seen through this lens, "place" is a complex and multilayered process, not an indicator of physical fixity.[2] The authors revealed not only a diachronic process in the making of Asia but also a physical process, whereby stretches of land and sea were gradually brought into what we now define as "Asia," and were incorporated into these realities across three-dimensional geographical "scapes."[3] The three-way interactions among transformation of physical infrastructure, mobility of humans, objects, ideas, and capital, and efforts to fix processes in place run through all three of these volumes.

The motivating theme of this volume is "people"—those human beings in motion whose transit "made" and "makes" Asia. People are not just the third leg of this triad but also the subjects who enable both time and space to work on the concept of "Asia" in meaningful ways. How did these human actors tie these threads together, in both historical and contemporary times? First of all, we find clues in the transient histories of "people on the move," through voluntary or involuntary circulation, either part of chosen paths (such as migration) or the radials of coerced journeys (such as slavery or the dislocations wrought by conflict). But in every case the fluidity of human movement acted to render the evolution of "Asia" more complex, both by reinforcing older connections across time and space and by forging new connections. This volume highlights human agency and the multifaceted connections that disrupt geographically conceived continental divides such as East Asia, Southeast Asia, South Asia, and beyond. We switch our gaze from state-centered units to oceans, littoral regions, oasis towns, and caravan routes. We stress mobilities across vast land-sea divides and suggest that objects that appear out of spatial and temporal contexts are in fact organically connected to their material / historical environments. Perceptions of their "displacement" often come from static, bounded conceptual categories. We therefore need to be acutely aware of our analytical blinders (Amrith 2016).

In sum, what we see in all three of these volumes is the continual process of "becoming," both for Asia as a unit and for the people who call the world's largest continent their home.[4] This is a humanistic project, focusing on how human beings created the times and places that surrounded them, but we also pay attention to both objects, such as shells, carpets, texts, and medical herbs, that accompanied our travelers and the cultural practices and knowledge (food, language, music, and religious rituals) that they circulated and reshaped as they moved through Asia. There can have been no more important process than the unfolding of these patterns. What we see are agentive energies of mobile generations that have left footprints in a variegated landscape and presented voices in a nonlinear historical narrative full of contingencies and surprises. We hope that teamwork in these volumes has been able to present the empirical substance and conceptual tools to appreciate them.

Mobility and Fixity

Erik Harms's fascinating chapter, "Mobility's Spatial Fix," not only examines particular cultural forms of spatial construction in Vietnam but also provides a general framework that informs many of the following essays. Harms sees mobility and its meaning to the Vietnamese almost as an accordion or folding fan—a concept that bends, expands, contracts, and then opens again into all sorts of possibilities. Though the notion of "homeland" as a fixed geographic space is very important to Vietnam, the realities and day-to-day exercising of Vietnamese spatiality is anything but fixed.[5] Vietnamese move in constant circuits—through cities and to "edge cities"; across kinship networks that play on place but that (in fact) explode place altogether; and across the national boundaries of what Thongchai Winachakul has called the "geobody," as Vietnamese in diaspora, in overseas work contracts, and so on (Thongchai 1993). Punctuated by the setting and resetting of policies such as the famous Doi Moi reforms of the mid-1980s, Vietnamese are in constant motion, across a range of registers, some of them grounded in the trappings of local identity, many of them trans-local, and danced to the realities of everyday "modern" life. Harms explores the dissonances between these two ideal forms as opposites and shows that most Vietnamese in fact live their lives somewhere in between the two ends.

This is not only contemporary ethnography but also geography and contemporary history, all poured into a single, complex narrative of what "mobility"

Rush hour in Hanoi. (Photo by Helen F. Siu)

might mean in a single Asian locale (Harms 2016, 2011). In a review essay on three books concerned with similar themes of movement and disjuncture in postreform China, Siu (2006) terms the people's agentive energies as "fast forward with historical baggage." Villagers or urban residents, migrant workers or elite school children buckling under family pressure to get ahead, they juggle with a lingering socialist bureaucracy, an unbridled market, and a nationalistic agenda to be modern.

Biao Xiang and Qiang Ma also look at the mobility of human beings in a late-socialist environment, through the evolving Muslim presence in two southeastern Chinese cities, Guangzhou (in Guangdong province) and Yiwu (in Zhejiang province). Guangzhou is one of the sites of the oldest Muslim activity in China, hosting centuries of multiethnic traders who came across the Indian Ocean and through the Strait of Malacca; in the Tang dynasty (618–907 CE) the first visiting Muslims likely entered China from here, including (apocryphally) the uncle of the prophet Muhammad. Four mosques in the city today cater to local Hui Muslims and foreign traders from the Middle East, South Asia, and Africa. Huaisheng Mosque (also known as Guang Ta, or Lighthouse Mosque) was built during the Tang and known to have been visited by Ibn Battuta in the Ming.[6] The one situated in the historic Muslim cemetery in the heart of Guangzhou (Saad bin Abi Waqqas Mosque), though architecturally fused with features of a traditional Chinese ancestral hall, accommodates large numbers of worshipers during religious festivities. A weekly bazaar frequented by Arab, African, and local Chinese residents of the city has also sprung up in the neighborhood.

Yiwu, by contrast, does not have a long history of Muslim settlement, but its Muslim population has grown by leaps and bounds over the past twenty years owing to the development of the world's largest small commodities market. Traders largely come from the global South, and some have settled with Chinese spouses and children. The authors argue for a notion of "assemblage," meaning a collection of disparate social elements that come together only in contingent circumstances. In this case, it means that local Muslims (mostly Hui), mixing with Muslims from China's far western provinces of Xinjiang and Gansu (sometimes ethnically Uighur), and foreign Muslims from South Asia, the Middle East, and Africa, have come to constitute new communities in these southeastern Chinese cities. Their analysis pushes against earlier, more simplified narratives that assumed that pockets of Muslims of various designations resided as veritable "ethnic archipelagoes" inside the vast

Historic Huaisheng Mosque in Guangzhou. (Photo by May Bo Ching)

Small Islamic commodity items in Yiwu. (Photo by Helen F. Siu)

"sameness" of the ethnic Han majority. Rather, their fieldwork and analysis of the extremely fluid situation on the ground in these two cities suggest that the Chinese Muslim spaces of southeastern China are continually being made and remade, as migrants, laborers, and job seekers continually cohere in new constellations of Muslim assemblage inside these cities (Xiang, Yeoh, and Toyota 2013; Xiang and Toyota 2013). By stressing the key role of Arabic-Chinese translators in promoting Islamic practices, they also demonstrate that language itself is a fluid cultural form, crossing ethnic and national boundaries.[7]

The Meaningful Worlds of Circulating Commodities

Representing a different line of inquiry, one centered on the circulation of commodities, David Ludden describes a world where cowry shells were king. In the early twentieth century, the anthropologist Bronislaw Malinowski highlighted Kula ring, the complex institutions of reciprocity, exchange, and power play involved in the circulation of cowry shells among the Trobriand Islanders in the Pacific (1961 [1922]).[8] As a historian of South Asia, Ludden extends the exchange network far back in time and in a vast, variegated space linking the Maldives (where the shells were collected) to the delta of Bengal, and up into the interior of "hill-track Asia," an arena now known academically as Zomia.[9] If there was a center to this world, it was Sylhet, a river port (in today's northeastern Bangladesh) that took the cowries and then distributed them elsewhere as a form of currency. Ludden's achievement has been to disentangle the webs of this world, showing how island chains, river mouths, and hill stations were all implicated in the forging of a geographic space dependent on passing shells. Human actors moved the shells, and it is through the activities of these actors that we see another, previously hidden face of *Asia Inside Out.* If Sylhet was a node in these movements, its history has been barely known, and its prominence now in Ludden's piece shows us how Asia expanded and contracted, depending on what exactly was in motion, in terms of both humans and the commodities they carried. Taken alongside the other pieces in the volume, Ludden's piece shows us why geography matters, as its contours led to connections that we have not often seen. Yet he also shows us the tense and sometimes tenuous relationship between human beings and things, and the ways in which their interactions helped prosecute history in new and unforeseen ways (Ludden 2012, 2011, 1999). Ludden's chapter, like others in this volume

Cowry shells. (Wikimedia Commons)

concerned with macro structures of power and politics, also features military activity and the British efforts to subdue the hill peoples who controlled the supply of the cowry trade.

Narges Erami, much like David Ludden with his use of cowries as a window into mobility, has taken Persian carpets as her "muse" in looking at patterns of human movement across Asia's putative boundaries. Though Persian carpets have had a venerable tradition of high value in the West and were (and are) sold for great sums, the isolating of the Iranian regime by Western governments since 1979 and the Revolution has forced both the government in Tehran and professional carpet dealers and manufacturers to rethink this dependency. East and Southeast Asia became an alternative market for their wares, and both the regime and the various economic actors interested in producing and selling carpets actively sought out ways to make Asia a new and complementary destination for their products.[10] Yet, as Erami shows, the relationship between the Iranian government and its merchants was always lukewarm at best. The manufacturers of carpets knew that the new middle-class Asian consumers, unlike Euro-American consumers, did not have a history of appreciation for traditional carpets, but they were not sure how to sell the idea of expensive "artisanal" carpet production as a superior alternative to mass production. Erami invokes the aesthetic theory of writers like Jacques Rancière to demonstrate that "taste" had to be made through human decisions. The traveling of a constellation of Iranian actors to points east began a process whereby carpets became a kind of diplomatic tool for a sometimes-cornered Iranian regime and its businessmen.

Erami narrates this process over the last several decades and shows how a "road was made" in unlikely places, such as Hanoi, Bangkok, and Kuala Lumpur. This was mobility being constructed in new ways, often because of the exigencies of international politics that could not be controlled by Tehran or by its economic subjects (Erami 2015, 2009). On the latter, the cultivation of taste among the new rich in Asia involved not only expensive commodities for new markets across geographical divides but also shrewd strategies in generating cultural capital for social and political mobilities. Today, the dramatic rise and fall in the value of exotic teas in Yunnan and of Chinese art objects (the prices of which have dazzled auction houses in New York and London) indicates a world of consumption as unpredictable as the impact of the anti-corruption campaigns now raging in Xi's China. How must the Iranian carpet merchants position themselves in their adventurous journey to the meaningful worlds of another "Orient"?

Practitioners, Texts, and Knowledge in Transit

Angela Leung also traces human mobility not only through the tracer-lines of objects but also through texts on these objects—in her case, on the *materia medica* corpus of and about barks, seeds, plants, and animal products that crossed between Sinitic and Vietnamese spheres. Starting off in the period of the Song and Yuan dynasties (the tenth through fourteenth centuries) and ending with the Ming to early Qing (the sixteenth through eighteenth centuries), she shows how the Sinitic regions of North China, Lingnan (South China), and Annan (the "Pacified South," roughly northern Vietnam in today's geography) were brought into a single medical sphere over the *longue durée* by traveling medical practitioners.[11] Many of these men sojourned between these arenas, but products and texts about them were also in transit, as were notions and ideas. Leung starts her essay with an early text (Recipes for defending life in the Lingnan region 1264) to illuminate processes of entanglement and differentiation in the evolution of a repertoire of medical knowledge. Medicinal items termed "strange things" *(yiwu)* and native healing practices were gradually adopted to tackle local afflictions encountered. Leung also argues that this "Southern" region had an "ecological coherence—extreme and perennial warmth and dampness, unique flora and fauna, and epidemiological environment—that generated shared human experiences." Doctors and civil servants who were charged with epidemiological matters, and who answered to different polities, knit these worlds together but also fashioned real divergences in the ways that medical knowledge was sustained and grew. The circulation of ideas in the medical texts illuminated an interface of multiple traditions—Confucian and Buddhist, on the one hand, and those more locally Lingnan and Vietnamese, on the other. Instead of neatly aligned regions and nation-states set off by linguistic and ethnic differences, a much more fluid reality existed on the ground.

Leung's chapter shows us the human agency in these transvaluations and provides a vital connective thread in piecing together how translocal mobilities simultaneously unified and forged dissonant traditions (Leung and Furth 2011; Leung 2009). As in Erik Harms's model, mobility both transmitted and fixed new practices in separate linked locations. In emerging conceptions of space and the making of regional identities, human imagination and improvised practices have been key elements.

Humans also traveled in virtual form through manuscripts, the subject of Mounia Chekhab-Abudaya's essay. Chekhab-Abudaya, a curator at the Museum of Islamic Art in Doha, Qatar, looks at the way pilgrimage manuscripts narrate human mobility in paper form, in the outstretched landscapes of the "greater Middle East." Though there are similarities here with Leung's chapter, this is an angle on human movement that we do not see much elsewhere in the volume, because Chekhab-Abudaya deals with traces, the detritus of objects (whether objets d'art or simply objects like manuscripts) in repositories and collections.[12] Her examples come from the vaults of a museum and, taken as a group, outline ways in which human senses of movement animate manuscripts on how to perform a pilgrimage properly. The pilgrimage in question is the Hajj, the once-in-a-lifetime goal of all Muslims and one of the five cornerstones of the faith. There are also "lesser pilgrimages," such as the *'umra* (also to Mecca) and *ziyara,* which are taken more often to a variety of tombs of saints. All this shows not only how mobile Muslim populations were in the "central Islamic lands" but also how vital it was deemed to record such travels, to the point where instruction primers survive in decent numbers. From a museological perspective, the preservation of such documents allows us a window into what really matters for a society—that which was kept safe and secure, in order to hand down such knowledge to future generations (Chekhab-Abudaya 2013, 2014).

Seekers and Unwilling Sojourners "at the Margins"

People themselves—both individuals and classes of human beings in agglomeration—also made these voyages. Seema Alavi takes us into a maritime world of mobility stretching from the Persian Gulf, to the Omani peninsula jutting out into the Arabian Sea, and to India, a thousand kilometers farther to the East. Linking these land- and seascapes together was the interest of the British Empire, resurgent in all these spaces as the Pax Britannica of the nineteenth century gathered pace. But this pax was never as peaceful as it sounded; Alavi shows us in particular how the Indian Revolt of 1857 reverberated through this corridor of the northern Indian Ocean and helped (at times hindered) the career of many Omani princes, who sought to take advantage of such disturbances. The Omani Empire was, at least in Indian Ocean terms, almost as vibrant as the British imperium. It had tendrils snaking south from Muscat to the eastern coast of Africa and particularly to Zanzibar. Merchant connections were also pushing east to India.[13] In this large sphere of action, Omanis held sway as merchants, politicians, and slavers, though the latter category of employment was increasingly closed to them because of British legislation as the nineteenth century wore on. Alavi shows us the ways in which East Africa, West Asia, and South Asia were linked in this period and forged a unitary world of sorts through the maneuvers and machinations of Omani elites. They dealt with the fabrication and ultimate unknitting of this world in novel and interesting ways, many of which play into the themes on offer in this volume as a whole (Alavi 2015, 2008). Alavi demonstrates that the Omani elites, like others acting on the borderlands between different empires (Tagliacozzo 2005), could profit from opportunities in illegal trades despite the best efforts of the imperial powers to regulate them.

Some proponents of globalization focus too much on the sunny side of global trade, neglecting the underground channels carrying unsavory products like weapons and coercive trafficking in human slaves. James Pickett, like Alavi in her study of Oman, looks at what he calls the "darker side of mobility"—a necessary and commensurate "flip side of the coin" to many of the processes described here. In the heart of Asia, along the grasslands of the

Old men at a market in Muscat. (Photo by Helen F. Siu)

steppe, Pickett (2016a, 2016b) sees an *ecumene* of Perso-Islamic culture that extends from the eastern doorway to Europe all the way out to the Indian subcontinent. This was the result of many years of trade, travel, and conquest—a fully coherent world of Islam along the central corridors of the continent that put much of West, South, and Central Asia in conversation with each other for hundreds of years. Ideas flowed just as people and commodities did. Yet Pickett sees a world circulating underneath (or at least alongside) this open cadence of the grasslands, one of refugees, political prisoners, and hostages, who also had a mobility that needs to be taken into account. These unwilling actors played an important and understudied part in the human movements that interest us in these three books, and they were vital in forging an order to the region. These "unwilling mobilities" were part and parcel of the evolution of this part of the world, from the *ecumene* that Pickett describes in early modern times to the much more fractured empires-then-nations fragmentation of the past two centuries. Coerced movement as part of this evolving system and also in opposition to it became a vital cog in unfolding processes

Multiethnic travelers at Zanzibar ferry. (Photo by Helen F. Siu)

and helps show us the price of modernity in a part of Asia that is often neglected, not least because of a lack of language expertise and extant sources.[14]

Tamara Loos, like Pickett, is also interested in the trope of exile. Yet where Pickett sees a class of people, all moving (or being moved) across the grasslands of Eurasia, Loos follows a single person, the exiled Siamese Prince Prisdang (1852–1935), through his circuits of Indian Ocean travel.[15] Prisdang was a member of the Thai elite, but his own predilections—and his willingness to speak up in a coercive system, with severe restrictions on what can be said in royal and semiroyal circles—led to his long exile from Siam in the decades around the turn of the twentieth century. He became part of an interesting and eclectic group of travelers, misfits, and seekers who were looking at ways to blend "East" and "West" together in novel and transformative ways. Though he spent time in London, where he was educated, his sojourns through Sri Lanka were particularly important for the purposes of our project. It was here that he sought ways to marry existing Thai systems and Buddhist cosmologies to Western worldviews. Prisdang was proud of his Theravada Buddhist roots and saw in this *ecumene* one that was similar in some ways to Pickett's Perso-Islamic one overland, though in Prisdang's case it was a sea-based, tropical web of connections based in monsoon Asia. He was emblematic of a number of sojourners who did not precisely fit in with their own local polities and the expectations of such places in a time of great change. Loos shows how reexamining the biography of well-known people can also lead us to look beyond the limits of a nation. Nationalist histories tend to omit the awkward times when their leading characters spent time in exile. Exiles are important only when they return to lead nationalist movements; in this account, Prisdang, like other famous exiles (including Sun Yat-sen and Ho Chi Minh), embedded himself in foreign societies and established multiple transnational networks. He and others are intriguing symbols of Asia "inside out" in singular, human form (Loos 2016, 2006).

The historical situations of seekers and unwilling sojourners at the margins are repeated in the modern times in the plight of those labeled as refugees. Driven by dire environmental calamities or forced out of their home communities by war, religious persecution, and/or ethnic cleansing, they endure torments whose scale of displacement and depth and immediacy of human suffering have been vividly brought to public view via global digital media. Much of the media have focused on the displaced populations in Syria and Iraq, the near total destruction of their communities, and the incredible violence inflicted on their lives. However, the desperate situations in West and

North Africa, and the equally heart-wrenching suffering of the Rohingya Muslim villagers, remain relatively "hidden" from view. Even back in 1995, Liisa Malkki's (1995) insightful review of "refugee studies" pointed to the inadequacies of treating displaced African populations under extreme duress as "refugees" despite the goodwill and resources poured into aid packages. She asked for more nuanced studies of these populations and of their complex worlds of meaning and sociality, rather than using hard policy categories and narratives that unintentionally truncate and dehumanize. The gnawing question remains: Have our analytical lenses since the 1990s caught up with an unexpected world of forced sojourners?

As for seekers, scholars have paid much attention to Asian migrant workers driven by family needs and economic aspirations—Filipina and Indonesian domestic helpers, bar hostesses, mail-order brides from Vietnam and China (Constable 2003, 2007, 2014; Faier 2009; Friedman 2014), information technology body shopping in India, African traders in Hong Kong, and sex workers across the Indonesia-Singaporean border (Xiang 2007; Mathews 2011; Lindquist 2010). The presence of massive numbers of these migrants in Asian cities such as Hong Kong and Singapore has created new urban ethnoscapes that are highly gendered. Issues about the abuse of these workers in home environments as much as on factory floors, their new identities and rights, and the adjustments of their families back home can be riveting and contentious (Chu 2010; Xiang, Yeoh, and Toyota 2013). Their plight involves moral issues of forging an encompassing environment in highly fractured societies, and institutional issues such as regulating agencies, legal recourse, and nationalistic agendas. Nonetheless, literature on past waves of migration also points to creative energies and agentive opportunities. How do we develop understandings of the new landscapes of power, of mobility and immobility, of connectedness and disjuncture that entangle people's lives at multiple levels in the twenty-first century? For the seekers and unwilling sojourners alike, could the zones at the margins have given them unexpected room for maneuver?[16]

Worlds in Motion: Soundscapes, Foodscapes, and Sportscapes

If several of our authors see mobility in the passage of *things* vis-à-vis human beings, May Bo Ching sees a mobility based on sound. Ching focuses on a Cantonese-speaking world—its song traditions and practitioners in South China, who made a living using such music from the mid-nineteenth to the mid-twentieth century. She traces a world in motion between Hong Kong, Guangzhou (Canton), and Macau, a triangle of port cities situated at different ends of the vast Pearl River estuary.[17] These cities have certainly been studied in relation to one another before, but Ching adds a new dimension by highlighting the intercity cultural flow, including Shanghai as an important node from the late nineteenth century on.[18] Her real contribution is to situate this vision in operatic and other performance traditions as an emerging soundscape (Ching 2008, 2010). From the humble footprints of blind itinerant singers in villages and urban working-class neighborhoods, to circuits of operatic stars staging their glamor and exquisite styles, to affluent connoisseurs, the Cantonese language in the lyrics and the music forged distinct social flows as well as cultural identities. The ethos spanned the Pearl River delta, colonial Hong Kong, and Macau and reached far into diasporic communities in Southeast Asia and across the Pacific to North America. This Cantonese-speaking world preceded and stood apart from the gathering of Mandarin-inflected realities of a Sinitic, nationalizing modernity. The mobilities under study here are regional in character and evidence of linkages and coherence that existed as part

Cantonese opera for community festival, Hong Kong. (Photo by Helen F. Siu)

Cantopop singer Denise Ho in concert. Permission of Denise Ho.

of the "great South" of China and beyond, a concept both historical and still intensely relevant in our own times.

Pushing into the late twentieth century, one found Cantopop. The genre started in Hong Kong in the 1970s when the cultural scene in China was just beginning to explore new moorings after decades of Maoist politics. Cantopop reached its height of glamor and style in the 1980s and 1990s. Powerful singers in Hong Kong such as Paula Tsui, Frances Yip, Lo Man, and Anita Mui and lyricists / songwriters such as Joseph Koo and James Wong dominated the stage and the lucrative recording industry. Its highly influential performance genre for the region is only the latest expression of the earlier cultural forms, Ching argues.

Improvisation has continued in the past two decades. The artistry of pop diva Denise Ho (HOCC) brings a novel but recognizable route for cultural circulation in the twenty-first century. Ho grew up in colonial-era Hong Kong and received an English-based early education there. She came of age in Montreal, where her family immigrated, and she returned to Hong Kong in 1998 just after the former British territory became a Special Administrative Region of China. Almost by chance, she became the protégé of the late Cantopop diva Anita Mui. Fluent in Cantonese, Mandarin, English, and French, Ho combines cross-dressing themes of classical Cantonese opera with Cantopop and the staging of rock music spectacles to capture new social and political imaginary in the past two decades for a digitally connected, inter-Asian public. We may be seeing a new soundscape in the making. But to understand the modern phenomenon of Cantopop and new creative energies across the region and globe, we must burrow in search of far older musical and linguistic roots, which Ching does in her wide-ranging essay.[19]

Emma J. Teng (2013, 2006) also looks at the role that culture played in the hybridities discussed in this volume, though in her case, food is the most important lens through which to view these transvaluations. She notes that awareness of and interest in Chinese food was uneven at first in China's interactions with the West; appreciation came even later. For much of the initial period of sustained Sino-Western contact in the nineteenth century when the Qing dynasty was in decline, most Westerners assumed that they had little to learn from the Chinese food cornucopia, and many cultural tropes of superiority played themselves out over matters culinary, as they did on almost everything else.[20] Yet Teng is interested in how this slowly began to change via both Chinese experimenting with food concepts in China and those who eventually left for the West and encountered new culinary worlds there. Cookbooks became part of this interface, and mobilities that were based on people able to move large distances also depended on cuisines making these journeys. As ideas on food traveled, the notion of "Chinese" and "Western" food changed to a degree, with the invention of new hybrid categories like "Chinese-American food" as part of the story. Teng traces this process both in China and among Chinese in America from the late nineteenth to the twentieth century, showing us how supposedly discrete worlds of culture actually merged in interesting and often unexpected ways. Chao Yang Buwei's cookbook not only generated greater appreciation for the sophistication of Chinese cuisine but also delivered a powerful critique of American wastefulness, stressing the common values of Chinese and Americans in wartime centered on frugality, and attention to the nutritional value of natural products. Chao's approach, using the analysis of the "foreign" as cultural critique in the home country, shares some features with Ruth Benedict's contemporaneous book on Japan, *The Chrysanthemum and the Sword* (2005 [1946]). In Clifford Geertz's (1988) interpretation, Benedict not only made Japanese more understandable to Americans by showing their cultural logic, but also delivered a biting critique of the limitations of American culture when contrasted with the values of an Asian country.

William Kelly also delves deep into the soft power of mobility, in what he calls the sportscape of the region, as seen primarily (but not exclusively) from Northeast Asia, namely, China, Korea, and Japan.[21] "Teams travel across the sporting continent," he says, "players move, investment capital flows, media and broadcast rights are fluid, and an industry of sporting goods is constituted by global commodity chains of production and lines of distribution (Weinberg 2015). Asia, from the perspective of sports, is all hubs and flows." While he appreciates the shared empirical features and analytical value of sports with popular music, fashion, cuisine, and graphic art such as manga and anime, he distinguishes it as a multifaceted but understudied phenomenon in Asia. "Sports—as participation and pedagogy, as spectatorship and rivalry, as media event and commercial profit, as national prestige and individual aspiration—have had deep roots in and dense connections across Asia for over a century." A community of scholarship is only beginning to emerge.

One might treat sports in the modern era as in the realm of mass entertainment and leisure, and to an extent civil society in action. However, Kelly notes that the movement of athletes across multiple paths of sports migration is not random or unhindered but institutionally embedded and hierarchically structured across continents. He shows how the creation and maintenance of sports federations was a salient part of postwar nation building in Asia, especially in countries ravaged by conflict. Sports served nationalism, but the development of competitions (like the Asian Games and the Asian qualifying rounds for the World Cup) also encouraged a kind of transnationalism (Kelly 2013; Kelly and Sugimoto 2007). Southeast Asia and eventually Australia and New Zealand also became part of the sports *ecumene* of Asia.

Kelly narrates this unique juxtaposition and asks, What kinds of mobilities would be brought about in a migration-driven world in the twenty-first century? What happened when individual athletes pursuing their multinational careers had to decide on the countries to represent? Korea and Japan might be archrivals in sports, but ethnic Korean soccer players who have been long-term residents in Japan but not entirely accepted as such might be presented with unexpected opportunities, such as playing for North Korea. These processes inform all the essays in our volume, whereby nation-states are not pinballs, bouncing off one another as ontological realities. Rather, Asia can

Japanese soccer fans at the 2016 FIFA World Cup. (Yukle.mobi)

be seen to be a collection of political entities that have always been more permeable than the colored maps on our walls let on.

Kelly's sportscape is thus an enduring and ever-changing complexity. It is a form of agonistic cultural performance and production long embedded in Asian history and consciousness. It has formal universal rules and institutional fixities, but it also encourages tactical improvisations and indigenization, thus cementing "the doubled effect of creating enduring solidarities and strong rivalries that bind neighborhoods, regions, and nations as [sports events] pit them against one another. Sports are connectivity through contestation." These features make sportscape a perfect site for exploring creative intersections of national and transnational human agency, in both empirical and analytical terms.

Do human beings make place? The essays in this volume suggest that they do, at least as much as time periods do, or that places do not have any claims to being ontologically "of themselves." The movement of people fabricates the bonds that construct locales, including the emotions and identities attached to them. It shows us that cities, hubs, and nodes are physical spaces, but they are also the products of human interactions with implicit and expressive meanings. It would not be an exaggeration to see Asia, in this scheme, as the sum of multiple component parts with the important dimension of human mobility connecting them. If the three-volume set of *Asia Inside Out* makes any contribution, it sees the world's largest continent as a stratigraphy of time, place, actors, and events. These strata constantly shift and change, and re-form in new shapes and guises. Therefore the "Asia" of our title signifies multiple realities and existences spanning centuries. As seen from the vantage of some three dozen authors, all with their own sets of fieldwork sites, archival repositories, languages, and methodologies, "Asia" looks like an incongruently organic entity. It is also infinitely knowable through the prism of interdisciplinary teamwork.

Big books with claims to reformulation seem inherently dangerous; paradigm shifts occur only rarely, and with good reason. Knowledge changes slowly and requires the input of many cognoscenti to weigh in on what is truly new and what is merely derivative. We make few claims to wholly changing existing paradigms of studying Asia, but we do hope we have stimulated a discussion on what Asia exactly *is*—as a concept and also as a lived reality of human relationships shared through culture, markets, and political economy. It has become increasingly fashionable to see the world in transnational terms, and we surely ride on that current wave of thinking as reflective of the world we live in. We also hope that by convening such a varied team of scholarly interests we have been able to ground our theories with solid empirical research, both in the field and in the archives. By looking at Asia over roughly half a millennium, and from Istanbul east to Tokyo, we have laid out some markers for those who come after us who wish to see connection where before there were only bounded lines on a color-coded map (Perdue 1998). To us, Asia unfolds like a fan through time, space, and the agency of mobile people, until some of the empirical facts and conceptual categories we thought we knew ultimately appear to be inside out.

Notes

1. Other scholars have tried approaches akin to this one; one that comes to mind is Andre Gunder Frank's stimulating and original *ReOrient: Global Economy in the Asian Age* (1998). For comparisons between three early modern Asian empires, see Islamoğlu and Perdue (2009). Yet because no scholar can hope to have the dozens of languages, field sites, and methodologies that a large, three-volume edited collection

can have, we hope we have been able to show the width and breadth of such an approach through three dozen pairs of eyes. This is one of the main interventions of the *Asia Inside Out* project, in terms of the kinds of coverage made possible by utilizing the insights and capabilities of a large group of scholars all at once.

2. A somewhat similar approach has been attempted by the great archaeologist/historian of Eurasia Barry Cunliffe, in his recent magnum opus *By Steppe, Desert, and Ocean: The Birth of Eurasia* (2015).

3. See Arjun Appadurai, "Global Ethnoscapes" in *Modernity at Large* (1996), on the emergence of "scapes," marked by the flow of technology, media, ethnic identities, and other fluid cultural dimensions of a global terrain. See also Anna Tsing, "The Global Situation" (2000), highlighting multilayered agency on a variegated global landscape. This is in tune with a large analytical literature on deterritorialization, starting with David Harvey's landmark study, *The Condition of Postmodernity* (1990).

4. The art historian/theorist John Berger talks about the idea of "becoming" as a quintessential way of seeing—in other words, seeing not only what is in front of us, as it exists, but also the possibilities in things and what they might become over time. See Berger, *Ways of Seeing* (2008).

5. For a historical look at some of these patterns, albeit written in a very different way (using verticality, ethnicity, and altitude to study some related themes), see Gerald Hickey, *Sons of the Mountains* (1982). For contemporary global flows, see Appadurai 1996 in "scapes"; Tsing 2000; for contemporary China, on the edges of expanding cities, see Siu 2007.

6. See BBC production on the travels of Ibn Battuta; also see Chaffee 2008 on the large multiethnic and Muslim communities in the city of Quanzhou during the Yuan dynasty.

7. The importance of this work is difficult to overemphasize; the number of people "on the move" in different forms of migration in China right now is simply staggering, in the hundreds of millions. When the Muslim element of these migrants is added in, the government looks at such numbers with skepticism, and often alarm. Policies in Western China among the Uighur (including new regulations on beard sizes, the use of the Koran, etc.) make this chapter particularly timely. For another unusual case where history of migration, ethnicity, and linguistic scripts intersected in Western China, see Jing Tsu's (2015) chapter in *Asia Inside out: Connected Places*. See also Elliott 2015.

8. His work was part of the century-long debates among social and economic anthropologists on worldviews of tribal populations and reciprocity and exchange in nonmarket economies. See also *The Great Transformation* by Karl Polanyi (2001 [1944]).

9. "Zomia" is a term first used by Willem van Schendel of the University of Amsterdam to describe certain hill inhabitants of Southeast Asian borderlands. The concept has been most fully articulated by James Scott in his book *The Art of Not Being*

Governed (2010). A number of the ideas expounded on in the volume are also in conversation with earlier work by Willem van Schendel (2015).

10. Though Erami's essay is contemporary in conception, there is in fact a history of long-distance trade between places in East Asia (like Bangkok) and the Middle East; see as a good example Kennon Brezeale, ed., *From Japan to Arabia: Ayutthaya's Maritime Relations with Asia* (1999). See also Siu and McGovern 2017 on historical connections between China and Africa over land and sea via the Middle East, and the historical importance of Guangzhou as a center for such trade. For that across the Indian Ocean, see Chaudhuri 1985. A combination of trade and diplomacy was also seen in tribute trade organized by China for many parts of the Asian world. See Hamashita 2008.

11. For an earlier vision of what this frontier world between South China and Southeast Asia looked and felt like, partially through material culture and partially through the poetry and missives of officials stationed in the border zones, see Edward Schafer, *The Vermilion Bird: T'ang Images of the South* (1967).

12. For an art-historical approach that takes into account some of these ideas on the pilgrimage, see Porter 2012.

13. Some good background on this triangle trade (and triangle diplomacy) being exercised in the Western Indian Ocean can be found in Sheriff 1987.

14. For an exception, see Anderson 2007.

15. This biographic method of studying sojourners in and around Southeast Asia has also been done in the reverse direction; for a good example, see Rush 1996.

16. For a theoretical work on meaningful spaces that might have escaped scholarly attention, see the work of the French anthropologist Marc Augé (2009 [1995]). On women's agency and unusual spaces for advancement in the highly commercialized South China region, see Siu 2010. See also Kelsky 2001 on adventurous Japanese women travelers in the United States and challenges to gendered hierarchies. On the flip side, see Siu 2007 on not equating displacement with physical movement. Instead, one can be severely "displaced" by being grounded for generations, like villagers in Maoist China.

17. For another historical elucidation of this South China world of the Pearl River delta, see Van Dyke 2005.

18. For the turn-of-the-century connections and the impact of a new, cosmopolitan culture in Shanghai and the accompanying world of leisure and entertainment, see Lee 1999. See also Lee 2010.

19. See Chow and De Kloet 2013. See also Yiu-Wai Chu 2017.

20. An interesting take on the linkages between Southern China and the United States vis-à-vis culture and mobility can be found in Hsu 2000. See also Sinn 2015.

21. For an earlier study of how games and amusements could forge commonality in an Asian region, see the relevant chapter in Reid 1988.

References

Alavi, Seema. 2008. *Islam and Healing: Loss and Recovery of an Indo-Muslim Medical Tradition.* London: Palgrave Macmillan.

———. 2015. *Muslim Cosmopolitanism in the Age of Empire.* Cambridge, MA: Harvard University Press.

Amrith, Sunil S. 2016. Review of *Asia Inside Out: Changing Times* and *Asia Inside Out: Connected Places,* eds. Eric Tagliacozzo, Helen F. Siu, and Peter C. Perdue. *American Historical Review* 121(4): 1228–1232.

Anderson, Clare. 2007. "Convict Passages in the Indian Ocean, c. 1790–1860." In *Many Middle Passages: Forced Migration and the Making of the Modern World,* eds. Emma Christopher, Cassandra Pybus, and Marcus Rediker, 129–149. Berkeley: University of California Press.

Appadurai, Arjun. 1996. *Modernity at Large: Cultural Dimensions of Globalization.* Minneapolis: University of Minnesota Press.

Augé, Marc. 2009 [1995]. *Non-Places: An Introduction to Supermodernity.* Translated by John Howe. New York: Verso.

Benedict, Ruth. 2005 [1946]. *The Chrysanthemum and the Sword: Patterns of Japanese Culture.* Boston: Houghton Mifflin.

Berger, John. 2008. *Ways of Seeing.* New York: Penguin Books.

Brezeale, Kennon, ed. 1999. *From Japan to Arabia: Ayutthaya's Maritime Relations with Asia.* Bangkok: Toyota-Thailand Foundation.

Chaffee, John. 2008. "At the Intersection of Empire and World Trade: The Chinese Port City of Quanzhou (Zaitun), Eleventh-Fifteen Centuries." In *Secondary Cities and Urban Networking in the Indian Ocean Realm c. 1400–1800,* ed. Kenneth Hall, 99–122. Lanham, MD: Lexington Books.

Chaudhuri, K. N. 1985. *Trade and Civilisation in the Indian Ocean: An Economic History from the Rise of Islam to 1750.* Cambridge: Cambridge University Press.

Chekhab-Abudaya, Mounia. 2013. *Hajj—the Journey through Art: An Exhibition Catalogue.* Doha: Museum of Islamic Art.

———. 2014. Mémoires du Hajj: Le Pèlerinage à la Mecque Vu à travers les Arts de l'Islam, la Production Intellectuelle et Matérielle de l'Époque Médiévale à l' Époque Contemporaine. Les Cahiers de l'Islam.

Ching, May Bo. 2008. "Where Guangdong Meets Shanghai: Hong Kong Culture in a Trans-regional Context." In *Hong Kong Mobile: Making a Global Population,* eds. Helen F. Siu and Agnes S. Ku, 45–62. Hong Kong: Hong Kong University Press.

———. 2010. "A Preliminary Study of the Theatres Built by Cantonese Merchants in the Late Qing." *Frontiers of History in China* 5(2): 253–278.

Chow, Yiu Fai, and Jeroen De Kloet. 2013. *Sonic Multiplicities: Hong Kong Pop and the Global Circulation of Sound and Image.* Chicago: Intellect.

Chu, Julie Y. 2010. *Cosmologies of Credit: Transnational Mobility and the Politics of Destination in China.* Durham, NC: Duke University Press.

Chu, Yiu-Wai. 2017. *Hong Kong Cantopop: A Concise History*. Hong Kong: Hong Kong University Press.

Constable, Nicole. 2003. *Romance on a Global Stage: Pen Pals, Virtual Ethnography, and "Mail-Order" Marriages*. Berkeley: University of California Press.

———. 2007. *Maid to Order in Hong Kong: Stories of Migrant Workers*. 2nd ed. Ithaca, NY: Cornell University Press.

———. 2014. *Born out of Place: Migrant Mothers and the Politics of International Labor*. Berkeley: University of California Press.

Cunliffe, Barry. 2015. *By Steppe, Desert, and Ocean: The Birth of Eurasia*. Oxford: Oxford University Press.

Elliott, Mark C. 2015. "The Case of the Missing Indigene: Debate over a 'Second-Generation' Ethnic Policy." *China Journal* 73: 186–213.

Erami, Narges. 2009. "The Soul of the Market: Knowledge, Authority and the Making of Expert Merchants in the Persian Rug Bazar." Unpublished doctoral dissertation, Columbia University.

———. 2015. "When Ties Don't Bind: Smuggling Effects, Bazaars, and Regulatory Regimes in Post-revolutionary Iran." *Economy and Society* 44(1): 110–139.

Faier, Lieba. 2009. *Intimate Encounters: Filipina Women and the Remaking of Rural Japan*. Berkeley: University of California Press.

Frank, Andre Gunder. 1998. *ReOrient: Global Economy in the Asian Age*. Berkeley: University of California Press.

Friedman, Sara L. 2014. "Marital Borders: Gender, Population, and Sovereignty across the Taiwan Strait." In *Wives, Husbands, and Lovers: Marriage and Sexuality in Hong Kong, Taiwan, and Urban China*, eds. Deborah S. Davis and Sara L. Friedman, 285–311. Stanford, CA: Stanford University Press.

Geertz, Clifford. 1988. *Works and Lives: The Anthropologist as Author*. Stanford, CA: Stanford University Press.

Hamashita, Takeshi. 2008. *China, East Asia and the Global Economy: Regional and Historical Perspectives*. New York: Routledge.

Harms, Erik. 2011. *Saigon's Edge: On the Margins of Ho Chi Minh City*. Minneapolis: University of Minnesota Press.

———. 2016. *Luxury and Rubble: Civility and Dispossession in the New Saigon*. Berkeley: University of California Press.

Harvey, David. 1990. *The Condition of Postmodernity*. Malden, MA: Blackwell Publishers.

Hickey, Gerald Cannon. 1982. *Sons of the Mountains: Ethnohistory of the Vietnamese Central Highlands*. New Haven, CT: Yale University Press.

Hsu, Madeline. 2000. *Dreaming of Gold, Dreaming of Home: Transnationalism and Migration between the United States and South China, 1882–1943*. Stanford, CA: Stanford University Press.

Islamoğlu, Huri, and Peter C. Perdue, eds. 2009. *Shared Histories of Modernity: China, India and the Ottoman Empire*. New York: Routledge.

Kelly, William. 2013. "Japan's Embrace of Soccer: Mutable Ethnic Players and Flexible Soccer Citizenship in the New East Asian Sports Order." *International Journal of the History of Sport* 30(11): 1235–1246.

Kelly, William, and Atsuo Sugimoto, eds. 2007. *This Sporting Life: Sports and Body Culture in Modern Japan.* New Haven, CT: Yale University Council on East Asian Studies.

Kelsky, Karen. 2001. *Women on the Verge: Japanese Women, Western Dreams.* Durham, NC: Duke University Press.

Lee, Leo Ou-fan. 1999. *Shanghai Modern: The Flowering of a New Urban Culture in China, 1930–1945.* Cambridge, MA: Harvard University Press.

———. 2010. *City between Worlds: My Hong Kong.* Cambridge, MA: Belknap Press of Harvard University Press.

Leung, Ki Che Angela. 2009. *Leprosy in China: A History.* New York: Columbia University Press.

Leung, Ki Che Angela, and Charlotte Furth, eds. 2011. *Health and Hygiene in Chinese East Asia: Policies and Publics in the Long Twentieth Century.* Durham, NC: Duke University Press, 2010.

Lindquist, Johan. 2010. "Putting Ecstasy to Work: Pleasure, Prostitution, and Inequality in the Indonesian Borderlands." *Identities* 17: 280–303.

Loos, Tamara. 2006. *Subject Siam: Family, Law, and Colonial Modernity in Thailand.* Ithaca, NY: Cornell University Press.

———. 2016. *Bones around My Neck: The Life and Exile of a Prince Provocateur.* Ithaca, NY: Cornell University Press.

Ludden, David. 1999. *An Agrarian History of South Asia.* Cambridge, MA: Cambridge University Press.

———. 2011. "The Process of Empire: Frontiers and Borderlands." In *Tributary Empires in Global History,* eds. Peter Fibiger Bang and CA Bayly, 132–150. London: Palgrave Macmillan.

———. 2012. "Spatial Inequity and National Territory: Remapping 1905 in Bengal and Assam." *Modern Asian Studies* 46(3): 483–525.

Malinowski, Bronisław. 1961 [1922]. *Argonauts of the Western Pacific: An Account of Native Enterprise and Adventure in the Archipelagoes of Melanesian New Guinea.* New York: E. P. Dutton.

Malkki, Liisa H. 1995. "Refugees and Exile: From 'Refugee Studies' to the National Order of Things." *Annual Review of Anthropology* 24: 495–523.

Mathews, Gordon. 2011. *Ghetto at the Center of the World: Chungking Mansions, Hong Kong.* Chicago: University of Chicago Press.

Perdue, Peter C. 1998. "Boundaries, Maps, and Movement: The Chinese, Russian, and Mongolian Empires in Early Modern Eurasia." *International History Review* 20(2): 263–286.

———. 2005. *China Marches West: The Qing Conquest of Central Eurasia.* Cambridge, MA: Harvard University Press.

Pickett, James. 2016a. "Enemies beyond the Red Sands: The Bukhara-Khiva Dynamic as Mediated by Textual Genre." *Journal of Persianate Studies* 9(2): 158–182.

———. 2016b. "Nadir Shah's Peculiar Central Asian Legacy: Empire, Conversion Narratives, and the Rise of New Scholarly Dynasties." *International Journal of Middle East Studies* 48(3): 491–510.

Polanyi, Karl. 2001 [1944]. *The Great Transformation: The Political and Economic Origins of Our Time.* Boston: Beacon Press..

Porter, Venetia, ed. 2012. *Hajj: Journey to the Heart of Islam.* Cambridge, MA: Harvard University Press, 2012.

Reid, Anthony. 1988. *Southeast Asia in the Age of Commerce, 1450–1680.* Vol. 1, *The Lands below the Winds.* New Haven, CT: Yale University Press.

Rush, James, ed. 1996. *Java: A Traveler's Anthology.* Kuala Lumpur: Oxford University Press.

Schafer, Edward. 1967. *The Vermilion Bird: T'ang Images of the South.* Berkeley: University of California Press.

Scott, James. 2010. *The Art of Not Being Governed: An Anarchist History of Upland Southeast Asia.* New Haven, CT: Yale University Press.

Sheriff, Abdul. 1987. *Slaves, Spices, and Ivory in Zanzibar: Integration of an East African Commercial Empire into the World System.* Athens: Ohio University Press.

Sinn, Elizabeth. 2015. *Pacific Crossing: California Gold, Chinese Migration, and the Making of Hong Kong.* Hong Kong: Hong Kong University Press.

Siu, Helen F. 2006. "China's Century: Fast Forward with Historical Baggage." *American Anthropologist* 108(2): 389–392.

———. 2007. "Grounding Displacement: Uncivil Urban Spaces in Postreform South China." *American Ethnologist* 34(2): 329–350.

———, ed. 2010. *Merchants' Daughters: Women, Commerce, and Regional Culture in South China.* Hong Kong: Hong Kong University Press.

———. 2014. "Key Issues in Historical Anthropology: A View from 'South China.'" *Cross-Currents: East Asian History and Culture Review* 13: 174–188.

———. 2016. *Tracing China: A Forty-Year Ethnographic Journey.* Hong Kong: Hong Kong University Press.

Siu, Helen F., and Mike McGovern. 2017. "China-Africa Encounters: Historical Legacies and Contemporary Realities." *Annual Review of Anthropology* 46: 337–355.

Tagliacozzo, Eric. 2005. *Secret Trades, Porous Borders: Smuggling and States along a Southeast Asian Frontier.* New Haven, CT: Yale University Press.

Tagliacozzo, Eric, Helen Siu, and Peter C. Perdue, eds. 2015a. *Asia Inside Out: Changing Times.* Cambridge, MA: Harvard University Press.

———, eds. 2015b. *Asia Inside Out: Connected Places.* Cambridge, MA: Harvard University Press.

Teng, Emma J. 2006. *Taiwan's Imagined Geography: Chinese Colonial Travel Writing and Pictures, 1683–1895.* Cambridge, MA: Harvard East Asia Monographs.

———. 2013. *Eurasian: Mixed Identities in the United States, China, and Hong Kong, 1842–1943*. Berkeley: University of California Press.

Thongchai, Winichakul. 1993. *Siam Mapped.* Honolulu: University of Hawai'i Press.

Tsing, Anna. 2000. "The Global Situation." *Cultural Anthropology* 15(3): 327–360.

Tsu, Jing. 2015. "Romanization without Rome: China's Latin New Script and Soviet Central Asia." In *Asia Inside Out: Connected Places,* eds. Eric Tagliacozzo, Helen Siu, and Peter C. Perdue, 321–353. Cambridge, MA: Harvard University Press.

Van Dyke, Paul. 2005. *Merchants of Canton and Macau, 1700–1845*. Hong Kong: Hong Kong University Press.

Van Schendel, Willem. 2015. "Spatial Moments: Chittagong in Four Scenes." In *Asia Inside Out: Connected Places,* eds. Eric Tagliacozzo, Helen Siu, and Peter C. Perdue, 98–127. Cambridge, MA: Harvard University Press.

Weinberg, Ben. 2015. *Asia and the Future of Football: The Role of the Asian Football Confederation.* New York: Routledge.

Xiang, Biao. 2007. *Global "Body Shopping": An Indian Labor System in the Information Technology Industry.* Princeton, NJ: Princeton University Press.

Xiang, Biao, Brenda Yeoh, and Mika Toyota, eds. 2013. *Return: Nationalizing Transnational Mobility in Asia.* Durham, NC: Duke University Press.

Xiang, Biao, and Mika Toyota, eds. 2013. "Ethnographic Experiments in Transnational Mobility Studies." Special issue of *Ethnography* 14(3).

I

Mobility's Spatial Fix

Finding the Vietnamese "Homeland" from the Outside In

ERIK HARMS

The May / June 2002 issue of *Heritage,* the Vietnam Airlines in-flight magazine, treated travelers to a beautifully illustrated bilingual feature article about the Vietnamese tradition of keeping detailed genealogical records. The article was titled "Gia Phả" in Vietnamese and "Family Records" in English. While the English translation of the main title is quite accurate, other aspects of the two versions convey markedly different tones. For example, the English subtitle, "We Are Family," flippantly plays on the name of a popular American R&B hit from the 1970s that was enjoying a second life in millennial Vietnam's karaoke houses—overall, the English-language article amounts to little more than a feel-good story about family heritage. The Vietnamese subtitle, by contrast, is much more serious, sending a moralizing message to readers about the importance of filial piety. "Uống nước nhớ nguồn," it reads, evoking a folk phrase popular not only in Vietnam but in China as well: "When you drink the water, remember the source" (Vietnam Airlines 2002).[1]

The article illustrates how the Vietnamese concept of the homeland is commonly described as spatially fixed, despite the empirical fact that Vietnamese people are constantly on the move. As the rest of this chapter will show, a similarly dynamic relationship between fixity and motion is evident within

Vietnamese kinship relations, which in turn inform historical movements of Vietnamese throughout Asia, around the world, and in more recent mobility practices as well. In this particular case, the article described the importance of patrilines in the Vietnamese tradition of kinship and explained how interest in preserving genealogies was revitalized alongside economic growth in millennial Vietnam. To show this, it documented the sentimental stories of several elderly men who had gone back to their ancestral villages in search of their families' genealogical record books. It ended with a poem written by one of those men, which the article's author, the anthropologist Nguyễn Xuân Kính, described as "rustic, and not written according to poetic conventions"; nevertheless, the author insisted, the poem was "able to awaken among the younger generations a sense of remembering the source." Part of the poem went like this:

Bùi, Lê, Ngô, Nguyễn vẫn một dòng	Bùi, Lê, Ngô, Nguyễn, the same line
Vấn tổ tìm tông ghi chép lại	Seek to write ancestral names
Nhắc cháu con nhớ mãi trong lòng	Help the young keep them in mind
Cây vững gốc mới mong tồn tại	Trees with stable roots remain
Người nhớ nguồn người sẽ thành công!	Remember the source and shine.[2]

In order to grasp the way it is possible for fixity and motion to produce each other, it is useful to imagine the context in which a modern and highly mobile Vietnamese person boarding this airplane would have read this magazine article about family genealogies. It appeared in the second year of the new millennium, twenty-seven years after the end of the Vietnam War, sixteen years after the market reforms known as Đổi Mới were introduced in 1986, and eight years after the end of the U.S.-imposed economic embargo (lifted by the Clinton administration in 1994). In 2002 Vietnam was right in the middle of its long process of gaining entry into the World Trade Organization (the process began in 1995 and Vietnam formally entered the WTO in 2007). In other words, when this article appeared, the nominally communist but increasingly market-oriented Socialist Republic of Vietnam was clearly committed to its "open door" policies of global economic integration. But if the country's leaders (and most Vietnamese people) were increasingly facing outward, the content of the article asked its readers to look inward, admonishing travelers to remember the source of their family identity—and not just *any* source, but *the* source; the singular, unique, identifiable *source of origins,* rooted in the land of one's father's ancestors. Such an emphasis on the importance of highly localized origins would not have been surprising to a Vietnamese reader: even today, every Vietnamese citizen carries an identity card that identifies his or her "original homeland" *(nguyên quán),* which is almost always the same as his or her father's ancestral home, even if the card holder was born elsewhere and has never even set foot in that place.[3] Furthermore, as this chapter will show, the tendency of Vietnamese to emphasize a strong sense of localized identity and place-based origins has long existed in a dynamic relationship with an equally strong emphasis on the importance of mobility and movement. This story about searching for origins in an in-flight magazine encapsulates this dynamic relationship almost perfectly: taking off on an airplane as one moves about the world integrating with the global economy is part of the process through which an idealized sense of origins is preserved.

The article's central proverb about drinking water and remembering the source clearly emphasizes this assumed sense of singular origins and offers an apt introduction to traditional Vietnamese conceptions of the ancestral patrilocal homeland. The central metaphor of "the source" *(nguồn)* evokes the traditional image of a family water well in a patrilineal homestead, its shaft bored straight down through the soil of an ancestral homeland, plunging through earth in a plumb line moving from the surface of the present to the source deep in the past. One might imagine the sediments and layers along the well's shaft as generation markers on the main trunk of a patrilineal family tree. It is those markers of the patriline, of course, that family records seek to document and trace. Ideally, a family's record book *(gia phả)* would be safely placed in the ancestral altar, which would itself be located in the most prominent position in the patrilocal home of a male descendant of the patriarch. And that home would be located in the most sacred of places, the ancestral homeland, known in Vietnamese as the *quê hương.*[4]

The standard dictionary translation of quê hương is "native land, fatherland" (Viện Ngôn Ngữ Học 1997). Although the word "quê" is not itself inherently gendered, the patrilineal assumptions that attach to the idea of homeland certainly are. The quê hương is not unlike the male-inflected idea of a patria, which Benedict Anderson calls "the wonderful Iberian word that can gently stretch from 'home-village,' through 'home-town' and 'home-region,' on to 'home-country'" (1998, 60). Like this understanding of the patria, the meaning of quê hương includes but also stretches beyond the notion of village origins to encompass more expansive geographical associations of national identity. Perhaps even more distinctly than the term "patria," the native place of the quê hương is typically associated with the father's lineage, as typified by the phrase one standard Vietnamese dictionary uses to illustrate the meaning of the word "quê" by way of example: *quê cha đất tổ* (father's native place and ancestors' land) (Viện Ngôn Ngữ Học 1997). In normal Vietnamese discourse, if one wishes to specify a mother's ancestral place, one must add the qualifier *ngoại* (outside) to form the composite term *quê ngoại,* which literally means something equivalent to "native place of the outsiders."

Heritage magazine article on "Family Records / Gia Phả." Courtesy of Vietnam Airlines Heritage magazine, May / June 2002.

All of these meanings mingle on the pages of the *Heritage* article and lend gravitas to its evocative descriptions of Vietnamese families searching to document their ancestors. As the airplane takes off, it is useful to imagine the traveler turning the page of the article. "Through genealogies," it explains, "people try to search for their native homeland (quê hương bản quán)" (Vietnam Airlines 2002, 15). The article evokes a search for rootedness precisely as the traveler lifts off the ground. Is this flight a part of that search? How can movement itself be bound up in rootedness? As this chapter will show, Vietnamese conceptions of mobility and movement abroad cannot be separated from efforts to reproduce the patria at home.

Movement and Rootedness

This image of highly mobile jet airplane travelers being admonished to remember their fixed patrilocal native places clearly illustrates how movement and fixity should not be understood as opposites, but as two parts bound together within a productive, mutually reinforcing relationship. As Kate Jellema (2007) has pointed out, the Vietnamese notion of leaving the homeland necessarily implies a return; in spoken Vietnamese one never simply says that one is "going" *(đi)* to one's ancestral home but always says that one is "returning to the homeland" *(về quê)*. Building from this observation, this chapter further shows that the dynamic relationship between leaving and returning, rootedness and unboundedness, or spatial constraint and expansiveness creates a conception of movement that spatially "fixes" the idealized concept of patrilineal kinship in a society that is decidedly on the move. This way of thinking about movement always returning to a homeland "fixes" the idea of the patriline in the sense of freezing it in place and making it appear spatially fixed and immutable, just like the homeland on one's identity card. This way of thinking about movement also "fixes" patrilineality, in the sense of offering solutions to its many inherent contradictions, not least of which is the impossibility of maintaining and reproducing a family on a small, bounded piece of land, or otherwise making a living in a resource-scarce world without casting forth into spatially unbounded hinterlands and the outer world of opportunity. Rather than looking at movement and fixity as irreconcilable opposites, careful attention to the actual practices of movement shows that moving and staying put form a dialectic of mutual coproduction. In the Vietnamese sense of the homeland, movement and stability configure each other as parts of the same process. The patrilineal ideal may be understood as mobility's spatial fix, and mobility, in its own way, fixes the contradictions of patrilineal social organization.[5]

On the Concept of the Spatial Fix

The way mobile Vietnamese evoke idioms of patrilocal fixity and rootedness in a world of incessant movement can be productively understood as a "spatial fix" for dealing with the challenges of global mobility. By insisting, on the one hand, that identities and roots are formally fixed in space while also recognizing, on the other hand, that human experience also requires movement, the spatial expressions and familiar idioms of Vietnamese kinship provide something of a solution to the problem of accumulating and making productive use of resources in a world inherently limited by scarcity in land, labor opportunities, and other forms of cultural capital, such as social prestige, status, and so on. In making this claim, I borrow from and rethink David Harvey's (2001) notion of the "spatial fix," a concept he developed to describe the process through which "capitalism" fixes the contradictions inherent to the crisis of overproduction and underconsumption. Harvey explains the concept as having two senses that play on a dialectic of fixity and movement. First, capitalism "fixes" or resolves its own internal contradictions by setting off on the move:

> I first deployed the term "spatial fix" to describe capitalism's insatiable drive to resolve its inner crisis tendencies by geographical expansion and geographical restructuring. The parallel with the idea of a "technological fix" was deliberate. Capitalism, we might say, is addicted to geographical expansion much as it is addicted to technological change and endless expansion through economic growth. Globalization is the contemporary version of capitalism's long-standing and never-ending search for a spatial fix to its crisis tendencies. (Harvey 2001, 24–25)

Second, Harvey argues that capitalism tries to "fix" itself by immobilizing some spatial dynamics that facilitate certain kinds of movement: "capitalism has to fix space (in immoveable structures of transport and communication nets, as well as in built environments of factories, roads, houses, water supplies, and other physical infrastructures) in order to overcome space (achieve a liberty of movement through low transport and communication costs)" (Harvey 2001, 25).

For Harvey, capital races around the world in order to reproduce itself in situations where money can be turned into commodities that produce more money. Furthermore, as this process proceeds, the surplus capital produced by these forays abroad also needs to come back "home." In fact, in the most advanced forms of capitalism made nimble by the miraculous spatial fixes of globalization (such as ATMs, fiber-optic cables, and financial instruments, to name a few), capital can almost magically race around the world at the very same time that it accumulates in the bank account of an increasingly enriched capitalist. It gradually annihilates the gap between circulation and accumulation. Telling a similar story, but illustrating it by focusing on the spectacular rise of global cities, Saskia Sassen (1994) also notes how the production of urban cores and high-rises results from this kind of capitalism, which simultaneously expands outward and accumulates inward, such that the production of global networks and highly localized urban spaces is part of the same process. Outward expansion into global peripheries mirrors itself in the form of massive accumulation in highly localized cores.

Pushing beyond Harvey's and Sassen's own fixations, however, it is worth noting that it is not just capitalism that is in on the fix. The coproduction of fixity and movement can be seen in several chapters in this volume, and the determinate forces are not always driven by the imperatives of capital alone. Angela Leung, for example, describes how the circulation of medical knowledge between China and the "southern people" in what is now known as Vietnam led both to inter-Asian connections and to the reification of distinct notions of place-based conceptions of self. While southern people certainly learned from northern medicine, the exchange also reinforced southern people's sense that they had particular bodily and hence medicinal needs rooted in their place in the world. Mounia Chekhab-Abudaya shows not only how the circulation of people and manuscripts creates a notion of a shared Islamic world, but also how this circulation reinforces the importance of multiple sites across the Islamic world, including, but not limited to, Mecca. The production of a miniature Qur'an and other portable manuscripts might be understood as a technological fix in its own right, designed to solve the challenges of globalized movement as pilgrims devised ways to carry their spiritual practices along with them. In another chapter, Tamara Loos describes not only how Prince Prisdang Chumsai's exile abroad took him away from Thailand to places such as Japan, China, Hong Kong, French Indochina, British Malaya, and British Ceylon, but also how his attempts to advocate for a form of transregional Theravada Buddhism led him to elevate his own king of Siam, Chulalongkorn, to the position of supreme unifier. His engagement with transnationalism ultimately reproduced Siam as the center of the world. All of these cases can be understood as spatial fixes, coproduced in tandem with mobility, and driven not simplistically by capitalism but by social-cultural forces like religion, understandings of the body and health, and so on. Likewise, Vietnamese kinship offers a spatial fix of its own that engages with movement in specifically Vietnamese idioms.

Vietnamese kinship models a productive dialectic between fixity and movement, which regularly reproduces ideals of a male-dominated society while nonetheless encouraging the central role of women in the reproduction of patrilineal households—in short, it oscillates between a pragmatic expression of expansive bilateral relations and more restricted patrilineal ideals. Spatially, the oscillation between a geographically expansive celebration of movement and more spatially constrained visions of the bounded homeland, coupled with broadly inclusive conceptions of kinship (construed in terms of the bilateral kindred) and the spatially fixed celebration of the patrilocal concept of home, can itself be understood as a spatial fix to the contradictions of a world that demands both movement and rootedness. If, following Harvey, the compulsion to globalize is capitalism's spatial fix, then the compulsion to simultaneously keep moving about while always longing to return home might be understood as the Vietnamese fix to the contradictions of globalization itself. If globalization is capitalism's fix to its own internal limits, then mobile Vietnamese respond with a spatial kinship fix of their own, one that lets them be mobile and rooted all at once.

Vietnamese Kinship Inside Out

Theorists of global flows and capitalism sometimes give the impression that it is only big-time capitalists who know how to move and stay put at once, and that the only thing being accumulated in the world is money capital and real estate. Anthropologists, however, have for a long time insisted that it is possible to accumulate a wide range of valuables, both in the material form of ritual objects, which are put into or withheld from exchange, and in the form of more intangible qualities of value, which include but are not limited to qualities such as prestige, authority, oratory prowess, and even "beauty." In my own research in Ho Chi Minh City, for example, I have shown how both Vietnamese kinship and spatial understandings of the city's inner and outer districts exhibit a similar "dialectic between fixity and movement" and that the way people navigate and control their movement across "inside" and "outside" spaces contributes to their ability to accumulate symbolic and material resources (Harms 2011b, 2011a). The Vietnamese kinship idiom itself actually enables social actors to oscillate between "inside" and "outside" relations, which in Vietnamese kinship refer to the male-oriented and female-oriented kinship relations (Luong 1989, 1990). The practical manipulation of inside *(nội)* and outside *(ngoại)* relations unifies the spatial and temporal elements of this oscillation. In a family, space-time is organized around the reproduction of the social person, embedded in kinship relations that are themselves grounded in terms of both space and history. Patrilineal relations—called *dòng nội* (inner lines)—emphasize linear history and spatial boundedness in an idiom of reproducing the family unit in a tightly bounded space but over long periods of time. Lineages traced through the mother—called *dòng ngoại* (outer lines)—emphasize short durations of ahistorical clock-time integrated into spatially expansive and socially inclusive networks. As they move between inside and outside, Vietnamese families are able to pursue a wide swath of resources while also maintaining a space in which to accumulate them.

Within this kinship system, which is both flexible and rigid at the same time, successful families do not permanently forsake one form of family organization for another. That is, they do not "choose" to become either fully bilateral or patrilineal; instead, they oscillate between both models, attempting to gain the advantages of both forms of spatial-temporal social organization. Kinship relations expand and contract in a cyclical process of family formation. People shift away from close spatially bounded patrilineal kinship ties during times of transformation and then eventually return to the patrilineal ideal in a time of consolidation. In the end, these apparently contradictory tropes and practices regarding the inside and the outside constitute integral parts of a larger pattern of spatial-temporal oscillation. Opposites are produced to carve a space of movement. Moving between ideals produces social power that is analogous to, if not intimately tied in with, the generation and accumulation of capital, but that cannot be reduced to monetary value alone. The ideals of the quê hương and of the civilized urban core are bound in a relationship of mutual self-constitution that oscillates between spatially and temporally constituted poles of social action epitomized by the opposition of inside and outside, *nội* and *ngoại*.

In other words, Vietnamese mobility is not simply a haphazard array of people running around the world seeking fortune for the sake of fortune alone, but it is made productive by the ways in which mobile peoples integrate their movement within meaningful and productive conceptions of space that are themselves infused with the meanings of Vietnamese kinship. People do not just move around, but productively oscillate across boundaries of inside and outside, simultaneously reproducing an idea of a spatially fixed homeland even as they spread around the world engaging in productive activities that will help them accumulate social and material resources that can be funneled back to that homeland. This relationship appears clearly in the *Heritage* article on how to reconstruct family genealogies. The very people who are traveling about, traversing social space, and generating and accumulating capital prove to be the most interested in re-creating an essentially rooted family history that establishes a localized sense of place and traces a family's connection to that place through deep historical time.

Conceptualized in this way, the Vietnamese kinship idiom and the circulation of capital operate on similar principles: both are in on the spatial fix. Movements outward and away can, in both cases, produce specifically grounded burrowings within localized space. The remainder of this chapter illustrates how this spatial fix plays out in several actual examples of Vietnamese mobility. I begin by giving a broad and sweeping overview of major patterns in Vietnamese mobility and movement during the twentieth century. I then describe a few ethnographic examples from contemporary Vietnam, all of which illustrate how movement toward the "outside" is entangled with social processes that reproduce the "inside."

Mobility in Action

In a recent review article tracing key aspects of movement and mobility in Vietnam, Ivan Small rightly insists that "Vietnam is a nation on the migratory move, both domestically and internationally" (2016, 82). A careful reading of the literature Small surveys highlights how relationships of outward movement are commonly configured with relationships that reproduce either the patriotic homeland as a whole or the family in more localized terms. In other words, nearly all of the outward movements described in his review contribute to the production of social status and prestige back in the sending community. "Questions of migration, and also transportation," Small emphasizes, "are of course entangled with issues of social mobility" (2016, 86). Moving about (the world) helps people move up (in society).

In the early twentieth century, for example, Vietnamese activists and students who traveled abroad famously developed revolutionary sentiments that fostered the many strands of Vietnamese nationalism that would subsequently emerge in French Indochina. At the start of the twentieth century, when resistance to French colonialism was growing, the anticolonial nationalist Phan Bội Châu traveled to Japan (in 1905) and began promoting the so-called Đông du (Eastern study) movement with the intention of fostering a heightened sense of national identity back home (Marr 1971, 120–155; Phan Boi Chau 1999; Sinh 1988). "For both activists and reformists," writes David Marr, "the next two and a half years represented the high point of this generation's anticolonial efforts" (1971, 127). The history of Vietnamese anticolonialism that soon followed is also replete with stories of Vietnamese Francophiles who went to study in France, only to develop strident nationalist sentiments that morphed into outright anticolonialism. Famous figures such as Nguyễn An Ninh went to study subjects like law in France and came back as revolutionaries (Tai 1992, 74–87; Werth 2005 [1926], 131). Even more famously, the story of "going away" in order to cultivate deep sentiments about the homeland has become a central trope in the life history of Ho Chi Minh.[6] As William Duiker has noted, "hagiographers in Hanoi" have made much of scattered remarks contained in Hồ's reminiscences characterizing "his decision to leave Vietnam as a mission to save his country" (2000, 45). To reconcile his long absence with his patriotism, Hồ's peregrinations have been retold in terms that emphasize a productive relationship between his revolutionary work inside the country and his journey abroad. The concept *ra đi tìm đường cứu nước,* which is translated as "go out searching for the path to save the country," has itself become a stock phrase for describing Ho Chi Minh's early travels abroad. Outward movements, in all of these cases, have powerful connotations for the reproduction of the patriotic inside.

In the same way that the movements nationalist Vietnamese took abroad could foster a deeply nostalgic sense of home, which later emboldened their demands for independence, movements within the country also fostered nostalgia for people's ancestral homelands. The nearly one million northern Catholic refugees (Bắc di cư) who fled from the region above the seventeenth parallel to resettle in the south during 1954 and 1955 eventually became active agents in the development of southern Vietnamese nationalism. But these

Catholics, who typically settled in parishes grouped according to their home villages, also maintained a long-lasting sense of cultural self-segregation from other southern Vietnamese. To this day, many "1954 northerners" living in the southern portions of Vietnam continue to cultivate a deeply localized sense of identity that emphasizes their origins in specific, identifiable places in the north from which they originally came (Hansen 2009). During the colonial and anticolonial periods, and also during the Vietnam War (both in the [southern] Republic of Vietnam and the [northern] Democratic Republic of Vietnam), the internal migration of ethnic majority Vietnamese *(Kinh)* migrants from the coasts and deltas up into the highlands and other marginal spaces was central to the way the nation itself became imagined as a coherent geobody (Hardy 2003; Hickey 1993; Lentz 2011; Salemink 2003). More recently, as Small (2016) notes, scholars have focused attention on domestic migration and remittances, rural-urban migration, the role marriage patterns play in migration, and changes in state policies regarding residence permits *(hộ khẩu)*. In all of these cases, the ethnographic and historical evidence regularly emphasizes how peregrinations that send migrants in search of fortunes "outside" their homelands reproduce relationships on the "inside" of their localized village communities.

This same productive relationship between inside and outside can also be seen quite clearly in postwar international migration patterns, which Vietnam scholars increasingly understand as part of a cycle entangled with politics back home. Immediately after 1975, in the period following the end of the Second Indochina conflict (known as the American War in Vietnam or the Vietnam War in North America and Europe), many Vietnamese from the southern portion of the country permanently migrated to the United States and western Europe. In many cases, gateway countries such as Hong Kong also became permanent destinations for people forced to flee the country primarily as economic or political refugees. Given the exceptional conditions of such postwar migration, Vietnamese migration patterns at that time appeared to be unidirectionally outward-facing. At the time, it was assumed that "Vietnamese boat people" were simply leaving and never coming back. However, as Ivan Small's review indicates so clearly, when viewed over the *longue durée,* Vietnamese migration either has more often played out in the form of circular migration or has been characterized by gifting relationships that intimately bind those who have gone away to those who have remained in the quê hương.[7] Writing in 2016, more than forty years after the end of the war, and thirty years after the introduction of market reforms in 1986, Small notes that a "new wave of research in anthropology and sociology on return diaspora migration is also emerging" (2016, 84), and the increasing numbers of Vietnamese Americans "returning" to Vietnam require a more dynamic understanding of the relationship between movement and conceptions of the homeland (Nguyen-Akbar 2014; Small 2012; Koh 2015). Small's own monograph on Vietnamese American remittances shows how remittances must be understood as gifts in the sense described by Marcel Mauss. That is, they forge social ties and social obligations, and the money sent back home is often integrated not only into the process of building homes or securing real estate but into rebuilding social ties to the quê hương (Small 2019).

As noted above, circular migration was certainly the norm for Vietnamese during the colonial era, and it was also always the case during the socialist period in the North, both during and after the war, when Vietnamese intellectuals and workers regularly traveled to eastern Europe and socialist sibling countries around the globe. As Christina Schwenkel has forcefully argued, the history of socialist exchange among Vietnamese moving across the former Soviet Bloc clearly reveals that there was an "oft-overlooked circulation of people, goods, knowledge, and capital between communist states before the collapse of the Soviet Union"—what she calls "socialist mobilities" (2014, 236). Put simply, Vietnamese have been on the move since long before academic interest in globalization developed, and their movement "out" has typically been constituted in relationship to a notion of either returning to or maintaining close gifting relationships with the "inside." Viewed over a longer period, the story of Vietnamese circular movement to countries in what was formerly known as the Eastern Bloc, in some cases really came full circle in the late 1990s and early years of the new millennium, when capital generated abroad began to return home to Vietnam, forming the basis for new investments.

Taken together, all of the cases described in this section show that there is an important connection between the shape of mobility both inside and outside the country and the larger relationship it has with the idea of social mobility within the locally defined conditions of the quê hương. Examples from recent ethnographic work also show that the migratory ideal is not just about going away but about going away in order to return or at least send something back, moving to the outside in order to reproduce the inside. In the next section, I show how a similar dynamic can be seen both in transnational migration beyond Vietnam and in internal migration within the country.

"The Village of Transnationals"

On the outskirts of the northern port city of Hải Phòng, the pseudonymous fishing commune of Hải Thành recently became known in the region as a "village of transnationals." In her outstanding dissertation on this commune, Linh Khanh Nguyen (2016) describes how it became famous in the 1980s and 1990s as a central departure point for oceanic refugees fleeing the economic dearth and political oppressiveness of postwar society. Because the villagers had a long tradition of leading fishing expeditions into the South China Sea, and because of the location relatively close to Hải Phòng, their boats provided the perfect cover for escape by sea, and Hải Thành became a key departure point. Later, as the economic and political circumstances in Vietnam improved toward the end of the 1990s and beyond, it was no longer common for people to escape by sea. Hải Thành, however, remained a hub of transnational mobility, and over the past decade or so it became famous as the commune that sends "the largest percentage, nationwide, of its young women abroad in transnational marriages" (Nguyen 2016, 3–4).

Linh Khanh Nguyen's ethnography details the dramatic transformations that the movement away from the commune had on the fishing village, which had previously been a rural area with the modest homes characteristic of such spaces. In a series of photographs, she depicts opulent new houses that have sprouted up throughout the village. She then describes how Hải Thành had become the center of a veritable building boom:

> Local people were wealthy enough to build sumptuous houses, renovate the small village pagoda into a palatial one, perform costly rituals, and organize an annual three-day new-year festival. While they maintain the local traditions, they also aspire to modernity, reflected, for example, by the Western clothes that youth wear, the birthday celebration with cake and torches. Hải Thành looked rosy from the outside and was famous within the city for its wealth and its numerous Việt Kiều (Vietnamese transnationals). (Nguyen 2016, 7)

The bulk of the wealth driving this building boom in the village comes from remittances sent by the young women involved in the transnational network of marriage migration. As the daughters of these fishing families are married off to foreign husbands, primarily from South Korea and Taiwan, the remittances they send home become an important source of wealth, which is then reinvested in the physical landscape of Hải Thành.[8] The process in some ways looks like a smaller-scale, and decidedly more rural, version of the processes described by David Harvey and Saskia Sassen regarding the globalization of capital. In this case, however, the symbolic medium of exchange is not just money but the transnational marriages that make the movement of money possible. These marriages impose certain moral obligations that redirect material resources back to the ancestral homeland.

An important secondary story in Hải Thành further highlights the ways in which international processes intersect with local sociocultural dynamics. As all the marriageable Hải Thành women increasingly moved away to marry foreign husbands, there were simply not enough local women left for the local men to marry. While Hải Thành bachelors faced diminished romantic prospects among women native to Hải Thành, they also tended to be the primary beneficiaries of the windfall of remittances that were being sent home by those Hải Thành women who had married abroad. The local men were supported financially by their generous sisters or, more properly, by their foreign brothers-in-law. As a result, the men of Hải Thành themselves became popular marriage partners for women living in the surrounding communities, and a secondary movement developed in which women from nearby agricultural communes increasingly started to marry into Hải Thành. From the perspective of rural villagers in surrounding areas, the men of Hải Thành played a structurally similar role to that which foreign men played in relation to the women of Hải Thành. They were "rich outsiders" to other villagers whose marriageable women moved to Hải Thành as outsiders in their own right, in order to reproduce the inner patrilines of Hải Thành men. What emerges is an entire transnational circuit of "outsiders" reproducing other people's patrilines. On the transnational scale, Vietnamese women from Hải Thành were marrying abroad, upholding a "traditional" patrilineal "Confucian" ideal for East Asian men, who in turn sent remittance money to Vietnamese patrilines, which in turn were and are supported by a regional network of Vietnamese villages.

What is especially fascinating about this example is that it simultaneously violates the standard "rules" about patrilineal kinship (e.g., that it is supposed to be the men who go outside in search of fortune, that women are the "general of the interior," and so on) and, without contradiction, goes on to reinforce the idea of the patrilocal homeland as a cherished space that must be reproduced.

This social response evokes a long tradition in scholarship focused on the ways in which women address through their actions what anthropologist Bette Denich has called the "patrilineal paradox," in which "the structure denies the formal existence of women, while at the same time group survival depends upon them" (1974, 260; see also Wolf 1972). More recently, the anthropologist Sara Friedman has further expanded on the ways in which transnational marriages are forced to negotiate patrilineal gender norms even though marriage practices were driven by more translocal dynamics. In the case she describes, Mainland Chinese women marrying into Taiwanese families were deemed a threat to patrilineal models of the Chinese family, and hence were forced to find alternative ways to articulate the importance of the family through idioms of the mother-child bond (Friedman 2010, 90). As in China, stereotypes of the patriarchal and patrilocal family model no longer fully explain the way marriages play out (Yan 1997).

In the case of the translocal marriages of women from Hải Thành, the circulations of wealth, both across and beyond the South China Sea into Korea and Taiwan and in the villages surrounding Hải Thành, both undermine and intensify the importance of the patriline. It is, after all, the women who have married abroad, and who are thus sending back the money that produces all the opulent houses rising up in Hải Thành. This contradicts the ideal patrilineal notion that daughters do not contribute to their originary patrilines; by going abroad they successfully reproduce the conditions within their own village that enable their brothers to become heads of patrilocal households back in Hải Thành. On one level, the patrilines of the town are maintained not by the sons but by the financial contributions of the native daughters who have been married "out" to foreign husbands, daughters who in the classic patrilineal traditions of inheritance would otherwise have been "lost to the family." On another level, these contributions play a central role in reproducing the village as a spatial locus of patrilineal prestige and authority. Together, the case shows how kinship models can be quite flexible in practice, even as the flexibility itself can be channeled in ways that reproduce idealized, traditional notions of authority that are often thought of as being rather rigid and fixed. This is precisely what I mean by mobility's "spatial fix": mobility produces a relationship in which an ideal of patrilineal kinship is reproduced as something fixed, even as a host of flexible patterns emerge that literally fix all the contradictions associated with patrilineal conceptions of inside and outside.

Internal Migration

Patterns of movement among migrant traders within Vietnam also show how movement "outside" can reproduce the structures of the "inside" while also transforming it. This is especially clear in a recent collection of ethnographic studies called *Traders in Motion: Identities, and Contestations in the Vietnamese Marketplace,* which shows that migrant traders are both always on the move and yet always entangled with the quê hương (Endres and Leshkowich, 2018). In particular, two ethnographic cases from that volume clearly illustrate how highly mobile traders also reproduce the same dynamic relationship between fixity and movement expressed in all the examples described throughout this chapter.

In the first case, Hy Van Luong (2018) discusses a network of mobile trinket traders who all hail from the same small central coastal Vietnamese town of Tịnh Bình, in Quảng Ngãi province, but who ply their wares in Ho Chi Minh City, the coastal resort town of Vũng Tàu, and points throughout the Central Highlands. If one were to encounter one of these traders in person, one might assume that the individual must be part of an uprooted, unmoored, and unconnected vagabond class. As Luong's research shows, however, they are not in fact uprooted; the traders themselves described their mobility as actually helping them facilitate their relationship with home, especially when compared with the inflexibility of other job opportunities. Summing up some of the interviews conducted with his research team, Luong explained that Tịnh Bình migrants "commented favorably on the time flexibility in itinerant trade in comparison with the strict industrial discipline on factory floors" and they especially appreciated how trading allowed them to return to their home village (2018, 93). One young male migrant extolled the virtues of itinerant vending by comparing it with factory work: "When I worked in a factory, if I wanted to go home for a visit, I had to apply. [. . .] As an itinerant vendor, I could go home whenever I wanted. Nobody said anything" (ibid.). A female vendor made a similar point: "As a factory worker, I can only go home once a year. As a peddler, I can go home to help my family during peak agricultural seasons, and return to my itinerant vending work without any problem" (ibid.). The evidence from this intensive study of itinerant traders clearly shows that many aspects of migratory trade are in fact structured by the relationship traders have with the sending community in Quảng Ngãi province. While these traders are out and about on their circuits of migratory small-time vending, they give the impression of being an unmoored class of disconnected traders. But it is precisely the flexibility of the trade that enables them to maintain the importance of their home base in Quảng Ngãi. For example, all of the traveling vendors actively mobilized kin networks when raising capital for their start-up costs, and all the traders were thus deeply entwined with extensive networks and social relations from their home village, which enabled them to mobilize their own connections but also bound them to their place of origins.

A very different example from the same volume also illustrates a connection between mobility and the reproduction of local places of origin. Minh T. N. Nguyen (2018a) discusses the production of wealth and masculinity among waste traders who circulate between Hanoi and a village in the Red River delta. Nguyen's discussion is important because she shows the way movement and masculine identity play out over the course of a life cycle. She vividly describes the stories of young, footloose men from the village who imagine themselves as casting off from convention when, in their late teens and early twenties, they rush into the wide world of migratory opportunity offered by Hanoi's waste trade. In the process of entering the trade, however, they gradually begin to reproduce preexisting gender roles, first in terms of the gendered division of labor in waste collection itself (in which men specialize in "electronics" and women specialize in recycling and "junk"), and soon after, as they begin to team up with women and eventually settle down by getting married and opening up waste depots.

Nguyen carefully shows how success in the Hanoi waste trade is often channeled back to the home village in the Red River delta. In the process, the home village is literally built out of Hanoi's waste. Furthermore, as these men settled down, they gradually began to reproduce the gender attitudes of their fathers. The adventurous entry of these young men into the waste trade was marked by a rhetoric of cosmopolitan abandon, reckless spending, and flirtatious sexual adventure; however, by the time they settled down, got married, and set up waste depots, these young men were eager to style themselves in a patrilineal mold as "protectors" of their families and lineages. They settled down, focused on building a household, and often invested in homes and properties back in the home village. By the time they became fathers themselves, their gendered disposition quite markedly began to reproduce the same gendered dispositions of their own fathers. As Nguyen (2018b) notes in a new ethnographic monograph on the same group of waste traders, all of these sociocultural dynamics were mirrored in the way their home village itself was quite literally built from the material fruits of all these migratory movements. In a poignant statement about the way junk trading has led to the rise of fortunes in the home village, one villager declared: "Our village used to deal in shit, and now we are rich!" (Nguyen 2018b, xi).

All of the examples in this chapter have shown how movement in search of opportunity and the reproduction of the spatially fixed quê hương, or native place, can be understood as one of the central preoccupations of contemporary Vietnamese mobility. For scholars like David Harvey, such a dialectical connection between movement and accumulation might be explained as little more than the obvious effects of "globalization and the spatial fix." While the role of capitalism cannot be denied, all the examples in this chapter have shown that the spatial fix of Vietnamese mobility is not determined by capitalism alone but plays out in contextually specific ways that in their own manner seek to fix capitalism. In particular, the transformations taking place across the country are all intimately structured by Vietnamese idioms of kinship and homeland. These patterns engage with the imperatives of global capitalism and seek to fix them in specifically Vietnamese ways by channeling the promiscuous movement of capital and other spatially unbounded opportunities back toward the spatially bounded locus of the quê hương. Such changes, depending on how they play out, may either bring a mobile traveler great anxiety or deliver them a certain form of satisfaction. The anxiety may result from the mobile person's heavy load of nostalgia, as well as no small moral burden to remember the source as something fixed, eternal, and unchanging. The satisfaction, however, comes from the same moral burden, from the sense that one's moral duty is to build and contribute to the site of one's origins.

There are parallels to this relationship across Asia. Benedict Anderson, for example, begins his essay on "long-distance nationalism" by evoking Lord Acton's mid-nineteenth-century musing that "exile is the nursery of nationality." Anderson, like globalization theorists since at least Featherstone (1990), highlights the fact that nationalist sentiment seems to sprout up across the globe at the very moment that the world becomes more interconnected, and that the proliferation of people removed from their homelands has the paradoxical effect of intensifying their connections to their homes. This "enormous process of disintegration," Anderson writes, feeds off and emerges from nationalist and local sentiments at the same time that "the world has become ever more tightly integrated into a single capitalist economy" (1998, 59). Turning these observations toward the processes that drive mobility both within and outside a country, it is clear that contemporary forces of migration and movement, ranging from transnational to internal forms of migration, cannot be separated from forces that compel people to foster inward contemplation about their space of origin. Modernizing Lord Acton's claims to the current era, one might quip that study abroad or labor migration is the nursery of nationalism; urban migration is the nursery of rural nostalgia; and a flight on an airplane is the nursery for reflections on an imagined home.

Notes

1. For more on the moralizing aspects of the Chinese version of this proverb, see Oxfeld 2010.

2. See Vietnam Airlines 2002 for a differently rendered English translation. I have retranslated the poem in order to emphasize the seven-syllable meter and A-B-A-B-A rhyme pattern of the Vietnamese original.

3. As Nina Glick-Schiller has noted, the enduring interest of the "ancestral homeland," often rhetorically stressed in the "language of blood," is commonly reinforced by governments trying to engage their global diasporas, a practice found not only in China but also in countries as culturally removed from East Asia as Haiti (2005, 578).

4. The terms *quê hương* and *nguyên quán* basically mean the same thing, although the first is a Vietnamese word with no traceable Chinese origin, and the second is a Sino-Vietnamese word (Nguyễn Quốc Hùng, n.d.). The first term is most commonly used in everyday speech, popular songs, poetry, and so on. The second term is largely bureaucratic and appears almost only in paperwork.

5. For the classic discussion of the contradictions of patrilineal social organization, and how social actors negotiate them, see Wolf 1972, 32–41.

6. Numerous "official biographies" of Ho Chi Minh are available at nearly every bookstore in Vietnam, in Vietnamese and often English and other global languages. For an extensive catalog of officially sanctioned Ho Chi Minh books, visit the website of Thế Giới (World) Publishers, the long-operating foreign-language publishing house run by Vietnam's Ministry of Information and Communications: http://www.thegioipublishers.vn/en/books/. For more scholarly approaches to documenting Ho Chi Minh's life and movement, see Brocheux 2007; Duiker 2000; and Quinn-Judge 2002.

7. Anthropologists have long recognized migration as part of a complete system. For an early review of the literature on return migration, see Gmelch 1980.

8. For a discussion of the marriage of foreign women across East Asia, see the work of Danielle Bélanger (2010).

References

Anderson, Benedict. 1998. *The Spectre of Comparisons: Nationalism, Southeast Asia and the World.* New York: Verso.

Bélanger, Danièle. 2010. "Marriages with Foreign Women in East Asia: Bride Trafficking or Voluntary Migration?" *Population & Societies* 469: 1–4.

Brocheux, Pierre. 2007. *Ho Chi Minh: A Biography.* Cambridge: Cambridge University Press.

Denich, Bette S. 1974. "Sex and Power in the Balkans." In *Woman, Culture, and Society,* eds. M. Rosaldo and L. Lamphere, 243–262. Stanford: Stanford University Press.

Duiker, William J. 2000. *Ho Chi Minh: A Life.* New York: Theia.

Endres, Kirsten W., and Ann Marie Leshkowich, eds. 2018. *Traders in Motion: Identities and Contestations in the Vietnamese Marketplace.* Ithaca, NY: Cornell Southeast Asia Program Publications.

Featherstone, Mike, ed. 1990. *Global Culture: Nationalism, Globalization, and Modernity.* London: Sage.

Friedman, Sara L. 2010. "Marital Immigration and Graduated Citizenship: Post-Naturalization Restrictions on Mainland Chinese Spouses in Taiwan." *Pacific Affairs* 83(1): 73–93.

Gmelch, George. 1980. "Return Migration." *Annual Review of Anthropology* 9(1): 135–159.

Hansen, Peter. 2009. "Bắc Di Cư: Catholic Refugees from the North of Vietnam, and Their Role in the Southern Republic, 1954–1959." *Journal of Vietnamese Studies* 4(3): 173–211. doi: 10.1525 / vs.2009.4.3.173.

Hardy, Andrew. 2003. *Red Hills: Migrants and the State in the Highlands of Vietnam.* Honolulu: University of Hawai'i Press.

Harms, Erik. 2011a. "Material Symbolism of Saigon's Edge: The Political-Economic and Symbolic Transformation of Hồ Chí Minh City's Periurban Zones." *Pacific Affairs* 84(3): 455–473.

———. 2011b. *Saigon's Edge: On the Margins of Ho Chi Minh City.* Minneapolis: University of Minnesota Press.

Harvey, David. 2001. "Globalization and the 'Spatial Fix.'" *Geographische revue* 3(2): 23–30.

Hickey, Gerald Cannon. 1993. *Shattered World: Adaptation and Survival among Vietnam's Highland Peoples during the Vietnam War.* Philadelphia: University of Pennsylvania Press.

Jellema, Kate. 2007. "Returning Home: Ancestor Veneration and the Nationalism of *Đổi Mới* Vietnam." In *Modernity and Re-Enchantment: Religion in Post-Revolutionary Vietnam,* ed. Philip Taylor, 57–89. Lanham, MD: Lexington Books.

Koh, Priscilla. 2015. "You Can Come Home Again: Narratives of Home and Belonging among Second-Generation Việt Kiều in Vietnam." *Sojourn* 30(1): 173–214.

Lentz, Christian C. 2011. "Mobilization and State Formation on a Frontier of Vietnam." *Journal of Peasant Studies* 38(3): 559–586.

Luong, Hy Van. 1989. "Vietnamese Kinship: Structural Principles and the Socialist Transformation in Northern Vietnam." *Journal of Asian Studies* 48(4): 741–756.

———. 1990. *Discursive Practices and Linguistic Meanings: The Vietnamese System of Person Reference.* Philadelphia: John Benjamins Publishing.

———. 2018. "A Mobile Trading Network from Central Coastal Vietnam: Growth, Social Network, and Gender." In *Traders in Motion: Identities and Contestations in the Vietnamese Marketplace,* eds. Kirsten W. Endres and Ann Marie Leshkowich. Ithaca, NY: Cornell Southeast Asia Program Publications.

Marr, David G. 1971. *Vietnamese Anticolonialism: 1885–1925.* Berkeley: University of California.

Nguyen, Linh Khanh. 2016. "Morality in Motion: Gendered Movement and Social Stratification in Contemporary Vietnam." PhD diss., Syracuse University.

Nguyen, Minh T. N. 2018a. "Money, Risk Taking, and Playing: Shifting Masculinity in a Waste-Trading Community of the Red River Delta." In *Traders in Motion: Identities and Contestations in the Vietnamese Marketplace,* eds. Kirsten W. Endres and Ann Marie Leshkowich. Ithaca, NY: Cornell Southeast Asia Program Publications.

Nguyen, Minh T. N. 2018b. *Waste and Wealth: An Ethnography of Labor, Value, and Morality in a Vietnamese Recycling Economy.* Oxford: Oxford University Press.

Nguyen-Akbar, Mytoan. 2014. "The Tensions of Diasporic 'Return' Migration in the Transnational Family." *Journal of Contemporary Ethnography* 43(2): 176–201.

Nguyễn Quốc Hùng. n.d. nguyên quán 元舘. In *Từ điển Hán Nôm* [Hán Nôm dictionary].

Oxfeld, Ellen. 2010. *Drink Water, but Remember the Source: Moral Discourse in a Chinese Village.* Berkeley: University of California Press.

Phan Boi Chau. 1999. *Overturned Chariot: The Autobiography of Phan-Boi-Chau.* Translated by Vinh Sinh and Nicholas Wickenden. Honolulu: University of Hawai'i Press.

Quinn-Judge, Sophie. 2002. *Ho Chi Minh: The Missing Years, 1919–1941.* Berkeley: University of California Press.

Salemink, Oscar. 2003. *The Ethnography of Vietnam's Central Highlanders: A Historical Contextualization, 1850–1990.* Honolulu: University of Hawai'i Press.

Sassen, Saskia. 1994. "The Urban Impact of Economic Globalization." In *Cities in a World Economy,* 15–44. Thousand Oaks, CA: Pine Forge Press.

Schiller, Nina Glick. 2005. "Long-Distance Nationalism." In *Encyclopedia of Diasporas: Immigrant and Refugee Cultures around the World,* eds. Melvin Ember, Carol R. Ember and Ian Skoggard, 570–580. Boston: Springer US.

Schwenkel, Christina. 2014. "Rethinking Asian Mobilities: Socialist Migration and Post-Socialist Repatriation of Vietnamese Contract Workers in East Germany." *Critical Asian Studies* 46(2): 235–258.

Sinh, Vinh. 1988. *Phan Boi Chau and the Dong Du Movement.* New Haven, CT: Council on South East Asia Studies, Yale Center for International and Area Studies.

Small, Ivan V. 2012. "Embodied Economies: Vietnamese Transnational Migration & Return Regimes." *Sojourn* 27(2): 234–259.

———. 2016. "Framing and Encompassing Movement: Transportation, Migration, and Social Mobility in Vietnam." *Mobility in History* 7(1): 79–90.

———. 2019. *Currencies of Imagination: Channeling Money and Chasing Mobility in Vietnamese Remittance Economies.* Ithaca, NY: Cornell University Press.

Tai, Hue Tam Ho. 1992. *Radicalism and the Origins of the Vietnamese Revolution.* Cambridge, MA: Harvard University Press.

Viện Ngôn Ngữ Học. 1997. *Từ Điển Việt-Anh* [Vietnamese English dictionary]. TP.HCM: Nhà Xuất Bản TP. Hồ Chí Minh.

Vietnam Airlines. 2002. "Gia Phả [Family records] 'We Are Family.'" *Heritage, Vietnam Airlines Inflight Magazine,* 10–16.

Werth, Léon. 2005 [1926]. *Cochinchine.* Paris: Éditions Viviane Hamy.

Wolf, Margery. 1972. *Women and the Family in Rural Taiwan.* Stanford, CA: Stanford University Press.

Yan, Yunxiang. 1997. "The Triumph of Conjugality: Structural Transformation of Family Relations in a Chinese Village." *Ethnology* 36(3): 191-212.

2

Mobility Assemblage and the Return of Islam in Southeast China

BIAO XIANG and QIANG MA (RAMADAN)

Since the end of the 1990s, a surge of Islam has been witnessed in the cities of Guangzhou in Guangdong province and Yiwu in Zhejiang province, both in southeast China. When one of the authors (Ma) visited the Light Minar Masjid (also called Huaisheng Mosque) in Guangzhou in 1994, the gate was locked and the place was empty. He was told that the mosque, the oldest in China, was not open to the public and was turned away. Disappointed and hungry, he looked for halal (*qingzhen,* 清真) eateries but found none. The other three historical mosques in Guangzhou were in the same sorry state. Ma thus concluded that Guangzhou, a major port through which Islam entered China in the Tang dynasty, was unlivable for a Muslim. When Ma revisited the city eight years later, however, all the mosques were full at Jum'a time. By the time Xiang started his field research in Guangzhou in 2015, nearly 15,000 people were estimated to attend Jum'a in the four mosques in total, including about 1,000 in Light Minar Masjid.[1] The change in Yiwu has been even more dramatic. A city that had no Muslim population before the late 1990s now has a mosque of 2,500 square meters that dominates a busy street in a primary location (Zou, 2015: 33) and is attended by 8,000 at peak times.[2]

No Muslim will go hungry in Guangzhou or Yiwu today. Halal restaurants are not only widely available but also regarded as more authentic and reliable than those in the northwest, China's Islamic heartland. Halal restaurants in the northwest commonly serve alcohol, but very few in Guangzhou and Yiwu do so. It is also in Guangzhou or Yiwu that some young Muslims from the northwest started performing daily prayers, experienced their first Ramadan fast, and (for women) started covering their hair.

The immediate cause of the (re)emergence of Islam in the southeast, as recognized by news reports and academic research, is the in-migration of Muslims. Guangzhou, for instance, had 20,000 Muslims from other parts of China and another 20,000 from overseas in the late 2000s. This amounts to four times the 10,000 deeply assimilated local Muslims (Guo, 2010). In Yiwu all of the 20,000 Muslims in the late 2000s were migrants (Ma Yan, 2013: 16). Most foreigners were traders from the Middle East, North Africa, and South Asia. The Chinese came from across the country, with the northwest being the largest place of origin.

Although it is self-evident that there would be no development of Islam had there been no in-migrations of Muslims, it is also clear that Muslim migration does not necessarily lead to a thriving of Islam. Muslim migration is not at all specific to the two cities. It is rather a common phenomenon, and an estimated 2.1 million Chinese Muslims (including Uyghurs) were on the move in China in 2011 (State Commission of Family Plan 2011 Report on Internal Migrants, cited in Mi, 2012: 228). Furthermore, migrations in other places are observed to cause the decline of religion. For instance, a survey conducted in the four cities of Nanjing, Tianjin, Shanghai, and Shenzhen in the 2000s found that migrant Muslims became less active in religion as measured by how often they visited mosques, how much they interacted with fellow Muslims, and how much they knew about Islam (You, 2012). In Lanzhou and Xi'an in the northwest, which are the main destinations of migrant Chinese Muslims, the decline is reported to be even more obvious. This is because the migrant Muslim population dispersed spatially and lost access to religious education (Mi, 2012: 234–235). A researcher thus predicted that "in a couple of generations' time [the Muslims in the northwest] will become similar to [those] in the southeast now," who maintain a Muslim identity but know very little about Islam (Mi, 2011: 5).

Then, what in Guangzhou and Yiwu has contributed to the vibrancy of Islam in addition to in-migration? A related question worth asking is, Is the surge ephemeral or sustainable? It is reasonable to speculate that the current development is short-lived. Most of the Muslims are transient migrants. The foreign traders typically visit China only a couple of times a year and stay less than a month each time. The Chinese Muslims are not likely to settle down either. According to Ma Qiang's surveys and interviews conducted in Guangzhou between 2004 and 2006, the majority of the Chinese Muslim migrants are from the countryside, have an education level below junior high school, work in informal sectors, and migrate alone without families (Ma Qiang 2006: 232, 217–219). Given the *hukou* system that distinguishes the locals from the migrants and the cities' strong bias toward the highly educated in offering settlement, few Muslim migrants can become new urban residents. Furthermore, both international and internal migrations are highly susceptible to external shocks. The market instability in the Middle East following the Arab Spring in 2011 and China's tightening of visa control since 2015, for instance, have already reduced the number of Muslims in southeast China. If the inflow of Muslims is the sole cause of the thriving of Islam, then the ebb is likely to bring the end.

We argue that the ongoing flourishing of Islam in southeast China is not caused by the Muslims' in-migration to the two cities per se; rather, it is a result of the coalescing of different types of mobilities that took place across much larger scales of space and time. In the two trading cities, previously unrelated Muslims encounter each other and form multilayered, mutually supplementary relations. These relations—instead of formal organizations or religious doctrines—give stability to the community, gain certain recognition from the government, and mobilize grassroots religious energy. Each type of mobility has its own history, which provides the mobile subjects with rich social resources including networks, knowledge, and inspiration. In sum, historically shaped mobilities of various types come together contingently and in turn create something new. We call this "mobility assemblage."

The notion of assemblage first denotes the "composition of diverse elements into a provisional socio-spatial formation" (Oakes and Wang, 2015: 7), which in our case means the relations among migrant Muslims. Second, following the geological definition of assemblage as "a group of fossils that, appearing together, characterize a particular stratum" (cited in Wise, 2005: 78), we emphasize the layered historical experiences and memories beneath ongoing social formation. The migrations of Muslims to Guangzhou and Yiwu are part of their much longer journeys. Third, by assemblage we emphasize gaps and frictions. The different groups do not fit perfectly into a coherent whole, nor do the histories of the mobilities unfold in a linear manner. In fact, the discrepancies between groups and the twists in history are important parts of the story as they propel the migrants to reflect on Islam and on the self more deeply. Finally, components of an assemblage come together as well as move apart. What disperse, however, are not the same as they were before they converged. Being part of an assemblage can be transformative.

As a result of the mobility assemblage, the surge of Islam in southeast China is likely to have lasting effects beyond this region. Guangzhou and Yiwu may or may not develop sizable settlements of Muslims, but they already play an important role in the rise of religious consciousness among Chinese Muslims, especially the Hui, across the nation. It is for this reason that we describe the thriving of Islam as a "return" rather than a "revival" (*fuxing,* 復興) or "eastward spread" (*dongjian,* 東漸). "Revival" and "eastward spread" are the two terms that are commonly used in existing literature to describe the same development. The word "revival" implies a continuous Islamic tradition in the region, while "eastward spread" highlights the centrality of the northwest. We describe it as "return" not in the sense that the same thing goes back to the old place, but to suggest that Islam is *reactivated* in the process of circulation. Circulation is not bound to locality, and the two cities are hubs in the ever-moving process of circulation. Thus it is a return *in,* rather than *to,* southeast China. Return is always re-turn. There is no clear departing point or destination. The returned always turns out something new. With the (re)emergence of Islam in Guangzhou and Yiwu, new ideas and practices are also developed. Some of the new elements move to the northwestern home places, which is another form of re-turn.

In what follows, we first delineate how Islam (re)emerges in the southeast as a result of a mobility assemblage consisting of three mobile subjects: (1) the foreign traders, (2) the petty entrepreneurs from the northwest, especially *lamina* (拉麵, hand-pulled noodle) restaurant owners and their employees, and (3) the Chinese-Arabic translators who work for Arabic-speaking foreign traders. The second part of the chapter zooms in on the translators who play a critical role in the return of Islam. We trace their current migratory and religious activities back to the historical assemblage of mobilities that they participated in as religious students.

This chapter is based on field research that was conducted separately by the two authors. Ma carried out his intensive field research among Muslim migrants in Guangzhou between 2004 and 2006, which is followed up by his regular revisits. He has also worked on the historical changes among Muslim communities in Xi'an, in which migration played an important part. This provides a valuable reference point for examining the situations in Guangzhou and Yiwu. Xiang visited Yiwu for the first time in 2008 and started intensive field research in Yiwu and Guangzhou in 2015. So far he has spent more than four months in the two sites and interviewed eighty-two migrant Muslims. Participatory observation and in-depth interviews are the main methods used by both authors. All the names used in the article are pseudonyms.

The Convergence of Mobile Subjects

We regard migrants as "mobile subjects"—namely, actors whose dispositions, social resources, and life plans are shaped by their past migratory experiences, which in turn affect their future migration trajectories. The encountering of different migrants, thus, should be understood as intersections of various dynamic, ongoing mobilities, rather than as a convergence of individuals or groups with fixed subjectivities.

"The Arabs" as the Symbolic Representative

"The Arabs are the Deity of Wealth *(caishenye)* for the local government!" This was how Su Junyi, an Arabic-Chinese translator in Yiwu, originally from Ningxia, explained that the Yiwu government had been surprisingly open in accommodating Muslim migrants' religious needs in the 2000s. In 2004, the Yiwu party secretary designated the premises of an abandoned silk factory in the city center to be converted into a mosque. The mosque then raised more than 20 million Renminbi to rebuild itself into a state-of-the-art landmark of the Arabic style in 2013.[3] "In order to have the Arabs to come [to Yiwu], they have to provide places for prayer," explained Ma Bin, an owner of a cargo logistic company in Yiwu originally from Henan province, central China. "[The government] also knew that in order to keep the Arabs here, they have to keep people like us here." The reason why the Arabs are attractive is obvious: between 50 and 80 percent of all exports from Yiwu, known as the world's largest market of light commodities, are sold to the Middle East.

Similar consideration was behind the Guangzhou government's support for the development of the old mosques. The significance of mosques first caught public imagination during Canton Fairs in the early 2000s. To make foreign Muslim traders feel more at home, the city government financed mosques to hire English- and Arabic-speaking Imams and to provide halal food and assistance to the traders. The 2010 Asian Games in Guangzhou also increased the legitimacy of Islam as part of the city's life. The government invested 20 million Renminbi to extend the main prayer hall of Sages' Tomb Mosque and set up prayer spots inside the Asian Games Village, and called in more than twenty people from the north to serve as Imams and assistants. As "Many heads of states [from Islamic countries] also came [during the Games]," commented Huang, a leather trader from Henan, "China would look really bad if there were no places for them to pray!" In this sense the foreign Muslims were representative of all migrant Muslims to the government and the mainstream society.

But this representation relation is highly symbolic. First, it is far from accurate to equate the foreign traders to "the Arabs." Arabs are only part of the foreign traders. There are traders from south Asia (Afghanistan, Pakistan, India, and Bangladesh) who arrived before the Arabs. There are also those from Africa, particularly Nigeria, Rwanda, Mali, Somalia, and Kenya, who are the most recent comers. Even among the traders from the Middle East, they can be more accurately described as "diasporic" than as "Arabic." The early arrivals often had established businesses in Thailand, Egypt, South Korea, or Malaysia and expanded or relocated their business to China, especially after the 1997 Asian crisis. A considerable number of traders are themselves refugees, stateless people, or repeated migrants—for instance, Palestinians living in Saudi Arabia, or Syrians in Jordan. Former students on Chinese government scholarships are an important subgroup too. Thus, the foreign traders are not at all a single group. They embody mobility assemblage. Nevertheless Chinese public media lump them all together as "Arabs," because the Arabs are regarded as the most economically advanced. Chinese Muslims sometimes use "Arabs" as a shorthand for foreign Muslims because Arab is a symbol of Islam, even though a sizable number of the traders are non-Muslims.

The representation relation is also symbolic because the interaction between the foreign traders and the Chinese Muslims is rather limited. According to Ma Qiang's 2004 survey in Guangzhou, 74 percent of Chinese Muslims described their relations to foreign fellow believers as distanced (Ma Qiang, 2006: 251, table 5.2.5). Arabic-Chinese translators are the only Chinese who have sustained interactions with foreign traders, but their relations are in most cases limited to business dealings. They rarely hold in-depth discussions about religion. Many translators are shocked when they see traders from the Middle East swear, smoke, drink, and visit brothels, despite their superior knowledge about Islam. Some are also disappointed by foreign traders' indifference to the Palestine cause and the dominance of the United States in the Middle East. The aforementioned survey by Ma reports that 74.8 percent of the Chinese Muslims regarded the foreign Muslims in Guangzhou as lacking religious piety *(jiaomen buhao)* (Ma Qiang, 2006: 251, table 5.2.5). The gap between the image of Arabs as "authentic" Muslims from the sacred land and the firsthand observations urge the translators to rethink what it means to be a Muslim. This also means that, while foreign traders are instrumental in opening up highly visible religious space (formal mosques), they are marginal players in the return of Islam among the Chinese Muslims in southeast China.

The "Lamian Economy" and the "Base Population"

Chinese Muslims call the formal mosques in Guangzhou and Yiwu *kesi,* "guest mosques," which serve "guests"—those who are passing through. This is quite the contrary to the mosques in the northwest that are owned and run by residents around the mosques. Guest mosques can be very busy during festivals and Jum'a, but are rather empty otherwise. In this context, what constitutes the backbone of daily religious life for most Muslims are the prayer spots *(libaidian).* Set up by Muslim migrants, the prayer spots are often converted from a two- or three-bedroom apartment close to where they live. These spots are where the migrants pray every day, including Fajr before dawn and prayers during the night, as well as where they socialize, kill time, and take naps, similar to mosques in the northwest and many other parts of the world (Tagliacozzo, 2013). New arrivals may stay there before they find accommodation. For them, the prayer spots are not only shelters but also places where they receive vital information about the city and the job market. In sum, a prayer spot is the defining center of a Jamā'at—a Muslim community based on daily, face-to-face communication, where religious and social activities are inseparable.

The earliest prayer spots were set up by Chinese migrant Muslim petty traders, particularly *lamian* restaurant owners. A *lamian* restaurant typically hires three to ten assistants. Most of the workers are male (a sharp contrast to non-Muslim restaurants) relatives of the owner. They all live and work together like a family. The owner often has family members who run *lamian* restaurants in the same city, and they form tight networks. A few owners may bring their employees to a restaurant to pray together (Liang, 2012; Ge, 2015: 278). Networks among *lamian* migrants are further tightened by their poor integration into city life. Most of the restaurants are unregistered. The government of Fudong district in Shanghai, for instance, estimated that more than 95 percent are unregistered (Ge, 2015: 226). The poor integration is in turn caused by their very high level of mobility, as a *lamian* restaurant often moves to a new city every few years (Liang, 2012: 259). In sum, the *lamian* migrants are particularly capable of setting up prayer spots that replicate the structure of *fang*—self-contained residential quarters surrounding a mosque in northwest China. If the Arabs are the symbolic representative, the *lamian* migrants constitute a "base population." The base population are less visible but much more sizable. They attend religious activities regularly and provide crucial social infrastructure for the community.

The *lamian* migrants not only set up the earliest prayer spots but also were the first, and so far the only ones, to gain government recognition for these spots. Among the nine prayer spots in Guangzhou in early 2016, only the one set up by *lamian* restaurant owners was allowed to register as "a site for religious activities" (*zongjiao huodong changsuo,* 宗教活動場所). In Dongguan, an industrial city located between Guangzhou and Hong Kong, all eight spots were officially registered in 2015 and they were all run by a *lamian* group. The legitimacy of the *lamian* migrants can be attributed to the nature of their mobility. The *lamian* migration, particularly from Hualong county of Qinghai province, has been encouraged by the local government of the sending place as a most effective means of poverty alleviation, especially after the central government decided to convert farmland in that region back to forest in 1999, which deprived the peasants of an agricultural livelihood. The county government of Hualong encouraged employees in the public sector to apply for loans for *lamian* migrants by using their salaries as securities. The Hualong government also registered "Hualong beef *lamian*" as a patented brand with the State Administration of Industry and Commerce in 2004 (Ge, 2015: 276). The nationally dispersed "*lamian* economy," as it is officially named in Hualong, is now an important part of the local GDP. The Hualong government stations cadres in large cities to serve the *lamian* migrants and help them set up associations for mutual assistance. Thus, while foreign traders help gain a legitimate public image of Islam in the cities, the *lamian* group wins recognition for its grassroots activities.

Translators as Activists

Most prayer spots in Guangzhou and Yiwu are unregistered, and their status is highly precarious.[4] The prayer spot in Tongdewei, a residential area in north Guangzhou, for instance, was shut down a few times and moved twice after it was set up in 2004. The spot was in limbo again in July 2016 when the local street office (*jiedao banshichu,* 街道辦事處) forced the owner of the premises not to extend the lease. The informal status and precariousness, according to organizers of unregistered prayer spots, made the prayer spots more genuine. Jin Goufu, an Arabic-Chinese translator and the central figure of the Tongdewei prayer spot, stressed that the government's refusal to recognize the spot is not necessarily a bad thing: "Had we developed it into a formal mosque, there may be internal strife, conflicts over interests, and we may become less united. [. . .] I always tell our brothers [a commonly used phrase for Muslims, especially of the same Jamā'at] that pressure is a good thing. Faced with pressure, we will have to improve our work even more. Islam always develops in face of pressure."

What makes these prayer spots a central locus of the return of Islam is the people behind them. Although the organizers are not especially religiously devoted, they are enthusiastic about the development of Islam. They are keen to increase the influence of Islam in the mainstream society and are willing to spend time and resources to organize activities toward this end. They can be regarded as religious "activists."

The majority of these activists are Arabic-Chinese translators. There were about 4,000 translators working in Guangzhou and about 2,000 in Yiwu at any particular time between 2010 and 2016 (Ma Ping, 2012: 217; interviews by Xiang). They assume the role of activist first because they are young. Most translators are between twenty-five and forty years old, an age when one "reaches mature understandings of Islam," as our informants put it. Most of the translators are men, which gives them the authority to act publicly. They are also religiously active because they are economically well off. About 70 percent of them work as employees at trading companies set up by foreign or Chinese traders, and the remaining 30 percent either have their own firms or work as individual intermediaries. Their average annual income was estimated to be about 20,000 RMB a year (Ma Ping, 2012: 217). A few have accumulated so much capital that they moved to manufacturing. The translators' activist role is also related to the temporality of their mobilities. Because most foreign traders visit Guangzhou and Yiwu only a few times a year, translators have a large amount of free time though they have hectic schedules during busy seasons. Unlike the *lamian* migrants who move to a different city every few years but can hardly move within a city on a daily basis because of the business, translators tend to work in Guangzhou and Yiwu for many years but move around across China frequently, including visiting home places. This makes them both more attached to Guangzhou and Yiwu and better connected to Muslims in other places.

The translators became activists also because of their intermediary position between foreign Muslim traders and Chinese non-Muslim suppliers. Their Muslim identity is the single most important factor, probably more important than their Arabic proficiency, in winning the foreign traders' trust. The translators are all known to their foreign partners by their Arabic names (*jingmin,* literally names from the Books). But a more important push comes from the Chinese suppliers, to whom translators are known by their Chinese names. The Chinese suppliers and others constantly ask them such questions as "What is Islam?" and "Why do you pray just like the Arabs?" Faced with these questions and feeling that they are being watched, the translators developed a new sense of the religion—that is, they have to be responsible for providing the correct answer and demonstrating the right behavior. Yang Fuyou, a translator from Ningxia, experienced significant changes in recent years. "Before, I read books hastily without much thinking. Now I have to assess them. My criterion is: Is this good for China's Islam? These years' mobilities *(liudong)* have given me a consciousness of the collective, a sense of mission. I feel responsible for Chinese Islam." In addressing the questions from non-Muslims, some translators have also started preaching, which is a very rare practice for Chinese Muslims. Jin Guofu commented on his interactions with non-Muslims this way: "When they asked these questions, I told myself: good! An opportunity has come. I will seize the chance to tell them what Islam is. Every time when I explain Islam, it is also a chance to reinforce my faith."

As such, the activists set up prayer spots not merely to reproduce the *fang* structure but also to actively develop Islam. Unlike the *lamian* population who came from a very limited number of places and whose prayer spots are mini replicas of Qinghai Ihwān mosques, the translators have originated from many more places and their prayer spots do not follow a particular religious order. The activists make an effort to accommodate diversity. The committee of the Tongdewei prayer spot is unusually large, comprising more than twenty members. This is because they want to make sure that Muslims from all provinces in China have their representatives involved. Activists' prayer spots are special also in that some of them do not have Imams, which is rare for mosques in China. As the translators are well versed in Arabic and Islamic theology, they lead prayers and deliver Hutbah (sermons during Jum'a) themselves. Some translators are qualified Imams themselves. Often called "quasi-ahong" or "non-official ahong" *(minjian ahong)* in the community, they are sometimes more respected than the officially appointed Imams in the guest mosques. Ma Qinghu, a translator from Xinjiang, explained, "In official mosques *(gongjiasi)* the Hutbah needs to be reviewed by the government the day before! [The Imams] just repeat again and again the red letter headed documents (*hongtou wenjian,* meaning "issued or approved by the government") from the Islamic Colleges. We are an entirely different subject *(zhuti).* We are independent." The Hutbah given by the activists tend to address concrete issues directly related to daily life—for instance, how one should face the economic downturn and how to deal with the reliability of the information on social media.

The activists thus bring new dynamics to the prayer spots. Young Muslims are excited to see that, unlike the mosques in the home place that are visited by the elderly only, prayer spots in Guangzhou and Yiwu are full of young people. The atmosphere at the spots is much more open and less hierarchical, and anyone can volunteer to lead prayers. One informant put it this way: "In the home place we are all numbed. We go to the mosque [there] because we are supposed to go; in the mosque we see our fathers and uncles. In Guangzhou we always meet new friends in the mosque [*sic;* they use this word for both formal mosques and prayer spots]. We come here because of our faith. We can sit down to have a conversation. The discussion is much deeper."

The activists also reach out to Muslims who appear to have lost their faith. For example, Zhou Mingyong, a key activist of the Tongdewei prayer spot, would remind his friends of prayers by mobile phone messages. One of the friends ignored all the messages, but Zhou persisted. When the friend's wife gave birth to their first child, Zhou urged him to think about the meaning of life as a father. The friend became an activist. To attract more young people to "return" to Islam, activists organize home-based discussion sessions, barbecues, and sightseeing tours. Su Binyan, a translator in his late thirties, called these activities "work of thought" (*sixiang gongzuo,* 思想工作), a well-established Communist Party term. Islamic "work of thought," according to Su, hardly exists in the northwest. "It is easier to do the work (*zuogongzuo,* 做工作) in Guangzhou. In our home places we are all either friends or relatives. We have nothing to do at home; we just play cards or chitchat. Time passes quickly. You can't persuade people [to think about religion]." In the southeast, in contrast, "we are all busy and have proper jobs to do," therefore making in-depth discussions more likely.

Activists also play a bridging role among different Jamā'ats in Guangzhou and Yiwu. A number of translators, including the aforementioned Su Junyi and Zhou Mingyong, visit different prayer spots regularly to develop connections across groups. Their visits are sometimes called *kechuan,* a term normally meaning an entertainer who acts as an occasional host at another entertainer's television show, as they often give brief speeches and hold group discussions after the prayer. They pass information from one community to another. For instance, if one spot faces financial difficulties, others will know immediately and will take action to assist. The activists also engage with Muslim communities far beyond Guangzhou and Yiwu. Recent initiatives include raising funds for Rohingya (and sending representatives to Myanmar to hand over the money), launching programs to assist Muslim university students, donating to Muslim elderly care houses, and supporting girls' education in the northwest.

The activists reach out to local government bodies even though they are keen to maintain independence. The Tongdewei committee invites cadres of the Street Office to participate in Eid. When they held a gala in 2015 for the completion of an Islamic studies course by about forty children, organized by the spot, they invited leaders of the municipal bureau for ethnic and religious affairs. On the eve of the mid-Autumn festival and Chinese New Year, mooncakes and fruit were handed out to the police and security guards of the residential compounds where the Muslim population was concentrated.

To reach out to a broader audience, a group of translators set up an Internet-based Bulletin Board System forum called "Muslims' Mutual Support Community in Guangzhou" in 2002. It provided a lively forum for discussing issues that concern young Muslims, such as employment, marriage, and faith. The BBS proved to be very popular. Online participants also organized offline events, creating strong synergy between the virtual and the actual and therefore a unique type of Jamā'at. The BBS was the precedent of the largest Muslim internet portal in China today, the Chinese Muslim Networks (Zhongguo musilin wang, 中國穆斯林網). This is a powerful testimony of the impact the translators, though small in number, may have on Chinese Islam.

The activists are thus different from the leaders who are based in official mosques or Islamic associations, who have limited grassroots connections. The translators are also different from community leaders in the northwest, who can be divided into two types: the "traditional" ones and the "modern" ones. The "traditional" ones have their authority based on their age, lineage, and ultimately personal reputation and status. The "modern" ones are young, wealthy Muslims (a similar trend is observed among the Cham Muslim minority in Cambodia; see Tagliacozzo, 2013). In recent years an increasing number of entrepreneurs have been elected as the heads of mosque committees, which are a central organization of the community that represents the *fang* to manage individual mosques. Entrepreneurs emerged as new leaders because they are an important source of funding for the mosques. The activists are seen by migrant Muslims as more genuine leaders than both the traditional elderly and the currently wealthy.

The biggest difference between the activists and the conventional community leaders is that many of the activists were "problem youth." Many were school dropouts or were even involved in street gangs. They learned Arabic not because of their interest in Islam but as a last resort after failing their formal education. Ma Jinbao, a well-built, talkative translator who was always in sportswear, said that he was a well-known troublemaker in his hometown of Jilin in northeastern China. No neighbor wanted to greet him on the street. He never entered a mosque by himself until one day, at the age of sixteen, when he heard a new voice of *bangke* (Adhan, the call to prayer) coming out of the local mosque. The *bangke* was sung by a visiting Imam from the northwest. The tone, moving and powerful, instantly reminded him of his favorite rock song, "I can't bear myself" (*Wudizirong,* 無地自容) by the popular Chinese band Black Puma in the early 1990s. This opened the door to Islam for him. The translators' humble backgrounds helps them become activists. Their own experiences convince them that every Muslim, and every human being indeed, will eventually "return" to Islam sooner or later. They are therefore less rigid about theological doctrines, less judgmental about others' behavior, and open to everyone. Their rich, often tough, life experiences also taught them the skills of interacting with different people. They do mental labor amid the grassroots.

To understand how the translators go from being problem youth to becoming activists, we need to trace their earlier migration journeys as religious students, the subject we now turn to.

Layered History of Mobilities

Yang Fuyou, who was quoted above for his newly developed sense of responsibility toward Chinese Islam, dropped out of high school at the age of fifteen. His grandfather, a devoted Muslim, urged him to become a *manla* (religious student in a mosque). But after learning the Arabic alphabet, he dropped out of the mosque because he found the study boring. After working as a casual construction worker in Xinjiang for two years, he returned to his home village jobless. Fellow villagers were worried about his future and suggested to his parents to send him to an Arabic language school (ALS), one of a group of small private schools focused on Islamic and Arabic language teaching. "I was told that studying in an ALS is not like being a *manla*. ALSs are not very strict. They have desks and blackboards, and the students do not sit on the floor." He agreed to go, and went to Zhangjiachuan ALS in Gansu province alongside two friends from the same village. A year later he moved to Guanghe ALS in the same province because he heard the teaching there was more fun.

After graduation, Yang was introduced by a teacher at Guanghe ALS to a mosque in Pingliang, also in Gansu, to work as a teacher. He did not like the job. "I feel I am not suitable to teach in a mosque. In an ALS you can ask questions, but in a mosque you cannot think much." He planned to go to Saudi Arabia for further study in 2004. After spending more than 200 RMB to prepare the required documents and waiting for more than a year, he had to give up as he could not get a passport. Muslim out-migration at that time was tightly controlled in China, and Muslims had special difficulties in obtaining passports. Soon after, he married a Muslim in Pingliang. A former schoolmate at Guanghe who was now studying in Yunnan suggested to him to take up a teaching job at his school in Yunnan. He went to the south for the first time.

Yang liked the new job, but he was concerned about the salary (especially after his first daughter was born in 2008), which was just over 200 RMB a month. He shared his concern with the schoolmate from Guanghe, who had since moved from Yunnan to Guangzhou to work as an Arabic-Chinese translator. The friend's immediate response was, How about Guangzhou? Finding a job as a translator in Guangzhou, however, turned out to be harder than expected. Yang started trading clothes, sourcing them from Guangzhou and selling them in Pingliang. The venture lost 30,000 RMB in three months. He was in Guangzhou again after closing the shop in Pingliang:

> This time I was determined to stay. In the first two months I couldn't find a job. I relied on schoolmates. They gave me money without me asking. In the evenings they asked me to go out for dinner. After eating, they would hand me a few hundred. After I started working [for an Egyptian trader who was also introduced by a school friend], they still asked me from time to time "do you have enough to spend?" If they sensed that I have difficulties, someone would take the initiative, make phone calls, then a few close school friends would meet up for dinner, and give me money again. There is no obligation to return the money, as long as you spend the money for that purpose [as the friends expect you to do]. You can use the surplus to help others. It is common that school friends stick together to fight hardships *(yiqi daping)*. For instance those who haven't found jobs stay with those who are working [for free].

ALS networks, as Yang Fuyou's experience shows, play a critical role in the lives of the translators. To appreciate the significance of the ALS networks, we need first to understand how ALSs developed. Initially aimed at training modern Imams and Islamic scholars,[5] ALSs break with traditional mosque education (*jingtang jiaoyu,* 經堂教育) in multiple ways. Unlike mosques, where the main daily learning activity is reciting Islamic scripts (particularly the "thirteen books") in *jingtangyu* (經堂語, literally "madrasa language," an artificial language that mixes classical Chinese, Arabic, and Persian), ALSs model themselves after mainstream public schools. They teach Arabic as a living language and use Mandarin as the medium. With the passage of time, ALSs became increasingly "secularized." They evolved into a kind of vocational education and became more distanced from Islamic teaching than originally envisioned. Paradoxically, however, the secularization enables the ALS education to lay a foundation for the translators to become activists later.

This is because the secularization made the ALSs more popular among youths. As vocational teaching institutions, ALSs attracted considerable numbers of youths who would otherwise never have considered learning Arabic and Islam. Even Linxia ALS, unquestionably the most reputable ALS in China, set it as part of its mission to "provide drop-outs and unemployed young people with an opportunity to re-enter school" (*Baidu Baike*, n.d.). ALSs are also popular because, with a strong focus on contemporary Arabic, they are seen as the most direct path to international mobility. Larger ALSs established contacts with universities overseas, especially in Malaysia, Thailand, Saudi Arabia, the United Arab Emirates, and Jordan, to send graduates there for further study. ALSs became particularly popular in the 2000s when it was known that many graduates went to the southeast to earn quick money by working as translators, and ALSs thus acquired the moniker of "translator schools." Among the eleven registered ALSs in Ningxia Hui Autonomous Region, six were set up after 2004 (Ma Yan, 2012: 66-67)—that is, after the most rapid increase of the migration of Arabic-Chinese translators to Guangzhou (2003) and Yiwu (2004). Nearly 1,000 students and more than 20 teachers from Baofuqiao School in Yinchuan, the capital city of Ningxia, became translators in Yiwu by 2011 (Ma Yan, 2012: 68).

Secularization also gave ALSs in most parts of China much more freedom to expand than mosque education. While religious teaching in mosques is subject to regulations of at least four authorities (religious bureau, Islamic association, education bureau, and the residents and committee of the *fang*), ALSs answer only to the education bureau. ALSs developed at the same time that government control over religious teaching in mosques was tightened (for instance, in the 2000s, mosques needed approval before taking on students, and the number of students each mosque recruited was capped). By reducing religious elements in the curriculum and renaming courses on Islamic thought as moral studies courses, Linxia ALS was upgraded to Linxia Foreign Language College in 2007 and enjoyed full support from the government. In a similar manner, Guanghe ALS was developed into Guanghe Foreign Language Vocational College shortly thereafter.

Thanks to the ALSs' popularity and legitimacy, ALS students are able to carve out a social space based on their extraordinarily high level of mobility. Students constantly drop out and join new schools. Our interviews suggest that less than one-third of the students completed the three-year course in a single school. Why do they move so frequently? One commonly mentioned reason is the desire to learn more. Different schools have different strengths—for instance, Zhangjiachuan ALS is said to be strong in linguistic training, and Guanghe is known for its emphasis on Islamic thought. Changing schools is also said to help students concentrate on their studies, as a familiar environment makes one lax.

Most importantly, translators stress that they moved frequently simply as a continuation of the tradition of "travel learning" (*youxue,* 遊學).[6] *Youxue* traditionally means the rotation of Imams as well as the movement of their *manla* between different mosques and often across great distances. When an Imam moves to a new mosque every few years, most of his *manlas* follow. An Imam may also recommend his *manlas* to mosques in other places for further study in order to widen their exposure. *Manlas*' parents sometimes "send their children afar and deliberately to unfamiliar locales" in order for the students to fully concentrate on studying; this separation "initiates a career which itself is marked by numerous partitions and incessant movements" (Guangtian Ha, 2014: 234).

ALS students are even more footloose than *manlas* because they can migrate anytime without the master's approval and recommendation. Transfers across schools are academically easy as the theological teaching of most ALSs follows broad Hanafism instead of particular orders or *menhuan,* and their language curricula are based on standard Arabic textbooks published by Beijing Second Foreign Language University. ALSs take the students' going and coming as a matter of course. When a new student appears, a teacher holds a brief conversation with him (female students are much less mobile, though it is common for female students to study in provinces other than their home places; women do develop their ALS networks but the scope and impact are much more limited than men's) and then arranges "inserting" *(chaban)* him in a class according to his linguistic proficiency. Another reason ALS students are highly mobile is that ALS certificates mean little in the mainstream society. Students do not care much whether they have that piece of paper in the end, and they are ready to leave whenever they receive a job offer or hear about a school that offers interesting courses.

The student mobility has led to nationwide ALS alumni networks. The networks are critical in leading ALS graduates to jobs as translators. One of the first groups of translators in Guangzhou arrived in the fall of 2000. They did not come to work as translators but to join a Ponzi scheme specialized in massage devices. It was only after they discovered the scheme was a scam that they started working as translators and intermediaries. They were all recruited to the pyramid sales through ALS networks, and they also turned themselves into translators collectively through the same networks. The ALS networks are particularly important for the northwesterners. Early comers from the northwest were first introduced to the occupation of translator by ALS friends from Yunnan and Shandong. Ha Lijian, an ALS graduate who used to work as an ALS teacher but now works as a translator, explained: "Yunnanese [Muslims] have a stronger foundation in Chinese than us, so they learn new things faster than us northwesterners. People from Shandong, Yunnan, and the Central Plains [central China] are more alert about business opportunities." ALS graduates from Yunnan and Shandong were among the first who established contacts with foreign traders. In other words, ALS networks create synergies between northwestern Muslims, who are linguistically proficient, and those from the south and the east, who are more business savvy.

But ALS friendship is not a random happenstance. The networks are based on the common faith. To remain in the network, one needs to perform his faith even if he is not particularly religious. But not every religiously pious Muslim can join these networks. The translators approach Islam differently from other Muslims. "We know how to discuss, how to reason," Su Junyi explains, in regard to why ALS friends organize family gatherings to discuss religious questions, while other groups hardly do so. Although ALSs do not turn all students into devoted Muslims, the education equips them with the knowledge and discourses to think religiously and reflexively. Some ALS graduates proudly distinguish themselves from the students of the government Islamic colleges. According to them, students of the Islamic colleges may have better theological knowledge, but they do not have enough fear and reverence for Allah *(jingwei)*.

The religious underpinning of the ALS networks in turn facilitates their economic functions. This is evidenced by the reflection of Ma Anfu, a translator who set up his own trading company in 2013 and then invested in a jean manufacturing plant outside Guangzhou, on his ALS circle:

> Since 2015, we began to collaborate in business, for instance we set up companies together. Business collaboration requires [the partners to have] deep understandings of Islam. Those who have deep understandings have common language with each other. An elite cannot work with a common man. Neither a poor man nor a nouveau riche is easy to collaborate with. You need both economic foundation and religious piety [to be a good collaborator]. Cooperation is very complex, there will be a lot of disputes if the religious faith is weak *(jiaomen buhao)*; they cannot work together.

Just like economic prosperity, which takes years to accumulate, deep religious understanding, the activists repeatedly emphasized, is a result of long-time learning. The activists believe that it is their faith that brings them wealth, but the opposite is also true. Their faith deepens in the process of pursuing wealth. This is because both wealth and piety are accumulated through interactions with ALS alumni.

The return of Islam in southeast China is not driven by the in-migration of Muslim populations per se; it is more importantly a result of *interactions between different types of mobilities,* including those that took place before and outside the region. We call the contingent but consequential coalescing of mobilities "mobility assemblages." From the perspective of mobility assemblage, the important questions are how one mobile subject complements another structurally, and how one type of mobility leads to another historically, rather than whether the Muslims will settle down or move on, as conventional migration studies may focus on. Gaps and frictions internal to the assemblage are an important part of the assemblage and they bring in new dynamics. For instance, the Arabic-Chinese translators' disappointment with the behaviors of some of the Arab traders makes the translators more reflexive and confident. The apparent "secularization" of the ALS education creates new social space that enables religious development.

The perspective of mobility assemblage is particularly pertinent to understanding the surge of Islam in China today. This can be illustrated by a comparison to what happened in the 1980s. Noticing the rise of Islamic consciousness owing to international contacts in the 1980s, Dru Gladney suggested that "expanded awareness of the importance of Islam to Hui identity leads local government officials to revise policies that had previously encouraged a stricter distinction between ethnicity and religion. Many of these policies were originally intended to encourage economic development and the Four Modernizations. In this process, they have allowed freer religious expression of Hui identity" (1996: 330). In other words, it was the policy liberalization after the Cultural Revolution that led to increasing religious practices and international contact, which simultaneously strengthened Chinese Muslims' religious and national identity (Gladney, 1996: vii–xii). The past two decades have witnessed a reverse of this policy trend, and state control over religion has become stricter, especially after the late 2000s. In this context, mobility assemblage creates new opportunities for religious development. Mobility assemblage can have this effect because of its multifacetedness. For instance, the economic contributions of the Arab traders and *lamian* population win certain degrees of legitimacy for religious activities. The legitimacy makes the environment less hostile for the activists. At the same time the "secularization" of religious education makes it possible for future activists to develop their widespread networks. As part of the multifaceted mobility assemblage, religious developments became inseparable from transnational trade, educational advancement, and poverty alleviation through migration. Thus, the otherwise suspicious appears as something permissible or even desirable. Furthermore, mobility assemblage enables Islam to thrive in the process of constant circulation that is harder to monitor and control for the state.

The mobility assemblage perspective raises the question of how the "localization" paradigm in the study of Chinese Islam, which has been predominant in both Chinese and English literature, should be reassessed. As Frankel pointed out, "Regional specificity is one of the major characteristics of the wave of scholarship that has come to dominate the field over the past decade or so" (2011: 258). Lipman (1997: 39) in particular emphasized the need for "careful research, which must be local rather than generalized," on Chinese Muslims. The development of Chinese Islam as we observe, however, has become national, or more precisely, Sinophonic. Ideas, discourses, and connections are formed increasingly on a national scale. On the other hand, the perspective of mobility assemblage cautions us about the limit of the transnational paradigm, which has been predominant since the 1990s. Cross-nation contacts are clearly growing, but they by no means constitute a main driving force for the return of Islam in southeast China. The historical composition of mobility assemblage, as delineated in this chapter, shows that the reemergence of Islam has primarily grown out of traditions in China, both long-established and newly emerged.

Notes

1. Imam Wang Guanxue, interview by Xiang, Light Minar Masjid, Guangzhou, July 21, 2016.

2. Guanxue, interview.

3. Ma Bin, a key member of the mosque committee, interview by Xiang, September 10, 2015.

4. According to the State Council Regulations on Religious Affairs (*zongjiao shiwu guanli tiaoli,* Decree No. 426, November 30, 2004; revised at the 176th executive

meeting of the State Council on June 17, 2017), those planning to set up spots for religious activities must apply for permission from the county government. But such applications are rarely approved. This is not because the government forbids such spots altogether—they are often tacitly permitted—but because the government wants the prerogative to close them down anytime deemed necessary.

5. The setting up of ALSs in the 1980s was an attempt to resume a movement with the same goal in the early twentieth century.

6. Transregional networks among scholars were crucial for the development of Islamic thought in late Ming and Qing. See Zvi Ben-Dor Benite 2005.

References

Baidu Baike. n.d. "Linxia Alaboyu Xuexiao" [Linxia Arabic School]. Accessed June 2, 2017. http://baike.baidu.com/link?url=mZKbGFe3lTO5V77ygQywAyVnOTbl2hknPySVdmZ8K_e3NjXLoOFjDO97DrxJNO3t_Wmj5T15QTqoviIk8NtoI71XDPXsonp4FJWl-2T_iVhkBBZ2wWiv4j7Yp_3PoVA91xhbBJR39uF4L7N1h4kSpXceplF5DlUuYnnAthj3PMm.

Frankel, James D. 2011. "From Monolith to Mosaic: A Decade of Twenty-First Century Studies of Muslims and Islam in China." *Religious Studies Review* 37(4): 249–258.

Ge Zhuang. 2015. *Chang sanjiao dushi liudong musilin yu yisilan jiao yanjiu* [A research on migrant Muslims and Islam in Yangtze River delta cities]. Shanghai: Shanghai shehui kexueyuan chūbanshe [Shanghai: Shanghai Academy of Social Sciences Press].

Gladney, Dru. 1996. *Muslim Chinese: Ethnic Nationalism in the People's Republic.* 2nd ed. Cambridge, MA: Harvard University Press.

Guangtian Ha. 2014. "Religion of the Father: Islam, Gender, and Politics of Ethnicity in Late Socialism." PhD thesis, Columbia University.

Guo Chenzheng. 2010. "Zhongguo xibu musilin liuru dongbu yanhai dachengshi xianzhuang yu zhangwang" [Current situation and prospects of the influx of Muslims from western China to metropolitans in the eastern coast]. *Zongjiao yu Shijie* [Religion and the world], no. 3. Accessed June 1, 2017 (pages missing). http://www.sara.gov.cn/llyj/4488.htm.

Liang Jingyu. 2012. "Liudong musilin de xiandaixing yu shiminhua—jian lun musilin shaoshu minzu nongcun renkou liudong de shehui wenti" [Modernity and citizenization of migrant Muslims, also on the social problems of the migration of rural minority population of Muslims]. In *Zaoyu yu tiaoshi: Xiandaihua beijingxia de chengshi musilin xueshu yantao hui wenji* [Encounter and adaptation: A proceedings of the symposium on urban Muslims in the context of modernization], eds. Ma Qiang and Ma Fude. Lanzhou: Gansu Nationalities Publishing House: 225–261.

Lipman, Jonathan N. 1997. *Familiar Strangers: A History of Muslims in Northwest China.* Seattle: University of Washington Press.

Ma Ping. 2012. "Musilin 'dongjian' yu yanhai diqu chengshi de fenbu geju bianhua" [The eastward spread of Muslims and the changes in its distribution pattern among coastal cities]. In *Zaoyu yu tiaoshi: Xiandaihua beijingxia de chengshi musilin xueshu yantao hui wenji* [Encounter and adaptation: A proceedings of the symposium on urban Muslims in the context of modernization], eds. Ma Qiang and Ma Fude. Lanzhou: Gansu Nationalities Publishing House: 214–224.

Ma Qiang. 2006. *Liudong de jingshen shequ: Renlei xue shiye xia de guangzhou musilin zhemati yanjiu* [A mobile spiritual community: A study on the Guangzhou Muslim Jamā'at from an anthropological point of view]. Zhongguo shehui kexue chuban she[Beijing: China Social Science Press].

Ma Yan. 2012. *Yige xinyang qunti de yimin shijian: Yiwu musilin shehui shenghuo de minzuzhi* [The migration practice of a faith group: An ethnography of the social life of Muslims in Yiwu]. Zhongyang minzu daxue chubanshe [Beijing: Central University for Nationalities Press].

———. 2013. "Shixi Yiwu musilin zuqun rentong jiqi tedian" [An analysis of the ethnic identity of Muslims Yiwu and its characteristics]. *Zhongguo Musilin* [Chinese Muslims], no. 3: 16–20.

Mi Shoujiang. 2011. "Xu" [Preface]. In *Shuxi de moshengren: Da chengshi liudong musilin shehui shiying yanjiu* [Familiar strangers: A research on the migrant Muslim's social adaptation in metropolitans], by Bai Youtao, You Jia, Ji Fangtong. Yinchuan: Huanghe chuban chuanmei jituan, ningxia renmin chubanshe [Yinchuan: Yellow River Publishing Media Group and Ningxia People's Publishing House]: 1–6.

———. 2012. "Zhongguo huizu musilin dushi hua de qushi: Sanshi nianlai zhongguo huizu musilin shehui de zhongyao bianhua" [The trends of Muslii urbanization in China: Important changes in the Muslim society in China over the last thirty years]. In *Zaoyu yu tiaoshi: Xiandaihua beijingxia de chengshi musilin xueshu yantao hui wenji* [Encounter and adaptation: A proceedings of the symposium on urban Muslims in the context of modernization], eds. Ma Qiang and Ma Fude. Lanzhou: Gansu Nationalities Publishing House: 228–235.

Oakes, Tim, and June Wang. 2015. "Introduction." In *Making Cultural Cities in Asia: Mobility, Assemblage, and the Politics of Aspirational Urbanism,* eds. June Wang, Tim Oakes, and Yang Yang. London and New York: Routledge: 1–14.

Tagliacozzo, Eric. 2013. *The Longest Journey: Southeast Asians and the Pilgrimage to Mecca.* New York: Oxford University Press, chapter 10.

Wise, Macgregor. 2005. "Assemblage." In *Gilles Deleuze: Key Concepts,* ed. Charles J. Stivale. Montreal: McGill-Queen's University Press: 77–87.

You Jia. 2012. "Lun liudong musilin de zongjiao shenghuo yu chengshi shehui shiying: Yi dongbu yanhai chengshi weili" [On migrant Muslims' religious life and adaptation to urban society: Taking the coastal cities as an example]. In *Zaoyu yu tiaoshi: Xiandaihua beijingxia de chengshi musilin xueshu yantao hui wenji* [Encounter and adaptation: A proceedings of the symposium on urban Muslims in the context of modernization], eds. Ma Qiang and Ma Fude. Lanzhou: Gansu Nationalities Publishing House: 189–200.

Zou Lei. 2015. "Xin sichouzhilu shang zongjiao yu maoyi de hudong: Yi Yiwu, Ningxia weilei" [The religion-trade interactions on the new silk road: Taking Yiwu and Ningxia as examples]. *Shijie Zongjiao Wenhua* [World Religious Cultures] No. 3: 32–37.

Zvi Ben-Dor Benite. 2005. *The Dao of Muhammad: A Cultural History of Muslims in Late Imperial China.* Cambridge, MA: Harvard University Asia Center.

3

Cowry Country

Mobile Space and Imperial Territory

DAVID LUDDEN

Cowry shells *(Cypraea moneta)* had served as currency for millennia before people living among open spaces of mobility spanning South and Southeast Asia used cowries to form the unique multicultural commercial environment that I call Cowry Country: it stretched overseas from the Maldives (a string of coral islands off the western coast of the Indian peninsula), along rivers of deltaic Bengal, and across tropical mountains of Burma and Yunnan, connecting agrarian frontiers of Mughal India with Qing China and Indian Ocean trade networks. In the watery parts of its commercial space, merchant ships sailed the Bay of Bengal and Sylheti boatmen sailed the Meghna River, where Sylhet was the pivotal inland port, in northern Bengal, at the base of the mountains (now in Meghalaya). Above Sylhet, Khasia traders hiked jungle pathways connecting lowland Bengal with highland Burma. Cowry Country included the so-called Southwestern Silk Road and Horse and Tea Road, winding through China, Tibet, Nepal, Burma, Bengal, and North India (Anderson 2009; Yang 2004). Tribal peoples who traveled these routes used cowries more than metal coins stamped with symbols of lowland imperial authority. In the late eighteenth century, Cowry Country used more cowries than other regions in the world, at a time when cowries facilitated trade among littoral societies from China around Africa to the Americas (Wicks 1992; Yang 2004, 2011).

Tiny Maldives cowry shells served as the cheapest coin all around the Indian Ocean when the Europeans arrived, and were the first article of British trade from the Maldives to India (Hogendorn and Johnson 1986; Perlin 1993: 152–163, 270; Wicks 1992: 28–72). Bengal was a famous market for cowries (Deyell 2010), which dominated the Maldives export economy (along with coir for ship building) (Maloney 1980: 112, 126, 137, 417). In Bengal, however, only the northern Sylhet region had no coins in circulation except cowries. Sylhet District Records—manuscript correspondence preserved in the Bangladesh National Archives that records local knowledge gathered by British officers—make that fact crystal clear. In 1788, for example, the first resident district collector, a Scotsman named Robert Lindsay, reported that "there is not above 6 or 700 rupees to be found in Sylhet and these are bad Arcots. . . . No copper coins of any Species passes through the District. The Revenues are paid in Cowries and all mercantile transactions are carried on through the same currency" (SDR297.44:17May88).[1]

Sylhet town is nestled among rivers in a slight rise in the floodplain below the monsoon-drenched mountains (of today's Meghalaya), which loom over Bengal and send torrents annually down the Meghna River. Sylhet was a port of trade unique in Bengal not only for its exclusively cowry currency but also as a Mughal and then East India Company regional headquarters in what was typically described as a "wild frontier," whose residents were mostly mobile and largely ungovernable. In the eighteenth century, many mobile settlers had recently arrived from North India, called Afghans and Turks in the district records, and they fought for local control over land and labor on farming frontiers in the jungle. Many other residents were peripatetic hunters and fisherfolk, and many were tribal Khasias with mobile homesteads in the mountains and plains, who farmed, hunted, and traded all across Cowry Country. Yet for Mughal and British authorities, the most important—and best documented—residents of Sylhet were not the unruly mobile folk but rather tax-paying settled Hindu and Muslim Bengali peasants, landlords, officers, and merchants, who identified with, depended on, and sustained state authority in agrarian territory constantly disrupted by fighting and flooding (Eaton 1994; Ludden 2011).

The ungovernably mobile mingling of peoples in this mixed tribal, Hindu, Muslim, highland, and lowland social space sustained the local monopoly of cowry currency: it was clearly the preferred object of value standardization for commercial transactions in this open space of mobility outside the reach of state authorities, who stamped their symbols of power on metal coins. Eighteenth-century Sylhet sent shiploads of goods south—into lower Bengal, southern India, and the Maldives—and shiploads of cowries arrived in return. Cowries traveled from Sylhet into the mountains to bring countless mountain products into the plains (listed below) for local consumption and long-distance trade. Cowries then worked their way east through highland exchange into Yunnan.

Cowry Country's commercial value and vitality grew as agrarian frontiers expanded into the mountains of the southern tropics: from the west, in Mughal India; from the east, in Qing China; and from the south, in Alaungpaya (Kon-baung) Burma and Chakri Siam. As imperial expansion in the rice-growing lowlands demanded more goods from the mountains, tribal peoples living outside imperial control traveled connective commercial pathways among territories in India, Burma, Tibet, Siam, and China using transcultural cowry currency. This anarchic commerce provided highland wealth for agrarian empires as it also increased the wealth, power, and vulnerability of tribal polities in the highlands (Sinha 1987).

Cowry Country disappeared into those Asian agrarian empires in the century after 1750 (Giersch 2006). In Sylhet, it was squeezed from Bengal and Burma. Imperial Burma conquered Arakan (1785) and then Manipur (1814) and Assam (1819). The Bengal (Mughal) Nawab (governor) occupied Sylhet with a military *faujdar* and land grant frontiersmen, and the English East India Company settled a permanent resident revenue collector there in 1778 (Robert Lindsay). The Company soon confronted imperial Burma, above Sylhet, in Assam, which British India conquered in the 1820s (Ludden 2014). The incorporation of Cowry Country into lowland imperial territory ended the cowry's monetary monopoly in Sylhet. Cowry shells became merely cheap coins that symbolized old ways (Deyell 2010; Heimann 1980; Yang 2011).

A turning point in the spatial transformation of western Cowry Country occurred in 1790: Khasias were expelled from lowland Sylhet, then mixed Bengali-Khasia ethnic communities began to disappear (Ludden 2017). After 1824, silver rupees became the official coin in Sylhet and Assam. Trade still flowed among the mountains and plains: limestone from quarries above Sylhet built Calcutta. But modernity buried Cowry Country in maps of empires and nations (Ludden 2003b).

Mobile Space

Modern geography immobilized space by constructing its contours in fixed territorial terms. In that light, a region called Zomia has recently emerged as a territory inside official state boundaries but outside state control, in the heavily forested tropical mountains of interior mainland Southeast Asia, and by extension, also in the mountain borderlands of Tibet and Nepal, Hindu Kush, and the Kunlun Range (van Schendel 2002; Kratoska, Raben and Nordolt 2005; Scott 2009).

The production of Zomia territory was part of a long-term process during which states incorporated mobile peoples all over Asia. Zomia represents the incompletion of that process in contested spaces where people still manage to retain relative autonomy from state authority by various means (Ludden 1999, 2014; Scott 2009). Cowry Country highlights another aspect of that process: old human spaces of open-ended mobility disappeared into state territories controlled by modern methods that include maps and spatial representation (Ludden 2003b; Edney 1997). Modern maps carved up old mobile spaces of migration, trade, travel, and resettlement that sprawled across Asia from prehistoric times. Victor Lieberman (2003) describes spaces of migratory mobility and resettlement in mainland Southeast Asia, where the Khasias were one group among many. Ancient Khasias came from Vietnam into India, bringing betel nut cultivation with them (Ludden 2008, 2017).

Khasias became the most prominent citizens of western Cowry Country, as described in English East India Company records in Sylhet, where the mountains of Southeast Asia (now in the Indian states of Meghalaya, Assam, and Tripura) meet the riverine plains of Bengal. Sylhet was well known as a mountain region, from the days of Ibn Battuta; it was also a port of trade, as defined by Karl Polanyi (1963): a strategic location facilitating exchange at the juncture of contrasting ecological zones, in this case, highland jungle tropics and lowland rice-growing floodplains. Company records indicate that cowries traveled easily among diverse currency environments, including those where no state exercised territorial authority. Cowries served Cowry Country commerce on the external frontiers of expansive empires along routes where trade was organized by kinship and political alliances in tribal societies (Ludden 2011; Sinha 1987).

After 1650, imperial states enclosed such spaces of mobility with increasing force. Tribes were transformed in the process, as people deployed strategies that Albert Hirschman (1970) called "exit, loyalty, and voice." Asia's dry northern steppe and southern tropics provided very different opportunities for pursuing these strategies. On the northern steppe, horse warrior nomad tribes could exit only by riding away into open land. Their interactions with agrarian empires had strengthened imperial militarism to the point that, after 1650, empires in Russia, China, Iran, and India could close steppe frontiers to conquer and assimilate nomad warrior tribes (Perdue 2005; Rieber 2014), whose exit options disappeared.

Not so in the south, where tribes in the tropics confronted empires expanding over land and sea. Khasias faced Mughals and British, who followed Mughals up the Meghna River into Sylhet. Nevertheless, everywhere in the tropics, and also around the Hindu Kush, some upland peoples were able to retain the exit option in mountain bastions that provided space for retreat and self-defense and also provided natural resources for subsistence and trade. Famous examples in Zomia today are the so-called Golden Triangle and Golden Crescent regions of interior Southeast Asia and Afghanistan.

As those opium-growing regions indicate, mountain peoples and resources were also vital components in Asian commercial networks. European overseas expansion had in fact begun with a forceful drive to acquire direct access to pepper and spices from tropical Asian mountains. Constant mobility connected mountains, plains, and sea. Transhumant pastoralism brought people up and down slopes, seasonally, with flocks and herds, as mountain people also traveled, settled, conquered, plundered, traded, mingled, and intermarried among peoples in the plains (Guha 1999). Commerce connecting mountain tribes and Indian Ocean networks brought precious cargoes to Europe from ancient times (Hall 1993). Eventually, it provoked Europe's age of exploration, which carried the onslaught of agrarian and seaborne empires into the old tribal commercial tropics. There, in Sylhet, mobile Khasias pursued options of exit, loyalty, and voice.

A Port of Trade

The sharp ecological contrast between jungle highlands and wet rice-growing riverine lowlands, near the coast, formed a dynamic commercial complementarity on Asia's southern littoral, from Bombay to Shanghai. Lightweight tropical mountain products dominated the premodern Indian Ocean trade: pepper, cardamom, cinnamon, and cloves. Other forest products are less well known but were also important, notably elephants and tusks (ivory), sandalwood, and other forest flora and fauna, including insect dye-making materials and medicinal plants (Shaffer 1994; Chandra 1977). Along the coast, all these forest products were also in high local demand, while shipbuilding for local fishing and distant sea travel alike relied on mountain timber.

In these commercially active coastal spaces, many sorts of people mingled and intermarried. Seagoing immigrants and merchants formed multicultural settlements (Malekandathil 2010, 2016). Inland agrarian elites spread along the coast and river basins, and traveled overseas. Tribes of forest dwellers traveled river routes connecting the coast with Asia's interior. This mingling of peoples produced distinctive coastal cultures that were eventually dominated by inland agrarian elites, as in Bengal, and by overseas settlers, notably the English. In the records of Cowry Country, we see tribal upland peoples playing active roles in the social life of premodern Bengal and in the making of Asia's early modern commercialism.

The tiny cowry shell uncovers buried histories of Khasias around Sylhet. Cowries have served as coins longer than any other material. The shell is easily portable, very durable, easily recognized, difficult to counterfeit, and standard in size. It has become valuable as money, decoration, charms, and divination, and it is used in games (like chess). Its shape has also made it a fertility symbol. It was used as money in ancient north China, and its image became part of the Chinese characters for "money," "coin," "buy," and "value." The cowry that became money in ancient China, however, was not native to seas near China; rather, it came from southern seas. The Chinese word for "cowry" also seems to be a loanword from languages in southern regions, where Indian Ocean cowries were widely used among Malay, Khmer, and Khasia peoples.

Cowry Country emerged in these southern regions. Its recorded history begins in the eighteenth century, when cowries had become prominent in the Indian Ocean trade, carried in shiploads as ballast and traveling ashore as coin. Boatloads of cowries may have begun to arrive in Bengal by the fourteenth century, when Ibn Battuta pursued opportunities in the Maldives and then traveled to Bengal. Eighteenth-century Mughal and East India Company records describe the social dynamics and political economy of cowry commerce around its major inland Bengal port of trade, Sylhet.

Seventeenth-century Mughals built the first lasting state territory in Sylhet, which remained a frontier *faujdari* military outpost until Nawab Murshid Quli Khan began to develop the region, after 1719, with land grants for forest clearance and the extension of taxable cultivation (Eaton 1994: 260–261; SDR299.22:19Oct89; Ludden 2008). By that time, many groups had settled in Sylhet. Waves of Hindu colonization arrived from the seventh century, when one inscription described Sylhet as land "outside the pale of human habitation, where there is no distinction between natural and artificial; infested by wild animals and poisonous reptiles, and covered with forest outgrowths" (Eaton 1994: 73–77). Bengal sultans (1303–1612) sent settlers into the region. A Sufi warrior mystic, Shah Jalal, led an army of followers who conquered local rajas and established Islam in 1303. Ibn Battuta described the region in 1346 as including Khasias, Garos, Hindus, Muslims, and others (Ahmed 1999; Choudhury 1999).

Gangetic territorialism moved into Sylhet slowly and late compared with other parts of Bengal (Morrison 1970). Sylhet's vast inundation explains why. The Surma and Kushiara are the biggest of many rivers descending from the high mountains of Meghalaya, Tripura, Manipur, and Assam (Chakrabarti 2001; Bagchi 1944; Strickland 1940). Thumping earthquakes and river siltation routinely destabilized rivers to send floods in unpredictable directions. Tectonic shifts and river gouging deepened and shifted *haor* depressions (Rashid 1978: 24). The Brahmaputra shifted course suddenly in 1787 (M. A. Islam 1997). The Sylhet floodplain often became a turbulent inland freshwater sea that deterred settlers and made the raised land in the northern basin more accessible from the north via Assam. Settlers from India's Gangetic imperial heartland began arriving regularly only around 1300.

Mixed societies evolved on moving eastern frontiers of Gangetic territorialism, where many non-Bengalis in the highlands and lowlands hunted, farmed, and fished without settling down permanently (Eaton 1994: 258n78; Gupta 1931). These mobile tribal peoples lived in jungles. Their cultural and social practices, including matrilineal kinship, marked them as primitive aliens for incoming Hindus and Muslims, and, eventually, for Europeans, all of whom invested in territories of permanent sedentary cultivation, urbanism, state revenue, and state authority. Medieval Hindu land grants represent royal authority on sparse agrarian frontiers; Mughal land grants show a much more powerful regime patronizing local supporters who acquired more power to turn forests into farmland and subdue or expel jungle people (Ludden 1999: 60–129).

Seventeenth-century Sylhet was thus a Mughal frontier on river highways into highlands held by Khasias, Garos, Ahoms, Dimasas, Boros, and other tribal groups (Nathan 1936: 158–166, 171–233). Mughal conquest was never absolute in the lowlands: Afghans escaped into densely forested hills and deeply flooded *haor* basins, where Hindus had escaped Afghans three centuries earlier; and myriad escape routes into the hills made much of Sylhet Sarkar impossible to conquer, let alone govern. Eighteenth-century Sylhet remained a borderland for the English East India Company, which made Sylhet District a new version of the Mughal Sylhet Sarkar, in 1762.

In Company correspondence, phrasing such as the following became standard: "Sylhet is a frontier province inhabited by a turbulent and disaffected set of people" (SDR294.156:12Dec86). In 1779, one land dispute brought 600 armed locals against Company soldiers, who were "immediately cut down and shot." Attackers fled to the forest (SDR291.55: 3Nov79). Unconquered rebels roamed the lowlands, where highland rulers wielded substantial influence. Khasias held most land north of the Surma and ruled the mountains above (Pakem 1987). Jaintia Khasia rajas held land north and east of Sylhet town. Upland Cachar rajas held the lower Barak valley. Tripura hill rajas ruled southern uplands and adjacent plains. Northwest of Sylhet town, communities of Bengali Khasias formed by alliances between mountain Khasias and lowland Bengalis respected Mughals and Nawabs in the revenue estate *(jaghir)* of Omaid Reza, but they resisted the Company Raj, as we will see (SDR297.164:18Dec88; SDR298.7:20Dec88).

Sylhet's forest, flood, and wild frontier kept East India Company tax revenue tiny, compared with other Bengal districts, but not commerce. As far back as 1345, Ibn Battuta saw "water wheels, gardens and villages such as those along the banks of the Nile in Egypt," and said, "For fifteen days we sailed down the river passing through villages and orchards as though we were going through a mart" (Eaton 1994: 258). He did not describe market towns, and Sylhet still had no big market towns in 1780. Even Sylhet town was a spatially dispersed collection of riverbank markets, with no locally rich resident merchants or big bankers (Mohsin 1997: 217). No European Company made commercial investments in the Surma basin. Bills of exchange *(hundi)* were so hard to find that money moved almost entirely in cash (SDR294.112:15Nov85; Lindsay 1858: III, 170). But in 1790, Sylhet had over 600 named marketplaces (*hat, ganj,* and *bazaar*) (Datta 2000: 208; SDR299.128–9:8May90; SDR300.89–90:24Nov90). Sylhet town itself was an "inconsiderable bazaar," according to Collector Lindsay (Lindsay 1858: III, 167), but it became more active when Manipur and Tripura rajahs built a new jungle road to it in the 1790s (Buchanan [1798] 1992: 135–137).

Sylhet District markets were thus small and filled with small local transactions (SDR299.128–9:8May90), but long-distance trade also moved through them, up and down the Meghna, to and from Dhaka, Narayanganj, and Bakarganj, up and down the Barak valley, and to and from Manipur, Assam, and Burma. James Rennell described the natural basis of this trading environment as follows, "The Kingdom of Bengal, particularly its Eastern Tract, is naturally the most convenient for trade within itself of any country in the world; for its rivers divide into just a number of branches that the people have the convenience of water carriage to and from every principal [place]" (quoted in Chaudhuri 1997: 36).

In the highlands and lowlands that formed the combined basin of the Barak, Surma, and Kushiara Rivers, supply and demand met in countless transactions among people who lived in economically differentiated localities, where markets received little input from major urban centers. Rice and fish were the only important commodities produced in the lowlands. The major *(boro)* rice crop was harvested in the lowlands before heavy flooding from April to June. On higher ground, farmers planted *(aman)* rice to harvest from November to January. Fish in "immense quantity" and "every variety" were "left in the pools on the plain" when floodwaters subsided. They were gathered, dried in the sun, and carried to market. Lindsay further reported that hill people "roast the fish gathered on the plains, and convey them to the mountains in great quantities, as a delicacy to their chieftains" (1858: 169–170).

Freshwater fish from overflowing rivers and rice from fields carved out of flooded forests dominated lowland diets, but homestead gardens and horticulture at the hem of the hills produced fruits, vegetables, and betel nuts. Lowland rice markets were also lively because of flood-induced uncertainty in local output. Crop failures sustained rice markets in farming localities, where people who specialized in fishing, horticulture, hunting, trade, transportation, crafts, finance, and administration also bought rice. The lowlands thus fostered a lively cash economy, and rulers from Mughals onward received Bengal taxes only in cash (Allami 1927: 34).

Sylhet's commercial geography spanned a topographic continuum running into high mountain forests, where shifting *jhum* cultivation prevailed. Sylhet became a classic port of trade that was not just a price-setting marketplace but also a cultural meeting ground for transactions embedded in social relations among diverse peoples living in hills and plains; it was a connective site for mobility among contrasting ecological zones.

Lindsay came from Scotland and quickly saw profits in the hills. His memoir is worth quoting at length:

> The districts contiguous to the hills were . . . producing sugar, cotton, and other valuable crops. The high country had also other resources, well deserving the attention of the enterprising merchant: For example, the mountains produced wood of various kinds, adapted to boat and ship building, and also iron of a very superior quality and description. . . . It is brought down from the hills in lumps of adhesive and sand, and being put into the furnace, produces excellent malleable iron without ever undergoing the process of fusion, the hammer and fire discharging the dross and coarser particles at once, thus producing what is called virgin iron, superior to any made in Europe with charcoal. Silks of coarse quality, called *moongadutties,* are also brought from the frontiers of China, for the Malay trade; and considerable quantities of copper in bars, and a small quantity of European goods, are carried up to barter for these commodities. The adjoining mountain is also an inexhaustible source of the finest lime and lower down the river there is abundance of fuel for burning it. . . . The country under the mountains, where the ground undulates, but is not precipitous, furnishes elephants of the best description. (Lindsay 1858: 174)

Ecological diversity supplied markets. Khasias farmed *jhum* on high slopes and grew rice to sell in lower Jaintia. In high valleys and on low slopes, Khasias grew areca nuts, betel nuts, and turmeric to sell in the plains, along with honey, wax, gum, ivory, medicinal plants, cloth, "and, in the fruit season, an inexhaustible quantity of the finest oranges, found growing spontaneously in the mountains" (Lindsay 1858: 176). Mountain Khasias specialized in iron mining and smelting. They would denude whole forest tracts to stoke their cowhide blow-bag iron furnaces before moving on to exploit new sites of wood fuel. "An immense quantity" of Khasia iron along with steel and metal tools traveled river routes, down from the hills, along with gold, silver, other metals, and ornaments (Bareh 1987: 264–267; SDR312.141:7Apr1800). Khasia merchants carried commodities up and down hills and plains (SDR300.56–7:2Sept90). Elephants, wax, iron, cloth, and ivory traveled downhill, as salt and rice moved up the mountains (Lindsay 1858: 164).

Lindsay reported believably that "at least five hundred elephants were caught annually" in Sylhet (Lindsay 1858: 190; Allami 1927: 295). His successor, John Willes, did a brisk business in elephant tusks: in four years before 1792, he bought 480 tusks in Cachar, and tusks were also available in Jaintia and Pandua. Aloe wood and China-root appear as Sylhet products in the *Ain-i-Akbari* (Habib 1982: map 11B). Timber, sandalwood, cane, ivory, rubber, cotton, and silk came from Cachar and Manipur (Buchanan [1798] 1992: 137; Bhattacharjee 1987: 186). Cotton came from Tripura. The mountains behind Sunamganj held the finest limestone in Bengal.

In 1783, Lindsay dramatized the commercial value of the mountains to demonstrate a profitable method for converting cowry shell cash taxation into silver rupees. He used Sylhet revenues to buy loads of limestone, burnt lime, and other mountain products from Khasias in the hills. He then had the mountain goods loaded onto six seagoing ships, built in the mountains with forest timber, and had those ships sailed on the rising flood down from the mountains, down the Meghna, to the port of Bakarganj, where his agents sold forest products and bought rice to sell in Madras (Lindsay 1858: 198–202; SDR292.57:29Mar83).

Imperial Territory

Lindsay's ships may have returned loaded with cowry shells for Sylhet markets. In his day, coin varieties defined commercial space, and fifty-two kinds of rupees circulated in Bengal. Each region had its own set of coins. Most coins in Rangpur were French Arcot rupees, minted in Pondichery, and Narainy rupees, minted in Cooch Behar, because Rangpur did heavy trade with French Chandranagore and Cooch Behar. In Mymensingh, English Arcot rupees prevailed, because Mymensingh merchants sold loads of rice in Calcutta. Specific coins were also attached to individual commodities: for example, in Dinajpur, merchants used Sonaut rupees to buy rice and other grains, but used French and English Arcots to buy ghee and oil, and used only French Arcots to buy hemp and gunny. Most metal coins in Bengal had been minted in southern India and arrived by sea, mostly from Arcot and Pondichery, indicating Bengal's attachment to the Indian Ocean (Mitra 1991: 70–79).

In Sylhet, metal coins circulated only in its southernmost market, Habiganj, which formed a border with lower Bengal (SDR300.106:30Dec90). In

Sylhet town, gold mohurs and silver rupees were used only in ceremonies. Sylhet imported almost nothing from lower Bengal except cowries, which merchants brought from the Maldives to Chittagong and Calcutta, stored in Dhaka, and carried to Sylhet in boats that returned downstream with rice, fish, and upland products (SDR293.126–131:24Sept84).

Sylhet's cowry currency posed a problem for imperial finance that bedeviled East India Company tax collectors. Mughal officers had spent their Sylhet tax revenue locally, buying local products for meager administrative necessities; but the Company had to convert cowry taxes into Sicca rupee revenue to serve its expansive commercial purposes. When Lindsay struggled to explain his predicament, he could say only that cowries were everywhere the cheapest coin, serving petty transactions among poor people, so their dominance in Sylhet had to result from the region's poverty (SDR293.126–129:24Sept84). Now, that poverty looks rather more like the monetary externality of an agrarian frontier and the economic marginality of imperial borderlands. Sylhet lay outside networks of imperial revenue finance that promoted financial flows denominated in metallic currency. No ruler had the means or the need to send royal coinage into Sylhet, except for a few scattered rituals, and locals did not need metal coins to pay taxes.

States had never played any significant role in the commercialization of Cowry Country. Indeed, copper, iron, and silver from the mountains above Sylhet traveled downstream to become official coins that never returned to Sylhet. Everywhere in the agrarian lowlands of South Asia, silver, gold, and copper coins stamped with symbols of state authority served as units of measure and value in ritual transactions connecting property owners to states that stabilized rural social hierarchy and state power. By the seventeenth century, state power was thoroughly woven into commercialization through state military, financial, and legal support for frontier investors, who turned jungles into farmland and built markets and roads, and through vast state purchase of goods to support military power, elite consumption, and urbanization. State taxation financed commercial and agricultural expansion (Datta 2000; Habib 1982; Ludden 1999, 2011, 2017), but, before the nineteenth century, never extended as far as Sylhet with enough force to propel the local proliferation of state metallic currency.

The cowries that served Sylhet commerce traveled from the Maldives, across the Indian Ocean, across the Bay of Bengal, through Calcutta, up the Meghna River, into Sylhet, and then into the mountains. Along the way, they dispersed into Mughal territory, where they served as the empire's cheapest coin; but imperial metal currency that dominated the Mughal lowlands did not travel into the mountains: it reached only as far north as Habiganj, on the borders of Comilla and Tripura, where imperial territory faded into mountain frontiers.

Cowry Country was mountain country, connected to the sea across Bengal rivers, rather than commercial space integrated like the lowlands into imperial space; and Sylhet is thus described repeatedly as a "mountain region" from the fourteenth century onward (Allami 1927: 136–137). Mountains and plains around Sylhet composed a coherent regional economy, where cowry coins remained in circulation for decades after Company rupees became officially dominant in the 1820s (Mitra 1991: 90; Martin 1976: III, 128), when East India Company armies conquered Assam and adjacent Burma along routes leading to Yunnan.

Before 1820, attaching Cowry Country economically to British India presented a uniquely troubling currency conversion problem, which Lindsay sought to solve by using Sylhet District cowry revenues to finance his own private ventures and thereby generate rupee profits for himself and the treasury. He specialized in limestone trades and in building riverboats, armed with swivel guns, which carried his own goods as well as Company cash, goods, mail, soldiers, and officials. By 1781, Lindsay "had a speculation in hand of very considerable magnitude," and his agents were selling his cargoes in Calcutta, while "fleets of boats now covered the rivers and the trade increased so rapidly as to keep five or six hundred men in constant employ" (Lindsay 1858: 164–165, 176–180, 198). Lindsay and partners also bought Company cowries in Sylhet and Dhaka, used them for downstream trades, and delivered drafts payable in rupees to the Company treasury in Calcutta.

Lindsay became rich and claimed to have ended the "vast exportation of cowries" to meet the Company's rising revenue demand in Sylhet (SDR293.126–131:24Sept84), but he did not in fact stop cowry exports. Cowries left Sylhet in less massive quantities after 1783, but exports remained high and unrequited. Cowries piled up in Calcutta and Dhaka, depressing their price and inflating the cost of conversion (SDR294.113:15Nov85). In 1791, Collector Willes again decried the negative impact of cowry exports as revenue collections almost doubled (SDR304.9:20Apr93). Willes repeated the old refrain that Sylhet did not generate sufficient downstream commerce to bring enough cowries back into Cowry Country (SDR297.59:12May88).

By 1790, imperial financial pressure from London and Calcutta had thus increased to force the incorporation of Sylhet more firmly into the embrace of British Bengal's political economy. This was an old imperial process: the intensification of state control over borderland frontiers, using territorial instruments of law and order, had financed imperial expansion for many centuries (Ludden 2011). This specific transition in Sylhet was also propelled by dramatic disruptions in the decade of the 1780s. Massive floods and local rebellions had violently destabilized imperial resource control. In that context, pressures of imperial finance mingled with local profiteering when floods sent needy people in all directions to seek subsistence and thus provide desperate cheap labor for investors who now focused more attention on farming higher ground, covered with jungle, above the flood.

Upland frontier agrarian investors sought to expand permanent farm cultivation in hills where they faced fierce resistance from local resident forest dwellers, who also fought road-building efforts through the jungles to Manipur (Buchanan [1798] 1992: 135–137). At the same time, lowland merchant investors—like Lindsay—expanded their operations into the mountains, sparking conflict over trade routes and forest assets. Like the Mughals, and many rulers before, the Company used its law and order regime to support these investors with force and finance; in return, investors paid taxes and bribes to establish and secure rights to land and travel, amid challenges from locals who fought invading investors and their state backers. By 1790, a motley, violent, chaotic mixture of British imperialism and local enterprise pushed agrarian Sylhet forcefully into upland frontiers of Cowry Country.

A transition toward the permanent establishment of property rights in land had begun in Sylhet. It was part of a traditional process of state territorial expansion in the new global context of the late eighteenth century. Property rights had provided legal, cultural, and symbolic anchorage for state authority in South Asia for a thousand years before the British got into the game (Heitzman 1997; Karashima 2009; Ludden 1985, 1999). The novelty of the eighteenth-century English obsession with individual private property rights arrived with Company collectors in Sylhet, along with the rest of Bengal, in the 1780s (R. Guha 1963; Sartori 2014), as Company territory acquired a less transactional and more cartographic conceptualization (Edney 1997). Sylhet still had no land maps in 1820 and no boundary markers; but by 1791, the idea was firmly established in official circles that Sylhet District included all the land north to the mountains, including jungle: whoever lived there was therefore subject to Company authority, whatever their attitude toward ritualized judicial and tax transactions with state authorities. To enforce this official diktat, in 1791 the government produced a Sylhet cadastral survey (Hustabood) and Bandobast record of tax collections, which together described the official landscape for the 1793 Permanent Settlement of Bengal Presidency in Sylhet (SDR305.41–2:30Nov93).

Private enterprise and state power marched together into the jungle as floods forced local farmers into forest uplands and distant urban demand sent merchants into mountains filled with Khasias who lived outside spaces controlled by imperial authority. Khasia hunting, betel nut farming, shifting cultivation, trade in cowries, and rights over land and people did not require state authority, and Khasias had never bowed down to the Mughals. Cowry Country was mountain country and also largely Khasia country, mingled with Bengal lowlands. Expanding English territorial ambitions promoted the pursuit of upland opportunities by local investors to expand the imperial tax base in new areas for agricultural colonization and merchant enterprise where the Company's authority would assign rights to property and trade, in return for taxes. Markets in state-defined property rights attracted local buyers who invested in state power to secure their investments in land and commerce. Financial speculation and revenue collection formed cross-cultural partnerships, as the expansion of the British Empire into Cowry Country entangled political economies on local, imperial, and global scales.

Spatial Power

Mughal and English imperial territory expanded north from Dhaka across Bengal's deltaic lowlands toward the mountains into spaces controlled by Khasias who traveled and settled across high tropical mountains, foothills, and flood plains. Khasias formed their own distinctive brand of territorial order, all around Sylhet. As one collector explained, in 1798, "the lands of the [Khasia] Rajahs of Chachar and Jointah are blended with those of this District; indeed, the Rajah of Jointah possesses lands adjacent to the town of Sylhet" (SDR308.150:22Feb98).

The Raja of Jaintia was the major Khasia figure in Sylhet. Diverse Khasia groups—in the northern high mountains, lower uplands, and floodplains—respected his authority. He negotiated boundaries with the English as he would have done with Mughals, first by testing the imperial military with troops armed in Khasia fashion with "a large shield over the right shoulder, protecting nearly the whole of the body, the mountain sword, a quiver suspended over the left shoulder, full of arrows, and a large bamboo bow" (Lindsay 1858, 181). When musket-wielding Company troops pushed the Raja back into a reduced Jaintia territory, he released his personal claims to Company lands where Khasias loyal to him continued to settle nevertheless. The Khasias still paid tribute to their own Raja, not taxes to the Company (SDR298.52:12Jan89); and they settled disputes in traditional forms of warfare rather than petitioning Company courts (SDR298.50:12Jan89; SDR298.11:27Dec89).

A large area where Khasia and Company authority overlapped lay above Chhatak and Sunamganj in the foothills and flooded forests that remained "covered with an impenetrable jungle and so infested by elephants, tigers, and other wild beasts that . . . clearing and cultivation [was] attended with great difficulty and expense" (SDR294.126–7.3May86). In 1779, elephants provided most of the income for the few forest Zamindars (Company landowners) who paid taxes (sometimes) in this area (SDR291.48–9.8Sept79), and Khasia rajas in high mountains above exercised sporadic authority among local Khasias. The Company could no more conquer mountain Khasias than could Mughals, for as Lindsay explained, "You might as well attack the inhabitants of the moon" (1858: 186).

Like the Jaintia Raja, other Khasia rajas conceived Khasia territory as extending to wherever their loyal Khasias settled: Khasia territorialism was thus mobile and strictly ethnic, even when Khasia territory included non-Khasia people, which it normally did. Unlike the Jaintia Raja, however, most Khasia rajas in the northern mountains never performed rituals of submission to lowland rulers; indeed, their families may have fled the plains to avoid submission. Their claims to land were more purely indigenous, based on loyalty, family ties, and victories in battle.

One old form of imperial territory did, however, embrace mountain Khasia rajas and their lowland subjects: it was the *jaghir* of Omaid Rezah, whose home was in Bannyachang, in southwestern Sylhet, in the lower Kushiara floodplain. The Rezah's family had received a Mughal *jaghir* for protecting Sylhet Sarkar against Khasia warriors. He was the last in a long line of Mughal frontier commanders, called Tankadars, who had served Mughal Faujdars by protecting recipients of Nawabi forest land grants. As Nawabi land grants multiplied, the Rezah's *jaghir* expanded from Bannyachang into the mountains (SDR304.11–

17:20Apr93); and for the English who inherited the Nawab's authority, Omaid Rezah became the largest "landlord" in Sylhet: Willes called him "the only true zamindar in the district" (SDR299.72–4:15Jan90). His *jaghir* sustained the mobile ethnic mixing of Khasias and Bengalis who formed an ethnic territory combining Bengali and Khasia cultural forms, including violent feuds that offended Company elites. As Willes explained, Khasias "inhabit the hills and come down to the plains in search of necessities of life and articles of commerce," and their "intercourse and intermarriages" with Bengalis produced "the degenerate Race called Bengalee Cosseahs," who lived mostly inside Omaid Rezah's *jaghir* (SDR298.7:[n.d.]Dec88).

Violent conflicts involving Khasias, merchants, peasants, frontier investors, and Company soldiers increased as Omaid Rezah's authority declined. In 1790, Willes described this once-commanding figure as "a respectable old man but entirely incapable." At the Rezah's death, in 1792, his estate was hopelessly in debt; Bannyachang had drowned in 1791's floods (SDR302.29:13Mar92); and legal struggles over his estate brought litigants from as far as London to fight in Calcutta courts. By 1793, the collector had carved his *jaghir* into a motley collection of taxed parcels.

Commercial competition traveling through Omaid Rezah's *jaghir* triggered conflict over control of mobility between mountains and plains on routes through Bengali Khasia territories connecting the lowland river port of Sunamganj and the mountain river port of Pandua, which Lindsay described as being, along with Jaintia, Sylhet's main port for trade with Assam (SDR293.126–129:24Sept84). Conflict around Pandua began by 1779, when Greek, Armenian, and "low European" merchants complained to Lindsay of "Hill Rajahs compelling them to dispose of their goods at arbitrary prices." Lindsay stationed a military Havildar and "strong force" at Pandua to protect trade amid battles in the mountains pitting merchants and forest zamindars against Khasia rajas (SDR291.41: 26Jun79).

Lindsay used Company cowries and troops to gain limestone and his own private quarry rights from Khasia rajas who "breathed nothing but peace and friendship," resembling to him "[Scottish] Highlanders when dressed in the Gaellic costume." The rajas treated Lindsay to a feast of "six or eight large hogs . . . roasted in . . . a hole dug in the ground, lined with plantain leaves, and filled with hot stones," and they gave him the rights to "a large portion of the mountain, where the quarries are worked . . . including the most favourable situation for access to [his] boats, so as to afford [him] the fullest command of the water-carriage." Lindsay also received permission to build a fortified villa for his personal summer retreat (Lindsay 1858: 177–178).

Lindsay could not, however, control conflict over access to mountain profits (SDR300.57–9:2Sept90). As more Bengalis and Europeans invested in the limestone riding the rapids downriver to Sunamganj, on its way to Calcutta,[2] and as more Khasia mountain rajas enriched themselves at the source, conflict increased. It burst open in 1783, when Bengali Havildar at Pandua insulted a Khasia raja; on the same day, "toward the evening, the shrill war-whoop was heard in every direction, as the Cosseahs retired to the mountains," and "not a man was seen below for several weeks . . . [until they] descended in considerable force" to attack a fort of copper merchants (Lindsay 1858: 186; SDR292.50–1: [n.d.]1783). Lindsay then stationed a "whole Sebundy corps" at Pandua. Nevertheless, by 1784, Khasias had "taken possession of all the neighboring jungles." Lindsay sent in more troops and built a new fort at Pandua, to store merchant goods and house troops. He also had to end his mountain holidays (SDR293.119:4Sept84).

Meanwhile, below the mountains, Bengali Khasias in the lowlands and foothills faced threats from investors in farmland. One major investor in this agrarian frontier was Lindsay's friend and colleague Gowar Hari Singh, Sylhet's treasurer (*Peshkar*), private banker (*shroff*), and revenue farmer (*Waddadar*). Singh bought his first land at government auction in 1783, during the cowry scarcity, when he had privileged access to Company cash. In 1784, as the first major flood of the decade began, he bought two large upland parcels whose owners had refused to pay a 25 percent increase of tax demand (SDR294.69:6Sept84; SDR304.38:30June93). He and other investors bought land at government auctions that favored well-connected men close to Lindsay (SDR297.113:1June89). Their upland investments began to pay off and attract more interest as floods in 1784, 1787, 1791, and 1793 forced farmers onto higher ground and thus lowered the cost of clearing jungles for farming. In the 1780s, the state-property market in Bengal generally was buoyant (Datta, 1990, 146–147), and in Sylhet it benefited from agricultural and commercial expansion in the northern uplands.

The territorial expansion of farming in upland jungle frontiers is visible only indirectly in revenue records. For example, in 1791, an earthquake was followed by torrents that destroyed crops and drowned Ajmeriganj, Beejoorah, and Banyachang, but the overall Sylhet harvest was still adequate because of good later crops on high farmland that was jungle and not farmed in 1784 (SDR301.29–30:21May91; SDR301.59:26July92). In 1793, upland property bought in 1781–1784 could readily support a 43 percent higher tax demand *(jamma).* In 1793, thirty-five upland estates sold for an average price six times their *jamma,* and all but six sold at government auction that year went for more than twice their *jamma* (SDR304.11:20Apr93; SDR305.8–19:[n.d.]Sept93).[3]

Controlling Mobility

The expansion of farming in the north that is indicated by revenue records—but not recorded on any extant cadastral survey—shows that investors in land as well as in trade were moving north into the hills of Cowry Country. Imperial authority traveled with them to facilitate and secure their territorial mobility by expanding state border control. The immediate Company goal was to increase and stabilize state revenue in territories of secure landed property rights where proprietors were tied to the Company by tax transactions that anchored local livelihoods. The means to that end was organized state violence: the Company used its Indian sepoy army to discipline spaces of mobility in Cowry Country, securing and expanding the mobility of Bengali peasants and various nationalities of merchants, and restricting the mobility of Khasias between highlands and lowlands that destabilized frontiers of Company imperial territory in Cowry Country. The war that began as Lindsay left Sylhet launched a transformation of this old mobile commercial space that continues today in the Northeast Indian region of Zomia (Vadlamannati 2011), where state power is still turning old spaces of mobility into immobile territories of property rights marked by static borders of modern geography.

Preparations for the war that began the transformation of Cowry Country started in 1787. Lindsay argued then that military protection of northern frontiers "against incursions of Hill people" had been a central concern of Mughal government, and that rapidly increasing revenue demands and indefinite boundaries of landed property aggravated conflict in a region where people "are of unsettled disposition and have no fixed abode or native place like others," moving in "wretched hordes" from one place to another (SDR295.122–130:[n.d.]Nov87). Lindsay claimed that floods and Khasia incursions had killed the 1788 revenue and that zamindars had paid nothing for eight months and would never repay the securities advanced by bankers. As remedies, he prescribed lower taxes on insecure farms, fierce protection from Khasia incursions, and a fixing of boundaries for the district and for all its landed property (SDR297.17:1Feb88).

Collector Willes took office in 1788 and pursued only the latter two remedies. He focused first on mountain Khasias. Citing "Mr. Lindsay's narrative" and tingeing his prose with apprehension, he wrote: "Government have been informed of the uncivilized state of these [Khasia] people, of the minute division of their country into small independencies, and their incessant disputes with each other which are frequently decided on the bordering lowlands in the Company's jurisdiction." He exaggerated the frequency of Khasia attacks and stoked fear of French intervention, saying the French had formed "connections with the Cosseah Rajahs." Telling his superiors in Calcutta that Lindsay had "courted the Rajahs who look up to its authority," he warned that the French sought alliances that would divide Khasias into "French and English Rajahs," whose quarrels would spill into Sylhet.

Willes argued that increasing trade with the hills would increase conflict "if every trader be allowed to form whatever connections he thinks may be conducive to his own interests," and he therefore sought authority to regulate private trade in the hills, saying that, "these [commercial] connections have within the last six months brought forward four times the Number of Principals ever known before" (SDR297.48–50:29Mar88). But he warned that free trade could be dangerous, because trade in weapons could tilt the military balance. Problems would arise, "if Hill people acquire arms" and "learn the [use] of them from the wandering lowland Europeans, Moguls, Greeks, and Armenians who infest this district." If this should happen, he feared, "the Company's territories even as low as Dacca may be subjected to [mountain Khasia] incursions." He said that Lindsay had "stopped several foreigners who were going off to the Hills with arms for the purpose of barter," and that "within these [past] few weeks [in 1788] a large party of armed Moguls have been stopped and prevented from going off to the Hills to assist in the predatory wars of these inimical Rajahs" (SDR297.54–61:12May88).

Willes soon discovered that mountain Khasias were not his only problem. In 1788, as he negotiated with hill rajas to rebuild markets destroyed in battle and bring merchants back to Pandua (SDR297.93–5:5July88), conflict erupted among Bengali Khasias (SDR297.93–5:5July88). One of their leaders, Ganga Singh, "calling himself the Zemindar of Barrakeah," burned to the ground a neighboring zamindari and killed its proprietor, another Bengali Khasia; their land dispute became a "blood feud." Ganga Singh then captured both sides of a river carrying mountain trade with Sylhet. Pandua fell to mountain Khasias; and Bengali Khasias under Ganga Singh and other chiefs expanded control over land below the hills in "open hostility to the Company," seizing people, goods, and boats on the river (SDR298.45:12Jan89).

Willes described Ganga Singh as a Bengali Khasia who "possesses territory on the hills and also holds many pergannahs [villages] on the lowlands . . . [and] rents many villages from dependent zamindars of Sylhet." Willes found that this practice of letting and selling lands to the Cosseahs [had] been adopted by many of the Sylhet zamindars" and was "extremely injurious to the Company's interests." Willes had a simple remedy: "nothing but coercion will suit the dastardly and savage disposition of the Bengalee Cosseahs of the lowlands" (SDR297.154:15Dec88). Thus, in April 1789, he launched a war in the mountains around Pandua and in the jungles behind Sunamganj and Chhatak. He proposed a boundary to separate Khasia and Bengali territories. Saying Khasias are "not inherently warlike," he argued that they might be kept under control with little force but for their entanglements with Bengali landowners (SDR299.24:19Oct89).

By the end of 1789, a new spatial order had begun to emerge: Willes had begun to recruit investors in forest upland agricultural expansion, but rebellious Bengali Khasias remained a problem. Willes wrote that "the people to the northwest of the Surmah are a troublesome Race . . . tho' I am satisfied that the exertion of temperate severity . . . will effect the wishes of government." That "temperate severity" came to include a massacre of Bengali Khasias around Ganga Singh's home village, where Company soldiers (sepoys) captured 33 Khasia and Bengali prisoners, seized 290 cattle, and stopped grain and salt going to the hills, before being attacked, which led them "to use military rigour . . . by burning and destroying every village [they] came near, and putting to death as many of the enemy as were unable from their wounds to make their escape" (SDR85.37:20Jan90).

Sepoys captured Ganga Singh in 1790. Immediately, "about 400 Cosseahs . . . came down from the hills and burnt villages around Chhatak" (SDR299.67:7Jan90). Khasia warriors then came down in large numbers to within five miles of Sylhet. At this point, military action drove mountain Khasias into the mountains and secured Sylhet's northern boundary. Their job complete, the Thirty-Fifth Sepoy Battallion left Sylhet in November 1791, and the Company drew a notional boundary for Sylhet in the mountains below Pandua.[4]

This boundary acquired a reality based on Khasia victories in the mountains and British victories below, separating territories controlled by Khasia rajas and the English East India Company. It bisected the route from Sunamganj to Pandua. It marked the northern limit of British Bengal, which only then extended indisputably to the base of the mountains, and equally indisputably, did not include Pandua or high mountains. The primary justification for the boundary was that it secured Company territory against threats to British authority posed by unregulated mobility between mountains and plains. The English drew the boundary to restrict mobility and sever social bonds between people in the mountains and those in the lowlands. This boundary and the war that produced it expanded Bengal territory, truncated Cowry Country, defined northern mountains as alien Khasia territory, and made Khasias resident aliens in Bengal, where all the farmland became Bengali and Khasias remain a depressed minority to this day.

Mobility connecting hills and plains did not disappear and British territory continued to expand, grabbing what became Northeast India and Burma in the 1820s. What the new boundary did do was to inscribe on the land the state's modern ambition to control mobility inside official borders. It sought to curtail the fluidity and indeterminate vagueness of an old spatial order where state authority was immersed in unbounded, mobile geographies of land use, commerce, and culture, and often fell hostage to the whimsy of people living outside the reach of state authority. The boundary's modernity came with its intention to subordinate all geography to the state. Zomia began taking shape, as Cowry Country disappeared.

Notes

1. Archive citations appear as follows: SDR297.44.17May88 = Sylhet District Records, Volume 297, page 44, Collector Correspondence dated 17th of May 1788.

2. In 1790, seven Europeans owned 120,000 ferrahs of chunam in Sylhet markets, and fifty Natives owned 50,000 ferrahs. (1 ferrahs = 1 Maund, 10 Seers.) SDR300.57–9, 63:2Sept90.

3. This jamma comparison is based on a Board of Revenue report in 1791, which said that the "price of revenue lands sold, out of Calcutta, [never] exceeded the revenue [*jamma*] of two years." India Office Records, *Bengal Revenue Consultations,* P/52/31, 10 June 1791, quoted in Datta 2000, 146–147. For more detail, see Ludden 2003a, 2008.

4. SDR298.98:17April89; SDR298.116–18:13Jun89; SDR299.80:21Jan99; SDR 299.104:5Mar90; SDR305.55:6Jan94. Correspondence on the Khasia boundary war

occupies much of SDR volumes 85 (received) and 298, 299 (sent). For more on the boundary, see Ludden 2003a.

References

Ahmed, A. B. M. Shamsuddin. 1999. "Muslim Administration in Sylhet, 1303–1765." In Sharif Uddin Ahmed, *Sylhet: History and Heritage,* 335–339.

Allami, Abul Fazl. 1927. *Ain-I-Akbari.* Translated by H. Blochman. Vol. I. Delhi: Low Price Publications.

Anderson, James A. 2009. "China's Southwestern Silk Road in World History." *World History Connected* 6, 1. http://worldhistoryconnected.press.illinois.edu/6.1/anderson.html.

Bagchi, Kanangopal. 1944. *The Ganges Delta.* Calcutta: University of Calcutta.

Bareh, Hamlet. 1987. "Khasia-Jaintia State Formation." In Sinha, *Tribal Polities,* 261–306.

Bhattacharjee, J. B. 1987. "Dimasa State Formation in Cachar." In Sinha, *Tribal Polities,*177–212.

Buchanan, Francis Hamilton. [1798] 1992. *Francis Buchanan in Southeast Bengal (1798).* Edited by Willem van Schendel. New Delhi: Manohar.

Chakrabarti, Dilip K. 2001. *Ancient Bangladesh: A Study of the Archaeological Sources with an Update on Bangladesh Archaeology, 1990–2000.* Dhaka: University Press Limited.

Chandra, Moti. 1977. *Trade and Trade Routes in Ancient India.* Delhi: Abhinav Publishers.

Choudhury, Dewan Nurul Anward Hussain. 1999. "Hazrat Shal Jalal (R) and His Life—A Source Study." In *Sylhet: History and Heritage,* ed. Sharif uddin Ahmed, 129–172.

Datta, Rajat. 1990. "Merchants and Peasants: A Study of the Structure of Local Trade in Grain in Late Eighteenth Century Bengal." In *Merchants, Markets, and the State in Early Modern India,* ed. Sanjay Subrahmanyam, 146–151. Delhi: Oxford University Press.

———. 2000. *Society, Economy, and the Market: Commercialization in Rural Bengal, circa 1760–1800.* Delhi: Manohar.

Deyell, John S. 2010. "Cowries and Coins: The Dual Monetary System of the Bengal Sultanate." *Indian Economic Social History Review* 47(1): 63–106.

Eaton, Richard M. 1994. *The Rise of Islam and the Bengal Frontier, 1204–1760.* Berkeley: University of California Press.

Edney, Matthey H. 1997. *Mapping an Empire: The Geographical Construction of British India, 1765–1843.* Chicago: University of Chicago Press.

Fuquan, Yan. 2004. "The 'Ancient Tea and Horse Caravan Road,' the 'Silk Road' of Southwest China." The Silk Road. http://www.silkroadfoundation.org/newsletter/2004vol2num1/tea.htm.

Giersch, Charles Patterson. 2006. *Asian Borderlands: The Transformation of Qing China's Yunnan Frontier.* Cambridge, MA: Harvard University Press.

Guha, Ranajit. 1963. *A Rule of Property for Bengal.* Paris: Mouton.

Guha, Sumit. 1999. *Environment and Ethnicity in India, 1200–1999.* Cambridge: Cambridge University Press.

Gupta, K. N. 1931. "On Some Castes and Caste-Origins in Sylhet." *Indian Historical Quarterly* 7: 725–726.

Habib, Irfan. 1982. *Atlas of Mughal India: Political and Economic Maps with Notes, Bibliography and Index.* Delhi: Oxford University Press.

Hall, Kenneth R. 1993. "Economic History of Early Southeast Asia." In *The Cambridge History of Southeast Asia,* I, ed. Nicholas Tarling, 185–186. Cambridge: Cambridge University Press.

Heimann, James. 1980. "Small Change and Ballast: Cowry Trade and Usage as an Example of Indian Ocean Economic History." *South Asia: Journal of Southasian Studies* 3(1): 48–69.

Heitzman, E. James. *Gifts of Power: Lordship in an Early Indian State.* New Delhi: Oxford University Press, 1997.

Hirschman, Albert O. 1970. *Exit, Loyalty, and Voice: Responses to Decline in Firms, Organizations, and States.* Cambridge, MA: Harvard University Press.

Hogendorn, Jan, and Marion Johnson. 1986. *The Shell Money of the Slave Trade.* New York: Cambridge University Press.

Islam, M. Ataharul. 1997. "Population and Environment." In *History of Bangladesh, 1704–1971,* ed. Sirajul Islam. Vol. II. Dhaka: Asiatic Society of Bangladesh.

Karashima, Noburu. 2009. *South Indian Society in Transition: Ancient to Medieval.* Oxford and New York: Oxford University Press.

Kratoska, P., R. Raben, and H. Nordholt, eds. 2005. *Locating Southeast Asia: Geographies of Knowledge and Politics of Space.* Singapore: Singapore University Press.

Lieberman, Victor B. 2003. *Strange Parallels: Southeast Asia in Global Context, c. 800–1830.* Cambridge: Cambridge University Press.

Lindsay, Robert. 1858. "Anecdotes of an Indian life." *Lives of the Lindsays; or, A Memoir of the Houses of Crawford and Balcarres.* Vol III, pp. 147–227. London: John Murray. Digitized and available at Hathi Trust: https://babel.hathitrust.org/cgi/pt?id=wu.89006038434;view=1up;seq=17

Ludden, David. 1985. *Peasant History in South India.* Princeton, NJ: Princeton University Press. http://quod.lib.umich.edu/cgi/t/text/text-idx?c=acls;;idno=heb02438.

———. 1999. *An Agrarian History of South Asia.* The New Cambridge History of India, volume IV, part 4. Cambridge: Cambridge University Press.

———. 2003a. "The First Boundary of Bangladesh on Sylhet's Northern Frontiers." *Journal of the Asiatic Society of Bangladesh* 48(1): 1–54.

———. 2003b. "Maps in the Mind and the Mobility of Asia." *Journal of Asian Studies* 62(3): 1057–1078.

———. 2008. "Investing in Nature around Sylhet: An Excursion into Geographical History." In *Contested Grounds: Essays on Nature, Culture and Power*, ed. Amita Baviskar, 77–105. New Delhi: Oxford University Press.

———. 2011. "The Process of Empire: Frontiers and Borderlands." In *Tributary Empires in Global History*, eds. Peter Fibiger Bang and C. A. Bayly, 132–150. London: Palgrave Macmillan.

———. 2014. *India and South Asia: A Short History*. 2nd ed. London: One World Publishers.

———. 2017. "Country Politics and Agrarian Systems: Land Grab on Bengal Frontiers, 1750–1800." *Modern Asian Studies* 51(2): 319–349.

Malekandathil, Pius. 2010. *Maritime India: Trade, Religion and Polity in the Indian Ocean*. Delhi: Primus Books.

———. 2016. "Circulation of People and Patterns of Maritime Migrations in the Indian Ocean during the Pre-modern Period." In *Migrations in Medieval and Early Colonial India*, ed. Vijaya Ramaswamy, 259–286. London: Routledge.

Maloney, Clarence. 1980. *People of the Maldive Islands*. Bombay: Orient Longman.

Martin, Montgomery. 1976. *The History, Antiquities, Topography, and Statistics of Eastern India (Comprising the Districts of Behar, Shahabad, Bhagulpoor, Goruckpoor, Dinajepoor, Puraniya, Ronggopoor, and Assam)*. Vol. III. Delhi: Cosmo Publications.

Mitra, Debendra Bijoy. 1991. *Monetary System in the Bengal Presidency, 1735–1835*. Calcutta: K. P. Bagchi.

Mohsin, K. M. 1997. "Mughal Banking System." In *History of Bangladesh, 1704–1971*, ed. Sirajul Islam. Vol. II, 204–224. Dhaka: Asiatic Society of Bangladesh.

Morrison, Barrie. 1970. *Political Centers and Cultural Regions in Early Bengal*. Tucson: University of Arizona Press.

Nathan, Mirza. 1936. *Baharistan-I-Ghaybi: A History of the Mughal Wars in Assam, Cooch Behar, Bengal, Bihar and Orissa during the Reigns of Jahangir and Shahjahan*. Gauhati: Narayani Handiqui Historical Institute.

Pakem, B., and Surajit Sinha. 1987. "State Formation in Pre-colonial Jaintia." In *Tribal Polities and State Systems in Pre-colonial Eastern and North Eastern India*, 261–306. Calcutta: K. P. Bagchi.

Perdue, Peter C. 2005. *China Marches West: The Qing Conquest of Central Asia*. Cambridge, MA: Harvard University Press.

Perlin, Frank. 1993. *Monetary, Administrative, and Popular Infrastructures in Asia and Europe, 1500–1900*. Brookfield, VT: Ashgate.

Polanyi, Karl. 1963. "Ports of Trade in Early Societies." *Journal of Economic History* 23(1): 30–45.

Rashid, Haroun. 1978. *Geography of Bangladesh*. Boulder, CO: Westview Press.

Rieber, Alfred J. 2014. *The Struggle for the Eurasian Borderlands: From the Rise of Early Modern Empires to the End of the First World War*. Cambridge: Cambridge University Press.

Sartori, Andrew. 2014. *Liberalism in Empire: An Alternative History.* Berkeley: University of California Press.

Scott, James C. 2009. *The Art of Not Being Governed: An Anarchist History of Upland Southeast Asia.* New Haven, CT: Yale University Press.

Shaffer, Lynda. 1994. "Southernization." *Journal of World History* 5(1): 1–21.

Sinha, Surajit, ed. 1987. *Tribal Polities and State Systems in Pre-colonial Eastern and Northeastern India.* Calcutta: K. P. Bagchi.

Strickland, Cyril. 1940. *Deltaic Formation with Special Reference to the Hydraulic Processes of the Ganges and the Brahmaputra.* Calcutta: Longmans, Green.

Vadlamannati, Krishna Chaitanya. 2011. "Why Indian Men Rebel? Explaining Armed Rebellion in the Northeastern States of India, 1970–2007." *Journal of Peace Research* 48(5): 605–619. http://www.uni-heidelberg.de/md/awi/professuren/intwipol/peace.pdf.

Van Schendel, Willem. 2002. "Geographies of Knowing, Geographies of Ignorance: Jumping Scale in Southeast Asia." *Environment and Planning D: Society and Space* 20: 647–668.

Wicks, Robert S. 1992. *Money, Markets, and Trade in Early Southeast Asia: The Development of Indigenous Monetary Systems to A.D. 1400.* Ithaca, NY: Cornell Southeast Asia Program.

Yang, Bin. 2004. "Horses, Silver, and Cowries: Yunnan in Global Perspective." *Journal of World History* 15(3): 281–323.

———. 2011. "The Rise and Fall of Cowrie Shells: The Asian Story." *Journal of World History* 22(1): 1–25.

4

Persian Rugs in Southeast Asia

Cultural Production and Taste Making in a New Market

NARGES ERAMI

> Persian rugs are the only practical pieces of fine art in the world. No other investment grows in beauty as it ages.
>
> —Attributed to Geoffrey Orley[1]

> All around the world, Iranian carpets are the symbol of poetical luxury.
>
> —Attributed to Arthur Upham Pope[2]

In the latter part of the twentieth century and the beginning of the twenty-first, Iranian rug producers—in response to economic sanctions of goods made in Iran by Western nations—began to seek alternative markets that had been partially or marginally penetrated, namely in East and Southeast Asia. The professional union of carpet merchants identified the desirable sizes, designs, colors, and materials that would enchant and entice a new generation of consumers and connoisseurs that made up the markets to the East. This call to change has led to recurring questions of traditional and indigenous designs that have been historically associated with aesthetics of bourgeois European and American taste. These days, innovation in design has become a key semiotic value in order to understand the "new" Asian market and an emerging middle class that would represent idealized consumers of Persian rugs. The novelty markets now are those predominantly in Southeast Asia. The carpet producers negotiate how Persian rugs can retain their autochthony as the merchants renew their glance eastward to carve out indigeneity, aesthetics, and an emphasis on craftiness over tradition. The carpets with these "new" primordial designs have attributes inalienable to the place and people they come from, or more precisely, they belong to. A visceral sense of belonging to a place and a practice would be typified by traditional designs. This is not just a claim to authenticity but an inalienable connection to a place (Iran), to a time (the ephemeral Persian Empire), and to a practice (creating enchanting manifestations of a singularly Persian identity). This chapter questions the assumption that Persian rugs embody a national art form while arguing that in fact rugs as an art form are by nature and design transnational in both content and form. By concentrating on Persian rug exhibitions as "cultural experiences," the Iranian embassy with the help of diasporic Iranian carpet dealers has promoted Persian carpets as a way to learn about Iranian handicraft and art in several countries, mainly Thailand, Malaysia, and Vietnam. In each case, the promulgation of carpets is an official tactic to promote tourism beyond simply looking for new consumers in new markets. The idea is to build curiosity and interest to travel to Iran and experience the people and land that produce the carpets. In what follows, I describe a conflictual relationship between state agents and carpet producers. This singular interest, the carpet, has garnered a tense yet comfortable alliance that has brought together disparate interests of Iranian carpet merchants and Iranian officials that momentarily converge in places like Bangkok, Kuala Lumpur, and Hanoi for the glorification of the Persian rug.

A New Market and the Role of Exhibitions

Ramin Safi is the founder of Neda Carpet Gallery in Bangkok, Thailand.[3] In the past decade, he has established a niche within the industry as the only Persian rug emporium that carries the finest carpets, from antiques to more contemporary pieces. Neda Gallery is "licensed" exclusively to sell carpets from established rug-producing families, often referred to as *farsh-i mārkdār,* or branded rugs, where the family names and the city where they are produced are woven into the carpet.[4] He has been motivated to understand the Southeast Asian market through immersion. After traveling between multiple countries in the region, he moved to Thailand with his wife and son, closing his family store in Tehran. Ramy, as he goes by, is a third-generation carpet dealer, and his move to Bangkok was prompted by a move away from Dubai and Hamburg. "This is about a different market," one of his suppliers told me, "and he knows this market because he lives there and he knows how to distinguish our carpets in an industry saturated with poor imitations and substitutions, because he knows how to educate this market." On his website he emphasizes this very point: "We hold a central position in the Asia Pacific market as a 'first source' for those people who loves [*sic*] ancient art and Persian carpet."[5] The gallery sees itself as a Southeast Asian geopolitical node in a network of people who pass through Bangkok. Neda Carpet Gallery maintains the website that promotes the history of Persian carpets with a gallery of pictures of carpets on display. But he has another gallery, where he is pictured with famous carpet producers, predominantly from one family that has dominated carpet production and innovation in design in the city of Isfahan. In the pictures, Ramy is standing with carpet producers in their homes or showrooms, with his arms around them, sometimes holding up an iconic carpet. There are pictures of his father with some of the same producers. The direct access Ramy is reproducing through these images has an appeal only for a clientele that would recognize the names and faces of these men and more importantly would know of the stellar reputation his father held as a carpet dealer. Ramy maintains that Neda can promote these carpets as distinct and singular through this direct and intimate connection.

Ali Hutan moved to Kuala Lumpur in the late 1980s, establishing what he calls the first Persian carpet dealership in Malaysia. He describes a consumer market geared toward expatriates made up of his first clients, but he, in the same manner as Ramy, claims his gallery is a gateway to the Southeast Asian market. There is a lot of cooperation between the galleries in Malaysia and Thailand, but Ramy has preferred a different method in terms of gaining the trust of the local population. He has a history of working with the Iranian embassy as well as the Iranian Carpet Company, Shirkat-i Farsh-i Iran, or ICC in Thailand. He is, after all, a pioneer in setting up a direct connection between the Iranian Carpet Company and the embassy as one of its first "carpet ambassadors." He once approached the Iranian ambassador in Vietnam to create a cultural exhibition of Persian carpets. One of his suppliers described the strategy as highlighting what the finest Persian carpets would look like for a nonspecialist audience. "There is not a tradition of expertise or established authenticity at the level of the European or American market here and what was accomplished by *Ustad* Pope in America, does not exist in this market."[6] This reference to Pope is quite common among multigenerational carpet-producing families, including my grandfather, who loved to tell stories of hosting Pope in his home and showing him the latest carpets on the loom while seeking his advice on what colors Americans preferred. It was safe to say that in the case of Ramy and Ali Hutan, the carpets they wished to portray as the finest to future consumers in Thailand, Malaysia, and Vietnam were very similar to those meant for a Euro-American market. I suggested this to another carpet dealer from Kuala Lumpur, Hussein Ghani. He disagreed, shaking his head pointing to a picture of a carpet inspired by the house of Versace:

> We are wary of cheap imitations from Pakistan and elsewhere; first we want to show what the best of the best looks like and then bring in the very best designed carpets, but these will be different, not the dark blue, thick carpets that Americans in the East like or the creamy khaki hues and muted reds with geometric patterns that are favored in the west [coast of the United States]. These will be delicate, silk with pink and black, and gold, lots and lots of variations of gold. We are telling the producers to create more of these colors and really change the designs—carpets that will stand out in a room, create art [*hunar*].

Yet the emphasis that Persian carpets are art and an art form unique to Iranian culture is still linked to Arthur Pope's categories that helped define the field of Persian art. The gesture to Versace's designs brings forth the ways in which designs have always been informed by global reception and the moments of encounter with another cultural art form. The carpet producers therefore function much like film producers. They envision the reception of their designs as a moment of encounter with another culture, where the act of becoming familiar with this unfamiliar design will begin to become memorable and comfortable. Yet the carpet's mystery and uniqueness are still retained. Film theorist Bill Nichols explains how Iranian films are received by viewers in international film festivals, much like tourists coming in contact with a new and unknown place, by calling it an "ephemeral moment in which an imaginary coherence renders Iranian cinema no longer mysterious but still less than fully known" (1994, 27). As Nichols goes on to point out, the significance of film festivals for introducing the world to global yet local cinema can have a jarring effect. "Hovering like a specter, at the boundaries of the festival experience, are those deep structures and thick descriptions that might restore a sense of the particular and local to what we have now recruited to the realm of the global" (27).

In 2009, the first Persian carpet exhibition in Hanoi went on display at the Sofitel Hotel. Neda Carpet Gallery in Bangkok provided nearly 200 carpets for the exhibition. A local news story (in English) introduced the exhibition with the headline "Capital city takes a magic carpet ride." The article went on to say:

> Vietnamese people will learn more about Iranian culture through this first exhibition in Ha Noi, said the Iranian ambassador to Viet Nam, Seyed Javad Ghavam Shahidi. . . . The collection is a presentation of culture through research and will surely benefit those who admire Persian art and heritage. The art of carpet weaving will benefit from the promotion of this collection. People will be informed about the unique qualities found in Persian carpets, particularly in designs and patterns, said a representative from the [Neda] Carpet Gallery.[7]

Ramy wanted the exhibition to mirror an art gallery, emphasizing the experience with expert lighting to frame and showcase carpets, some of which were suspended from the ceiling, while the audience would walk around and over layers of carpets. There was always the possibility to purchase any of the carpets on display, but the space was set to awe and inspire. There were noted antique and semi-antique carpets that were roped off, as if on display at a museum.

Anthropologist Alfred Gell (1998) describes the moment of encounter with art (in various cultural and social contexts) as both magical and ineffable, art as object takes on an agentive role. What gains significance for Gell is the way objects exhibit the impact of their agency. This is not about their anthropomorphic qualities but about the capability of the object to mesmerize and enchant. The "halo-effect of resistance," according to Gell, gives art its special value, its fictive quality that becomes a source of enigma for humans to comprehend what they do and how they exist, which is partially, or in some cases, always, conditioned by our understanding of how they come to be (2010, 471). The "technology of enchantment" is art; more clearly it is the social strata that gives art its distance from humans and raises it to an unfathomable status (468). Iranian government officials were enticing people drifting in and out of the hotel salon to experience the process and visit where these carpets were created. Meanwhile, Neda employees, using proxy mediators as local translators, did their best to tell tales of Persian carpet history and the natural and unique tradition that gave rise to such an unrivaled art form. This was done with an emphasis on how long it would take to create the carpet and the technological savvy that would come only through tradition over generations. The traditional tales that were told during the exhibition were set to excite the imagination as to the "creative agency" that could not be imitated but only appreciated, even without knowing for certain the process of artistic creation (473). There was a missing component from the exhibition—the artists. Their presence and explanations could have made the carpets more tangible. Instead, the staff were relied on to answer the viewers' questions.

In 2014, when the second Persian carpet exhibit was displayed at the Melia Hotel in Hanoi, a new ambassador was at the press conference emphasizing state relations: "'The mutual understanding between the two peoples has been hindered by lack of information in the past few years,' said Hossein Alvandi Behineh, Iranian Ambassador to Viet Nam."[8] Experiences with art are politically constructed because of how the critical players—namely, the artists, consumers, and producers—are captured in a framework that is all about the creation of power differentials and social hierarchies. The process of trying to understand and recognize the way art is created becomes an impossibility for the consumer to figure out as he or she is encountering the art not just as the individual but the object itself. It is also accomplished through the power of the institutions, the governments, or the global market that dictates such power relations.

The politics of viewing should include an interaction with the artists, so at this second exhibition, Ramy brought with him two carpet producers from different cities but both from families who were represented in the gallery of images on the store's website. The producers were introduced as "artisans." The term "artisan" does not have an equivalent job description within the carpet industry in contemporary Iran. The division of labor within the carpet industry is a result of a historical transformation that began with foreign firms setting up workshops and factories in major carpet centers with the increase in production of carpets exported to satisfy European and American demands in the nineteenth and twentieth centuries. In 1883, foreign investors attempted to enter the carpet trade, when the Anglo-Swiss firm of Ziegler and Co., based in Manchester, set up its own factory in Sultanabad. The Ziegler factory was never successful in fully penetrating the close-knit world of carpet producers and merchants, but its methods of commercialization, mass production, and cultivation of European tastes for the "oriental" would prove highly influential in the development of the international rug trade (Ittig 1992).

Ramy thought that introducing the two producers as "producers" did not translate what their job entailed. The division of labor can be largely autonomous, but it relies heavily on a symbiotic relationship. At the top of the local hierarchy is the producer *(tawlid-kawnandih),* the key merchant who provides the capital for production and formally employs all other workers (except for the pile producer, who sells handmade or factory-made wool and silk to the producer). The producer must first consult with the master artist to arrive at a favorable design for a given rug. After colors are chosen for the design, the producer and dyers work together to find appropriate dyes for the wool or silk, based on prevailing market trends and availability. The design and dyed material are then turned over to the producer's overseer, who in turn provides the design in piecemeal to weavers, usually working at home on looms loaned from the producer. After the weaving is completed, the rug is taken off the loom by the warp winder, and it is then washed, trimmed, and straightened before being returned to the producer for sale in the bazaar. In Qum, where one of the producers in Hanoi was from (as opposed to most carpet-producing

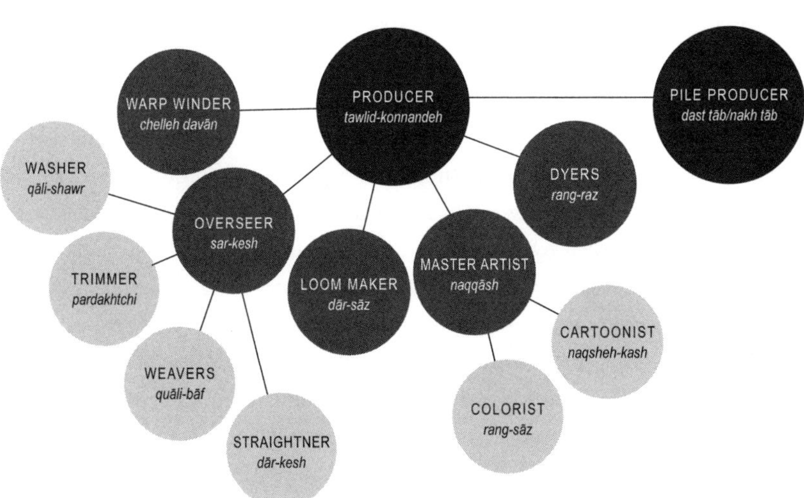

Division of labor in the rug industry. (Chart provided by Narges Erami)

cities), the producer, his master artisan, the dye factory, the weavers, and nearly every occupation mentioned above reside in different cities. In most other production centers, the various contractors are all from the same city or at least from the same province. The difference here is that Qum is a young(er) manufacturing center, embryonic compared with Isfahan, where the other producer at the event hailed from. Qum's production began in the 1920s, while the urban workshops of Isfahan date back to the seventeenth century.

The choice of not disclosing the full division of labor and instead referencing producers as artisans is a tactical tool to challenge what is visible and what is hidden within the artistic formula of the carpet. If the carpet is presented as art and representing art while reaching across the cultural divide as more than aesthetically pleasing and desirable, then this is a renewed measure of introducing design to a new market. The idea is to make the unfamiliar and even alien object attainable while maintaining the mystery behind its ordinary utilitarian function.

The Exhibition of Arthur Upham Pope

When the famed Iranist Arthur Upham Pope, along with Phyllis Ackerman (his wife and academic partner), published *A Survey of Persian Art* in 1939, he had already established a definitive place, if not a hierarchical preference, for Persian carpets.[9] In particular, he pioneered the standards that help define the quality and status of hand-knotted carpets in general, with Persian carpets ranking at the top of the heap, marked as the finest carpets from the region (Kadoi 2016b). Pope preferred carpets produced in urban areas such as Isfahan (where he and Ackerman are both buried), Tabriz, Kashan, and Kerman to tribal floor coverings made by nomadic women (Hillenbrand 2016). In *A Survey of Persian Art,* he wrote, "For several centuries Persian art has been best known in the west by the carpets" (quoted in Kadoi 2012, 9).

The complicated patterns and designs used on urban carpets that resemble inlays, earthenware, and calligraphy, which embrace the walls and doors of mosques, madrasas, mausoleums, and domiciles, set the tone for what is still considered "fine" Persian carpets. He spearheaded the field of Persian art in the United States as he went on to dominate the field, including research methodologies for identifying Islamic art that included Persian carpets (Silver 2016). He (and decades later his students) set the parameters for carpets to always be judged against the urban centers of production in Iran. With Pope advising private collectors such as John D. Rockefeller Jr. and William Randolph Hearst, as well as museums and academic institutions, Persian carpets with some of the more complicated designs became the most sought after in the United States. It is no surprise that the Islamic art historians Sheila Blair and Jonathan Bloom (2003) refer to Pope as an "entrepreneur," as it was through these lucrative private connections that he was able to fund catalogs and bulletins, as well as various exhibitions. In 1928, he helped establish the American Institute for Persian Art and Archaeology, which later became known as the Asia Institute in New York City (Frye 2012). In 1931, he established the first International Exhibition of Persian Art in London, which yielded various influential publications and shows.

It is through the legacy of Arthur Pope and his students that Persian rugs as an art form have developed throughout the world. Persian rugs signify "art" in the Western consciousness, but art in and out of particular contexts, not as timeless objects judged by the immutable criteria of traditional aesthetics. They act as appropriations, as thefts, as "subversive transformations," as moveable history (Culler 1986). It is such a dialectic that creates a "culture" for the colonization of taste. A taste may be encoded first as an elite aesthetic judgment of a precious object, and representations of that object are circulated as "unproductive expenditure" in Bataille's (1985, 118) sense. Once cultivated, the taste for an expenditure with no end beyond itself (e.g., "art for art's sake") generates new significations for new audiences. Under European capitalism, bourgeois fascination with elite displays of expenditure has triggered immense shifts in the flow of prestige goods from other parts of the globe. European entrepreneurs have in many cases taken it upon themselves to seek out the new productive technologies that can transform a commodity from luxury to commonplace (as, for instance, with the mechanized production of cotton, silk, and other formerly scarce textiles). In the popularization of taste beyond an elite audience, the once-precious goods may lose all traces of preciousness. But if continually aestheticized, a commodity may retain a vestige of its former representation as elite expenditure, signifying a luxuriousness available to the masses.

"Aesthetics" refers to our articulation and identification of the arts in which we establish what Jacques Rancière (2013) calls "the distribution of the sensible." In this process, aesthetics and politics come together to establish something common within agents in a society (a commonsense perception), while simultaneously establishing exclusive niches within this greater whole. When aesthetics is involved with politics, occupations begin to matter in that they reveal who can partake in the activity of "aesthetics" (and mistakenly, "art") and therefore have a stake in what is sensible. Following Rancière (2013), then, a distinction is made between "aesthetic practices" and "*artistic* practices." Whereas the former is a highly visible performance that places (or perhaps displaces) artistic practices in a "sensible" occupation, the latter refers to general ways of doing and making in a natural state of being.

The eventual domestication of European taste of Oriental rugs surely bears out this transformation. After all, the culture of taste for rugs remained embryonic before the explosive demand of the late nineteenth and early twentieth centuries. Early aestheticizations peer out of Dutch paintings of the sixteenth century, perhaps most famously represented in Hans Holbein's *The Ambassadors* (1533). Holbein, a German painter employed in the court of King Henry VIII, was commissioned to paint a portrait of a visiting French ambassador, Jean de Dinteville, with the bishop Georges de Selve. Art historians have long dissected the significance of all the objects arrayed on a table behind the two men: a celestial globe; a terrestrial globe highlighting Europe and showing the coast of a recently discovered America; numerous scientific instruments measuring time and space; a mathematics book; a case of flutes, a lute, and a Lutheran hymnal. Many have pointed to the puzzling elements of the painting, which seem to be caveats against worldly vanity, and reminders of the transient nature of human existence: a broken string on the lute, a crucifix of Jesus peering out from behind the curtain, and most startling of all, the distorted image of a skull in the foreground produced by the process of anamorphosis, a fashionable device in the sixteenth century. The macabre imagery, not uncommon to the sixteenth century, seems joltingly unfamiliar and uncanny in a post-Enlightenment age. It reminds us that behind the perfect transparency hoped for by European universalism, behind the smooth exchange of objects and language without translation, hide phantasmatic intimations of mortality (Foister, Roy and Wild 1997).

One item in the painting lies directly in the center of the canvas: an "Oriental" rug of geometric design covering the table. Holbein frequently incorporated this style of rug in his works, so much so that rugs with this type of pattern, believed to be of Anatolian (Turkish) origin, are known to Western collectors simply as "Holbein rugs." The rug reminds us of the long history of the importation of "Oriental" commodities to adorn the best homes of Europe, even before the massive influx of Asian goods beginning in the eighteenth century. The rug also reminds us that the cultivation of "civilized" European tastes was never a one-way process from the West to the Rest; rather, the aesthetic sensibilities of Europeans were long shaped by their encounters with the "East." But the very fact that this type of rug came to be known as a "Holbein rug" suggests that Eastern commodities could be fit into a universal scheme, immediately recognizable to consumers via representations like paintings and guidebooks. The carpet exhibits in Hanoi were aiming for this universal scheme. European connoisseurship for exotic luxury goods sought to encompass the world's beautiful objects through universalist representations, once again on the ideal of a world without the need for translation. Ramy and other rug dealers sought to create a space for Southeast Asian connoisseurship, specifically what they had encountered in Bangkok, and they hoped to garner similar tastes in Malaysia and Vietnam. Initially, buyers from these countries—with Ramy's guidance—would mimic the European history of cultivating taste for Persian carpets. This formation of acquired taste preconditioned and redirected by new aestheticizations shaped trade and even diplomacy between Europe and Iran, and would do so for Southeast Asia. Establishing commercial trade concomitant with diplomatic gestures was exactly the venture that brought government agents and carpet merchants together. Carpets represent an entirely different confluence of commerce and aesthetics inasmuch as there is a paradox of aesthetics. At the same time that aesthetics frees art to the world by making it visible, it pollutes art's essence by linking it to social order and occupations. The controlled space of the hotel ballroom was a far cry from visiting workshops and villages in Iran. This is all about creating a desire to visit Iran and go through the experience of buying a carpet in the bazaar, a member of the diplomatic crew explained. Ramy and other dealers sometimes were at odds with this direction of the market in Southeast Asia. The dealers maintained that this could be an advantage for them. Only a particular class and a select few would be able to travel to Iran and purchase carpets there. Most would want to imitate the ownership of an investment like fine carpets and would look to nearby markets like Singapore and Thailand. Ramy said, "Seeing our galleries in their home country, means carpet buying has been established and since carpets need special care of mending and maintaining, like expensive cars, having a local mechanic only ensures the investment." The government agents imagined more mobility not just in terms of the carpets but in terms of people as well. "Iran needs to be a destination for tourism; if carpets can bring people to Iran, that is even a better form of transportation, why not promote that magical venture but it can only happen in Iran," a member of the embassy in Thailand told me recently.

The exhibits served the purpose of creating the hegemony of taste. In the intercourse of production and consumption that brings into being the elusive entity known as "taste," certain kinds of manipulation are at play. An analysis of taste construction might examine how consumers are subjected to the manipulations of commodity producers and their techniques of publicity, or conversely it might judge the extent to which producers bend to the desires of their consuming audience. The focus of analysis depends crucially on one's view of commodity consumption as a passive or active process. Anthropological interpretations of taste might concentrate on its symbolic and ritual roles under the banner of aesthetics, or else on its "utility" in various functionalist readings. But a full discussion of taste and its constitution would need to move beyond these arguments and take into consideration the relative status and social positionality of the participants in the process. We need to ask, therefore, who are the "taste makers" in a given aesthetic / commercial realm of interaction, and what are the social mechanisms at their disposal for the successful reproduction of their judgments? This question has been approached sociologically by Bourdieu (1984), symbologically by Sahlins (1976), and experientially by Rancière (2004). What their studies help foreground is that the twin structuring processes of commoditization and aestheticization should not be generalized in universal terms, but rather specified in cultural uniqueness. The key, then, to understanding the aesthetic valuation and fetishization of prestige goods is the appreciation of distinctive articulations among cultural practices relating to production, exchange, and acquisition.

Aesthetic Sensibilities

At the exhibit in Hanoi in 2014, family members of Mohammad Seirafian, the famed carpet producer from Isfahan, held pictures of one of his most famous designs that was gifted to the United Nations headquarters in New York City in 2005 by the Iranian government. The carpet has the twelfth-century poet Sa'adi's auspicious verse dubbed "The Oneness of Mankind" woven in gold:

The sons of Adam are limbs of each other,
Having been created of one essence.
When the calamity of time affects one limb
The other limbs cannot remain at rest.
If you have no sympathy for the troubles of others,
You are unworthy to be called by the name of a Human.

The carpet's extraordinary presence was told to the viewers at the exhibition, and members of the Seirafian family were there to discuss the significance of the carpet and its place as the highest form of indigenous art, both through poetry and textile. The Seirafians explained how the carpet was made, and what it means to aesthetically appreciate the craft of a Seirafian rug that has a special place.

> "This is a great carpet; this is the kind of carpet you should aspire to own," claimed a family member.
>
> "Study the carpets here from the Seirafians and use them as a reference to find something similar," said a member of Neda Gallery.
>
> "By showing great carpets, it is just common sense now, what is great and what is cheap imitation and what they [Vietnamese] should look for," added one carpet producer.

It is this common sensibility of indigenous art forms that plays into the politics of perception and the politics of the presence. In the introduction to the collection of his short interview-essays, Jacques Rancière defines aesthetics as "a regime for identifying and reflecting on the arts: a mode of articulation between ways of doing and making, and their corresponding forms of visibility" (2013, 10). In *The Politics of Aesthetics*, Rancière claims that the political sphere is circumscribed by the limits of sight and response. Art both delimits and is limited by these sensible distributions.

What, then, causes this affinity between aesthetics and politics? Why do the two seem to be intrinsically linked? To understand this, Rancière presents two distinct regimes of art. The first is a poetic (representative) regime of arts, which identifies the substance of art, particularly within the general ways of doing and making. In contrast, the second is the aesthetic regime, which establishes certain sensible modes (the distribution of the sensible) to specific artistic products. The Seirafian carpet enriched with a geopolitical prowess of location as advertising to global elites typifies this distribution of the sensible.

A final point needs to be made regarding the semiotic transformations of rugs as commodities—namely, the question of "alienability," a crucial notion in Marx's (1990) framing of commodity fetishism (brought into opposition to Maussian constructs of the gift). It could be argued that the continued aestheticization of rugs as "authentic" art objects has served to render them as somehow impervious to alienating processes, as Annette Weiner (1985) writes of "inalienable goods" in the Pacific. The dichotomy that ascribes inalienability to "gift economies" and alienability to "commodity economies" has been successfully critiqued, and the critique would find further grounding in the case of Persian rugs (Appadurai 1986; Gregory 1982; Kopytoff 1986). The rugs can be seen as promiscuous objects / subjects with various degrees of "alienation" with respect to the participants involved in sectors of the industry—the weavers, the producers, the merchants, and the consumers (Helfgott 1994; Spooner 1986). The very idea of "inalienability" linking the rug to the weaver may be expertly maneuvered by merchants and marketers attuned to global connoisseurship, as well as the orientalist desire for lingering traces of the authentic exotic, the "Benjaminian aura" (Benjamin 1968). As Nicholas Thomas writes, "The cultural violence in seizing a headdress or ornament and listing it in a curiosity catalogue or squabbling over its price can be appreciated only if its initial, singular, inalienability is specified" (1991: 19).

If we believe that this desire for the inalienable comes about constructed as an imagined exchange, then we may follow Georg Simmel's (1978) argument to identify where that exchange occurs at the meeting point of matching desires and demands. The regimes of exchange, abstracted into the epiphenomenal world of money, can then be seen as transformational power surging into the object / subject (Sahlins 1994 & 1996). The "commodity phase in the social life of anything" is variable according to cultural and historical particularities, allowing objects to move back and forth on clines of alienation and commoditization (Appadurai 1986, 13). Moving through different eras and in different hands, Persian carpets float across representational spaces of commodity and gift, utility and art, need and desire.

The Highest Bidder

The Persian carpet or rug and carpet-weaving are an essential part of Persian art and culture. Persian carpets can be divided into three categories: *farsh* or *qali*—bigger than 6 ft. × 4 ft.; *qalicheh* which means "small rug"—

> 6 ft. × 4 ft. or smaller; and *gelim* or *zilu,* known as nomadic carpets. The earliest Persian carpet is said to have been woven some 2,500 years ago, in 500 B.C. Materials used in making one of these collector's items include silk, wool, cotton and even camel hair. The most expensive carpet in the world is a seventeenth-century Persian rug sold in June 2013 at Sotheby's in New York for US$33.8 million. It was reported that four bidders fought over it for ten minutes after which an anonymous caller won the bid for the carpet with rare "vase" technique patterns.[10]

The above write-up in a local paper in Kuala Lumpur reads more like an advertisement for a carpet gallery than a news story. The mention of the world's most expensive carpet captures aesthetics measured globally. A seventeenth-century Kerman carpet was auctioned at Christie's in 2010. When the carpet fetched $9.6 million, it became known as the most expensive carpet ever sold. In 2013, as described earlier, Sotheby's trumped the record. Carpet sellers love to talk about these antiques as possibilities for the career of any fine Persian carpet. These "museum quality" items are in demand for their rare design and perfect condition. They signal a return to the past as an ultimate value of the modern project. In "Artistic Regimes and the Shortcomings of the Notion of Modernity," Rancière (2013) discusses how Western history has seen the development of several aesthetic and thus political regimes, or several ways of delimiting the political or civil sphere. In Plato's "ethical regime of images," images were defined only by their origins or their "making," and their ends or what they were meant to teach and impart to specific audiences. Rancière gives divine images as one example. In the "poetic or representative regime," representation and mimesis organize and delimit art, which is defined as "ways of doing and making." The "aesthetic regime" moves beyond the representative. Rancière makes a Heideggerian move here. He claims that in the aesthetic regime, art allows form to be experienced for itself and reveals the fundamental formation processes of life through identity of opposites and instances of suspension. This seems rather similar to Heidegger's (1977) concepts of "becoming" and "revealing." For both Heidegger and Rancière, art objects draw us through them, allowing us to approach their formal essences and thus the essence of the forms of life (i.e., truth).

Ramy began his search for a new market through an invitation by the carpet association in Tehran. In March 2002, a group of rug producers from Tehran, Tabriz, and Qum organized an exhibition in Bangkok, Thailand, with the intention of focusing on the Southeast Asian market's interest. This initiative was prompted by the events of September 11, 2001, in New York City and the war waged in nearby Afghanistan. The Iranian Carpet Company (ICC) had a presence at this exposition as spectators rather than sellers: members abandoned traditional tasks by monitoring interest in Persian rugs rather than market prices, and hoped to promote Iranian culture rather than their particular designs. Carpets would lead the way as a commodity but would also serve to promote an ancient culture that cannot be viewed by other artistic media—namely, cinema and modern art.

Before the group set out for Bangkok, many of the carpet merchants were interested in the ICC's creating pamphlets promoting the history and origin of rug designs to function as a basic guide and highlight how to identify an authentic rug pattern autochthonous of a region, and warn consumers about fake rug patterns masquerading as a Persian rug from a specific region. The promoters figured that describing the history of Qum's first rug would resonate with the consumers and emphasize the origin of the Persian carpet industry in Qum over the city's identity as a center for the *'ulama* and religious learning. During the discussion, members of the ICC were dumbfounded to discover that the first truly Qum design was created by a member of the *'ulama.* "This will not be part of the exhibition; there is a danger in seeing this design affiliated with a *mu'amam* [a turban wearer]," a leading agent said. And the group decided that the identity of the first designer was not as important as the city in which it was designed. The history of rug designs was abruptly dropped from the exhibition's leaflets. This was not the market where Islam and carpets were to be conflated.

Visual Difference and the "Violence of Seeing"

Though there is nothing sacred about the actual rug design, the paisley design has been repeated all over the rug inside and outside the borders. Nor is there any implication of impropriety associated with this image, as in the contemporary carpet community the links to the members of the *'ulama* are never advertised. Official government agencies such as Agri-Jihad (Ministry of Construction Crusade),[11] the ICC and the National Carpet Museum in Tehran all deny this history of the modern Qum carpet. At the museum the rug representing Qum does not bear the name of its original designer—Haj Aqa Sayyid Kazem Mohseni. Both the ICC and Agri-Jihad feature the famous design on the cover of their pamphlets and informational sources on the carpet industry in Qum, but make no mention of Aqa Kazem.

Rugs associated with religion are regulated and relegated to a specific visual-cultural practice, namely among Shi'i Muslims where images of the Prophet and his son-in-law and cousin Imam 'Ali and his sons Imams Hasan and Hussein are portrayed. These images of religious icons are referred to as *tableaux*—rugs designated to be framed and hung on walls. Similarly, rugs with Qur'anic verses and images of the Ka'ba are also *tableaux,* as opposed to those with poetry framing a scene depicted on the rug, which are thrown on the ground.[12] The authorities of the Islamic Republic sanctioned the association to a cleric by deeming the affiliation as "danger in seeing." The history of this image's association or "icontext" is then removed and destroyed, to be substituted with an "unknown" or an "absent" designer. This creates a visual difference where the practice of experiencing a sense of familiarity in seeing the image obfuscates the origins of the design.[13] The concept of visual difference is inspired by W. J. T. Mitchell's definition of visual culture and the study of images as a "social construction of the visual experience" (1995a, 540, 1995b).

By enforcing visual difference, the various agencies involved in promoting rug production were denying the life of this particular design and the image associated with it. Yet the idea that the first Qum design was created by a cleric may indeed make the rug design or bring an illusion, a visual knowledge of a "sacred gaze"[14] to the paisley design or Qum carpets in general. The design had to be separated and stripped from any association with the infamous seminary, the Grand Ayatullahs who have resided in the city and the pilgrimage sites of Sacred Fatimah (Sister of the Eighth Shi'a Imam) and the Mosque of Jamkaran.

The deeply symbolic act of removing any mention of Aqa Kazem's paisley—or more importantly his significant role as a well-known preacher whose sermons allowed his presence in intimate spaces—facilitated his role as a carpet producer. David Morgan's (2005) term "violence of seeing" is revealing in framing the debates among merchants in the early 2000s about why this particular lacuna by both sets of groups—government agencies and the community of *bazaaris*—was seen as "dangerous." Ramy was keen on controlling the types of stories told by merchants about the biography of the carpet. He and others concentrated on the Southeast Asian market as uncharted territory, with full control of what kinds of carpets are demonstrated as exemplary, and how the viewer identifies the carpet as both utilitarian and artistic. At the exhibition in Hanoi, both merchants and agents had to start with cultivating taste coupled with tactical tourism and visual difference.

Notes

1. This and the following quote are found on the home page of Neda Carpet Gallery (accessed December 18, 2016). Neda is a pseudonym for the gallery discussed in this chapter. Geoffrey Orley is a well-known carpet dealer in Florida who, along with his partner, has promoted a return to natural materials, basic technologies, and "forgotten" methods of weaving as well as "neglected" designs of the past. This is an oft-quoted praise that is reproduced on various Persian carpet promotional websites. See Ann Gilbert, "Persian Rugs: Beauty, Value, Increase with Age." *Antiques and Arts Around Florida,* 2009. http://aarf.com/persiansf03.htm (accessed December 18, 2016); "Unique Antique Bakhtiari Commissioned Carpet." *Rugs and More: Fine Oriental Rugs and Home Furnishings*, January 9, 2016. http://rugsandmore.com/tag/persian-carpet (accessed December 18, 2016); "Persian Rugs: The Only Practical Pieces of Fine Art" *Curious History*, August 10, 2015. http://www.curioushistory.com/persian-rugs-the-only-practical-pieces-of-fine-art/ (accessed December 18, 2016).

2. The quote is attributed to the art collector and historian Arthur Upham Pope, but I cannot find the source of this quote except that it is used frequently by carpet gallery and tourist promotional websites. See "Persian Carpets and Rugs". Persia.Tours.Com http://first.persiatours.com/dt_places/persian-carpets-ruggs/ (accessed December 22, 2016); "Informed Carpets." Embassysa.ir http://www.embassysa.ir/emb/Iran%20Info/Carpet.htm (accessed December 22, 2016); Carpettour.net http://www.carpetour.net/fa/part.asp?r=s&Aid=9050&u= (accessed December 22, 2016).

3. Names have been altered.

4. I use "carpets" and "rugs" interchangeably, which correspond to the Persian terms *farsh* and *qālī,* respectively. In the vernacular, all carpets and rugs are considered to be handwoven unless it is noted that they are made mechanically. Machine-made carpets are always modified by the qualifier "machine-made" but only as *farsh,* such as *farsh-i māshīnī.*

5. Website accessed December 14, 2016.

6. Interview via skype, August 29, 2015.

7. "Capital City Takes a Magic Carpet Ride." *Vietnam News: The National English Language Daily*, January 4, 2009. http://vietnamnews.vn/life-style/arts-craft/186681/capital-city-takes-a-magic-carpet-ride.html (accessed December 15, 2016).

8. "Ha Noi Hotel Rolls Out Enormous Carpet Show." *Vietnam News: The National English Language Daily*, November 15, 2014. https://www.vietmaz.com/2014/11/ha-noi-hotel-rolls-out-enormous-carpet-show/(accessed December 10, 2016).

9. For a detailed discussion of Pope's influence on the field of Iranian art, see Kadoi 2016a.

10. "Persian Masterpieces." *The Sun Daily*, May 25, 2015. http://www.thesundaily.my/news/1429182 (accessed December 2, 2016).

11. Agri-Jihad was created immediately after the founding of the Islamic Republic. The goal was a crusade against poverty by empowering the men and women living

outside major urban centers. In Qum, Agri-Jihad was involved in separating the weavers from the urban-dwelling carpet producers by making the women of the villages their own producers, essentially their own boss. The venture failed by all accounts.

12. Prayer rugs are a totally different matter. They have no religious insignia designating them as prayer rugs. They are mostly machine-made and small in size. There is a rug design that is referred to as "prayer rug design," which has a specific framing but no religious images to denote it as such.

13. "Icontext" is a visual textual unit that cannot be seen disparately as text or image. See Wagner 1995.

14. By "sacred gaze" I employ David Morgan's useful definition here: "allows images to open iconically to the reality they portray or even to morph into the very thing they represent" (2005, 276), and "sacred gaze" is a term that designates the particular configuration of ideas, attitudes, and customs that informs a religious act of seeing as it occurs within a given cultural and historical setting. A sacred gaze is the manner in which a way of seeing invests an image, a viewer, or an act of viewing with spiritual significance (20).

References

Appadurai, Arjun. 1986. "The Social Life of Things." In *The Social Life of Things: Commodities in Cultural Perspective,* ed. Arjun Appadurai, 3–63. Cambridge: Cambridge University Press.

Bataille, Georges. 1985. *Visions of Excess: Selected Writings, 1927-1939.* Translated by Allan Stockl, Carl R. Lovitt, and Donald M. Leslie Jr. Minneapolis, MN: University of Minnesota Press.

———. 1991. *The Accursed Share: An Essay on General Economy.* Translated by R. Hurley. Vol. 1, *Consumption.* New York: Zone Books.

Benjamin, Walter. 1968. *The Work of Art in the Age of Mechanical Reproduction. Illuminations.* New York: Schocken.

Blair, Sheila S., and Jonathan M. Bloom. 2003. "The Mirage of Islamic Art: Reflections on the Study of an Unwieldy Field." *Art Bulletin* 85(1): 152–184.

Bourdieu, Pierre. 1984. *Distinction: A Social Critique of the Judgment of Taste.* Cambridge, MA: Harvard University Press.

Culler, Jonathan. 1986. *Ferdinand de Saussure.* Ithaca, NY: Cornell University Press. Original edition, 1976.

Foister, Susan, Ashok Roy and Martin Wyld. 1997. *Making and Meaning: Holbein's Ambassadors.* London: National Gallery Publications.

Frye, Richard N. 2012. "Asia Institute." *Encyclopaedia Iranica.* Accessed December 15, 2016. http://www.iranicaonline.org/articles/asia-institute-the-1.

Gell, Alfred. 1998. *Art and Agency: An Anthropological Theory.* Oxford: Clarendon Press.

———. 2010. "The Enchantment of Technology and the Technology of Enchantment." In *The Craft Reader*, ed. G. Adamson, 464–482. New York: Berg.

Gregory, Chris A. 1982. *Gifts and Commodities*. Vol. 2. Vancouver: Academic Press.

Heidegger, Martin. 1977. *The Question Concerning Technology and Other Essays*. New York: Harper & Row.

Helfgott, Leonard M. 1994. *Ties That Bind: A Social History of the Iranian Carpet*. Washington, DC: Smithsonian Institution.

Hillenbrand, Robert. 2016. "The Scramble for Persian Art: Pope and His Rivals." In *Arthur Upham Pope and a New Survey of Persian Art*, ed. Yuka Kadoi1, 3–45. Leiden: Brill.

Ittig, Annette. 1992. "Ziegler's Sultanabad Carpet Enterprise." *Iranian Studies* 25: 103–135.

Kadoi, Yuka. 2012. "Arthur Upham Pope and His 'Research Methods in Muhammadan Art': Persian Carpets." *Journal of Art Historiography* 6(n / a): 6-YK / 1.

———. 2016a. "Arthur Upham Pope and a New Survey of Persian Art." In *Arthur Upham Pope and a New Survey of Persian Art*, ed. Yuka Kadoi, 1–12. Leiden: Brill.

———. 2016b. "The Rise of Persian Art Connoisseurship: Arthur Upham Pope and Early Twentieth-Century Chicago." In *Arthur Upham Pope and a New Survey of Persian Art*, ed. Yuka Kadoi, 233–265. Leiden: Brill.

Kopytoff, Igor. 1986. "The Cultural Biography of Things." In *The Social Life of Things*, ed. Arjun Appadurai, 64–94. Cambridge: Cambridge University Press.

Marx, Karl. 1990. *Capital: A Critique of Political Economy*. New York: Penguin.

Mitchell, W. J. T. 1995a. "Interdisciplinarity and Visual Culture." *Art Bulletin* 77(4): 540–544.

———. 1995b. "What Is Visual Culture?" In *Meaning in the Visual Arts: Essays in Honor of Erwin Panofsky's 100th Birthday*, ed. Irving Lavin, 207–217. Princeton, NJ: Princeton University Press.

Morgan, David. 2005. *The Sacred Gaze: Religious Visual Culture in Theory and Practice*. Berkeley: University of California Press.

Nichols, Bill. 1994. "Discovering Form, Inferring Meaning: New Cinemas and the Film Festival Circuit." *Film Quarterly* 47(3):16-30.

Pope, Arthur Upham, and Phyllis Ackerman, eds. 1938–1939. *A Survey of Persian Art from Prehistoric Times to the Present*. London: Oxford University Press.

Rancière, Jacques. 2004. *The Philosopher and His Poor*. Translated by Andrew Parker. Durham, NC: Duke University Press.

———. 2013. *The Politics of Aesthetics: The Distribution of the Sensible*. Translated with introduction by Gabriel Rockhill. London and New York: Continuum.

Sahlins, Marshall. 1976. *Culture and Practical Reason*. Chicago: University of Chicago Press.

———. 1994. "Cosmologies of Capitalism: The Trans-Pacific Sector of 'The World System.'" In *Culture/Power/History*, eds. Nicholas B. Dirks, Geoff Eley, and Sherry B. Ortner, 412–456. Princeton, NJ: Princeton University Press.

———. 1996. "The Sadness of Sweetness: The Native Anthropology of Western Cosmology." *Current Anthropology* 37(3): 395–428.

Silver, Noël. 2016. "Pope, Arthur Upham." *Encyclopaedia Iranica.* Accessed December 15, 2016. http://www.iranicaonline.org/articles/pope-arthur-upham.

Simmel, Georg. 1978. *The Philosophy of Money.* Translated by T. B. a. D. Frisby. Boston: Routledge and Kegan Paul.

Spooner, Brian. 1986. "Weavers and Dealers: The Authenticity of an Oriental Carpet." In *The Social Life of Things: Commodities in Cultural Perspective,* ed. A. Appadurai, 195–235. Cambridge: Cambridge University Press.

Thomas, Nicholas. 1991. *Entangled Objects: Exchange, Material Culture, and Colonialism in the Pacific.* Cambridge, MA: Harvard University Press.

Wagner, Peter. 1995. *Reading Iconotexts: From Swift to the French Revolution.* London: Reaktion Books.

Weiner, Annette. 1985. "Inalienable Wealth." *American Ethnologist* 12(2): 210–227.

5

A "South" Imagined and Lived

The Entanglement of Medical Things, Experts, and Identities in Premodern East Asia's South

ANGELA KI CHE LEUNG

One merit of doing medical history is that epidemics, healing materials and practices, experts, and patients, because they are not confined by national boundaries, naturally define a region rather than a nation, revealing regional coherences often distorted by political divisions.

The "south" of East Asia connecting southern China to the Gulf of Tongking area, bearing old names such as Lingnan (嶺南, "south of the mountain ranges"), *Nan Yue* (南越, Southern *Yue,* becoming Vietnam, 越南, since 1803), Annam (安南, Pacified South), or *Jiaozhi* (*Giao Chi,* 交趾),[1] was not usually conceptualized as an integrated region. Its shifting political boundaries did not do justice to the region's ethnic, linguistic, and cultural complexities or to its ecological coherence.[2] Chinese and Vietnamese nationalist historiography often disregards the temporal and spatial interconnectedness of the region for political reasons. Similar to the modern idea of the "tropics," the "south" in the East Asian context would be a much more productive regional concept if framed not by political boundaries but by its ecological coherence—extreme and perennial warmth and dampness, unique flora and fauna, and epidemiological environment—that generated shared human experiences. The comparison with the Mediterranean region suggested by

Denys Lombard and Li Tana is another useful way of rethinking this region.[3] This chapter aims to demonstrate the cultural coherence of this region by tracing the historical processes in which circulations of medical things, knowledge, practices, and especially experts were inextricably interwoven with the region's unique natural environment, complex ethnic configuration, and changing political mediation. The seemingly controversial "China" element in the construction of Vietnamese identity,[4] in this context, was no more than one among many factors in the historical structuring of the region's rich culture.

The Chinese early imagination of the South as a region was nourished by a special literati genre, called records of *yiwu* (*yiwu zhi*, 異物志, Records of extraordinary things), or "exotic monographs"[5] on plants, animals, and stones in the extreme south. The term *yiwu* highlights the exotic nature of "things" imagined to thrive in remote, untamed, and uncivilized regions with extreme climates,[6] including antidotes to treat vile southern poisons.[7] The first of these mostly lost texts was authored by Yang Fu (楊孚), a Cantonese of the Eastern Han (first century), and collated in the early nineteenth century with more than one hundred items.[8] One later example, *Nanfang caomu zhuang* (南方草木狀, Plants of the southern region), attributed to Xi Han (嵇含, 263–306) but more likely a twelfth-century compilation,[9] was cited by sinologists as the first botanical work on the region inclusive of today's southern China and northern Vietnam, describing more than seventy different herbs, trees, fruits, and bamboos. The *yiwu* genre proliferated after the fourth century with more than twenty known titles, describing items that eventually became part of China's *materia medica*. It disappeared after the twelfth century, by which time many of the most representative items, such as betel nuts and rhino horn, had become routine ingredients in Chinese medical recipes.[10]

The typical Sinocentric explanation of the disappearance of this literary genre is that, with the progressive penetration of Han Chinese civilization in the South, the "strangeness" of southern things and customs, or the marked "differences" between Han and southern cultures, was gradually erased or at least rendered insignificant for the civilized Chinese in the "north."[11] It assumed a straightforward Han cultural assimilation of this South.

This chapter unravels the complex process of cultural interaction between the politico-cultural center in the north and the South after the twelfth century by highlighting the role of human actors in the entanglement of medical things, knowledge, practices, and identity formation in this region in two phases: the thirteenth through fifteenth centuries, and the sixteenth through eighteenth centuries.

Thirteenth through Fifteenth Centuries: Miasmatic Lingnan and Annam

Becoming more accessible, the miasmatic south was now depicted with human players: northern medical experts interacting with native patients. The experts began to scrutinize and describe the region's ecology, and its epidemiological situation characterized by ubiquitous miasmatic (*zhang*, 瘴) diseases and "uncivilized" native customs. The most representative medical text of this process is of course the *Lingnan weisheng fang* (嶺南衛生方, Life-preserving recipes for the Lingnan region, 1264), built on a collation of shorter, preexisting texts produced between the twelfth and the thirteenth centuries and compiled by Buddhist monk Jihong (繼洪) from northern China (Hebei) in the thirteenth century.[12] It is the culmination of a developing genre emerging in the Tang period.[13]

The eyewitness accounts reveal several developments in the South by the thirteenth century. They show that the region was by then easily accessible from the north: sojourning monks, scholar-officials taking up office in the region, and traveling doctors were the typical visitors. They made firsthand observations on local pathological conditions and offered preventive or therapeutic recommendations.[14] However, *Lingnan weisheng fang* suggests that despite its greater accessibility, this "South" remained an alien land to northern visitors. Being a land of permanent *yang* (depleting warmth), it was considered dangerous for northerners (*beiren* 北人), whose bodies were more vulnerable to the *zhang* miasma, whereas the natives (*turen* 土人), or southerners (*nanren* 南人), were more resistant as "part of the *qi* of the (local) soil and water"[15]. The "South" was alien also because the natives were physically and culturally different and inferior: they were, in general, "emaciated with a sallow complexion". When sick they did not take medicines, but "made offerings to ghosts.[16]

We also learn from this book that by this time, native "southern" doctors, learned in medical classics, were present and active. But they were criticized by northern experts for being crude in their therapeutic skills, such as mindlessly applying purgative recipes using strong ingredients (particularly *mahuang* [麻黃, ephedra]) recommended by classics of the Cold Damage School, not knowing that such methods would do more harm than good for bodies depleted of *yang*. Northern medical experts claimed that "the *zhang* miasma [of the South] may not kill the sick, but the [southern] doctors do"[17](1: 5a). On the other hand, the authors of the thirteenth-century text no longer distinguished between northern and southern medicinal herbs, formerly known as *yiwu* (strange things). By the twelfth century these had already entered mainstream *materia medica* and even "domesticated" as part of "Chinese" medical culture:[18] betel nuts and *agastache rugose* (藿香, *huoxiang*) for treating diarrhea and febrile conditions; rhinoceros horn for fevers; coix seed (薏苡仁, *yiyiren*) for dispelling dampness; tangerine peel (陳皮, *chenpi*) for dissolving phlegm and toxic *qi;* and *Dichroa Febrifuga Lour* (常山, *changshan*) and *Herba Artemisiae Chinghao* (青蒿, *qinghao*) for recurrent fevers. Generally of warm nature with quick healing effects befitting northern elite doctors' preferred healing strategies, these southern *materia medica* were gaining currency in popular medicinal recipes published by the Song government.[19]

This book represents the northern Sinocentric perspective on southern healthcare. Dismissing the role played by native experts, the northern authors claimed with satisfaction that "northern doctors are gradually reaching this region, so that [correct medical methods] could be studied and transmitted here"[20] The complex process of interfertilization of medical knowledge and practices was interpreted as a one-way civilizing process. To a large extent, the Red River delta was similarly understood by northern Chinese as a region of *man* (蠻, "barbarian").[21] Sinocentric interpretations of the "civilizing process" of this period could be read in historical sources written in Chinese.[22] Fine medical skills were said to be slowly introduced by doctors from China, some being military doctors captured during the Song-Yuan dynastic transition in the late thirteenth century; even Chinese ritual healers were much sought after.[23]

On the other hand, in the early fifteenth century when Jiaozhi was being brought under direct Ming control, the Chinese military was clearly unprepared for the toxic miasma as the Yongle Emperor remained greatly concerned with the epidemiological conditions of the region and suggested the deployment of native ethnic Miao troops who were more resistant to the endemics. At the same time, he summoned famed Viet medical doctors and ritual healers to be sent to the Ming court together with other skilled artisans and experts. In 1407, a well-known Jiaozhi doctor, Zou Dongxuan (鄒洞玄), was sent with imperial auspices.[24]

Yongle's request was a continuation of early Ming policy of exchange of monks and other healthcare experts between China and Jiaozhi. In 1385, the Ming government began to request monks to serve in the Chinese capital of Nanking because, according to Đại Việt sources, they were better ritualists than the Chinese;[25] in 1395 the imperial court again summoned "monks, masseuses and castrated servants" to be sent from Jiaozhi, though only the eunuchs were definitely kept.[26] Castrating young boys of deprived or non-Han background in the South to be trained as servants in powerful households or the court was a custom common since the Tang.[27] It was banned by the Hongwu Emperor in 1372 in Guangdong and Fujian provinces,[28] but continued in Jiaozhi. Chinese official sources such as the Ming Veritable Records (*Ming shilu,* 明實錄) of the same period also recorded movements of Viet experts to the Ming capital. Zou Dongxuan was in fact one of 9,000 Jiaozhi experts, including outstanding scholars, talented fighters, craftsmen, ritualists, medical experts, and mathematicians, sent to the imperial court.[29] According to Chinese sources, these movements were part of the process of civilizing Jiaozhi as these experts were to undergo training in China before they were sent back to serve their own people as bureaucrats. Chinese-style local bureaus were actually set up in Jiaozhi in 1414 to regulate medical and ritual matters.[30]

But in Vietnamese historical memory, these movements of experts, together with the burning and seizure of local books, represented blatant Chinese imperialist attempts to destroy Vietnamese indigenous culture. In the field of medicine, it is believed that most existing medical and religious expertise of value in Jiaozhi was confiscated or destroyed by Ming emissaries controlling the region in the early fifteenth century.[31]

It was precisely in this period that modern Vietnamese historians of medicine situate an icon in Vietnamese medical history, monk Tuệ Tĩnh (慧靖), known for coining the term *Nam dược* (南藥, southern medicine) for "authentic Vietnamese medicine" in a text attributed to him, *Nam dược thần hiệu* (南藥神效, Miraculous drugs of the South), considered the foundation of "authentic" Vietnamese medicine. His biographical details, however, are inconsistent and confusing. A nineteenth-century Vietnamese historical text described him as active during the twelfth century: "Lê Đức Toàn (黎德全), active between the Lý and the Trần dynasties (1010–1399) called himself Chan (Zen) master Tuệ Tĩnh . He collected southern herbal plants to cure southerners. He was well known in the [Chinese] Southern Song dynasty (1127–1279). When the Empress fell ill, an emissary was sent to take him into service. He then lived in the Jiangnan region (in China) and died there. The Song Emperor buried him and set up a stone stele to commemorate his deeds." It was Emperor Lê Dụ Tông (黎裕宗, 1679–1731) who ordered the repatriation of the stele and granted him the honorific name Giác Tư (覺斯). A temple was built in his name in the mid-nineteenth century.[32]

Other accounts of the monk's medical activities span from the eleventh to the nineteenth century. A popular version of his biography suggests 1330–1389 as his dates, and that he was sent to the early Ming court in Nanking as a tributary gift in 1385.[33] Dương-Bá-Bành, author of *the* "standard" history of Vietnamese medicine written in 1947–1950, on the other hand, considered Tuệ Tĩnh an eighteenth-century monk, while the Japanese medical historian Mayanagi Makoto thinks that a courtier in 1717 published a medical work in the name of Tuệ Tĩnh.[34] These conflicting dates suggest the likelihood that several monks bearing the religious name Tuệ Tĩnh might have merged in the popular imagination of the mythical founder of "authentic" Vietnamese medicine.[35] Because the treatise attributed to Tuệ Tĩnh was said to have circulated in manuscript form and did not appear in print until the eighteenth century, it is simply impossible to determine who first drafted it, when, and how it was reedited before it was fixed in print form.

Rather than trying to solve the impossible puzzle of the "authentic" Tuệ Tĩnh,[36] it may be more productive to use his story to deepen the understanding of the historical exchange of medical experts and knowledge between northern Chinese and Đại Việt in the period, especially during the early Ming occupation. The most obvious point to note is that medical monks played a key role in the circulation of medical knowledge and practice, as demonstrated by both Tuệ Tĩnh and Jihong, compiler of the thirteenth-century *Lingnan weisheng fang*. Monks were the most accessible medical experts on indigenous herbs and experts of ritual healing, an inseparable part of "Southern" medical culture up to the modern period.[37]

The episode of Tuệ Tĩnh being taken to the Chinese capital to treat the (Southern Song or Ming) empress, where he wrote his seminal medical treatise and died, could be read in the context of the early Ming requests for experts from Jiaozhi to Nanking. Tuệ Tĩnh's story highlights a defining feature of the premodern identity construction of the "South": political compliance in exchange for cultural empowerment, the north / south division being conceptualized on unequal cultural relations rather than political opposition.[38] This empowerment would eventually strengthen the Vietnamese (and southern

Chinese) pursuit of their own regional agenda, while elite Chinese scholars to the north would continue to revive tropes describing this region as relatively uncivilized.[39]

But the most intriguing point in Tuệ Tĩnh's story is his being crowned the master of "Southern medicine," synonymous with "genuine" Vietnamese medicine. This system was the alternative of northern medicine (*thuốc Bắc,* 藥北), synonymous with "Sino-Vietnamese medicine,"[40] a system based on Chinese medical classics with greater theoretical sophistication, and using more expensive "Chinese" pharmaceuticals. These two categories are still used today to frame Vietnamese traditional medicine.[41]

What exactly was "genuine" southern medicine? David Marr's insightful interpretation of *thuốc Nam* as a practice of necessity, as "the poor man's medicine, generally using ingredients readily available nearby and involving a minimum of processing," is worth pondering. Marr's comment echoes an observation recorded in a late nineteenth-century Chinese text on Annam, "There are a lot of medicinal herbs in this country. However, the Annam people do not know how to process them. So [these herbs] are all sent to China to be processed. When [the processed] herbs returned to Annam, the natives call them northern medicine *(thuốc Bắc).*"[42] This remark, not without exaggeration, reveals how Viet southerners would distinguish between southern and northern medicines by the degree of processing: raw ingredients were "genuinely" southern, but of less value than processed ones. Chinese pharmaceutical processing technology reaching a high degree of sophistication in the late imperial period[43] may symbolize Chinese culture in the South, where "raw" native herbs constitute the natural, or sometimes better, counterpart.

The authenticity of "southern" medicine was also constructed linguistically. Native names and local pronunciation of the names of truly "southern" medicinal ingredients were considered indicators of their native origin. The fact that Vietnamese medical writings, especially those attributed to Tuệ Tĩnh, are considered crucial in the historical development of Chữ Nôm (字喃), Vietnamese ideograms re-created from traditional Chinese characters, suggests that medical things and knowledge played a key part in the construction of the Viet identity. The treatise *Nam dược thần hiệu* was an important text in the history of the creation of Chữ Nôm ideograms that phonetically expressed local names of indigenous *materia medica.*[44] The textualization of *thuốc Nam,* therefore, was concurrent with an emerging sense of native and even protonationalist identity, and the critical question becomes: *When* exactly did the

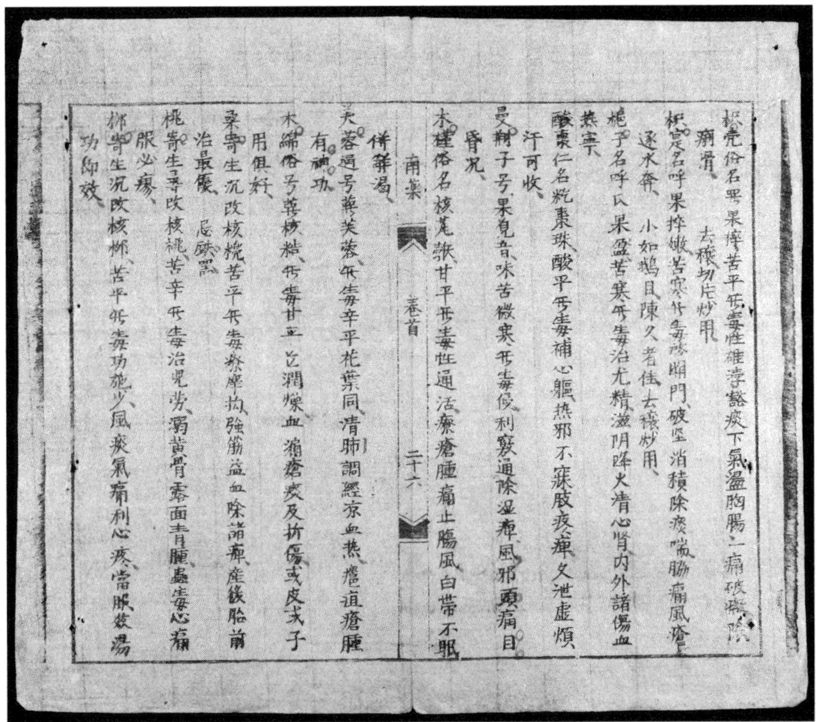

南藥 卷首 二十六

A nineteenth-century print of *Nam dược thần hiệu.* Chapter on southern herbs showing ample use of Chữ Nôm. Reproduced from a copy in the National Library of Vietnam.

South / North dichotomy attributed to *Nam dược thần hiệu* begin to shape "traditional" medicine as a knowledge system in the Vietnamese south? A look at Vietnamese medical texts in the following period, when the authorship became more individualized, may provide some clue to this question that the undatable *Nam dược thần hiệu* cannot answer.

Sixteenth through Eighteenth Centuries: Indigenous Southern *Materia Medica*

Two entangled developments, one commercial and the other political, shaped East Asia's "South" in this second period: the arrival of global traders and European missionaries in transoceanic vessels, and the traumatic dynastic change in China in the mid-seventeenth century where the Ming court found refuge in this South, resisting Manchu forces for more than two decades before succumbing in 1668.

It was during this critical period of intensifying globalization that the first pioneering study on indigenous *materia medica* in Guangdong province was published.[45] He Kejian (何克諫, native of Panyu, Guangdong) did fieldwork and compiled *Shengcao yaoxing beiyao* (生草藥性備要, Essentials of medicinal quality of raw herbs)[46] in the mid-seventeenth century while socializing with a group of Ming loyalists. His loyalist identity[47] may have explained the text's late and less than elegant publication under a pseudonym.[48]

This text listed 311 herbs native to Guangdong province, most of which were not registered in Li Shizhen's magnum opus of 1596, *Bencao gangmu* (本草綱目, Systematic *materia medica*).[49] The text circulated in manuscript form before

鷄屎藤 味苦性辛其頭治新内傷痰肉食補虛益腎除
火補血洗瘡止痛消热散毒其葉擂米加糖煎
食止疴痢葉有蔴芋有毛者佳
枸杞菜 味甜性寒明目益腎虛安胎寬中退热治婦人
崩漏下血立止其根即是地骨皮其葉炒米茶
益精氣
石菖蒲 味辛性温祛風消腫治心氣痛通竅洗疔瘡百
上生的一寸九節者佳
荷錢葉 味劫性寒擂汁治白濁存性治遺精其花陰
乾貼瘡節立消

Late nineteenth-century edition of He Kejian's work on native herbal plants described in the Cantonese dialect. Reproduced from a facsimile copy of Shengcao yaoxing beiyao by He Kejian, published by Guangdong keji chubanshe, Guangzhou, 2009, in author's collection.

it was first printed in Guangdong in 1711, after the 1668 military pacification of the region, and probably after He's death. It had at least three nineteenth-century editions, four Republican editions, and two modern annotated editions (1995, 1999) and inspired numerous research articles in contemporary China. It formed the basis for subsequent compilations of Guangdong native *materia medica* in the Qing and Republican periods. This work was put under the spotlight in the late 1950s when the Guangdong government commissioned a province-wide survey of native plants and old recipes.[50]

This first compilation of Guangdong *materia medica* is marked by the free use of the Cantonese dialect for plant names and descriptions of taste and nature, indicating that the printed text was very much in the form of field notes.[51] Descriptions of herbs were sometimes followed by popular recipes, especially for external application to treat boils and skin diseases, snake bites, tumors, diarrhea, and other problems of the natives' everyday life. The author of this linguistically crude text nonetheless claimed this research as part of Confucian learning, demonstrated his knowledge in sophisticated processing (recommended for certain listed herbs), and in ritual healing as part of the local practice.[52] The author was consciously building local knowledge in the Cantonese dialect, excluding ingredients already incorporated in standard *materia medica* such as tangerine peel. This book clearly articulated the idea embedded in the Viet notion of "Southern medicine" without mentioning the word "south."

While He Kejian chose to lead a hermit's life in Guangdong in the face of the Manchu invasion, other Chinese southern loyalists opted for migrating to Jiaozhi given its political sympathy for the Ming regime.[53] These emigrants from southern China, many of whom were in the herbal trade, were known in Đại Việt as "people transmitting Ming rituals" (*Minh Hương*, 明香).[54] Văn Giang (文江) in the province of Hưng Yên (興安) in the Red River delta was famous for Chinese pharmaceutical trade dominated by a few Fujianese lineages that took advantage of the rich herbal resources in the region and their mastery of processing technology. They purchased raw herbs in nearby regions that they processed with tools brought from China.[55] The duly processed herbs that were actually grown and processed in the "South" became highly valued "Northern medicines." Other towns in the same region, such as Hải Phòng (海防), also became major trading ports where processed Chinese medicines were imported, a trade monopolized by the Cantonese.[56] Anecdotes in the official history of the Nguyễn Dynasty compiled in the mid-nineteenth century also illustrate the economic and cultural importance of Chinese pharmaceuticals in the region,[57] which explains the appearance of new medical institutions in Hà Nội in the nineteenth century.[58]

It is against this background that the Lãn Ông (懶翁) phenomenon emerged. Hải Thượng Lãn Ông (海上懶翁, a laid-back man from the Hải Thượng region) was the pen name of Lê Hữu Trác (黎有倬, 1724–1791), the second medical master in Vietnamese history. David Marr considered him the "Father of Vietnamese medicine, not only the traditional branch, but also as authentic home-grown precursor of the meticulous clinical approach underlying modern cosmopolitan medicine."[59] From a literati family with both his grandfather and father as licentiates of the Vietnamese court examinations (*jinshi,* 進士), Lãn Ông was the product of the Neo-Confucian culture planted in Đại Việt since the fifteenth century. His comprehensive medical work *Hải Thượng y tông tâm lĩnh* (海上醫宗心領) was a fine representation of the Jiangnan medical tradition. Written in a mixture of Chinese and Chữ Nôm, in twenty-eight volumes and sixty-six chapters, but published well after his death, in 1880–1885, this text notably contains two chapters on indigenous "Lingnan" *materia medica.*

Modern Vietnamese historians of medicine praise Lãn Ông mostly for his theoretical innovation: claiming the nonexistence of Cold Damage (*shanghan* 傷寒) clinical patterns in the South, and the danger of ephedra in treating local diseases.[60] In fact, the caution against ephedra, a northern ingredient, had already been pointed out in the thirteenth-century Chinese text *Lingnan weisheng fang* and was not a new idea.[61] But Lãn Ông's strong-worded claim that *shanghan* clinical patterns were totally irrelevant to the extreme South and that local ailments required a very different therapeutic strategy showed a clear southern subjectivity. The Vietnamese scholar Nguyễn Trần Huân, who translated into French Lãn Ông's autobiographic chapter in this medical book, points out that the author was a pioneer in writing in the first person in the eighteenth century.[62] In this case the first person in *Hải Thượng y tông tâm lĩnh* was flagged as a Lingnan native.

Lãn Ông's presentation of native medicinal herbs in his book—the two chapters entitled "Lingnan" *materia medica,*[63] separate from the one on standard "pharmaceuticals" (藥品, *yaopin*)—was equally revealing. The list of 500 items, of which 241 are plants (others were animal- or human-based, minerals, or stones), is intriguing in two ways: First, the two chapters are identical to the chapter on pharmaceuticals of *Nam dược thần hiệu* (南藥神效) attributed

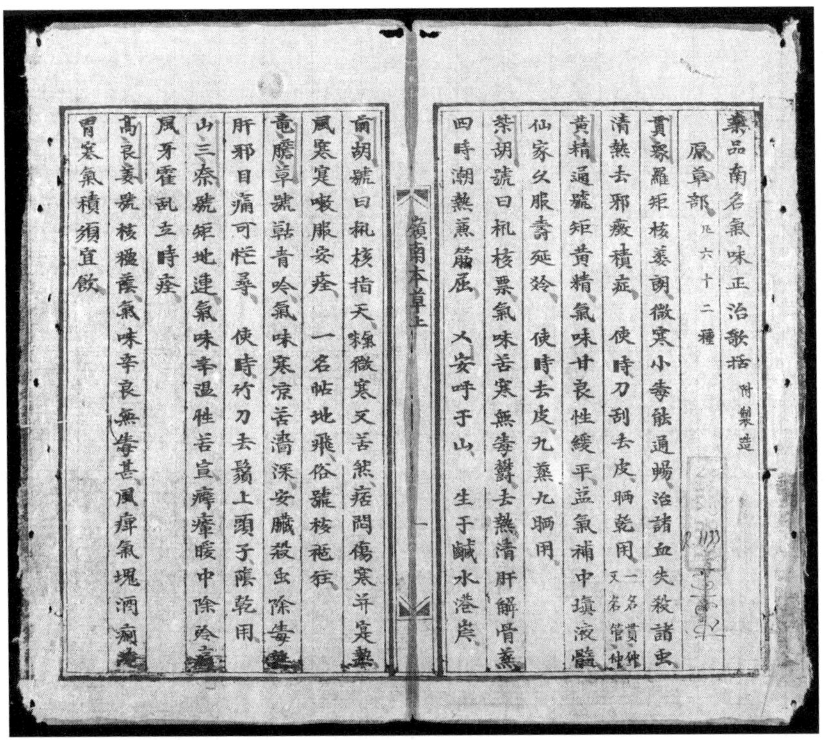

藥品南名氣味正治歌括 附製造
原草部 凡六十二種
貫衆羅矩核萎朗微寒小毒能通腸治諸血失殺諸虫
清熱去邪痰積症 使時刀刮去皮晒乾用 一名貫仲 又名管仲
黃精通號矩黃精氣味甘良性緩平益氣補中塡液髓
仙家久服壽延紾 使時去皮九蒸九晒用
柴胡號曰枙核票氣味苦寒無毒蠲去熱清肝解骨蒸
四時潮熱薫𦶜㞸 又安呼于山 生于鹹水港岸

嶺南本草上 一

前胡號曰楓核指天糠微寒又苦然痞悶傷寒并寒熱
風寒寔嗽服安痊 一名帖地飛俗號核衼狂
亀膽草號鵲青吟氣味寒凉苦濇深安臟殺虫除毒蠱
肝邪目痛可㤥尋 使時竹刀去鬚上頭子蔭乾用
山三奈號矩地連氣味辛溫性苦宣癖癢暖中除冷蠱
風牙霍亂立時痊
高良姜號核㰖蓔氣味辛良無毒甚風痺氣塊洏痢疴
胃寒氣積須宜飲

Nineteenth-century edition of Lingnan *materia medica* in Lãn Ông 's eighteenth-century treatise. Reproduced from a copy of Hải Thượng y tông tâm lĩnh by Lãn Ông in the National Library of Vietnam.

to Tuệ Tĩnh. The classification of these ingredients was clearly post-*Bencao gangmu,* thus unlikely to be published before the seventeenth century. One can reasonably speculate that a common master list circulated among Vietnamese experts in the eighteenth century. Lãn Ông, and not Tuệ Tĩnh, was a possible compiler. Second, the style of describing the herbs is similar to the slightly earlier work by the Cantonese He Kejian of the mid-seventeenth century: descriptions in dialect or Chữ Nôm, inclusive of processing methods and formulae for mostly "external" problems such as snake bites, skin diseases, diarrhea, and so forth. The list of 241 native plants was shorter than He's 311 with some 20 bearing exactly the same Chinese names, compared with the 610 "standard" ingredients listed in Chinese "elitist" *materia medica* texts by the late seventeenth century.[64] The two southern lists show that around the mid-seventeenth century, native southern experts, Chinese and Vietnamese alike, began to be conscious of the importance of organizing local plant knowledge for better and more practical healthcare based on immediately available raw herbs. These activities were probably part of an intellectual trend inspired by the publication of *Bencao gangmu* in the late sixteenth century. In the South, moreover, they were also prompted by nascent local identities expressed in linguistic forms.

"Chinese" Medicine for Western Missionaries in the South

At the same time, trading and missionary activities dominated by the East India companies and the Jesuit Society added yet another layer of complexity to the circulation of medical things and experts in this "South." These activities began by more tightly connecting different parts of East Asia's south. One early actor was the Jesuits' dispensary of St Paul in Macao (1562–1762). Being a key station for Jesuits working in Asia, Macao was visited by priests working in Vietnam, Hainan, southern China, and Japan. During the 200 years of the existence of the dispensary of St Paul, Portuguese Jesuits developed interest and knowledge in Chinese *materia medica* and imported Chinese ingredients from Canton for use with European ones, creating hybrid recipes.[65] It was the best-stocked dispensary for global travelers in the region where European missionaries also learned about Chinese medical things and practices. Seventeenth-century Portuguese Jesuits in Đại Việt, such as Christoforo Borri, also witnessed the abundance of native doctors who knew how to cure diseases unknown to European physicians.[66]

Jesuit experts traveling in this southern maritime region wasted no time in publishing their versions of the region's flora and *materia medica* considered as "Chinese": the Polish Jesuit Michal Boym's (ca. 1614–1659) illustrated *Flora Sinensis* (1656) depicts tropical fruits and animals such as mangoes and rhinoceroses as "Chinese"; *Les secrets de la médecine des Chinois* (1671) by an anonymous Frenchman working in Canton portrayed Chinese medical methods as unreliable; and Boym's attempt to introduce Chinese pulse medicine to Europeans in *Specimen Medicinae Sinicae* (An outline of Chinese medicine, 1682) and *Clavis Medica ad Chinarum Doctrinam de Pulsibus* (Medical key to the Chinese doctrine on the pulse, 1686) were important examples.

Boym's cases, thoroughly studied by Hanson and Pomata,[67] deserve attention. Active in East Asia's south between 1643 and 1659, in Macao, Hainan, Guangdong and Guangxi provinces, and Tonkin[68] during the Manchu conquest of south China, Boym, son of a physician, developed great interest in Chinese medicine and *materia medica* based on what he could find as texts and pharmaceuticals circulating in the region.[69] Besides translating the Chinese text on pulse medicine, he was also building a catalog of Chinese pharmaceuticals that he could find in Macao. Boym was certainly not the only expert keen about the project. A list of 298 pharmaceuticals accompanying Boym's *Specimen,* called *Medicamenta simplicia quae a Chinensibus ad usum medicum adhibentur* (Simple medicine used by the Chinese for medical purposes), with medicinal names in Chinese characters, Romanization, and descriptions in Latin, was the likely work of the Belgian Jesuit Philippe Couplet (1627–1693), Boym's collaborator and editor.[70]

Couplet's list of 298 Chinese pharmaceuticals of mostly southern herbs, excepting 22 minerals and 22 animal ingredients, is an excellent sample of local knowledge built in the seventeenth-century South that is worthy of further research.[71] The Romanization of herbal names reveals southern pronunciation, and the explanations in Latin show local understanding of the ingredients, sometimes erroneous. One example is the item *awei* 阿魏 (asafetida), item 61 on the list, a Central Asian resin with a strong stench shipped to China via Canton since the Song.[72] The item was Romanized as *ō gúej,* clearly a southern pronunciation, with the following descriptions: "I don't exactly know what it is. They say it is the excrement of a small animal of a certain plant. This medicinal substance comes from the province of Leâo tum."[73] Probably, informants for the Jesuits included not only medical experts but also local merchants for the compilation of the list, which clearly is an assemblage of circulating medical things and knowledge mediated by various experts in this southern region, reflecting a complex medical culture integrating different medical traditions and breeding new regional identities.

We have seen the flows of medical things and experts in two phases. In the first phase, we saw the northern movement of southern medical ingredients (formerly known as *yiwu*) to become an integral part of the Chinese standard *materia medica.* We also saw the southern movement of experts (monks, bureaucrats, doctors, etc.) into the miasmatic Lingnan region using southern ingredients to treat local ailments. These flows of things and people opened up Lingnan as an accessible space for medical observation and experimentation, still imagined in North / South hierarchical cultural relations. As noted by Liam Kelley, by the fifteenth century, "Southern envoys did not wish for any other differences to prevail between their domain and the one to their north. Instead, they endeavored . . . to ensure that their domain stay on 'the same tracks' as the Middle Kingdom. They did this out of a belief in the 'benefit' that participation in this larger world would bring . . . [to the southern kingdom]."[74] Political boundaries were not a major issue.

In the second phase, broader global flows of medical things and experts created a tighter southern network shaped by European commercial and religious interests and activities, and the political crisis in southern China in the mid-seventeenth century. These forces, facilitated by the ecological coherence and shared pathological environment of the region, seemed to have generated spaces of indigenization and emerging southern agency within the broad Lingnan region. New constructions of local medical knowledge based on native medical things in interaction with external commercial and political forces were dynamic and multisited. The spaces grew not only in response to the traditional political and cultural center to its north[75] but also increasingly in interaction with commercial and religious forces coming from its west.

Notes

1. On the significance of the names of the region, see Baldanza 2016, especially 1–6.

2. The cultural coherence of the region centered at Hanoi and Guangzhou has recently been treated in Cooke, Li, and Anderson 2011. See Li 2011. See also the rigidity of political terms of "China" and "Vietnam" that prohibits productive regional imaginations, in Kelley 2005, 27–28; for a *longue durée* treatment of the changing power relations between southern chieftains and China, see Anderson and Whitmore 2014.

3. Lombard 2007; Li 2011, 3.

4. See Woodside 1971, in which the notion of "Little China" for Vietnam is raised; more recently, Kelley 2005 (citing Keith Taylor 1992) provides a different view: "In contrast to the assertions of the little China theory—that it was the Chinese elements in society and government that made Vietnam strong—Taylor argued that these elements had led the Lê to alienate themselves from their own people, a phenomenon which in turn produced centuries of 'prolonged civil wars' and 'internal divisions'" (15).

5. Term used by Métailié (2015, 129) for a list of such texts.

6. A point well illustrated first by Schafer (1963).

7. Chen 2013, 430–433.

8. This text was first reconstructed in the first half of the nineteenth century by Cantonese literati, and the current version was fixed in print in 1851. See Wu 2010, 16–17.

9. See Ma 1978.

10. Betel nuts were introduced in China before the seventh century but for a long time were imported only as diplomatic gifts. See Chen 2013, 138–139.

11. Wu 2010, 9–10.

12. The extant text is based on a mid-nineteenth-century Japanese reedition of a sixteenth-century Chinese publication (with at least two editions in 1513 and 1576).

13. The official dynastic history of the Tang recorded a number of medical formulae for Lingnan ailments, some, judging from their titles, being travel guides. None of these texts are extant. This genre of medical texts on Lingnan medicine, contrary to the *yiwu* genre, continued to thrive after the Song period.

14. These medical experts included sojourning monks (Jihong, the compiler of the book), scholar-officials, and doctors: Li Qiu 李璆 and Zhang Zhiyuan 張致遠 (magistrate in Guangzhou in 1138), doctors Wang Nanyong 汪南容, Lo Andao 婁安道, and Zhang Jie章傑, author of *"Lingbiao shi shuo"* (嶺表十說, Ten features of the southern pathological environment) *Lingnan Weisheng fang,* Beijing: Zhongyi guji chubanshe based on the 1841 Japanese edition, "Foreword," 1–3; see also He Shixi 1991, 624.

15. *Lingnan weisheng fang*, I: 10a.

16. Ibid., II:1a-b; I:7b.

17. Ibid., 1:5a.

18. The proliferation of encyclopaedic compilations on medical formulae using such *materia medica* since the tenth century witnessed this development. See the table showing increasing use of foreign ingredients in Chinese medical recipes from the Tang to the Song established by Hartwell (1989, 477–480).

19. This period was also marked by increasing use of spiced ingredients in recipes, which had swift effects; see Zheng 2005, 49, 151.

20. *Lingnan weisheng fang*, II:4a.

21. A region where rites and music were not established, as described by the first Ming emperor. See Baldanza 2016, 57.

22. Notably *Đại Việt sử ký toàn thư* 1984–1986.

23. *Đại Việt sử ký toàn thư,* entry on the Vietnamese need of silk and pharmaceuticals coming from China, I: 348–349 (year 1274); entry on ritual healing introduced, I: 391–392 (year 1310); entry on prominent captured Chinese military doctors during the Song/Yuan transition serving the Vietnamese court, I: 419, 425 (year 1339); see also Zhu 1981, 127–129.

24. Li 1996, 2: 706–707. Yongle suggested the deployment of the ethnic Miao troops to replace the Chinese.

25. *Đại Việt sử ký toàn thư,* I: 458 (year 1385).

26. *Đại Việt sử ký toàn thư,* I: 470 (year 1395), 483 (year 1403).

27. Rideout 1949, 54–56.

28. *Ming shilu* 1966, Records on Taizu, *juan* 73: 1353; *Đại Việt sử ký toàn thư,* I: 490 (year 1406). A few early Ming Jiaozhi eunuchs rose to prominence; see *Ming shigao* 1962 [1732], *juan* 178: 7a–b. See also Li Tana 2010, 96.

29. *Ming shilu,* Records on Taizong, *juan* 71: 997, 1001.

30. Ibid., *juan* 68: 962–963; Đại Việt sử ký toàn thư, I: 496. See also Whitmore 1985, 121–131, on the establishment of Chinese institutions.

31. Dương Bá Bành 1947–1950, 38; Hoàng Bảo Châu, Phó Đức Thực, and Hữu Ngọc 1993, 12. Li 1996, 2: 707–708 on book burning and confiscation; Ong 2010 on the Ming emperor's motive to impose Neo-Confucian ideology; *Đại Việt sử ký toàn thư,* II: 516 (year 1418).

32. Phan 1965, book 3: 380. Mayanagi concurs with Dương Bá Bành that the major medical text *Hồng Nghĩa Giác Tư Y Thư* (洪義覺斯醫書) attributed to Tuệ Tĩnh was written by an eighteenth-century courtier in the name of Tuệ Tĩnh. See Mayanagi 2010, 275.

33. Thompson 2015a, 16–19.

34. Dương Bá Bành 1947–1950, 41–42.

35. Thompson (2015b: 3) proposes this hypothesis that seems plausible.

36. The late development of printing in Vietnam was part of the problem as manuscripts were copied, collated, edited, and reedited before most of them became fixed printed texts only in the nineteenth century. See McHale 2004, 12–17.

37. Zen Buddhism in Vietnam reached its apogee in the Trần Dynasty (1225–1399), and this version of Buddhism was considered to be the "Chinese version" of Buddhism in Vietnam. See Trần 1985, 3: 83. Religious training of indigenous doctors remained strong even in the twentieth century; see the autobiography of Quang Văn Nguyễn in Nguyễn and Pivar 2004.

38. Kelley 2005, 25–26.

39. The intensive human and cultural flows between Đại Việt and Ming China in the fifteenth century were crucial for the subsequent development of the Red River delta into a dense human hub comparable to the Pearl River delta. See Li 2010, 83–103. On Đại Việt's use of Neo-Confucian methods in the cultivation of indigenous beliefs and practices, see Whitmore 2014, 252–254. See Baldanza 2016, 10, on the growing political clout of Đại Việt between the fourteenth and sixteenth centuries despite the persistent Chinese view of the region as culturally inferior.

40. Dương Bá Bành 1947–1950, introduction: 2.

41. See Hoàng Bảo Châu, Phó Đức Thực, and Hữu Ngọc 1993. This book begins by indicating the two components of Vietnamese medicine as *thuốc Nam* and *thuốc*

Bắc, but later admits that "there was no strict dividing line" between the two (7). Monnais, Thompson, and Wahlberg 2012; and chapter 1 by Thompson (2015a: 97–99). Marr 1987: 169.

42. Yao 1877–1897, 50: 74. The author of this text provides stereotypical descriptions of Vietnamese things and customs, considering the Vietnamese culture as comparatively crude and inferior, its people less hardworking and trustworthy, and so forth.

43. Zheng 2005: 212–213. Processing technology matured in the Song dynasty and peaked in the Ming / Qing period. Modern Chinese experts have the following definition for northern pharmaceuticals: northern medicines (*bei yao* 北藥) were those that needed processing before use, mostly grown in northern China, whereas southern medicines (*nan yao* 南藥) were those that could be used in their raw form, produced mostly in the south. See also Guan Peisheng 1995: 5.

44. Shi 1993, 2: 55–58. According to Ngô Đức Thọ 吳德壽 (2015), Vietnamese scholars' use of Chữ Nôm in their writings became more widespread in the thirteenth and fourteenth centuries.

45. Though a few earlier doctors who had sojourned in Guangdong province, such as Zhang Jike (張繼科 sixteenth century) and Chen Zhi (陳治 early Qing), continued the tradition of *Lingnan weisheng fang* in observing Lingnan miasmatic ailments in their writings as classically trained doctors from the "north." See Zheng 2009, 226–238.

46. The extant printed copies of this text are mostly dated late nineteenth to early twentieth century. It is uncertain that the title of the text was the original one given by He. It could be given by nineteenth-century publishers and printers.

47. His name is listed in Chen Botao's 陳伯陶 1919 *Compiled biographies of Ming loyalists in Guangdong* (Shengchao Yuedong yimin lu 勝朝粵東遺民錄). One of his close associates was the famous Guangdong loyalist Chen Gongyin 陳恭尹 (1631–1700); see preface of Guan 1995, 3–8; see also Xian 1980, 3: 21–22.

48. He's other work, published in a finer print, 增補食物本草備考 (1732) also had an unsigned preface. His notoriety as a Ming loyalist may be the reason for this anomaly.

49. This is stated in the preface (supposedly written by He himself) of the printed version; see the facsimile of the late nineteenth-century Shoujing tang edition, Guangzhou: Guangdong keji chubanshe 2009, 3.

50. A 1960 version of the survey was said to have been destroyed during the Cultural Revolution but can be found online.

51. Like the frequent use of the adjective *jie* (*kip* in Cantonese) 劫to designate the "acrid" taste.

52. He Kijian 2009, 1a, preface on Confucian learning. His descriptions of steaming and sunning ingredients while maintaining their intrinsic nature were

frequent throughout the text. Ritual healing such as incantation was also mentioned (*juan xia:* 33a).

53. On the interdependence between the Southern Ming regime and Đại Việt during this political crisis, see Baldanza 2016, 204–206.

54. Choi 2004, 85–100; Yan 2007; Feng 2002.

55. Phan and Li 2002.

56. Yan 嚴璩1983, 59.

57. For example, the biography of Nguyễn Kỳ 阮紀, a middle bureaucrat appointed in 1802, states: "When young, Nguyễn Kỳ lived in the house of a Northern visitor (Chinese *beike* 北客) and studied with him. He developed stomach ailments during this period but was cured after taking medicines provided by the Northern visitor. Later, the military commander of the region got the same ailment and Kỳ cured the commander by offering him the same medication. [After this, Kỳ] acquired the reputation of a "famous doctor." The Northern visitor later returned to Qing China and entrusted his wife to Kỳ. After his death, Kỳ married the wife and started a business with the man's estate. See Phan 1965, 135.

58. For example, in 1831 temples were built for the worship of mythical Chinese medical figures and famous historical doctors. See *Gudai Zhong-Yue guanxi shi ziliao xuanbian* (古代中越關係史資料選編) 1982, 626; Dương Bá Bành 1947–1950, 47–48.

59. Marr 1987, 171–174.

60. Zhang 1992, 166; Mayanagi 2010, 278–279; Nguyễn, Du, and Wang 2013.

61. Jihong discussed in length the unsuitability of ephedra in treating southern Cold Damage–like patterns; see *Lingnan weisheng fang,* 2: 25b–27a.

62. Nguyễn 1972, xvii.

63. Interestingly, the two chapters (in *juan* 13 of the work) were almost identical to the one supposedly authored by Tuệ Tĩnh on local (southern) herbs. From the format and system, I would judge that this chapter is more likely a post-eighteenth-century text than a fourteenth-century one, as it shows the influence of Li Shizhen's classic in the classification of herbs.

64. The early Qing medical philologist Zhang Zhicong (1644–1722) claimed that by his time, a total of 610 herbs were named and used as medical ingredients, with an additional category of 153 named but unused (Zhang 1982 [1670], 99).

65. Amaro (1999, 116) noted that a 1625 letter sent by priests in Macau showed that many ingredients used in the dispensary were already imported from Canton. See also Amaro's compilation of what she considered as hybrid recipes used in Macau society, *Mal-de-ar in Macau* (Macau: Instituto internacional de Macau, 2011).

66. Dror and Taylor 2006, 119–120.

67. See Hanson and Pomata 2017, 1–25 on Boym's work, 4–6 on other contemporary works.

68. Pelliot 1934, 95–151.

69. Cook 2011, especially 215–219.

70. Hanson and Pomata 2017, 14–15, while Edward Kajdanski (1987, especially 174–175) thinks that the list was compiled by Boym himself.

71. Of the 252 plant ingredients circulating in this region and brought to the attention of European experts, at least 21 can be identified in He Kejian's (2009) book, and about 60 in Lãn Ông's list of Lingnan *materia medica.*

72. See the study on the history of this ingredient by Leung and Chen (forthcoming).

73. I thank Gianna Pomata for showing me the list and for translating the Latin description for me.

74. Kelley 2005, 32–34, 197. Kelley considers that by the late fifteenth century, as shown by *Đại Việt sử ký toàn thư,* the South had identified itself as the domain of *wen* 文 civility but with ambivalence, as it was not on the same par as the Chinese North.

75. See Wang 2015, 1–15, for a discussion of the Sinocentric and northward-looking perspectives of southern histories.

References

Amaro, Ana Maria. 1999. "The Influence of Chinese Pharmacopeia in the Prescriptions of the Jesuit Dispensaries." In *Religion and Culture: An International Symposium Commemorating the Fourth Centenary of the University College of St. Paul,* eds. John W. Witek and Michel Reis, 111–129. Macau: Instituto Cultural de Macau; Ricci Institute for Chinese-Western Cultural History of the University of San Francisco.

Anderson, James A., and John K. Whitmore. 2014. "Introduction: The Fiery Frontier and the *Dong* World." In *China's Encounters on the South and Southwest: Reforging the Fiery Frontier over Two Millennia,* eds. James A. Anderson and John K. Whitmore, 1–55. Leiden: Brill.

Baldanza, Kathlene. 2016. "Introduction: The Power of Names." In *Ming China and Vietnam: Negotiating Borders in Early Modern China,* ed. Kathlene Baldanza, 1–12. Cambridge: Cambridge University Press.

Chen Ming 陳明. 2013. *Zhonggu yiliao yu wailai wenhua* 中古醫療與外來文化 [Medieval medicine and external cultural influences]. Beijing: Beijing daxue chubanshe.

Choi, Byung Wook. 2004. "The Nguyễn Dynasty's Policy toward Chinese on the Water Frontier in the First Half of the Nineteenth Century." In *Water Frontier: Commerce and the Chinese in the Lower Mekong Region, 1750–1880,* eds. Nola Cooke and Li Tana, 85–100. Singapore: Rowman & Littlefield.

Cook, Harold J. 2011. "Conveying Chinese Medicine to Seventeenth-Century Europe." In *Science between Europe and Asia: Historical Studies on the Transmission,*

Adoption and Adaptation of Knowledge, eds. Feza Günergun and Dhruv Raina, 209–232. Netherlands: Springer.

Cooke, Nola, Li Tana, and James A. Anderson, eds. 2011. *The Tongking Gulf through History.* Philadelphia: University of Pennsylvania Press.

Đại Việt sử ký toàn thư 大越史記全書 [Complete historical chronicle of Đại Việt]. 1984–1986. 3 vols., ed. Chen Jinghe 陳荊和. Tokyo: Tokyo Daigaku Toyo bunka kenkyujo.

Dror, Olga, and K. W. Taylor, eds. 2006. *Views of Seventeenth-Century Vietnam: Christoforo Borri on Cochinchina and Samuel Baron on Tonkin.* Ithaca, NY: Cornell University Press.

Dương Bá Bành. 1947–1950. "Histoire de la mèdecine du Vietnam." Manuscript. Hanoi.

Feng Lijun 馮立軍. 2002. "Gudai Zhong-Yue zhong yiyao jiaoliu chutan" 古代中越中醫藥交流初探 [Preliminary study on medical exchange between China and Vietnam in the early periods]. *Haijiao shi yanjiu* 1: 52–53.

Guan Peisheng 關培生. 1995. *Zengding shengcao yaoxing beiyao* 增訂生草藥性備要 [Augmented edition on "Essentials of the medicinal nature of raw herbs"]. Hong Kong: Juxianguan Wenhua youxian gongsi.

Gudai Zhong-Yue guanxi shi ziliao xuanbian 古代中越關係史資料選編 [A selection of historical sources on old Sino-Vietnamese relations]. 1982. Beijing: Zhongguo shehui kexue chubanshe.

Hanson, Marta, and Gianna Pomata. 2017. "Medicinal Formulas and Experiential Knowledge in the Seventeenth-Century Epistemic Exchange between China and Europe." *Isis* 108(1): 1–25.

Hartwell, Robert. 1989. "Foreign Trade, Monetary Policy and Chinese 'Mercantilism.'" In *Collected Studies on Sung History Dedicated to James T. C. Liu in Celebration of His 70th Birthday,* ed. Kinmugawa Tsuyoshi, 477–480. Kyoto: Dohosha.

He Kejian 何克諫. 2009. *Shengcao yaoxing beiyao* 生草藥性備要 [Essentials of medicinal quality of raw herbs]. Guangzhou: facsimile reprint of the Shoujingtang edition.

He Shixi 何時希. 1991. *Zhongguo lidai yijia zhuanlu* 中國歷代醫家傳錄 [Biographies of medical experts in Chinese history]. Beijing: Remin weisheng chubanshe.

Hoang Bao Chau, Pho Duc Thuc, and Huu Ngoc. 1993. *Vietnamese Traditional Medicine.* Hanoi: Gioi Publishers.

Jihong 繼洪 ed. 1983. *Lingnan Weisheng fang* 嶺南衛生方 (Life-preserving recipes for the Lingnan region). Beijing: Zhongyi guji chubanshe based on the 1841 Japanese edition.

Kajdanski, Edward. 1987. "Michael Boym's Medicus sinicus." *T'oung Pao* LXXIII: 161–189.

Kelley, Liam. 2005. *Beyond the Bronze Pillars: Envoy Poetry and the Sino-Vietnamese Relationship.* Honolulu: University of Hawai'i Press.

Leung, Angela, and Chen Ming. Forthcoming. "The Itinerary of *hing/awei/* asafetida across Eurasia, 400–1800." In *Entangled Itineraries: Materials, Practices, and Knowledges across Eurasia* (University of Pittsburgh Press), ed. Pamela Smith.

Li Tana. 2010. "The Ming Factor and the Emergence of the Viet in the 15th Century." In *Southeast Asia in the Fifteenth Century: The China Factor,* eds. Geoff Wade and Sun Laichen, 83–103. Singapore: NUS Press.

———. 2011. "Introduction." In *The Tongking Gulf through History,* eds. Nola Cooke, Li Tana, and James A. Anderson, 1–21. Philadelphia: University of Pennsylvania Press.

Li Wenfeng 李文鳳. 1996. *Yue Qiao Shu* 越嶠書 [Correspondences from the Viet mountains] 1540 preface. Facsimile reprint in Siku quanshu cunmu congshu series. Vol. 162. Tainan: Zhuangyan wenhua.

Lombard, Denys. 2007. "Another 'Mediterranean' in Southeast Asia." *Asia-Pacific Journal* 5(3): 1–15.

Ma, Tai-Loi. 1978. "The Authenticity of the *Nan-fang Ts'ao-mu chuang.*" *T'oung Pao* 64(4–5): 218–252.

Marr, David G. 1987. "Vietnamese Attitudes Regarding Illness and Healing." In *Death and Disease in Southeast Asia: Explorations in Social, Medical and Demographic History,* ed. Norman G. Owen, 162–186. Singapore: Oxford University Press.

Mayanagi Makoto 真柳 誠. 2010. "Yuenan yixue xingcheng di guiji" 越南醫學形成之軌跡 [Tracing the development of medicine in Vietnam]. In *The 2nd Joint Symposium of Japan, China and Korea Societies for the History of Medicine/Summary of Collected Papers,* Mito, May 2010: 274–283.

McHale, Shawn. 2004. *Print and Power: Confucianism, Communism, and Buddhism in the Making of Modern Vietnam.* Honolulu: University of Hawai'i Press.

Métailié, Georges. 2015. *Traditional Botany: An Ethnobotanical Approach.* Science and Civilization in China IV: 6. Cambridge: Cambridge University Press.

Ming shigao 明史稿 [Draft of Ming history]. 1962 [1732]. Taibei: Wenhai chubanshe.

Ming shilu 明實錄 [Veritable records of the Ming]. 1966. Taibei: Institute of History and Philology, Academia Sinica.

Monnais, Lawrence, C. Michele Thompson, and Ayo Wahlberg, eds. 2012. *Southern Medicine for Southern People: Vietnamese Medicine in the Making.* Cambridge: Cambridge Scholars Publishing.

Ngô Đức Thọ 吳德壽. 2015. "Yuenan Nom zi xingcheng di fazhan luecheng ji Yuenan Hanzi shuweihua di yi xie kaoliang" 越南喃字形成的發展略程及越南漢字數位化的一些考量 [The formation of Chữ Nôm in Vietnam and considerations of digitalization of Vietnamese Chinese characters]. *Gujin lunheng* 27: 34–35.

Nguyen, Quang Van, and Marjorie Pivar. 2004. *Fourth Uncle in the Mountain: A Memoir of a Barefoot Doctor in Vietnam.* New York: St. Martin's Press.

Nguyễn Thị Lý 阮李氏, Du Yinxin 杜尹心, and Wang Yin 王寅. 2013. "Yuenan Lê Hữu Trác 'Hải Thượng Y Tôn Tâm Lĩnh' shuping" 越南黎有卓『海上醫宗心領

』述評 [Comments on Lê Hữu Trác 'Hải Thượng Y Tôn Tâm Lĩnh' of Vietnam"]. *Yunnan zhongyi xueyuan xuebao* 36(3): 82–84.

Nguyễn Trần Huân (traduction et annotations). 1972. "Introduction." *Lãn-Ông: Thượng Kinh Ký Sự* 上京記事 [Relation d'un voyage à la capitale] [Narration of a trip to the capital]. Paris: EFEO.

Ong, Alexander. 2010. "Contextualising the Book-Burning Episode during the Ming Invasion and Occupation of Vietnam." In *Southeast Asia in the Fifteenth Century: The China Factor,* eds. Geoff Wade and Sun Laichen, 154–165. Singapore: NUS Press.

Pelliot, Paul. 1934. "Michel Boym." *T'oung Pao.* 2nd ser., 31(1–2): 95–151.

Phan Đại Doãn 潘大允 and Li Na 李娜, trans. 2002. "Yuenan Duoniuxiang di Fu xing jiazu yu Zhong yao jingying" 越南多牛鄉的傳姓家族與中藥經營 [The Fu lineage and Chinese medical trade in Duoniu village in Vietnam]. *Dongnanya zongheng* 12: 32–38.

Phan Thúc Trực 潘叔直, ed. 1965. *Quốc sử* di *biên* 國史遺編 [Supplement to national history]. (Original copy in Ecole française d'Extrême Orient, Hanoi) with an introduction by Chen Jinghe. Hong Kong: Chinese University of Hong Kong, New Asia Institute of Advanced Chinese Studies.

Rideout, J. K. 1949. "The Rise of the Eunuchs during the T'ang Dynasty." *Asia Major,* New series 1, part 1: 53–72.

Schafer, Edward. 1963. *The Golden Peaches of Samarkand: A Study of the T'ang Exotics.* Berkeley: University of California Press.

Shi Weiguo 施維國. 1993. "Cong Yuenan gudai yizhu kan Chữ Nôm de tedian" 從越南古代醫著看字喃的特點" [The characteristics of Chữ Nôm seen in Vietnamese old medical texts]. *Xiandai waiyu* 2: 55–58.

Thompson, C. Michele. 2015a. *Vietnamese Traditional Medicine: A Social History.* Singapore: NUS Press.

———. 2015b. "The Posthumous Publication and Promotion of the Works of Tuệ Tĩnh, by the Le Dynasty (1428–1788)." Manuscript.

Trần Văn Giáp 陳文玾. 1985. "Yuenan fojiao shi lue (2)" 越南佛教史略 (下) [Part 2 of a brief history of Vietnamese Buddhism]. *Dongnanya Yanjiu ziliao* 東南亞研究資料 [Southeast Asian Studies] 3: 83.

Wang, Gungwu. 2015. "Introduction: Imperial China Looking South." In *Imperial China and Its Southern Neighbours,* eds. V. Mair and Liam Kelley, 1–15. Singapore: ISEAS Publishing.

Whitmore, John. 1985. *Vietnam, Hồ Quý Ly, and the Ming (1371–1421).* New Haven, CT: Yale Center for International and Area Studies.

———. 2014. "Northern Relations for Đại Việt: China Policy in the Age of Le Thanh Tong (r. 1460–1497)." In *China's Encounters on the South and Southwest: Reforging the Fiery Frontier over Two Millennia,* eds. James A. Anderson and John K. Whitmore, 252–254. Leiden: Brill.

Woodside, Alexander. 1971. *Vietnam and the Chinese Model.* Cambridge, MA: Harvard University Press.

Wu Yongzhang 吳永章, ed. 2010. *Yiwu zhi ji yi jiaozhu* 異物志輯佚校注 [Annotated record of strange things edited from retrieved texts]. Guangzhou: Guangdong remin chubanshe.

Xian Yuqing 冼玉清. 1980. "Jicheng Guangdong caoyao di xianbei He Kejian" 繼承廣東草藥的先輩何克諫 [To inherit the legacy of He Kejian, pioneer in Guangdong herbal medicine]. *Xin Zhongyi* 3: 21–22.

Yan Caiqin 閻彩琴. 2007. "Shiqi shiji zhongqi zhi shijiu shiji chu Yuenan huaqiao yanjiu (1640–1802)" 17世紀中期至19世紀初越南華商研究 (1640–1802) [A study on Chinese merchants in Vietnam, 1640–1802]. PhD diss., Xiamen University.

Yan Qu 嚴璩. 1983. "Yuenan youli ji" 越南游歷記 [A record of travel in Vietnam]. In *Wan Qing haiwai biji xuan* 晚清海外筆記選 [A selection of overseas writings in the late Qing], ed. History Department of Fujian Normal University. Beijing: Haiyang chubanshe.

Yao Wendong 姚文棟. 1877–1897. *An Nan xiao zhi* 安南小志 [A short history of Annam]. Late nineteenth century, in the collection *Xiao Fanghuzhai yudi congchao.* Vol. 50. Shanghai: Zhuyitang.

Zhang Xiumin 張秀民. 1992. "Yuenan di yixue mingzhu *Lãn Ông tâm lĩnh*" 越南的醫學名著『懶翁心領』 [A famous Vietnamese medical text *Lãn Ông tâm lĩnh*]. In *Zhong-Yue guanxi shi lunwenji* 中越關係史論文集 [Collection of essays on Sino-Vietnamese relations], 165–168. Taibei: Wenshizhe chubanshe.

Zhang Zhicong 張志聰. 1982 [1670]. *Lüshantang leibian* 侶山堂類辯 [Debates at the Lüshan studio]. Nanjing: Jiangsu Kexue jishu chubanshe.

Zheng Hong 鄭洪. 2009. *Lingnan yixue yu Wenhua* 嶺南醫學與文化 [Medicine and culture in Lingnan]. Guangzhou: Guangdong keji chubanshe.

Zheng Jinsheng 鄭金生. 2005. *Yaolin waishi* 藥林外史 [Social history of pharmaceuticals]. Taibei: Dongda Tushu Gonsi.

Zhu Yunying 朱雲影. 1981. *Zhongguo Wenhua dui Ri-Han-Yue di yingxiang* 中國文化對日韓越的影響 [Chinese cultural influences on Japan, Korea and Vietnam]. Taibei: Liming Wenhua shiye.

6

Traveling Manuscripts

Understanding Pilgrimage in Central and Eastern Islamic Lands

MOUNIA CHEKHAB-ABUDAYA

As is still the case nowadays, the book characterizes the cultural, educational, and intellectual development of the society (Atiyeh, 1995: xiii–xiv). The diffusion of paper in the Islamic world had an important role in the process of democratizing the book as a vehicle of cultural and intellectual development (Bloom, 2001: 47–89; Loveday, 2001: 17–27). From the middle of the eighth century onward, paper and papermaking were introduced in the Islamic world from China through Central Asia and progressively replaced the use of parchment in the Middle East.[1]

Despite the archetypal image of a Muslim society based on oral transmission, the book is indeed a witness to the prestigious value given to writing and is, in fact, used in the context of mosques or madrasas in the process of oral transmission. The production of manuscripts is linked to the development of patronage by sovereigns and princes, who both possess and enrich libraries but also have manuscript workshops under their auspices. The process of learning in the Islamic world through the large-scale production of books begins with the Abbasid *Bayt al-Hikma* in eighth-century Baghdad (Balty-Guesdon, 1992) and continues to develop through the Persian *kitabkhane* from the thirteenth and fourteenth centuries onward (Szuppe, 2004). Translation, transcription, and bookselling go alongside the rise of libraries as well as scribes (*katib* pl. *kuttab*) and calligraphers (*khattat* pl. *khattatin*), who earn an important social and political status at the court. Books can also serve political aims, or sometimes propaganda, and both workshops and libraries act as institutions in the spread of knowledge on various topics.

Islamic pilgrimage routes have most certainly influenced the production of manuscripts, not only for those intended to be transported by pilgrims but also for commercial transactions related to the pilgrimage itself. However, very few studies have been published on the process of diffusion of manuscripts in the Islamic world. Pilgrimage and the mobility of the pilgrims have encouraged the development of manuscripts of several genres, whose function has played a role not only in the canonization of the rituals but also in the standardization of the representations of sacred places and in the use of such manuscripts as instruments of devotion. The word "pilgrimage" needs to be understood here in its plural meaning: it involves more sites of the Islamic world than just Mecca. This chapter does not aim to present the different types of pilgrimages or their nature. The idea is to put forward that, even if an establishment of the tradition of pilgrimage existed in the pre-Islamic era, it is accompanied by the diffusion of manuscripts in the medieval period, which translate not only this social and religious phenomenon but also the mobility of the populations that such a phenomenon implies.

The central and eastern Islamic lands, lands of pilgrimages, have counted since the fourth century many sacred sanctuaries in cities such as Mecca, Medina, Jerusalem, and Damascus, alongside the tombs of religious figures considered holy or martyrs in Egypt, Syria, Palestine, Iraq, and the Arabian Peninsula (Porter, 2012: 69), as well as Iran and Central Asia. While obvious objects such as pilgrims' flasks are examples of assets a pilgrim would take with him on his journey, the handwritten text, whether a scroll, a bound volume, or a talismanic document, also transcribes the material reality of this journey, whatever the destination and whatever the stage on the itinerary. These documents are part of the spiritual dimension of this itinerary, since pilgrimage can be considered a phenomenon that goes beyond the rituals undertaken at the sacred site itself and highlights a practice of numerous devotional habits before, during, and after the trip. Thus, manuscripts and their mobility represent the temporal and spatial reality of pilgrimage in Islamic lands. Such a presentation could be based on a multitude of manuscripts, which is why we choose here to present only examples preserved in the Museum of Islamic Art in Doha.

Pilgrimage Manuals: Guides for the Holy Sites

Pilgrimage and travel in Islam have influenced the production of several types of texts, including not only travel accounts (*rihla* in Arabic and *safarnâma* in Persian) but also guides for visiting sacred sites (for either the *'umra, hajj,* or *ziyarat*) and obtaining blessings there *(baraka).* We will take here the examples of the *Kitab Futuh al-Haramayn* and the *Dala'il al-Khayrat,* both of which are the most copied and widespread pilgrimage-related texts in the Islamic world from the sixteenth century. These two examples could be used as visual or textual guides for the places to visit and the rituals to undertake. They can also be considered devotional books, valued for their literary significance and sometimes copied in the sacred sites. Both works can be either the physical or spiritual or both parts of the objects transported by the pilgrim on his journey or used during his journey, or as literary items.

Futuh al-Haramayn

Muhyi' al-Din Lari (d. AH 933 / 1526–1527 CE), a disciple of the philosopher Jalal al-Din Muhammad al-Dawani, was Persian, and is the author of the *Kitab Futuh al-Haramayn* (Revelation of the two sanctuaries). This book is a description of Mecca and Medina and the rituals of the pilgrimage. This versified account (including some poetry of Jami) was written in AH 911 (1506 CE) and dedicated to Muzaffar bin Mahmud Shah of Gujarat (r. AH 917–932 / 1511–1526 CE). This famous book was regarded as a guide or manual for pilgrims going on the Hajj. It was especially valued for its paintings, which feature all the important places of Mecca and Medina with titles and captions written in Persian as well as Arabic and Turkish. Many copies were made, mainly in Turkey during the sixteenth century and later in India from the seventeenth to the nineteenth century. The text includes prayers for the different stages of the journey (Berthels, 2002: 478).

Two Indian copies are preserved in the Museum of Islamic Art in Doha. MS.171.2007 is a seventeenth-century Mughal, copied either in India or in Mecca. This copy is written entirely in Persian, each page being laid out in two columns of *nasta'liq* written in black ink with internal headings in red throughout the manuscript, as is generally the case in Persian poetry manuscripts such as *masnavis*. It includes eighteen illustrations in red, blue, and green and highlighted with gold. A seal impression begins the manuscript and is dated to the thirty-ninth regnal year, which suggests the reign of Aurangzeb (1658–1707), the longest reign of the seventeenth century. The seal can then be dated to 1697, but nothing gives further indication about the owner, whether it was a royal official or that the manuscript belonged to a specific library.

The paintings represent locations near Mecca and Medina (including pilgrimage-related sites and other mosques, cemeteries, and mountains). The manuscript was recently rebound in modern European binding with marbled paper. The general aspect of the paper and the fact that the manuscript has been rebound, most likely owing to the poor condition of its spine, might indicate that it was highly used and that it might have traveled. Whether it was copied in Mecca or India is uncertain, but it further demonstrates the transmission of manuscripts from or to India during the Mughal period. Its format (18.2 × 10.2 cm) and the small number of pages (forty-four) also underline the portability of the copy.

MS.594.2007 is another Mughal copy and is dated AH 1124 (1712). It also includes eighteen paintings, and the text is also arranged in two columns written in black ink with some words, headings, and prayers for the different stages of the journey inscribed in red ink. It has been rebound in modern green leather binding.[2] Although of a higher quality than MS.171.2007, this copy has also been highly used. Several brown stains indicate that it suffered water damage. Insect holes and channels are still visible on several pages of the manuscript. The presence of Indian decorated paper inserted at the location of illustrated pages shows the use of interleaving papers in India to protect the paintings and avoid pigments from offsetting from one page to another. It also shows another stage of restoration of this manuscript that happened after the water damage—because the brown stains and insect holes are not visible on these interleaves—but probably before the replacement of its original binding with the current green leather one. The format of the manuscript (28.5 × 20 cm, book closed) is bigger than MS.171.2007, and its damage history does not necessarily corroborate its use during travel; the damages could have happened in a library.

However, the similitude between both manuscripts demonstrates the large diffusion of the *Futuh al-Haramayn* as a popular guide for pilgrims but also

Illustration of the *haram* of Mecca in MS.171.2007 (f. 21r.). Courtesy of the Museum of Islamic Art, Doha. Photo by Samar Kassab, Multimedia Department.

Illustration of the Jabal ʿArafat in MS.594.2007 (f. 20r.). Courtesy of the Museum of Islamic Art, Doha. Photo by Samar Kassab, Multimedia Department.

as an object of devotion. The paintings of MS.594.2007 were executed using different shades of green, brown-purple, and black, highlighted with gold. This copy shows that the illustrator might have been part of a higher-skilled workshop, especially given the attention to details and the use of different shades of colors. However, the same places are represented with very few differences between some of the mounts or tombs visited.[3] The number of illustrations is the same, and the same flat projection, typical of the *Futuh al-Haramayn,* has been used in both manuscripts. Similar characteristics were highlighted by Milstein, who compared it with a corpus of sixteenth-century *Futuh al-Haramayn* (Milstein, 2006). All included fifteen to twenty illustrations of the sites visited during the *hajj.* Starting from the sixteenth century, there has been a change in the representations of the holy sites, not only in pilgrimage certificates but also in related texts such as the *Futuh al-Haramayn.*[4] The first illustrations of the *Futuh al-Haramayn* followed a fairly realistic frontal topography and served primarily to provide information on the sacred sites. These illustrations have subsequently become a decorative and symbolic character, probably because of their devotional function, and their practicality has become less important as pilgrims increasingly visit the holy sites. Moreover, more models seem to circulate and are illustrated at a larger scale, particularly in Mecca's markets to be sold as souvenirs. Such productions show that holy sites are also cosmopolitan cities, where pilgrims from all places of the Islamic world may settle, thus bringing with them their skills.

Sixteenth-century Jewish pilgrimage guides show similarities with the Muslim pilgrimage manuscripts. The context of production was probably the same, as we notice some standardized elements such as the frontal representation of buildings or the representation of hanging lamps under the arches at the gates of the Temple (Berger, 2012: 225–251).

Dala'il al-Khayrat

The *Dala'il al-Khayrat* (The ways of edification or Guide for the good deeds) is one of the most successful and favored kinds of prayer books in the Islamic world, often carried by pilgrims on their journey to Medina. It reads as a long litany of blessings over the prophet Muhammad to be recited daily after the *subh* prayer. The text was written by the Moroccan mystic Abu 'Abdullah Muhammad Ibn Sulayman al-Jazuli, who was killed in AH 869 (1465). After studying in Marrakech and mainly at the Qarawiyyin library in Fez, he is initiated to the *shadiliyya* sufi order before travelling to Mecca and Medina. On his way back from pilgrimage, he stops in Cairo where he follows *sufi* instructions of the Qadiri order at the al-Azhar mosque. Upon his return to Morocco in 1453, he writes the prayer book that made him famous throughout the Islamic world. He establishes himself in Safi, where he founds a *zawiya*. The number of his followers grew rapidly, recognizing him as the long-awaited *mahdi*. The governor of Safi had him expelled or killed (Porter, 2012: 52, 54–55). This book also illustrates the importance of the visit to Medina in the journey of a pilgrim, with daily prayers provided in the text.

Usually, *Dala'il al-Khayrat* manuscripts include illustrations showing elements of the Prophet's mosque in Medina, including the *minbar,* the *mihrab,* the tomb of the Prophet and those of Abu Bakr and 'Umar, sometimes associated with views of the Great Mosque of Mecca.[5] Depending on the place of production of the manuscript, the paintings reflect a local style. Most of the copies of the text are eighteenth- and nineteenth-century copies from Morocco, Turkey, India, and Southeast Asia. The Doha collection holds four Turkish copies and one Moroccan.

MS.419.2007 is a late eighteenth-century copy of the text (17.5 × 12.2 cm), signed by Sherife Emine Safvet, daughter of the famous scribe Mustafa Kütahi (Safwat, 2000: 206–207; Derman, 1998: 90).[6] The text is written in *naskh* script with some red comments in Turkish on the margins, and executed on European laid paper with watermarks on some folios that are not identifiable. The manuscript is of quite medium quality, especially with the poorly dyed paper and the use of a copper alloy for the gilt paint instead of pure gold. The book has clearly been used extensively: there are several fingerprints and the spine has been recently repaired. Several blank sections (mainly missing chapter headings and paintings) indicate that the manuscript was never completed. The only paintings included in the manuscript are those of the *Masjid al-Haram* (f. 17v), including the Ka'ba with the *maqams* and the Prophet's mosque in Medina (f. 18r), with the dome, the *rawda,* and the courtyard. These paintings have been executed in a very naive style, using red, green, blue, white, black, and brown watercolors. Many pigment losses and traces of water stains or fingerprints are visible on both paintings. The pigment losses on the Green Dome might be fingerprints if we consider that people used this type of imagery as devotional tools and pressed their fingers on the dome or the Prophet's tomb to get blessings, as is the case for the Prophet's sandals on some manuscripts. Both illustrations associate the bird's-eye-view perspective with the flat, two-dimensional representation. The tombs are not clearly identifiable, and both paintings look very similar in style. The elements illustrated are not easy to identify, because of the schematic style that has been used to represent them.

Two other examples of the Doha collection are of exceptional quality and might have been commissioned by a member of the Ottoman court. Probably not used on a journey, they are mainly devotional pieces, meant to be admired and probably used for blessing their owners.

The first example is MS.391.2007 (14.8 × 10.5 cm), a later copy dated 15 sha'ban AH 1237 (May 7, 1822) and signed by Seyyid Ibrahim, known as Sukuti, who was a student of the famous calligrapher Osman Efendi and who also held a position as a guard at the Sultan's palace (Safwat, 2000: 214–219). Written in black *naskh* on brown polished paper, some words, such as *Allahumma,* are written in red, whereas the headings are executed in white on a gold background, similar to what we will see below with MS.427.2007. The two illuminated pages represent Mecca and Medina (8v and 9r).

Other depictions follow the tradition of putting the paintings of Mecca and Medina on two facing pages: the seal of the Prophethood *(muhr al-nubuwwa)* on f. 10r, described in the *hadiths* as worn by the Prophet between his shoulders. Combining the *thuluth, naskh, riqa',* and *ghubar* scripts, the seal also includes the *shahada* at the center in white on a gold background. The *hilye,* describing the physical attributes of the prophet Muhammad, is represented on folios 10v and 11r, which also include several Qur'anic inscriptions related to the Prophet.

The second copy is MS.427.2007 (23.4 × 16.7 cm), a manuscript dated AH 1216 (1801) and copied in Istanbul (Safwat, 2000: 208–213; Chekhab-Abudaya and Bresc, 2013: 128). The colophon bears not only the name of the calligrapher, Mehmed Emin, but also the name of the illuminator, Hafiz Mehmed Nuri. It mentions Mehmed Emin as being the head clerk of the Imperial Chancery in Istanbul at the time the manuscript was completed.[7] The manuscript is written in black *naskh* with headings for the time and day of each prayer written in white *riqa'* on a gold background. It has been executed on an oriental brown-toned polished paper with gilt paint executed with pure gold leaves in three tones of gold. There are no traces of dirt, just a few insect holes probably due to its storing in a library.

In this manuscript and most illustrated copies of the *Dala'il al-Khayrat,* the double images of Mecca and Medina (f. 16v and f. 17r) come directly after a passage that reads: "This is the depiction of the blessed garden in which the

Illustrations of Mecca and Medina in MS.391.2007 (f. 8 v and 9 r.). Courtesy of the Museum of Islamic Art, Doha. Photo by Samar Kassab, Multimedia Department.

Prophet of God, peace be upon him, was buried with his two companions Abu Bakr and Umar—with whom God was pleased." The text also refers to a fourth tomb, presumed to be that of Jesus Christ. It is perhaps this specific part of the *Dala'il al-Khayrat*'s text that initiates later on the representation of Jerusalem in later Ottoman devotional manuscripts, including this specific mystical text.

The illustrations of Mecca and Medina are very interesting as they differ from those of other Ottoman copies of the *Dala'il al-Khayrat:* they combine the flat, two-dimensional representations already encountered in the *Futuh al-Haramayn* with some elements in perspective but do not correspond to the three-quarter bird's-eye perspective seen previously with the two other examples. The Prophet's mosque in Medina clearly depicts the three tombs under the green dome and another one below that might represent the tomb of Jesus Christ, but also the tomb of Fatima, sometimes depicted (Witkam, 2009: 29). The *minbar* and *mihrab* are also depicted in addition to date-bearing palm trees in the courtyard.

The folio 3r also bears the depiction of a pink rose, a well-known metaphor of the prophet Muhammad's physical attributes often represented in Ottoman manuscripts (Gruber, 2014). Several other double illuminated pages with texts and diagrams are encountered through the whole volume.

The examples presented so far in this chapter were produced in Central Islamic Lands and the eastern part of the Islamic world and show the use of a set of sacred iconography related to Medina and the prophet Muhammad, whose function is discussed later on. In addition to the Ottoman examples, it is important to present the production of *Dala'il al-Khayrat* in Morocco to provide a scale for further comparisons. MS.420.2007 (7 × 9.5) is an example of the eighteenth or nineteenth century (Safwat, 2000: 278–281), and its square format is characteristic of one of the formats used in North African and Iberian Qur'ans until the fourteenth century and revived during the eighteenth and nineteenth centuries for small prayer books like the *Dala'il al-Khayrat.* This miniature manuscript is written in black *maghribi* script on a white European paper, with some words, such as "Allah" or "Muhammad," highlighted in brown, green, red, and blue inks and gilt paint. It includes decorative medallions and headings illuminated throughout the manuscript, as well as abstract diagrams representing the *mihrab* and *minbar* of the Prophet's mosque in Medina and the Rawdah with the three tombs (f. 23v and 24r), a simplified version of what has been presented so far in the Ottoman versions. The

Illustrations of Mecca and Medina in MS.427.2007 (f. 16 v. and 17 r.). Courtesy of the Museum of Islamic Art, Doha. Photo by Samar Kassab, Multimedia Department.

Illustration of the three tombs in MS.420.2007 (f. 23 v.). Courtesy of the Museum of Islamic Art, Doha. Photo by Samar Kassab, Multimedia Department.

distinctive design can be associated with the Awlad al-Hilu craftsmen who worked in Fez (James, 2006). It might have been used as a talisman during pilgrimages and taken by pilgrims during their journey to the holy places. The frontispiece pages, the headings, and the folios, including the representation of the holy places, have been protected with interleaves made of pink paper.[8] The binding is typical of Moroccan book binding production, with its red leather and the gilded eight-point star decorating it.

If we compare both Moroccan and Ottoman productions, their function and set of symbolic and devotional images differ from each other. The Moroccan ones, often associated with leather bags, seem to have been produced as manuscripts to be taken on the journey to Medina, whereas in the Ottoman Empire, the text was magnified with illuminations and high-quality calligraphy by the most famous calligraphers of the Ottoman court, most probably to glorify the Prophet and create devotional manuscripts for members of the elite.

The Moroccan copies, as well as examples from India and Southeast Asia (Porter, 2015: 107), follow the conventional flat projection, with schematic representations symbolizing Medina's mosque and the three tombs. The Ottoman copies of the text feature bird's-eye views, but the Moroccan ones continue the first tradition until the nineteenth century. Moreover, the Ottoman examples illustrate Mecca alongside Medina, although not directly related to the text itself but probably due to the uniformization of this type of representation in the different devotional and religious texts illustrated in the Ottoman Empire. Witkam also mentions a possible criticism toward the Prophet's veneration, especially after the spread of the Wahhabi movement in the eighteenth century (Witkam, 2007, 2009). This argument does not match the place given to the Prophet's attributes in most of the Ottoman manuscripts, with several examples of symbolic representations of the *hilye,* the seal of the Prophethood, and the rose or sandal of the Prophet. The large production of materials related to the Prophet by the Ottomans during the nineteenth century could be a response against Wahhabism in the peninsula and possibly establishes some artistic conventions: the representation of Mecca to legitimate the power of the Ottomans over the two holy sites.

The examples of the *Futuh al-Haramayn* and the *Dala'il al-Khayrat* presented here give a sense of the different functions of such manuscripts. Informative and decoratively illustrated documents, the prayers and rituals go alongside the locations of the sacred sites inscribed on each painting. They also demonstrate the spiritual and devotional dimension in the transfer of sacred images, either schematic or not, which are used as symbolic intermediaries between believer and God. The combination of the sacred nature of the text and its related iconography further demonstrates the beliefs in the healing and protective power of the written word. These two texts, because of their literary value, have been privileged as illustrated pilgrimage-related manuscripts, when compared with other texts that have rarely been illustrated, such as the *Manasik al-Hajj.* More than guides, they were also produced as gifts, whether before the pilgrimage in order to accompany the pilgrim and protect him on his journey, at the end of the pilgrimage (for manuscripts copied in Mecca), or for a personal devotional purpose. One may consider here the numerous markets, including those of Mecca, where manuscripts and sacred images were an essential part of the trade with pilgrims. Both texts also show that a shift occurs globally in the production of pilgrimage-related manuscripts that start to be illustrated in the sixteenth century with a clear transfer of models of representation. From the sixteenth century onward, topographic and bird's-eye-view representations have taken over flat projections, although still being used in the Indian copies of the *Futuh al-Haramayn*. This view that combines elevation and plan, and two-dimension and three-dimension, is used not only in manuscripts and pilgrimage scrolls but also in Iznik tiles. It gives an idea of the proportions of the buildings but still does not correspond to reality.[9]

Other Ottoman Devotional Miscellanies

As mentioned earlier, the Ottomans produced several texts related to the sacred pilgrimage sites.[10] Two examples of the Doha collection show a transfer of the motifs already described in the previous section. MS.389.2007 (16.3 × 10.5 cm) is a selection of Qur'anic surahs written in *naskh* and copied by the calligrapher Haci Ahmed Na'ili, who copied hundreds of Qur'ans and prayer books in the nineteenth century and was a pupil of Mustafa Kütahi's, mentioned earlier for MS.419.2007. The manuscript, copied in AH 1223 (1808), is composed of a set of images and diagrams including Mecca and Medina (f. 77v and 78r), the *hilye* (f. 81v and 82r), the seal of the Prophethood with the seal of Solomon[11] (f. 76v and 77r), the Blessed Palm Tree and the tree of Tuba, which grows in Heaven (f. 79v. and 80r), two roses inscribed with the names of Allah and Muhammad (f. 78v and 79r), and, among other illustrations, diagrams of the Prophet's hand and foot (f. 81v and 82r) (Safwat, 2000: 226–230).

Another manuscript, MS.399.2007 (24.8 × 17 cm), is also a devotional miscellany copied by Haci Mehmed Rasim and illuminated by Haci Ahmed Ayasofia, dated AH 1294 (1877). This volume is clearly a copy made for the Ottoman court, commissioned by Princess Refia in memory of her father the Sultan Abdülmecid who died in 1861.The text, combining black *naskh* script and white *riqa'*, is composed of a selection of Qur'anic surahs, prayers, and religious poems, with a gold double frontispiece decorated with a series of floral decorations typical of the layouts of late nineteenth-century Qur'ans. Several diagrams again complete the text: the seal of the Prophethood (f. 193r) followed

Illustration of the heavens in MS.399.2007 (f. 208 v. and 209 r.). Courtesy of the Museum of Islamic Art, Doha. Photo by Samar Kassab, Multimedia Department.

by two medallions bearing the names of Allah and Muhammad in *thuluth* script (f. 193v and 194r) and the names of Abu Bakr, ʿUmar and other companions (f. 194v and 195r). Other folios are illustrated with inscriptions glorifying God and the archangels (f. 205v) and the representation of the staff of Moses ending into snakes and surrounded by the Prophet's prayer rugs (206r). Following are the Prophet's axe, the rose, and the palm tree (f. 209v to 210v); then the heavens are symbolized with houses and a blue sky (f. 208v) and the tree of paradise with fruits and flowers; and finally flat projections of Mecca and Medina (f. 211v and 212r) (f. 209r), which are very different from the usual bird's-eye views seen in other nineteenth-century copies (Safwat, 2000: 268–274).

These two courtly manuscripts further demonstrate the devotional role of an Ottoman illustrated prayer book, which connects its owner to the afterlife, especially with the representation of several elements linked to heaven. The relics are also given a high importance, probably because they have been preserved in the Topkapı palace since the sixteenth century. Such examples also illustrate the importance for the elite of commissioning precious manuscripts for their own private libraries or for other institutions but also to be offered as gifts within the families and other members of the court. These manuscripts allow us to consider copies of lower quality, which indicate the cultural and social impact of the production of manuscripts produced by the elite but also the scale of diffusion of production criteria in smaller workshops.

Miniature Qur'ans: Travel Documents and Talismans

The Museum of Islamic Art in Doha owns several examples of miniature Qur'ans from different regions of the Islamic world: mainly Iran and Turkey, with respectively one example from Central Islamic Lands and India. Miniature Qur'ans have not been studied much, and their use or function is still not clear. However, these manuscripts were definitely easy to transport because of their size and because they were often accompanied by a metallic case or a small leather bag. As seen with the examples presented below, the metallic cases can house either a complete Qur'an or a section *(juz')*. Manuscripts of this kind can be interpreted as being traveling Qur'ans, probably during pilgrimage journeys. They could also have been worn as talismans by their owners, especially for the ones using the *ghubar* script, a minuscule script that was not meant to be read or was very difficult to read—*ghubar* meaning literally "dust," designating the small cursive script used in the later Islamic periods. The cases themselves can also refer to the latter function, when inscribed with verses from the Qur'an or invocations of God's power to protect.

Iranian Examples

MS.782.2011 is an early example, typical of eleventh-century Iranian production with its brown paper and its eastern Kufic script. This period marks in Iran the beginning of the production of single bound volumes and of small format (8 × 7.5 cm) using a smaller script. If we look at the quality and the rare use of gold as well as the script, this example is not of the highest value and might have been produced for personal use only, whether being transported on a journey or kept at home by its owner. However, it shows the emerging smaller square formats in this part of the Islamic world and recalls what will be seen later on in the Western Mediterranean and in the Sahara, often accompanied by custom-made bags for their transportation. The Moroccan binding is a later replacement, but the format of the manuscript was already roughly the current size. The latter remark shows an extensive use of the manuscript. A few seals of the Qajar period have been stamped on some pages, which show its use at later periods.

This early example also highlights the establishment of paper for copying Qur'ans in the eastern Islamic lands as opposed to the Western Mediterranean, although some examples of the same period have been copied on vellum (Déroche, 1992: 152–153).

From the sixteenth century onward, many octagonal-shaped miniature Qur'ans have been produced in Iran, mainly during the Safavid and Qajar periods. MS.367.2007 and MS.433.2007 are respective sixteenth- and seventeenth-century Safavid examples,[12] whereas MS.384, MS.364.2007.1, and MIA.2013.13 are later eighteenth- and nineteenth-century Zand and Qajar examples (Safwat, 2000: 70–73, 97, 194). These five examples have the same size (a diameter roughly between four and five centimeters), the use of a *ghubar* script more or less readable, and the use of metallic cases for two of them (MS.364.2007.2 and MIA.2013.13). They all show an extensive use, which can be seen in the condition of their bindings, whether restored or not. Such small Qur'ans would have a very fragile spine because of their size. MS.367.2007 is indeed the only example that does not have loose folios because of its restoration. Its binding is clearly composed of pieces of a bigger Safavid binding assembled

Miniature Qur'an with its case (MS.364.2007). Courtesy of the Museum of Islamic Art, Doha. Photo by Samar Kassab, Multimedia Department.

to create the octagonal shape. The frontispiece pages have also been cut from another manuscript to be adapted to its new format. The recto of the first folio bears a Qajar seal impression of the ruler Muzaffar al-Din Shah and dates to AH 1308 (1890–1891), which further indicates the use of the manuscript at later periods. The first folios of MS.384 have been replaced and the binding is also a later addition but in poor condition.

The two metallic cases are very similar to the amulet cases produced as well in Iran during the nineteenth century. The case accompanying MS.364.2007.1 is engraved with verses of the Qur'an (surah 61, v. 13, and surah 68, v. 51–52). MIA.2013.13's case is quite corroded, but the central medallion shows the repetition of the name of ʿAli, which associates it with a *shiʿi* context. As most of the Iranian miniature Qur'ans seem to be octagonal starting from the Safavid period, another example from the Doha collection highlights another type of the Iranian production. MIA.2014.415 is an interesting nineteenth-century Qajar Qur'an of approximately 6.1 × 3.7 cm (Adle, 1980: 28–31). It is dated AH 1092 (1680), but the date does not correspond to the style of the manuscript, which is clearly Qajar. Executed on very thin sheep skins, this Qur'an shows the use of rectangular formats for single bound volumes. The spine is damaged because of extensive use.

Other Examples

MS.308.1999 is an Ilkhanid *juz'* written in *rayhani* script of approximately 5.5 × 4.5 cm. According to the style of the double frontispiece, it is the first section of an Ilkhanid miniature Qur'an in thirty volumes produced in the early fourteenth century, perhaps in Iraq or Iran (James, 1992: 96–117).

MS.608.2007 is the smallest miniature Qur'an of the MIA group (2.8 × 3 cm) and clearly shows it was not meant to be read. This rectangular Ottoman example might have been kept in a small case or even a pendant case and used as a talisman. Written in black *ghubari* script with headings in red ink and some gilt illuminations, it is dated AH 1190 (1776).

MS.438.2007 (9.4 × 6.7 cm) is most probably an eighteenth-century Qajar copy. The format is very practical, and the *naskh* is clear and easily readable. Some loose pages and the medium quality of the illuminations indicate that it is probably a personal copy.

MIA's collection of miniature Qur'ans shows a certain pattern, characteristic of the small manuscripts that have spread in Turkey, Iran, India, North Africa, and sub-Saharan African from the sixteenth to the early twentieth century, mainly through warfare and trade and pilgrimage routes. Known as *sancak* ("banner"), they were enclosed in metal boxes *(muhafaza)* or textile purses and were traditionally worn by Turks on the battlefield as amulets. Placed on the standards or worn on waistbands *(kamarband)* or armbands *(bazuband)* on military costumes of Turkey, Iran, and India, their protection function under war circumstances might have spread to accompanying travelers and pilgrims on their journey; thus they were worn around the neck or over the left shoulder *(hama'il)* (Coffee, 2009 79–103).[13] The majority, as seen with the Doha examples, are octagonal, probably because of the symbolic association—often found in architecture as well—between the circle and the square as intermediaries between the earth and the heavens. Sometimes difficult to decipher, their legibility shows the spiritual effort that the reader should undertake. The portability and the use of small containers to carry them recall the practice of carrying portable manuscripts as well as metallic badges by pilgrims in the medieval Christian context. Some of these popular devotional items could have been acquired as well at the end of the pilgrimage as *memento* or souvenirs (Foster, 2012).

Manuscripts Copied in Mecca

Apart from their central role in Islam, pilgrimage places such as Mecca have represented areas of economic and intellectual influence throughout their history. They played a role in the production and transfer of manuscripts. Beyond its geographic significance, Mecca occupied an important place in the production of manuscripts since the advent of Islam, as the Qur'an, the exegesis *(tafsir),* and other works such as *Kitab Futuh al-Haramayn* were often copied there. It is certain that Mecca was a place of interest for copyists who sought to bring legitimacy to the production of manuscripts copied in the holy city.

The first Qur'ans were copied onto parchment in a vertical format in the so-called *hijazi* script, a reference to the Hijaz region, where Mecca and Medina are located. Produced at the end of the seventh century and the beginning of the eighth century CE, they might have been made in this region or in the Middle East. This type of format was supplanted by the "Italian" horizontal format in *kufic* script, with just a few lines per page in a far larger script than was the case for folios in *hijazi.* The *hijazi* folios were made primarily for practical reading; presumably their main purpose was to record the text in a format that made it easier to record and memorize.[14]

Ottoman Qur'ans like MS.786.2011 were made during the nineteenth century and bore gold double frontispieces with small cartouches representing Mecca and Medina using the bird's-eye-view perspective, and decorated in the rococo style with blue and pink stylized vegetation, very similar to MS.399.2007.[15] This Qur'an (18 × 12 cm) is dated AH 1259 (1843) and, similar to MS.419.2007, is signed by two women: a copyist named Fatima Bint Abdullah and an illuminator named Manal Kucuk.

MS.766.2011 (27.6 × 20 cm) is a *tafsir* of the Qur'an copied in Mecca by Kamal al-Din Husain al-Hafiz al-Haravi (d. 1504 CE), the scribe of the Safavid ruler Shah Tahmasp, who reigned from 1524 to 1576 CE and was famous for ordering the most beautiful examples of manuscripts, among which was the "Royal Shahnameh." According to the colophon, the scribe of the royal workshop most likely traveled to Mecca and copied this sumptuous *tafsir* in AH 955 (1548–1549) for the sovereign. It is said that Shah Tahmasp offered many gifts to the scribe when he arrived at his court and that Kamal al-Din refused them. The shah demanded of him a copy of the Qur'an and a *tafsir,* written in the holy city, to earn forgiveness for this insult. The quality of the script of the double frontispiece depicting the opening surahs of the Qur'an makes it one of the most elegant productions of *tafsir.* The Qur'anic text and the commentary, composed in *nasta'liq* script, are written, respectively, in gold and black ink with some white *thuluth* headings. Choosing the *nasta'liq* script for the Qur'anic verses was a very bold choice, as this script is more commonly used for Persian poetry and official documents and the *naskh* script is privileged for Qur'ans since the fourteenth century in Iran.

Between the ninth and fifteenth to sixteenth centuries, some geographers developed the "sacred geography," which consisted of placing Mecca at the center of the world as a cosmographical principle, without any geographic coordinates or scale, so that all the regions of the world faced the sacred sanctuary. MS.523.1999 (23.5 × 17.5 cm) and its related maps are part of the *Kitab Kharida al-'Ajayib wa Farida al-Gharayib,* copied by Abd al-Rahman ibn al-Surur Ghamadi in Bandar Jadda and dated AH 3 Safar 983 (May 14, 1575 CE). *Bandar,* a word of Persian origin, means "port" or "coastal town." So al-Ghamadi may have been an Iranian or Indian pilgrim who copied the text in the port of Jeddah before or after his pilgrimage. He also might have been part of the *mujawirun,* pilgrims who settled in the Hijaz, mainly coming from South Asia and Southeast Asia. This group included artists and calligraphers, who produced manuscripts and paintings as souvenirs in the holy city (Milstein, 2006: 167; Porter, 2015: 106–107). The original author, given at the beginning of the manuscript, is named "al-Marrakshi," but this *nisba* does not determine if this is indeed the astronomer and geographer Abu 'Ali al-Hasan bin 'Ali al-Marrakushi (thirteenth century CE). It also seems strange that al-Marrakshi is credited as the author at all, as this book is known to have been attributed to 'Umar ibn al-Wardi (d. AH 749/1348–1349 CE).

In the tradition of "sacred geography," many legends grew up around the history of the composition of the world. Among them is one recorded in texts such as the *Mu'jam al-Buldan* of Yaqut al-Rumi (d. 1229 CE), which states that the earth is supported on the horns of a bull, which itself is supported by a stone set on the back of a whale. On the map, the brown part represents the seas, and the "encircling ocean" surrounds the whole map. Mecca is in the center, inside a shape clearly recognizable as a whale (Chekhab-Abudaya, 2014: 20, 23, 24).

These courtly examples show the importance given to Mecca and Medina by Safavid patrons as well as members of the Ottoman court, especially knowing the role of the sultan as *khadim al-Haramayn.* Among other gifts to

Mecca-centered map in MS.523.1999. Courtesy of the Museum of Islamic Art, Doha. Photo by Samar Kassab, Multimedia Department.

the holy sanctuaries, Qur'ans were sent as part of the Hajj caravan from Damascus and Cairo to Mecca and Medina (Porter, 2015: 95–107). The production of manuscripts in the holy cities was certainly perceived as sacred, and the examples presented here show the transfer of Iranian and Turkish models in the Arabian Peninsula.

Scrolls and Paintings: Testimonies of the Pilgrim's Journey

Some manuscripts, whether in the format of individual documents or scrolls, are directly related to the pilgrim's journey. Several examples from the Doha collection show the evolution of such documents that held several functions, whether legal, symbolic, decorative, informative, sacred, or talismanic, similar to the manuscripts presented earlier.

MS.14.2006 is possibly a Fatimid or Mamluk[16] talismanic document and certificate referring to the visit to Medina. Measuring 32.4×11 cm, it bears diagrams of the prophet's mosque with a text glorifying the Prophet and describing the stages of a visit to his mosque as a privileged and pious act. In addition, it mentions the other places the pilgrim has visited alongside the mosque, such as the Mosque of the Two Qiblas (*Masjid al-Qiblatayn*) and the Baqi' cemetery. This document, probably from Fustat, is an early example of a folded talismanic document that bears a double function: a certificate attesting the visit to Medina and a talisman to protect or bless the owner after his visit.[17] The text starts with blessings on Medina, glorifications to God, and prayers on the Prophet. It is followed by the description of the *ziyara*—clearly designated as such in the text—and the list of rituals and sites visited by the pilgrim. The diagrams on the document represent schematically the mosque of the Prophet and its palm trees, and the cemetery of Baqi'. That the document shows traces of being folded indicates not only that it served as a proof of the visit to Medina, but also that it was carried and kept as an amulet probably after the *ziyara.*

Dated AH 21 Muharram 837 (September 6, 1433 CE), the pilgrimage certificate MS.267.1998 was made for a pilgrim named Sayyid Yusuf bin Sayyid Shihab al-Din Mawara al-Nahri, who undertook the *'umra.* With a length of 666 cm, it features the major Islamic sites, including the Ka'ba and the *Haram* of Mecca with the *mas'a* "trotting space" between Safa and Marwa, the Prophet's mosque in Medina with the *minbar,* the *mihrab,* and the tombs of Abu

Talismanic document referring to the visit to Medina (MS.14.2006). Courtesy of the Museum of Islamic Art, Doha. Photo by Samar Kassab, Multimedia Department.

Bakr and Umar, and the Prophet's sandal. Also included are the Dome of the Rock with the Aqsa Mosque illustrating the third holy place in Islam, Jerusalem, and finally the Cave of the Patriarchs, in Hebron *(al-Haram al-Ibrahim)* with the Iraqi shrines of ʿAli and Husayn. Alongside all these illustrations are inscriptions from the Qur'an and texts written in Arabic and Persian related to the pilgrimage with the name of the pilgrim and his six witnesses featured at the end (Chekhab-Abudaya, Couvrat-Desvergnes, and Roxburgh, 2016).

Pilgrimage certificates are considered as legal or juridical documents acquired by the pilgrim at the end of his pilgrimage, in Mecca or in another place during his journey, whether after performing *hajj* or *'umra*. This document was produced for the pilgrim to keep a personal and official record of the accomplishment of the pilgrimage. The certificates were mostly scrolls, as this was the easiest way to transport them. Arranged vertically, the contents generally follow the tradition of "sacred geography" with representations of the sites the pilgrim visited during his journey, starting with Mecca and the different places of the *hajj* or *'umra*, Medina, Jerusalem, and sometimes the shrines of Iraq. It features the pilgrim's itinerary and at the same time illustrates the topography of the holy places.

The earliest examples of pilgrimage scrolls go as far back as the Ayyubid period and the tradition continues up to the twentieth century, with various examples from the Saljuk and Mamluk eras with an important production from the sixteenth and seventeenth centuries during the Ottomans and Mughals. A large number of the certificates produced from the thirteenth century onward started being printed. Each certificate, when complete, usually bore at the foot the name of the person who performed the pilgrimage and the names of the witnesses. The representations as well as the content of the certificate gradually became standardized and conventional, as the components and style are very similar in the surviving examples of these documents. According to research carried out on the subject, it is likely that more *'umra* certificates were delivered than *hajj* ones. The uses of these documents are uncertain, but they might have been hung in places like mosques, or in the house of the pilgrim himself to illustrate his new social status. These certificates were issued until the mid-twentieth century, by which time they were simple documents in a printed format where the name of the pilgrim could be filled in along with the date he had executed the pilgrimage. Such documents signified the places visited by the pilgrim, after which he would receive a new title and gifts. They could also possibly be used as objects of devotion while transporting the viewer to the sacred places represented and providing blessings through the physical contact with these images (al-Saleh, 2014).

The conventions of the illustrations of both MS.14.2006 and MS.267.1998 set a precedent for what will later be found in the *Futuh al-Haramayn, Dala'il al-Khayrat,* and other devotional documents already presented in this chapter. Both talismanic documents and medieval pilgrimage scrolls have influenced the iconographic development of the modern production.

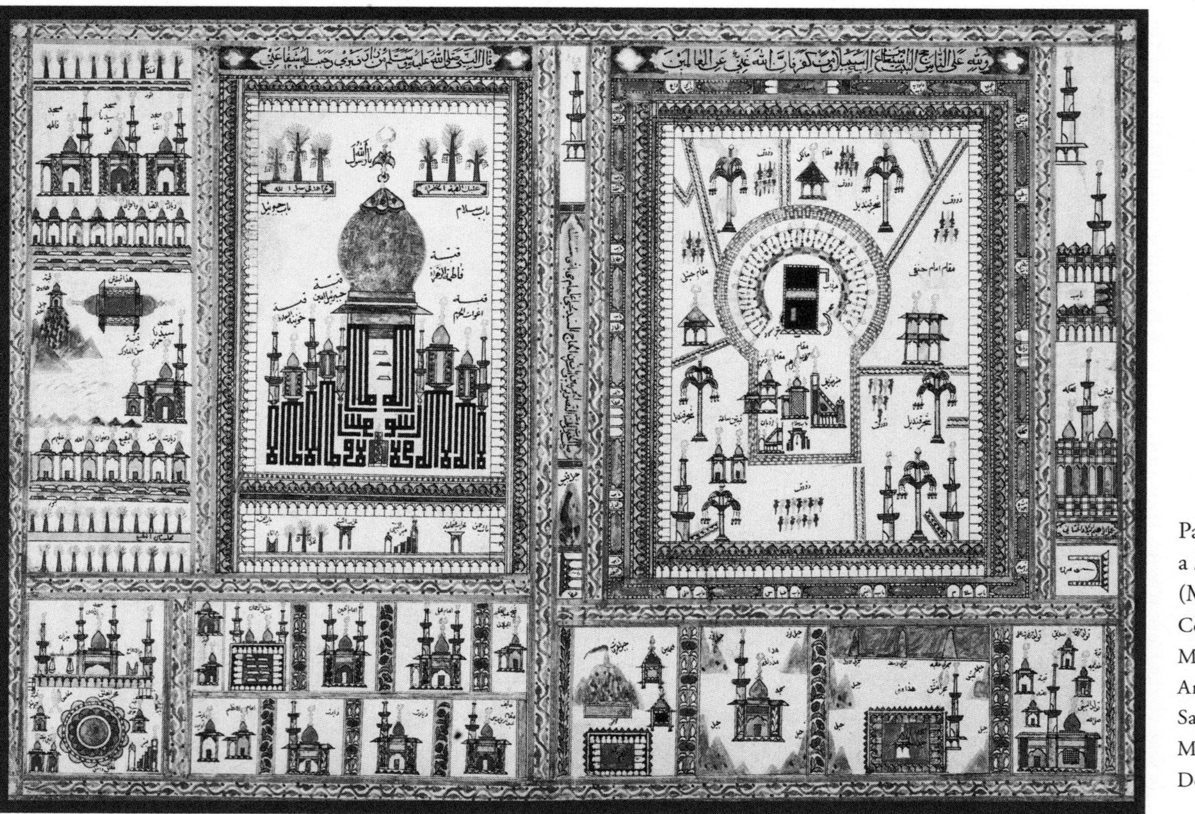

Painting, probably a *hajj* certificate (MS.740.2011). Courtesy of the Museum of Islamic Art, Doha. Photo by Samar Kassab, Multimedia Department.

MS.740.2011 (56.3×78.8 cm) is a painting, probably a Hajj certificate for a pilgrim named "Hajj Yahya." Dated AH 1223 (1808 CE), it has been executed by a painter named Ibrahim Efendi Daghestani. Depicted on this document are the two main sanctuaries and also many other sacred buildings, stations of the Hajj, and places of popular devotion. The right-hand part of the page is devoted to Mecca: we can distinguish the Haram, Muzdalifa, Safa and Marwa, Mount Arafat, the plain of Mina with two *mahmals*, the *jamarat* (stoning pillars), the birth place of the Prophet, and the tomb of his first wife, Khadija. On the left side, sacred places at Medina are illustrated: the main building, highlighted by a striking square Kufic inscription, is the Mosque of the Prophet with its green cupola and the graves of Muhammad, the first two caliphs Abu Bakr and Umar, and the grave of Fatima, the Prophet's daughter, with its palm trees. Beside it, one can also recognize the Quba Mosque (the oldest mosque in the world), the mosque of the two Qiblas, and Mount Uhud with the tomb of Hamza, the uncle of the prophet Muhammad. Several other places of Muslim devotion now lost are represented, mainly in connection with historical figures, relatives, and companions of the Prophet, such as shrines in the Jannat al-Baqi cemetery, next to the Prophet's mosque. Both the elements represented and the flat projection set this painting in the continuity of the Indian copies of the *Futuh al-Haramayn*.[18]

All the manuscripts presented in this chapter provide a scale of the importance of interpreting pilgrimage circuits as circuits for transfers of manuscripts, as well as artistic, religious, intellectual, and cultural knowledge, in particular through the use of Arabic, Persian, and Turkish often combined together. The mobility of the populations of the Islamic world has allowed the dissemination of knowledge, and the various forms of pilgrimage have participated in the elaboration of these intellectual and artistic transfers. Moreover, the spiritual dimension occupies a fundamental role in the manufacture or transport of some of these manuscripts. The traveler gives particular importance to the possession of his own manuscript, whether accompanying it in a pilgrimage or not. The place given to writing in the medieval and modern eras in the Islamic world often transcends patronage and official royal workshops. The mobility of manuscripts also raises the question of the development of specific formats related to pilgrimage journeys. With the variety of examples highlighted in this chapter, one may see that their formats were sometimes similar and, for most of them, easily transportable. The iconography of these pilgrimage-related works also demonstrates a certain form of standardization of the representations of holy places mainly from the sixteenth century. The *Futuh al-Haramayn* and the early Eastern copies of the *Dala'il al-Khayrat* are themselves reminiscent of the first pilgrimage scrolls where the representations were schematic and symbolic, without a topographical reality that starts appearing in nineteenth-century representations (Roxburgh, 2012; Mols, 2015; Marzolph, 2014). One may note as well the apotropaic function of some of these representations, intended to highlight the talismanic powers of certain attributes of the prophets (the Prophet's footprint or the seal of Solomon for instance), which would accompany and protect the person who touches, kisses, or carries them in his journey, his life, and his afterlife (Gruber, 2013, 2016). The process of pilgrimage, whatever the type, thus becomes a factor of understanding of medieval and modern Islamic society and its religious practices, alongside the dynamics of exchanges between the different regions.

Notes

1. In North Africa, parchment continued to be used in a religious context until the fifteenth century (Déroche, 2002: 387–392).

2. As observed by MIA paper conservator Amélie Couvrat-Desvergnes, folios 40 and 36 were misplaced within the text block probably during the restoration. The folio 40 is currently placed between the folios 2 and 3, and the folio 36 is between the folios 38 and 39, as the result of an incorrect pagination.

3. The main sites visited during the pilgrimage are depicted in almost the same order, except for the mosque of Abu Bakr, which is at the beginning of MS.171.2007 and almost at the end of MS.594.2007. The differences (three in total) appear only with the shrines and cemeteries that are not mandatory in the pilgrimage.

4. A manuscript similar to the *Futuh al-Haramayn,* the *Shawq Nâme,* has also been illustrated, and a sixteenth-century Ottoman example is published by Milstein (see Milstein, 2001). We can notice that the illustrations are very detailed, but, similar to the Ottoman copies of the *Futuh al-Haramayn,* other locations such as Jerusalem or Jeddah do not appear in Indian copies. See also Milstein 1994.

5. For an extensive research on the *Dala'il al-Khayrat,* see the PhD dissertation of Hiba Abid under the supervision of François Déroche and defended in May 2017 (Collège de France—ERC SICLE).

6. This element highlights the role played by female scribes in the Ottoman calligraphic sphere.

7. Mehmed Emin was also known as a teacher and chief assistant of the Agha who administered the Sultan's palace. Safwat adds that he is said to have studied with famous calligraphers such as Ebubekir Rashid Efendi (d. 1782) and Akmolla Ömer Efendi (d. 1777).

8. For more information on the use of interleaving papers in Islamic manuscripts, see the upcoming publications of paper conservator Amélie Couvrat-Desvergnes.

9. Comparative elements exist between Jewish, Muslim, and far-eastern Buddhist documents, such as the mandalas. The images illustrating these documents have in common the placing of the sacred element of each site at the center of the image, since they are considered as being at the center of the cosmos (Renard, 2001).

10. For other examples of an illustrated prayer book very similar to those presented here, see Gruber 2009 and Bain 1999.

11. The seal of Solomon, described as an apotropaic seal, is depicted as a hexagram on many supports and bears apotropaic properties.

12. MS.433 is dated AH 1024 (1615–1616) and is signed Muhammad Amin al-Katib al-Ghubari, in reference to the script being used and the status of the scribe as being a master of this technique.

13. Coffee mentions several sources of the modern and contemporary period, such as Chardin, Snouck, or Burton, describing the use of pocket Qur'ans as amulets, alongside talismanic scrolls carried in tubes.

14. The Museum of Islamic Art owns several *hijazi* folios, which are not included in this chapter.

15. MS.720.2010 is an early nineteenth-century Qur'an in the Doha collection that also bears similar representations on its double frontispiece, in addition to representations of Jerusalem and Damascus. Of fairly small format (15.6 × 10.3 cm), it is enclosed in a leather box decorated with gilt paint.

16. The dating of such documents is difficult. Although the script and format of the document with its visual content indicates it could be a ninth or tenth century certificate, the number of minarets corresponds to architectural modifications undertaken by the Mamluks in the fourteenth century.

17. Two other examples are respectively kept in the Dar al-Kutub collection (inv. 513/4383) and the Nasser D. Khalili collection (MSS 1079).

18. Another painting preserved in the Museum of Islamic Art, MS.801.2011, is signed Mahmud, probably Mahmud Malik, an artist of the court atelier of Fath 'Ali Shah (r. 1797–1834) (Chekhab-Abudaya and Bresc, 2013: 32–33). This painting, with its bird's-eye-view style, has been put in parallel by Porter with a painting of Muhammad 'Abdallah, a painter of Mecca with Indian origins, who might have been in contact with other painters through his workshop, including Mahmud Malik during his trip to Mecca (Porter, 2015: 105–106). Similarly, even Ibrahim Efendi Daghestani might have visited artists or manuscript workshops in Mecca.

References

Adle, Chahryar. 1980. *Ecriture de l'Union, Reflets du temps des troubles: Oeuvre picturale (1083–1124 -1673–1712) de Hâji Mohammad.* Paris: de Nobele.

Atiyeh, George N. 1995. *The Book in the Islamic World: The Written Word and Communication in the Middle East.* Albany: State of New York Press, the Library of Congress.

Bain, Alexandra. 1999. "The Late Ottoman En'am-ı şerif: Sacred Text and Images in an Islamic Prayer Book." PhD diss., University of Victoria.

Balty-Guesdon, Marie-Geneviève. 1992. "Le Bayt al-ḥikma de Baghdad." *Arabica* 39: 131–150.

Berger, Pamela C. 2012. *The Crescent on the Temple: The Dome of the Rock as Image of the Ancient Jewish Sanctuary.* Leiden: Brill.

Berthels, Evgenlĭ. 2002. "Muḥyi'l-Dīn Lārī." *Encyclopaedia of Islam.* 2nd ed., Vol. 7.

Bloom, Jonathan M. 2001. *Paper before Print: The History and Impact of Paper in the Islamic World.* New Haven, CT, and London: Yale University Press.

Chekhab-Abudaya, Mounia. 2014. *Mémoires du hajj—Le pèlerinage à la Mecque vu à travers les Arts de l'Islam, la production intellectuelle et matérielle de l'époque médiévale à l'époque contemporaine.* Paris: Les Cahiers de l'Islam.

Chekhab-Abudaya, Mounia, and Cécile Bresc. 2013. *Hajj: The Journey through Art.* Milan: Skira.

Chekhab-Abudaya, Mounia, Amélie Couvrat-Desvergnes, and David Roxburgh. 2016. "Sayyid Yusuf's 1433 Pilgrimage Scroll *(Ziyārātnāma)* in the Collection of the Museum of Islamic Art, Doha." *Muqarnas* 33: 345–407.

Coffee, Heather. 2009. "Between Amulet and Devotion: Islamic Miniature Books in the Lilly Library." *The Islamic Manuscript Tradition, Ten Centuries of Book Arts in Indiana University Collections.* Bloomington and Indianapolis: Indiana University Press: 79–115.

Derman, M. Uğur, and Nihad Çetin. 1998. *The Art of Calligraphy in the Islamic Heritage.* Istanbul: IRCICA.

Déroche, François. 1992. *The Abbasid Tradition: Qur'ans of the 8th to the 10th Centuries A.D.* Londres: Azimuth editions, coll. "The Nasser D. Khalili Collection of Islamic Art" (I).

———. 2002. "Note sur les circuits commerciaux du livre manuscrit dans le Maghreb médiéval." *Antiquités africaines,* nos. 38–39: 387–394.

Foster, Megan. 2012. "Pilgrimage through the Pages: Pilgrim's Badges in Late Medieval Devotional Manuscripts." PhD diss., University of Illinois at Urbana-Champaign.

Gruber, Christiane. 2009. "A Pious Cure-All: The Ottoman Illustrated Prayer Manual in the Lilly Library." *The Islamic Manuscript Tradition, Ten Centuries of Book Arts in Indiana University Collections.* Bloomington and Indianapolis: Indiana University Press: 117–153.

———. 2013. "The Prophet Muhammad's Footprint." *Ferdowsi, the Mongols and the History of Iran. Art, Literature and Culture from Early Islam to Qajar Persia. Studies in Honour of Charles Melville.* London: I. B. Tauris: 297–307.

———. 2014. "The Rose of the Prophet: Floral Metaphors in Late Ottoman Devotional Art." *Envisioning Islamic Art and Architecture: Essays in Honor of Renata Holod.* Leiden: Brill: 223–249.

———. 2016. "From Prayer to Protection: Amulets and Talismans in the Islamic World." *Power and Protection: Islamic Art and the Supernatural.* Oxford: Ashmolean Museum: 33–51.

James, David. 1992. *The Master Scribes: Qur'ans of the 10th to 14th centuries AD.* London: Nour Foundation.

———. 2006. "A Note on the Awlad al-Hilu: A Scribal Dynasty of Fas (Fez)." *Manuscripta Orientalia* 12(2): 3–7.

Loveday, Helen. 2001. *Islamic Paper: A Study of the Ancient Craft.* London: Archetype Publications.

Marzolph, Ulrich. 2014. "From Mecca to Mashhad: The Narrative of an Illustrated Shiite Pilgrimage Scroll from the Qajar Period." *Muqarnas* 21: 207–242.

Milstein, Rachel. 1994. "Drawings of the Haram of Jerusalem in Ottoman Manuscripts." *Scripta Hierosolymitana, XXXV: Aspects of Ottoman History.* Jerusalem: Magnes Press: 62–69.

———. 2001. "Kitab Shawq Nameh, an Illustrated Guide to Holy Arabia." *Jerusalem Studies of Arabic and Islam* 25: 275–345.

———. 2006. "Mapping the Sacred in Sixteenth Century Illustrated Manuscripts of Futuh al-Haramayn." *Mamluk and Ottoman Studies in Honour of Michael Winter.* London: Routledge: 166–194.

Mols, Luitgard. 2015. "Souvenir, Testimony, and Device for Instruction: Late Nineteenth- and Early Twentieth-Century Printed Hajj Certificates." *Hajj, Global Interactions through Pilgrimage. Mededelingen van het Rijksmuseum voor Volkenkunde* 43: 185–212.

Porter, Venetia. 2012. *Hajj: Journey to the Heart of Islam.* London: British Museum Press; Cambridge, MA: Harvard University Press.

———. 2015. "Gifts, Souvenirs and the Hajj." *Hajj, Global Interactions through Pilgrimage. Mededelingen van het Rijksmuseum voor Volkenkunde* 43: 95–111.

Renard, John. 2001. "Picturing Holy Places: On the Uses of Architectural Themes in Ornament and Icon." *Religion and the Arts* 5(4): 399–428.

Roxburgh, David J. 2012. "Visualising the Sites and Monuments of Islamic Pilgrimage." *Architecture in Islamic Arts, Treasures of the Aga Khan Museum.* Geneva: Aga Khan Trust for Culture: 33–40.

Safwat, Nabil F. 2000. *Golden Pages, Qur'ans and Other Manuscripts from the Collection of Ghassan I. Shaker.* London: Azimuth Editions.

al-Saleh, Yasmine F. 2014. "'Licit Magic': The Touch and Sight of Islamic Talismanic Scrolls." PhD diss., Harvard University.

Szuppe, Maria. 2004. "Circulation des lettrés et cercles littéraires: Entre Asie centrale, Iran et Inde du Nord (XVe–XVIIIe siècle)." *Annales. Histoire, Sciences Sociales* 5: 997–1018.

Witkam, Jan J. 2007. "The Battle of the Images: Mekka vs. Medina in the Iconography of the Manuscripts of al-Jazuli's Dala'il al-Khayrat." *Technical Approaches to the Transmission and Edition of Oriental Manuscripts, Beiruter Texte and Studien* 11: 67–82, 295–300.

———. 2009. "Images of Makkah and Madinah in an Islamic Prayer Book." *Hadeeth al-Dar* 30: 27–32.

7

Slaves, Arms, and Political Careering in Nineteenth-Century Oman

SEEMA ALAVI

In 1861, Lieutenant Colonel C. P. Rigby, the British consul at Zanzibar, expressed alarm at the heightened French involvement in the slave trade on the Persian Gulf. He was shocked that the trade continued despite the British campaign for its ban. He was equally intrigued at the involvement of the Omani princess in the imperial politics over the slave traffic. He attributed this to the impact of the 1857 Indian revolt that created the impression in the Gulf that the British were too preoccupied in India to protect their interests in the region. He wrote: "There had been no British agent or consul here [in Zanzibar] for 13 months; this was the period of the Indian mutinies and the French had persuaded the Sultan and the Arabs that the British had lost India, and that no British consul would ever reside here again."[1]

Rigby's comment reflected the connected worlds of India and Oman framed in the larger milieu of Western imperialism (Goswami, 2016; Sheriff, 1987). He was convinced that news of the 1857 debacle shaped politics in the Persian Gulf in no small measure. It affected the war of succession on the death of Sultan Syed Said (1856), heightened Western interference, and destabilized Oman. Indeed, the conjunctional moment of crisis reoriented lives and triggered mobility: Omani princes, imperial networks, merchants, slaves, and arms straddled India, Oman, and the Persian Gulf with renewed vigor. Together they constituted an attractive space where individual political careers could be nurtured.

This chapter forefronts the careers of the Omani princes as they made the most out of the mobility that the crisis triggered. The connected world of British imperialism, India, and the Persian Gulf offered them a range of opportunities. The princes weathering the impact of imperial decline saw in the British Empire a newly envisioned conceptual space where they could reconfigure their careers as they came to terms with the collapse of their own empire. And the freshly reconfigured British Empire recovering from its own crisis offered the enabling forum. The internal feuds of the Omani brothers over the division and inheritance of their late father's possessions and contest over his political legacy entangled with British imperial networks, rivalries with France, and its antislavery and arms trade campaign. The coming together of the Western imperial world and that of Asian empires in the age of crisis offered the perfect canvas to chart fresh political careers. Indeed, the age of crisis became the trigger for wider social and political change in the Western Indian Ocean.

Sultan Syed Said (1807–1856), ruler of Oman whose territories stretched from the southern Arabian Peninsula to Zanzibar on the east coast of Africa, died in 1856. He left behind seven sons who fought a bitter battle over his political legacy. The bone of contention was the inheritance of their late father's political sovereignty that was spread over his Arab as well as African possessions.[2] The claim of his third son, Syed Thuwayni (b. 1820), to be its sole inheritor was challenged by his siblings.

In 1840, when Syed Said shifted base from Muscat to Zanzibar, he put Thuwayni in charge of Muscat (1846). On the death of his younger son Khalid (1854), his fourth son, Syed Majid, was made overseer of his African dominions at Zanzibar. In 1856, Syed Majid was "elected" ruler of Zanzibar by the local people after Syed Said died at sea. This was in keeping with tribal tradition where the ruler was chosen from the most influential and popular persons available. Syed Majid used this occasion to assert his independence from Muscat and claim independent status. He contended that the yearly grant that he remitted to his brother Syed Thuwayni was a "friendly subsidy" and not tribute that recognized him as the sole sovereign of Oman.[3] Thuwayni vehemently contested this claim from Muscat, where, on the death of his father, he had declared himself the political sovereign of Oman.

Omani Political Careering and British Indian Subjects

From the early eighteenth century, mobile Indian merchants from the Western states of Sindh, Gujarat, Kutch, and Kathiawar had made Oman their home. This connection ensured that news of landmark events in India, like the transfer of power to the Crown, reached Oman instantly and created ripples in the Persian Gulf. If the Indian revolt triggered rumors of British preoccupation in India and its distraction from Gulf affairs, the transfer of power to Queen Victoria increased the confidence that a resurgent Britain could play an influential role in Gulf politics. Indeed, the news of Queen Victoria's coronation streaming in from India offered hope to the warring princes.

It was no surprise that in 1859 Commander Griffith Jenkins reported from the Persian Gulf that Sultan Thuwayni (1856–1866) celebrated with gusto the handing over of India to Queen Victoria. He pledged his loyalty and alliance to her and made a public display of his sentiments. Jenkins said:

> On evenings and nights of 6, 7, 8th March cities of Muscat and Muttra and other towns were illuminated. Monday 7th instant was kept as a strict holiday at Muscat and Muttra in honor of England. On that day Royal standard of Queen of Britain was displayed from mast head of principal flag staff in citadel of forts of Muscat and vessels in port dressed with all their flags. . . . The day was devoted at his capital to the honor of Queen and in prayer for her people.[4]

The celebrations at Muscat included even the sons of Sultan Thuwayni—Syed Salim and Syed Faisal—along with all the nobility and merchants of the city.[5]

Queen Victoria represented a more heavy-fisted and vigilant British Indian government. To divert attention from the 1857 insult she threw a wider net of imperial networks and articulated a political rhetoric that spilled beyond British India into the Western Indian Ocean rim. She was most emphatic on the anti-arms and slave trade campaign that traditionally knit Arabia, Eastern Africa, and Europe (Chew 2012). She offered hope in Oman as she put the spotlight on France and clamped down on its slave trade, so as to bring its profits back to local economies. Sensing the significance of the Persian Gulf and the Red Sea as critical commercial arteries for her India trade, she stepped up British influence in the region by consular presence in Muscat and Oman and direct interference in the sultan's succession disputes. These were critical to contain the European, in particular the French, competition for expansion in the region via its small arms trade supply (Chew, 2012: 98–160). The British concern for the region becoming an "international arms bazaar" and a slave market as a consequence of European rivalries over arms and slaves offered huge benefits for Omani princes. Indeed, her imperial trade wars with France and concern for the British Indian trading community in Oman offered the new conceptual space to both Syed Thuwayni and Syed Majid to recalibrate their politics and build their careers afresh. If managing the affairs of the Indian trading community in Muscat became the conduit for Thuwayni to access imperial networks and favors, the politics of the slave trade, centered in Zanzibar, provided a similar entry point to his brother Syed Majid, who was located on the island.

Syed Thuwayni and the British Indian Merchants: The Case of the Khojas

Muslim Khojas were a wealthy merchant community of Western India who migrated in the late eighteenth century (1740–1780s) to Oman from Kutch, Sindh, and Bombay. In Oman they were also known as Lotias. The region attracted them for trade, and they were actively involved in the pearl fishery, dried fish, dates, and textile and grain trades. They owned shops in Muttrah—three kilometers from Muscat—and doubled as artisans and carpenters (Goswami, 2016: 87–90). But Oman was also attractive to them because they felt they were closer to Persia, which was home to their spiritual leader Aga Khan. Living in Oman made it relatively easy for them to make their pilgrimage to him. Indeed, many Khojas settled also in the Iranian cities along the Persian Gulf: Bander Abbas, Meshd, and Yezd.

Khojas were innately philanthropic because of their religious belief that made each Khoja give one-fifth of his property annually for the Prophet and his descendants. The offerings were collected in all the towns in a prayer house–cum-depository called the *mehmankhanah*. Property and money of Khojas with no heirs also went into the Aga Khan's kitty. But many with legal heirs also opted to bequeath their assets to the spiritual leader on their death. The

Aga Khan owned properties not just in India and Oman but in Kabul, Kandahar, Balkh, Bokhara, and Badakshan.

In 1859 Muhammad Jafar Khan, nephew of the Aga Khan, reported from Muscat that the Indian Khojas were major investors in the economic growth of the port city.[6] Indeed, these British Indian subjects, with a long history of commercial dealings in Oman, constituted an important part of Syed Thuwayni's economic and social base, as they did of his late father. But in the period of imperial crisis they became even more important as they emerged as the perfect site where the interests of Syed Thuwayni and the British coalesced. Interference in their matters became the ideal stepping-stone for him to access British imperial politics for furthering his career. On their part, the British, shaken by the 1857 revolt, wanted to keep tabs on their subjects abroad. Muslim subjects in particular were under their surveillance. And the Omani princes were best suited to mediate and be the middlemen in this surveillance exercise. Managing the Indian émigré Khojas was thus of mutual political benefit.

Handling the Khojas with British advice and assistance was the perfect route to political careering in Oman. In 1859 Syed Thuwayni got the opportunity he awaited: a rebel faction of Khojas attacked the community's local place of worship and depository *(mehmankhanah)* in the Muttrah village. Syed Thuwayni used the issue to both cement his ties with British imperial administrative networks and showcase his clout with the influential Aga Khan.

The attackers took all the cash, gold, silver, and apparel, including Kashmir shawls, which had been collected there for many years. The supervisors took the matter to the British agent, Khoja Haskeel, and asked him to be a witness. But interestingly, the Aga Khan asked his nephew Muhammad Jafar Khan to take the matter to Sultan Thuwayni for redress. Thuwayni asked his son to ignore the opposition from the rebel Khojas and make arrangements for his stay at the *mehmankhanah.* Muhammad Jafar Khan waited for Thuwayni to return from his trip to Bander Abbas and Sohar to solve his dispute. The rebel Khojas continued to be abusive and violent toward Muhammad Jafar Khan each time they visited the *mehmankhanah* for their prayers. But Thuwayni was welcoming to him and extended his help as he negotiated with the Khojas.

Muhammad Jafar Khan, with the knowledge of Syed Thuwayni, submitted a petition to the British resident as well asking for help. But, like the Aga Khan before him, the resident, acknowledging Thuwayni's clout in Muscat, reverted the matter to the sultan. On his part, Thuwayni, keen to enter the administrative networks of the British and earn favors, referred the matter for complete investigation to their agent Khoja Haskeel, and asked him to prepare a report. Satisfied with the report, he handed over the *mehmankhanah* and the house to Jafar Khan and promised a written order for the same. On the question of the return of the property plundered from the house, he promised intervention and resolution of the dispute on his return from Zanzibar.[7]

It is significant that despite relying on the British agent and bringing him into the loop in addressing the grievance, he refused to have the agent countersign any order he issued. He also refused any request for inviting the agent to resolve the issue of plundered property, or even inform him that this matter remained unresolved even if the dwelling house and *mehmankhanah* had been handed over to Muhammad Jafar Khan.[8] On his part, Khan was dissatisfied and considered the matter unresolved. But Thuwayni had milked it to his long-term political advantage by leveraging himself with both the globally acclaimed spiritual leader of the Khojas and the hugely influential temporal power in Muscat—the British agent.

Princely Careers and Imperial Rivalries over the Slave Trade

Omani politics, which was based on portable empires and mobile merchant networks, was predictably diabolic. Plugging into British imperial politics and tapping its networks for career gains involved constant negotiation. It was a bumpy ride, as the extent to which Britain encouraged the arming of indigenous sultans and allowed them slave-trade profits was unpredictable. On both fronts Britain calibrated its moves keeping in mind its own interests in the face of imperial rivalries triggered by aggressive capitalist expansion in the Indian Ocean.[9] Thus if in 1859 the Bombay government leaned on Thuwayni to settle the Khoja affair, it did not stop Lord Elphinstone, the governor of Bombay, from accusing him of supporting the French in the slave trade on the east coast of Africa. Indeed, this made him justify his intervention in the princely wars. He said: "Syed Thoonee had been instigated by the French to attack his brother who has incurred their displeasure by his honest desire to act up to his engagements with us to suppress the slave trade."[10]

He suggested that Thuwayni be dissuaded from attacking Zanzibar and all help extended to it as it was an ally in the British campaign against the slave trade. Rigby lent weight to the case when he maintained that Thuwayni's fourth brother, Syed Bargash, who had rebelled against Syed Majid, was also "now under French protection and cannot be touched." He pointed out that the extent of French involvement was such that "the question of the right of succession to the government in Zanzibar would have to be settled in Europe."[11]

The Omani princes used the vicissitudes of imperial politics to their advantage. They knowingly implicated themselves in imperial wars over the slave trade whenever it suited them. In 1859, even if the Bombay government intervened and succeeded in preventing Syed Thuwayni from attacking Zanzibar, the mobilization of men and resources by both brothers remained intact. This was useful for future state building. Syed Thuwayni agreed to abandon the expedition to Zanzibar and refer his claims to the arbitration of Governor Elphinstone. Similarly, Syed Majid consented to abide in like manner through the intervention of Colonel Rigby. But their entanglements in Anglo-French imperial politics had critical bearing in consolidating their base and firming their political aspirations. The rise of Syed Majid as a powerful ruler of Zanzibar is an important case in point.

Slave Trade Wars and Syed Majid's Rise in Zanzibar

Syed Majid (1856–1870) asserted his claim as the independent sovereign of Zanzibar much to the chagrin of his brother Syed Thuwayni, who was convinced that he was its rightful sovereign. He claimed that the tribute paid to him by Syed Majid was an acknowledgment of his sovereign status. But Syed Majid contested this claim on grounds that the money he paid was not tribute. Despite these claims and counterclaims there was no denying that Syed Majid was the island's popular leader. He had been "elected" by the people in an almost "national revolution" style because he was the overseer of the tremendous economic progress Zanzibar had made in the period of his father (Bishara, 2017 9–10).[12] Like his father he too had contacts with the Indian commercial community and leaned on them for financial help (Bhacker, 1994: 214). He was the beneficiary of the political and commercial investments his father had made in the region, especially after he shifted his capital to Zanzibar in 1840.

It was widely believed in British circuits that Syed Majid asserted his independent sovereign status because he was riding the popularity wave, having cornered to his advantage the economic progress initiated by his late father.

The latter transformed Zanzibar's political economy by encouraging the Arabs from Oman to settle on the island. Earlier, the Arabs had viewed Zanzibar as a mere nursery for slaves. But once they settled they began to promote its agriculture and commerce using slave labor. In 1834 Commander H. M. S. Imogene described Zanzibar as having "little or no trade." This rapidly changed, and by 1859 the island possessed an aggregate trade estimated at 1,664,577 pounds sterling. Rigby noted that twenty-five years ago, Sultan Syed Said did not receive more than 50,000 crowns of annual revenue from the African possessions. But by 1847 it had increased to 145,000 crowns, and in 1860 it was 206,000 crowns.[13] Brigadier Coghlan, in his report on the island, noted that with Arab investments the African possessions surpassed the Arab territories in their economic value. There, "annual revenue exceeds the revenue of the latter to the amount of 77,000 crowns or pound 16,000 sterling."[14]

Syed Thuwayni was not impressed by this economic boom and challenged his brother's claim of being the island's political sovereign. He prepared to attack Zanzibar in 1859. Paradoxically, this impending collision became the trigger for the consolidation of Syed Majid's social and political base. And the ongoing Anglo-French politics on the ban of the slave trade offered Syed Majid the perfect route to navigate imperial rivalries to further his interest. To facilitate his political career, he openly exploited British overtures to be their ally in the anti–slave trade campaign. Career advancement was possible on the back of the slave trade wars because in this conjunctional moment of crisis (1859), the British aimed to dislodge the French from the slave trade and not to ban the trade per se. The pitch for a complete ban was articulated later in the 1860s with the abolition declared in 1873. Then too the restrictions on slave traffic were largely on British subjects—like the Indian Kutchi traders.[15] Moreover, slave traffic thrived as Arab and British slave owners as well as the abolitionists, such as David Livingstone, were complicit in using the slave as a clean slate on which to articulate their own identity and status. If the former used them as economic labor, the latter converted them to social capital. Even slaves had internalized the economic and social benefits of such ownership. Ironically, for slaves, freedom often meant becoming petty slave owners themselves (Prestholdt, 2008: 117–146). Thus, the antislavery campaign and the alliances against French participation in the trade did not end slave traffic. Nor were they meant to stop it. They merely shifted the use of slaves from mere economic labor to social capital on whose bodies ideas of blackness, race, and Africa were poised to emerge. They brought Arab and African slave owners in close alliance with both their British counterparts and the abolitionists. Syed

Majid welcomed the anti-French alliance as it opened the markets to local Arab and African merchants and helped consolidate his social base. Even the Kutchi traders looked to him for help when, as British subjects, the going got tough. The additional bonus for Syed Majid was the return support that the British promised in his succession dispute with his brother Thuwayni.

Slave Trade Politics and the Militarization of Zanzibar

Syed Majid put together a formidable army and militarized Zanzibar under the watchful eye of the British. This was not only good preparedness for any war with Muscat but also a means to weld together once again the Arab, Indian, and African communities that his father—the late Sultan Syed Said—had successfully nurtured as his enduring social base. This base had fractured in the age of crisis when the Arab and African possessions of the late sultan were split between his sons. The hostility between Muscat and Zanzibar had strained the relations between North Arabs from the Muscat area and the Arab and African tribes on the east coast of Africa, who in the past had together propped up the political economy of a united Oman.

Syed Majid put a check on these spiraling Arab-Afro tensions by recruiting 20,000 men that included Arabs, Baluchis, Makranees, natives of the Comro isles, and Swahilis of the east African coast. This mix of Arabs, Africans, and Baluchis was equipped with American muskets and carbines. The governor of Zanzibar—Syed Suleiman bin Ahmad and a confidant of the late Sultan Syed Said—doubled as the recruiting agent. He invoked the memory of the late sultan and used his influence over the Arab tribes to contain the Arab-Afro identity tensions. Colonel Rigby testified to the huge popularity of Syed Majid among the Swahili population of east Africa:

> When the invasion of the Zanzibar dominions by Sayyid Thoweynee was expected the inhabitants of the Sowahil rose en-masse to support Seyyed Majid. Many tribes under their own chiefs came over to Zanzibar . . . and when some of the dhows which had Seyyid Thoweynee's troops on board endeavored to procure wood and water, they were driven from every point at which they attempted to land, and at length were obliged in consequence to surrender to Seyyed Majid's ships of war.[16]

He added that at Zanzibar the Swahili population and the natives of the Comoro isles supported Syed Majid because they "feared and hated" the Northern Arabs [from Muscat], who they felt came to Zanzibar only to "kidnap their children and carry them away as slaves."[17]

Syed Majid's dependence on the British enabled much of this military buildup. His reliance on the British was evident when he was hugely relieved at the posting of Colonel Rigby as consul in 1858. Rigby reported that he could "scarce recognize him as the same individual" when he read Her Majesty's letter approving his succession, and a ship of war arrived from the Indian government.[18] Rigby was satisfied as to his loyalty and good governance: "All classes here the Europeans and American merchants, the Indian traders and the Arabs . . . bear testimony to the kind and amiable disposition of the Sultan, his justice and liberal policies, they all consider him a worthy successor to his father."[19]

Syed Majid's career was tightly framed in the interstice of the Anglo-French imperial politics over the slave trade. Indeed, with his help, the British dispersed congregations of "negro slaves" who were trafficked by the French private firms. They used the pretext of protecting British Indian subjects from the attacks of these armed "negro slaves" to park their ships in Zanzibar. These were to assist Syed Majid in the eventuality of an attack by his brother Thuwayni.[20]

Syed Majid benefited from being perceived as the much-sought-after figure in the imperial rivalries on the slave trade. In 1858 Colonel Rigby reported the renewed French efforts to wean away Syed Majid to their side by suggesting that he permit the export of "negro slaves" from his territories, as "engaged laborers" to the French island of La Reunion or any other French colony. The French laid out a detailed plan to classify slaves as "free labor" for export because Syed Majid was tied by treaty engagements with the British government that prohibited direct or indirect sale of slaves from the island.[21] The French backed their demand by stationing "war ships" in the Persian Gulf.[22]

Rigby was happy that Majid was continuing his late father's tradition of loyalty to and alliance with the British on the issue of slave exports to European colonies. Rigby pointed out that his late father too had agreed to the export of "free men" to be bought by French dealers for labor in their colonies, but had refused permission for those slaves imported from Africa and who had no idea of their position even when they were made "free men." He even refused permission for exports when told that the French could procure "freed slaves" from Zanzibar, and if unsuccessful they would buy them from his territories on the coast of Africa by force of warships. The late Syed Said had replied that if "you threaten to use force I cannot resist but I do not consent." He had openly declared his allegiance to the British when he said that "he was unable to resist the force of France but that the government with which he had a treaty for the prevention of the sale of slaves to Europeans would perhaps prevent France buying slaves in his territories."[23]

This anti-French stand also got him the support of his own Arab traders and brokers who were "averse to slaves being sold and taken away" in this way to French colonies.[24] Indeed, allying with the British made his subjects happier as restrictions on slave traffic were technically for British subjects alone.[25]

Syed Majid too showed similar political acumen and resisted the French demands. Allying with British efforts to ban the trade was particularly attractive to him because it helped garner local Arab and African merchant support. In 1857 he refused to yield to the continuous pressure from the French merchant Monsieur Reutone Rautony, of Bourbon, who wished to send his ships to Zanzibar ports to export "free slaves" at a profit to Syed Majid. He urged Majid to accept his offer, as it was morally proper to free slaves to "labor for wages in any country." And financially it brought high profits that would be shared between them: the slaves would be transported in a fast-moving French ship called *Paikur,* and profits would be immense as the ship would be able to perform voyages with speed. Even the price of the slaves sent from Zanzibar would be equally divided between the two parties after taking care of the expenses of shipping and passage. He made a demand for young and strong slaves. For every ninety male slaves he wanted ten female slaves between fourteen and sixteen years of age.[26]

Monsieur Reutone played on the Anglo-French competitive politics in the age of imperial crisis when he urged Syed Majid to "not pay attention to the words of the English Counsel" and instead work in the interest of his own people. He reminded him that the English imposed restrictions because they needed slaves for their sugar plantations in Europe and India. In contrast, France was desirous of "happiness of all mankind"; and in keeping with this idea, slaves on arrival at Bourbon and French colonies would be "taught labor" so that they may become "wise and clever."[27]

Sultan Majid not only refused the offer but also resisted French attempts to buy slaves from the African east coast. But this did not put an end to French efforts to procure slaves, and it resulted in grave economic consequences for Zanzibar: the price of slaves went up because of the high French demand. Additionally, the number of able-bodied slaves in Zanzibar declined as most were taken to the new market that the French opened south of the island of Monfsa. Finally, other trades, like that of ivory, were neglected as most tribes involved in it found "slave hunting" more profitable.[28] The limitations of Syed Majid's anti–slave trade drive notwithstanding, the Arab traders drew close to Syed Majid because, by putting hurdles in the unfettered French shopping for slaves, the local market became relatively free for them. Arab slave brokers and merchants supported him and constituted his social base.

Syed Majid continued his tirade against French slave merchants. In 1858 he objected to the French vessels' carrying his flag so as to avoid British surveillance. He threatened the French ship *Glamense* that he would deprive it of his flag and papers if it attempted to leave the port with "negroes" on board. He gave similar warnings to all buggalows belonging to the port.[29] The sultan's strictures against the slave trade were well known to his subjects, and these were conveyed to French ships that came for slaves escorted by warships to the first port of call on the east coast of Africa—Kisingia. But here, despite the resistance from local people, the French invariably had their way by force of arms. This small port was the destination of all "slave caravans" coming from the interior and from Lake Wanyassa. The French "Brigades of war" also came to the port with the express purpose of protecting vessels in procuring "negroes." Slaves were forcefully taken from here to be shipped to Zanzibar and other ports within its dominions. Syed Majid was incensed at the violation of his orders and not only complained to the English consul for help but also dispatched his own yacht to Kilwa port ordering his governor to stop this traffic.

Syed Majid forbade the Arab and Indian merchants to participate in the French export of slaves. He sent a proclamation to the same effect addressed to the Banians and other Indian residents at his ports urging them to exercise caution.[30] At Kilwa, his governor, Saif bin Ali, assured him that he had proclaimed publicly through "sound of horn" throughout the town that any of the subjects who disobeyed the order banning slave trade will be severely punished. He had also conveyed these commands to the chief of the Najoo tribe and to the chief of the Baluchis at Kilwa.[31] But despite his proclamations and the support he received from local trading communities, French war brigades accompanying vessels with slaves were a common sight on the ports of Kisingia, Kilwa, Pemba, and Comron; ships also embarked from the east coast of Africa to the slave depots at Nosa, Beh, and Mayotta. French slave ships were also sighted on the west coast of Madagascar.

And yet the resistance of the local people to the French continued. Indeed, this anti-French sentiment enabled Syed Majid to not only maximize profits of this trade but also heel himself in local society by garnering the support of his people. His subjects resisted and opposed French merchants on their ports. On the west coast of Madagascar there was a "deadly feeling of hatred" against all white men among the population. Their opposition was most evident when on one occasion they burned a French ship and killed its crew north of Monambo. This extreme step was triggered because a member of one of the Arab tribes was used to kidnap members of the other tribe to sell them to the French merchants. However, the French government continued to view the trade as legitimate and legal. It argued that the exported men were "freed slaves" or "free labor" and thus the trade did not violate any injunction or law of either Syed Majid or the British.[32]

Both Syed Thuwayni's and Syed Majid's political careering depended on curtailing French slave trade entrepreneurs, as this was to the advantage of communities that constituted their social base: Arabs, Africans, and Indians. Indeed, both vied for British attention and competed to plug into imperial wars on the slave trade as and when it suited their own political interest. It was thus not surprising that Syed Thuwayni too, even when suspected by the British for abetting the trade, complained to the British consul to curb this trade from his ports of Kilwa. He drew their attention to the "unprecedented amount of English coin" in which the payment for slaves was made to the French. Equally alarming for him was the "greatly increased demand for gunpowder" for the sale to "slave hunters" in the interior. This, he pointed out, "indicated the wide spread nature and scale of this trade."[33] Like his brother Majid, he too believed that the French demand for slaves adversely affected the trade in cloves and ivory, as Arab tribes neglected these commodities and instead got involved in "hunting" slaves for the French.[34]

The Canning Award, Arms Trade, and Rise of Syed Thuwayni in Muscat

After the 1857 Indian revolt, the British tightened their surveillance at Muscat and Bombay as intelligence reports revealed that arms from Europe had reached Indian rebels in the North West frontier via these two ports. While Bombay was under British administration, the stringent measures in Muscat applied only to British officers, subjects, and trade firms. The movement of both people and arms traveling between Muscat and Bombay came under stricter scrutiny as the British unified India under a single regulatory regime and began to dominate the markets through regulation (Mathew, 2016: 91). British regulations shook Muscat's political economy, which was largely dependent on profits from the slave and arms trades. They also affected the mobility of Indian traders and made British private firms look for new routes and reliable middlemen and brokers.

Syed Thuwayni, who had used imperial politics for his rise, was hit hard as the new regulations threatened Muscat's economic vibrancy. Kutchi Indian traders based in Muscat noted the decline of the city from the 1840s when Thuwayni's father, Sultan Syed Said, moved his base to Zanzibar. But its significance as a premier market for arms slumped drastically with the British clampdown on the private trade of slaves and arms after 1857 (Goswami, 2016: 102). Arms for even the personal use of Syed Thuwayni were difficult to get. In 1858 Messers Wallace & Company sought and obtained special permission from the Bombay government for selling thirty muskets with bayonets for the personal use of Syed Thuwayni in Muscat.[35]

But the enterprising Syed Thuwayni was unrelenting. He tapped new routes and ports, such as Bander Abbas in Iran, which he held in lease, to move traders and arms to India overland via Iran and Afghanistan. His ingenious politics ensured that arms shipped from Europe to Muscat moved in smaller boats to Bander Abbas for their onward overland journey via Iran and Afghanistan to India. A string of Arab, African, Indian, Persian, and Afghan traders kept this traffic going, avoiding British regulations in Muscat and its surveillance in Zanzibar and Bombay.

Indeed, the post-1857 conjunctional moment of crisis made Muscat the arms emporium par excellence (Goswami, 2016: 153–156; Mathew, 2016: 95). It attracted wealthy Kutchi merchants such as Ratansi Pushottam. He migrated to the city to take advantage of the new opportunities possible in the shadow of empires. In 1857 his uncle, already based in Muscat, welcomed him and mentored him in his ancestral firm Natha Mekhan (Mathew, 2016: 89–95). His firm, which dealt in arms in Muscat, flourished as it leveraged itself with the interests of Syed Thuwayni and the private European and British trading firms. And he was not the only one. The firm of another well-known Kutchi trader, Gopalji Walji, also had a meteoric rise in this period of clampdown and crisis.

The British did not remain idle spectators to these economic lifelines of Syed Thuwayni. As private Indian, Arab, and European commercial firms dug in their heels in Muscat, the British Indian government also zeroed in on the region. It stretched its long administrative arm to include the newly established British consulate in Muscat within its ambit. Brigadier Coghlan, in his recommendations for the new road map of the region, recommended the establishment of a consulate in Muscat that would report to the Bombay government. Indeed, he saw the lack of a consulate in Muscat and the control of its affairs by the consul in Zanzibar, who in turn reported to the resident in the Persian Gulf, as the main reason for the British mismanagement of princely disputes. Coghlan envisaged the reinvigorated Muscat as "the residence of the independent sovereign and the seat of the government of Oman . . . exercising considerable influence over a large portion of Arabi, including the Western shores of the Persian Gulf." He felt this was desirable because of British "commercial interests in that quarter."[36]

His top priority was the British administrative control of Muscat affairs, as there was too much at stake: the British Indian trading communities had to be monitored, the town of Muscat had become a station for the electric telegraph, and the arrival of steamers and steamships that linked Bombay and the Persian Gulf meant that they had to pass via Muscat. It was therefore essential to appoint a competent consul there who, in the words of Brigadier Coghlan,"should be well acquainted in the Arabic language, have some knowledge of Arab laws and customs, and together with firmness and disposition should possess a temper calculated to conciliate the natural impetuosity and obstinate puerility of the Arab character."[37]

The Canning Award and Syed Thuwayni

Brigadier Coghlan's formulations culminated in the famous Canning Award (1861), which divided Oman into the independent sultanates of Muscat and Zanzibar with the intention to politically and economically subordinate it to British interests. But Muscat was difficult to dominate and its economic vibrancy remained the site of contestation between Syed Thuwayni and the British. The award had limited success as it could not break the economic lifelines of Syed Thuwayni. In fact, like many other adversities, this too was milked by Syed Thuwayni with the complicity of private traders (both Arab and Indian Kutchi) as well as the private British and European trading companies[38] (Goswami, 2016: 82–84; Sheriff, 1987: 83). He avoided the British regulations for arms traffic on the Muscat-Zanzibar-Bombay route by using the Iranian port of Bander Abbas for entry into the Indian market. From here the arms moved via overland routes through Iran and Afghanistan and reached India, avoiding Bombay. He maximized the profits of arms trade by avoiding the Bombay vigil and focusing instead on the ports on the Persian coast that he held in lease.

Indeed, Muscat and Iran had a strong bond that was reflected in 1856 when, on the death of Sultan Syed Said, the shah of Iran sent Imam Quli Khan as his ambassador with presents and condolences for Thuwayni.[39] This was accompanied by the free access to the Bander Abbas port, which was off and on held in lease by Thuwayni. This was a huge concession as it made his entry into the port city of Sohar, where his brother Syed Turki posed a challenge, easy. It also provided the entry point of arms to India. From 1858 Thuwayni used Bander Abbas for both these ends.[40]

Throughout the last four decades of the nineteenth century, an illegal trade in arms that avoided British regulations in Bombay thrived in Muscat, energized by both local traders and middlemen, Indian merchants, and private European commercial firms. It worked via the Bander Abbas route that Thuwayni had ingeniously charted and that continued to flourish as late as 1880 when Qajar Iran began to seal its borders to private arms trade (Mathew, 2016: 90–91).[41] As Muscat became the key transshipment area for arms, it emerged as the arms emporium that ensured supplies to the new markets in India, Afghanistan, and Baluchistan via the Iranian port of Bander Abbas. British shipping companies, seeking to profit from the arms trade and unmindful of imperial politics, continued to ship guns and rifles to Muscat. From here they were put in small boats (*dhows*) and shipped to Bander Abbas in Iran en route to Afghanistan and the North West frontier.

Fracis Times and Company and Omani Entrepreneurship

The continuity of Muscat's influence in Bandar Abbas outlived Thuwayni. The routes and contacts his governor, Haji Ahmad, put in place ensured that Bandar Abbas remained the gateway to an illegal trade in arms to India well into the twentieth century. The history of operations of one of the oldest British firms in the arms trade, Fracis Times and Company, reveals how the wide ambit of commercial networks and trade routes that Thuwayni worked out following the Canning Award restrictions continued well into the end of the nineteenth century. This was a story that unfolded at the underbelly of empire, avoiding Bombay, where the British surveillance was strict, and relying instead on ports on the "edges of empire" to sneak arms into India and pump revenue into local economies. All the efforts by the British government to put an end to this trade failed. The entanglement of European and English private profits, imperial networks, anti-British sentiment, and the extraordinary web of ethnically diverse commercial communities that straddled Empires was difficult to break.

Fracis Times and Company had three partners: Fracis Times, of England, and Nassarwanji Dossabhoy and Dorabji Edalji Dharwar, both originally from Bombay. Nassarwanji generally traded between England and the Persian Gulf and had offices in Bushier and England. Fracis Times and Dharwar were located in England. The firm used a string of steamers—the *Turkistan,* the *Afghanistan,* and the *Baluchistan*—for its operations in the Gulf. Significantly, Fracis Times and Company had no direct dealings with Bombay. It traded only with the Gulf, and the arms transacted by this firm reached the North West Frontier of India only via Persia (avoiding ports controlled by the Bombay government).

At its major ports or importing stations it relied on local merchants and traders. Thus, in Bander Abbas its staff was almost entirely composed of Persian subjects, including Haji Muhammad Sharif Alavi, Sayyid Abdur Rahim Awazi, Haji Ali Aga Hussain Lari, Haji Mehdi Lari, Haji Hussain Galadari Awazi, Haji Nakhoda Ali, and Aga Hussain Lari. The staff also included three people from Shikarpur: Kishandas, Sakaram, and Lakhu. In Muscat, Fracis Times relied on a string of British Indian subjects: two that have been identified are Ratansi Purshotam, a Kutchi Bhattia, and Damodhar Dharamsi. The transactions in arms largely avoided Bombay after 1861. But the firm had an agent in the city for taking orders from local mechants. Dadabhai Chothia, a Parsi and an independent merchant whose office was in Hornby Road Fort, worked for the firm as its commissioning agent.[42]

The Bander Abbas Persian merchants, along with their Indian counterparts, played a key role in this illicit arms trade in an age of heightened surveillance and border controls. They moved via a chain of agents and contacts between Bombay and Persia, not just selling their wares but also taking orders along the way. Thus, the merchant Aga Hussain Lari traded in Bander Abbas but lived in Bombay and carried out his transactions in Bander Abbas via his agent from Shikarpur, named Tekchand (alias Waliram). These Persian merchants and their agents joined with caravans of Afghan traders at Bander Abbas once a year and also at the Persian cities of Kirman and Yezd every month.

The arms then passed via Meshd and Herat into Afghanistan. They were concealed in other goods so as to escape the restrictions imposed by the Persian authorities. Afghan traders carted dry fruits and ghee to Persia for sale, and in return bought tea, sugar, cloth, and so forth. But the principal trade was arms and ammunitions, which reached Kirman and Yezd from Bushier. The merchants also went to Bander Abbas from Muscat, Bushier, and Lingah in native boats. It was believed that they smuggled arms into the boats concealed in bags containing dry limes.[43]

This chapter uses "crisis" as a heuristic device and an analytical category to analyze individual political careers in the mid-nineteenth-century age of revolt and imperial rivalries. It puts the spotlight on those impacted by the idea of imperial decline, and elaborates, via their histories, the process by which the very illness and "crisis" of empires led to the creation of a wider space and scope for political and economic entrepreneurship in the Indian Ocean. This political entrepreneurship used imperial networks and rivalries even as it remained pitted against empires. It benefited from the shifty yet embracive nature of Western imperialism and the social community of traders and middlemen that straddled empires and often made them appear portable.

This chapter has argued that imperial networks and rivalries spread over India and the Persian Gulf proved very handy for the career mobility and advancement of Omani princes located between empires. Indeed, the moment of crisis offered both Syed Thuwayni and Syed Majid fresh political opportunities as the British government in India stretched itself to dabble in the affairs of the Persian Gulf to recover its political and economic standing after a drubbing in 1857. This diversion of British attention toward the Gulf intensified Anglo-French imperial rivalries over the arms and slave trades. Omani princes became critical pawns in imperial wars as the long arm of the British Indian government made its presence felt in the Gulf. It inaugurated the boom time for business as merchants, brokers, middlemen, and European firms straddled empires and used its angularities to maximize their profits. Both the Anglo-French rivalry and the commercial world of traders and middlemen that sustained it became the bedrock for Omani politics as sibling princes contested the political legacy of the dead sultan and fought for independent rule of his Arab and African territories.

Notes

1. Captain C. P. Rigby to C. E. B. Russell, 1 July 1861, Political and Secret Records, India Office Records / L / P&S/9/38, British Library, London.

2. The sovereignty was sustained by the nineteenth-century economic expansion of Oman into the Western Indian Ocean. Kutchi and Sindhi merchants from India and Swahili traders from the east coast of Africa were involved in the export of ivory, cloves, and slaves to the Indian and European markets. For the integration of this trade into the global capitalist economy in the long nineteenth century, see Sheriff 1987; Goswami 2016.

3. L No. 17, Brigadier W. M. Coghlan, in charge Muscat & Zanzibar Commission, to H. L. Anderson, Chief Secretary to Govt. Bombay, Dec. 4 1860, Report of Commission 1860, Sec. Consultations, 1861 No. 97, file no. 15, Secret Muscat & Zanzibar, Political Department (PD) 33 / 1861, Maharashtra State Archive (MSA), Bombay (henceforth Coghlan Report).

4. Commander G. Jenkins, Persian Gulf, to Commander G. G. Wellesley, C-in-C of Indian Navy, Muscat, 10th March 1859, File No. 597, Muscat, 1859, PD 120 / 1859, MSA, Bombay.

5. L No. 363, Ahmad bin Mahomed Ali, Sec. to Sultan of Muscat, to Commander Jenkins, 16 April 1859, Persian Dept. 19 April 1859, File No. 597, Muscat, 1859, PD 120 / 1859, MSA, Bombay.

6. L No. 440 of 1859, Persian Dept, 21st May 1859, Copy of letter from Muhammad Jafar Khan, nephew of Aga Khan, to Commander G. Jenkins, 4rth March 1859, tr. 20th May 1859, File No. 676, Muscat, 1859, PD 120 / 1859, MSA, Bombay. See also Goswami 2016, 88–90, for their settlements in Muscat and good relations with the sultan.

7. L No. 440 of 1859, Persian Dept, 21st May 1859, Copy of letter from Muhammad Jafar Khan, nephew of Aga Khan, to Commander G. Jenkins, 4rth March 1859, tr. 20th May 1859, File No. 676, Muscat, 1859, PD 120 / 1859, MSA, Bombay.

8. Ibid.

9. For a discussion on arming the indigenous allies for larger geo-political considerations, see Chew 2012.

10. Minute of Lord Elphinstone, Governor of Bombay, 2 Feb. 1859, Sec Consult, 21st Feb. 1859, File no. 161, Muscat-Zanzibar, Pol Dept, 1859, PD 121 / 1859, MSA, Bombay.

11. L No. 43, Captain C. P. Rigby, British Agent in Zanzibar, to H. L. Anderson, Sec. to Govt. Bombay, 11 April 1859, File No. 161, Muscat-Zanzibar, Pol. Dept. 1859, PD 121 / 1859, MSA, Bombay.

12. For Indian merchants in a credit network that was underpinned intellectually by jurisprudence as a philosophy that transformed the region.

13. Coghlan Report.

14. Ibid.

15. "Slave dealing and slave holdings by Kutchees in Zanzibar," 1870, IOR/L/PS/18/B90, British Library, London.

16. Ibid.

17. Ibid.

18. L No. 19, Captain C. P. Rigby, Agent at Zanzibar, to H. I. Anderson, Sec to Govt, Bombay, Zanzibar, 24rth August 1858, File No. 328, Secret, Muscat, 1858, PD 147/1858, MSA, Bombay.

19. Ibid.

20. L No. 19, Captain C. P. Rigby, agent in Zanzibar, to H. L. Anderson, Sec. to Govt. of Bombay, 17 Feb. 1859, Sec. Consultations, file no. 161, Political Dept. 1859, Muscat-Zanzibar, PD 121/1859, MSA, Bombay. Syed Majid's ships were *Shah Alam*, forty-four guns; *Piedmontese*, thirty-six guns; *Artemise,* twenty-two guns; *Setporna,* four guns; and *Africa,* four guns.

21. L No. 4 of 1854, Captain C. P. Rigby, agent in Zanzibar, to H. L. Anderson, Sec. to Govt. of Bombay, Zanzibar 13th April 1854, Sec Consultations, 1858, Political Dept., file no. 336, Muscat & Zanzibar, PD 148/1858, MSA, Bombay. In 1854 the French dealers offered the slave broker money to sell the slaves as "free men" to him. The slaves were then taken to a judge or Qazi to get the valid seal of free men and a certificate of the same. This certificate enabled the slave to be taken away as free labor to French colonies. In the colony he worked for five years at the rate of two dollars per month and rations. At the end of this term he became a free man.

22. L No.15, Captain C. P. Rigby, agent in Zanzibar, to H. S. Anderson, Sec. to Govt. Bombay, 20th August 1858, Sec Consultations, 1858, Political Dept., file no. 336, Muscat & Zanzibar, PD 148/1858, MSA, Bombay.

23. L No not given, Major A. Hamerton, Consul and Agent in the territories of the Imam of Muscat, to the Earl of Clarendon, Sec of State for Foreign Affairs, August 20, 1858, Zanzibar, Sec. Consultations, 1858 Political Dept., file no. 336, Muscat & Zanzibar, PD 148/1858, MSA, Bombay.

24. Ibid.

25. "Slave dealing and slave holdings by Kutchees in Zanzibar," 1870, IOR /L/PS/18/B90, British Library, London.

26. Enclosure No. 1, (Translation of French merchant Monsieur Reutone's letter to Syed Majid,) letter No. 25, Captain C. P. Rigby, Company Agent at Zanzibar, to H. L. Anderson, Sec. to Govt., Bombay, 21st Sept. 1858, Sec Consultations, 1858 Political Dept., file no. 336, Muscat & Zanzibar, PD 148/1858, MSA, Bombay.

27. Ibid.

28. L No. 21, Captain C. P. Rigby, Company's agent Zanzibar, to H. L. Anderson, Sec. to Govt., Bombay, 13th Sept. 1858, Sec Consultations, 1858 Political Dept., file no. 336, Muscat & Zanzibar, PD 148/1858, MSA, Bombay.

29. L No. 40, Captain C. P. Rigby, British Agent, Zanzibar, to H. L. Anderson, Sec. to Govt., Bombay, 24rth Dec. 1858, File No. 163, 1859, Political Dept., Muscat, PD 120/1859, MSA, Bombay.

30. L No. 20 of 1859, Captain C. P. Rigby, English Consul and agent at Zanzibar, to H. L. Anderson, Sec. to Govt., Bombay, 16th March 1859, file 163, 1859, Political Dept., Muscat, PD 120/1859, MSA, Bombay.

31. Saif bin Ali, Governor of the port of Keelwa, to Sultan Syed Majid, Keelwa, March 7, 1859, file 163, 1859, Political Dept., Muscat, PD 120/1859, MSA, Bombay.

32. L No. 20 of 1859, Captain C. P. Rigby, English Consul and agent at Zanzibar, to H. L. Anderson, Sec. to Govt., Bombay, 16th March 1859, file 163, 1859, Political Dept., Muscat, PD 120/1859,MSA, Bombay.

33. Ibid.

34. L No. 447, Captain C. P. Rigby, Company's agent at Zanzibar, attached translated letter, Syed Thuwayni, ruler of Muscat, to Commander G. Jenkins, 4rth March 1859, translated on 20th May 1859, Persian Dept., 24rth May 1859, File No. 163, 1859, Political Dept., Muscat, PD 120/1859, MSA, Bombay. Syed Thuwayni complained to the English consul that the slave trade was injuring commerce at his ports because Arabs were neglecting other trades on his coastline and engaging in the more profitable slave trade.

35. L No. 812, R. Spooner, Commissioner of Customs Salt and Opium to L. Anderson, Sec. to Govt., Bombay office of Commissioner of Customs Salt & Opium, 1st March 1858; L No. 1802, B. Crawford, Chief Commissioner of Police, Bombay, to R Spooner, Commissioner of Customs Salt and Opium, 12th May 1858, File No. 151, Political Dept., 1858, Secret, Muscat, PD 147/1858, MSA, Bombay.

36. Coghlan Report.

37. Coghlan Report.

38. Indian Kutchi traders, like Mowji of the legendry Bhimani firm and merchants of the Shivji Topan firm, were encouraged by successive sultans of Muscat to carry on their dealings in arms and slaves. Merchants like Saleh b. Haramil, were active in slave and arms trade as well.

39. L No. 73 of 1858, Persian Dept., 3rd Feb. 1858, Substance of letter from Heskeal bin Yusuf, acting native agent at Muscat, to the Persian Secretary to Government, 8th Feb. 1858, translated on 29th Jan. 1858, file no. 283, Sec. Muscat, PD 147/1858, MSA, Bombay.

40. L No. 1242 of 1858, Persian Dept. September 3, 1858, Haskil bin Yusuf, acting native agent at Muscat, to H. L. Anderson, Persian Sec to Govt., July 11, 1858, received and translated on 1st Sept. 1858, file no. 283, Sec. Muscat, PD 147/1858, MSA, Bombay. In 1858, Thuwayni marched to Sohar, where his army and that of Syed Turki clashed and he besieged the town.

41. The 1881 regulations of Qajar Iran that sealed the borders and the assertion of the state's monopoly of trade in arms created a hurdle. And yet, trade in arms never really stopped.

42. Enclosure 2, in Letter 151, H. Kennedy to E. C. Cox, 16 Aug. 1889, Part II, Foreign Office (FO) 881/7463.

43. Ibid.

References

Bhacker, Rida M. 1994. *Trade and Empire in Muscat & Zanzibar: The Roots of British Dominion.* London: Routledge.

Bishara, F. A. 2017. *A Sea of Debt: Law and Economic Life in the Western Indian Ocean, 1780–1950.* Cambridge: Cambridge University Press.

Chew, E. 2012. *Arming the Periphery: The Arms Trade in the Indian Ocean during the Age of Global Empires.* Houndmills, Basingstoke, Hampshire: Palgrave Macmillan.

Goswami, C. 2016. *Globalization before Its Time: The Gujarati Merchants from Kachchh.* Delhi: Penguin India.

Mathew, J. 2016. *Margins of the Market: Trafficking and Capitalism across the Arabian Sea.* Oakland: University of California Press.

Prestholdt, J. 2008. *Domesticating the World.* Berkeley: University of California Press.

Sheriff, Abdul. 1987. *Slaves, Spices, and Ivory in Zanzibar: Integration of an East African Commercial Empire into the World Economy, 1770–1873.* Athens: Ohio University Press, 1987.

8

The Darker Side of Mobility

Refugees, Hostages, and Political Prisoners in Persianate Asia

JAMES PICKETT

For nearly a thousand years, large swathes of Asia were permeated by a remarkably stable continuum of Perso-Islamic high culture. An educated individual could theoretically travel from Sarajevo to Kashgar to Delhi, and many (though certainly not all) of the skills and knowledge forms would remain fully commensurable. The same Persian verses were recited in Istanbul and Lahore, just as the same Islamic legal doctrines undergirded both societies. In the nineteenth century, this cultural ecumene—the cosmopolis—began to fray in the face of accelerating processes of modernity.[1] This chapter examines how cultural change impacted the ability of educated individuals to traverse the center of Asia. Members of the cultural-religious elite forced into exile or taken hostage found that virtues of the Persian cosmopolis were far less practically advantageous in the new colonial regimes that extended their tendrils across Asia, changing the rules of the game and catalyzing an epistemic rupture.[2]

Much like Seema Alavi's and Tamara Loos's respective chapters, this one follows the trajectories of select individuals to illustrate a larger point. If the "crisis" examined by Alavi was one of empires in duress, the crisis underlying the analysis here was one of cultural episteme in transition as the cosmopolis competed with colonial forms of knowledge—an equally fundamental and enduring paradigm shift, but also one never objectified by the historical actors in question or understood as under threat.[3] In recent years, much emphasis has been placed on mobility and travel connecting different arenas usually considered separately (Green 2014). The heroes in these stories often fit the mold of cosmopolitan intellectuals, at home in multiple cultural spaces at once, and moving between them fluidly (Alam and Subrahmanyam 2007). However, travel in the preindustrial world was risky business, particularly in politically fragmented territories such as those of central Eurasia.[4] Cosmopolitan intellectuals indeed moved voluntarily, but their many less fortunate contemporaries traversed Eurasia because they had no other choice. This chapter therefore focuses on the darker side of mobility: hostages, political exiles, and refugees.[5]

Some of the individuals considered—such as Mulla Akmal Tashkandi and Abdallah Beg Yakkabaghi—moved considerable distances across Eurasia without ever leaving the Persian cosmopolis or finding themselves wanting for employment. Others—notably Beg Quli-Beg and Jura Beg—traveled across very similar spaces but found themselves fishes out of water within the new colonial dispensation, their Persianate skill set less relevant in an unfamiliar context. What these wayfarers shared was that their peregrinations were *involuntary:* theirs was a world where most people stayed put most of the time, when they could possibly help it. Their ultimate fates, however, were quite different, and this chapter argues that the Persian cosmopolis at twilight served as a safety net for some, and its absence imperiled others, as its features gave way in the face of colonialism.

Refugees and Exiles

Mulla Akmal Tashkandi was born in Tashkent sometime in the mid-nineteenth century and was trained in myriad Perso-Islamic forms of knowledge. Just like so many of his colleagues, Mulla Akmal mastered poetry, Islamic law, and calligraphy—and quite likely other disciplines such as occultism and mysticism as well. It is not clear whether he left Tashkent in search of greener pastures or whether he was fleeing powerful enemies in the city.[6] His departure fell during the immediate aftermath of the Russian conquest of Tashkent in 1865, which eliminated certain positions available to Islamic scholars and fundamentally altered local power dynamics, and likely factored into his decision to depart.[7] What is clear is that he traveled to Kashgar to enter the service of Ya'qub Beg (r. 1865–1877), a military leader from the emirate of Khoqand who had thrown off Qing rule and established control of several cities in the Tarim Basin (Kim 2004). Ya'qub Beg appointed Mulla Akmal judge *(qazi)* of the newly formed state,[8] but when China retook Xinjiang, Mulla Akmal was forced back to Tashkent (Shar'i, 61a).

However, returning home to Tashkent did not mark the end of Mulla Akmal's dislocation. Mulla Akmal had scarcely set foot in his home city when he was once again driven out by unscrupulous naysayers and enemies jealous of his erudition (Shar'i, 61a).[9] This time he moved to Bukhara, which during his sojourn in Kashgar had gone from city-state to protectorate of the Russian Empire. Nevertheless, even under Russian protection, Bukhara was an active Persianate center. By the late nineteenth century, the Manghit dynasty of Bukhara was one of the few remaining active sponsors of Persianate courtly culture, and Mulla Akmal quickly secured patronage there.[10] He composed poetry *(qasida)* in Arabic and Persian in praise of the Bukharan amirs, both living and bygone.[11] This sufficiently endeared him to the ruler such that he secured a spot in the permanent retinue of the amir[12]—which was fortunate, given that he had already managed to make powerful enemies in Bukhara as well. Presumably for his safety, the amir took Mulla Akmal along on royal visits to provinces such as Shahrisabz, where he participated in dispute resolution councils[13] with local elite.[14]

Mulla Akmal's journey across three polities—Russian Turkestan to Ya'qub Beg's emirate in Kashgar to the protectorate of Bukhara—illustrates the practical, applied relevance of high culture to migration. But it also illustrates displacement in the face of uncertainty and upheaval. At most—if not all—junctures, Mulla Akmal moved unwillingly, whether from jealous rivals in the case of Tashkent, or an infidel *(kuffar)* onslaught in the case of China's reconquest of Xinjiang. Many of his peers voluntarily traveled equal or greater distances on pilgrimage (both to local shrines and on the Hajj), to propagate a Sufi order, and in search of education (Brower 1996; Can 2014).[15] Yet Mulla Akmal's case is hardly an outlier. Traveling across dangerous mountains and deserts was an endeavor undertaken only when the payoff was sufficiently great or—just as often—when the consequences of staying put were severe.

For Mulla Akmal, and many other refugees like him, the Persian cosmopolis was not only a literary-cultural complex; it was also a safety net. Bukhara and Kashgar were separated by imperial borders and hundreds of miles of mountains and deserts, but they were connected by an integrated Persianate high culture. In Kashgar, Bukhara, and Tashkent alike, Mulla Akmal could leverage the same Hanafi legal texts, recite the same Persian poetry, and produce the same kinds of bureaucratic documents.[16] His skill set was fully transferable throughout this cultural zone, which made him a valuable asset—even in exile. Strikingly, Mulla Akmal's political dislocation did not entail social or cultural dislocation.

Yet Mulla Akmal's cultural world of the eighteenth century was on the verge of displacement, whether he knew it or not. Steamships, locomotives, and print culture; passports, citizenship, and nationalities—all of these things brought with them new kinds of mobility, but premised on new cultural forms quite different from the ones Mulla Akmal and his colleagues had mastered. Ironically, it was precisely during the age of steam and print that the cosmopolis began to fray at the edges, displaced by narrower nationalisms and vernacular cultures.[17] Indeed, the fact that the idea of the premodern cosmopol*is* and cosmopolitan*ism* share etymology is a source of much confusion in the literature.[18] In the amir of Bukhara's court, the ability to compose an epic praise poem *(qasida)* was a powerful advantage that secured Mulla Akmal's livelihood; but such virtues of the Persian cosmopolis were far less useful in the imperial governments of the new hegemons of Eurasia.[19]

This point is illustrated by the similar trajectory—but very different fate—of another refugee fleeing the defeated emirate of Kashgar: Beg Quli-Beg, son and heir of Ya'qub Beg. After ruling an independent emirate in Kashgaria for over a decade, Ya'qub Beg died suddenly in May 1877—exactly when Qing troops were mustering to retake the region. This sparked a succession struggle between Ya'qub Beg's sons, as well as a number of other factions, from which Beg Quli ultimately emerged more or less victorious in October of that same year.[20] No sooner had Beg Quli secured his inheritance than Qing troops were at his door, driving him into exile in the Russian-controlled Farghana valley in December 1877. In the words of a Taranchi[21] poem circulating in the late nineteenth century: "In the month that Yaq'ub Beg died, misfortune befell the Beg Bachcha [i.e., Beg Quli-Beg]" (Pantusov 1901, 7).[22] This was probably around the time that Mulla Akmal Tashkandi fled for the exact same reasons, though we do not have precise dates for his itinerary.

However, the fortunes of Mulla Akmal and Beg Quli diverged sharply in exile. Whereas Mulla Akmal moved to the Russian protectorate of Bukhara—a polity still ruled by a precolonial dynasty, which continued to cultivate Perso-

Islamic high culture—Beg Quli tried his luck with the new colonial order. Beg Quli's father, Ya'qub Beg, had pursued an aggressively pragmatic foreign policy, maintaining friendly ties with the British, and granting favorable trade treaties to the Russians (Millward 2007, 123). And when Beg Quli's voice emerges in the Russian imperial archive, it is through his attempts to leverage these former diplomatic relationships to secure for himself a future in exile. Specifically, Beg Quli was petitioning the Russian colonial government to provide him with a stipend. His ability to secure such resources depended on his answer to a question explicitly posed by the Russian administration: "When Beg Quli-Beg independently ruled the entire country [of Kashgaria], precisely what services did he render to the Russian government?" (RGVIA F 400 O 1 D 2168, f. 43a).

It was a question that Beg Quli understood all too well. In his petition for a retirement salary, Beg Quli skillfully navigated the imperial grid, justifying his request for a stipend by his service to the Russian Empire. He wrote that when his father, Ya'qub Beg, was still among the living, in 1871 Tsar Alexander II himself had confirmed Beg Quli-Beg's right to inherit the throne: "Seeing the impossibility of resisting the enormous forces of the Chinese, and just when I was about to finish dealing with the internecine conflict [with pretenders to Ya'qub Beg's throne], I was forced to abandon the country and seek asylum with the Russian Emperor . . . to whom I had sent expressions of devotion and deep respect through numerous embassies."[23] Just like the British in India vis-à-vis princely states, Russian administrators were intensely concerned with succession dynamics in their client states, as engaging local politics in the borderlands was often critical to the imperial advance (Bayly 1996, 89; Gvosdev 2000, 84–85). Through this assertion of devotion, and by referencing his relinquishment of sovereignty over succession to the Russian emperor, Beg Quli performed the role of a loyal noble of the Russian Empire—one meriting the tsar's protection.

After the disaster that befell his emirate in 1877, Beg Quli wrote that he fled to Russian Turkestan, where Governor-General Konstantin von Kaufmann personally received him with great affection and invited him to settle wherever he wished in Turkestan.[24] Von Kaufmann also granted him periodic stipends to cover expenses. In exchange, Kaufmann asked for Beg Quli's help with resolving the "Ghulja question" with China (referring to Russia's occupation of the Yili valley from 1871 to 1881).[25] From the Russian perspective, Beg Quli was so far playing the role of a (temporarily) useful imperial servant.

It was Beg Quli's peregrinations after his settlement outside Tashkent that raised eyebrows. Beg Quli took a train and then a steamship across the Black Sea to Istanbul, where he had several audiences with the Ottoman sultan.[26] More worrisome, from the Russian standpoint, was Beg Quli's interaction with the British ambassador to Istanbul, Lord Dufferin. Beg Quli was well aware that interaction with the British could damage his self-portrayal as a faithful Russian subject, and insisted in his petition that he had "categorically refused" invitations by Dufferin to visit London and have an audience with the queen. Beg Quli similarly declined Dufferin's offer to provide a permanent, luxurious residence in Bombay on the British dime, though Beg Quli conceded that he had no choice but to take British funding for his return trip to Russian Turkestan via Kabul. On his way through Kabul, Beg Quli claimed that the amir of Afghanistan offered him the governorship of the "Four Provinces" *(Chahar Wilayat)* in the northern part of the country bordering Russian Turkestan. Throughout all of these temptations, insisted Beg Quli, he remained faithful to the Russian emperor (RGVIA F 400 O 1 D 2168, ff. 4b–5a).

None of which answered the basic question posed by the Russian officials: What, exactly, could Beg Quli do for the Russian Empire? None of the Persianate tools at Mulla Akmal Tashkandi's disposal were of use to Beg Quli in dealing with the Russians. The Russian governor of Turkestan was not terribly interested in epic Islamicate praise poetry, but Beg Quli had some ability to trade in currencies that were valued in the imperial context. For instance, he presented signed letters from the most famous governor-general of Turkestan, Governor-General von Kaufmann.[27] Just as Beg Quli claimed, the letters evidenced his father's service to the Russian Empire in delimiting an exact border between Kashgar and the Farghana valley. Russian officials in the Turkestan governor-generalship vouched for Beg Quli's loyalty in correspondence with the Supreme Headquarters *(Glavnyi shtab)* of the Russian military, and—more significantly—that he might prove useful in "exerting influence over the native population of Central Asia" (RGVIA F 400 O 1 D 2168, f. 44a).[28]

Whatever Beg Quli's potential to serve the Russian crown, superiors in St. Petersburg were unimpressed—as expressed in the following resolution in 1898: "I do not see sufficient basis in this petition. Beg Quli-Beg never independently ruled a country. He provided no services to the [Russian] Government. . . . During my visit to the Kashgar embassy in 1876, Beg Quli-Beg behaved toward our embassy very suspiciously" (RGVIA F 400 O 1 D 2168, f. 43a). Ultimately, the Russian War Ministry directed the Turkestan governor-generalship to finance Beg Quli's stipend using its own discretionary funds, if he was so important. Those funds appear never to have materialized, leaving the exiled prince from Kashgar out in the cold.[29]

Beg Quli-Beg's more famous father, Ya'qub Beg, was able to offer the Russian Empire the *possibility* that Kashgar might become the next Bukhara: a loyal, semiautonomous buffer state. No amount of training in Persian poetry or Islamic law could change the fact that Beg Quli-Beg had nothing concrete with which to bargain except a keen understanding of Russian imperial discourse (which did indeed sustain him for a time). Like all colonial regimes, the Russian one incorporated on native intermediaries, but Beg Quli was not offering his services as a *munshi* (Persianate secretary): he was performing the role of service aristocracy, and the window for the permanent absorption of Muslim nobility in the Russian Empire had long since closed.[30] There was a place for client states such as Bukhara, Khiva, and—potentially—Kashgar in the Russian Empire, but the empire was not reliant on the services of a native landed gentry.[31]

The divergent careers of Beg Quli-Beg and Mulla Akmal Tashkandi offer insight into the rapidly shifting cultural and political landscapes of the nineteenth century. In the local Taranchi poems of Xinjiang, Beg Quli appears as a pious Islamic ruler, not so different from how Mulla Akmal would have portrayed the ruler of Bukhara in his praise poetry: "If you go to Andijan, say a prayer for Beg Bachcha [i.e., Beg Quli-Beg]; If they ask where his ladies are, say they're in the infidels' hands" (Pantusov 1901, 7). But that skill set was irrelevant from the perspective of the empires colonizing Eurasia. Instead, Beg Quli reimagined himself as a roving cosmopolitan in the age of steam and print.[32] That movement required playing a very different game, one with rules dictated by service to empire and engagement with national-vernacular cultures (though the latter does not factor into the story captured in the Russian archives). Beg Quli met this challenge with some initial success, only to eventually find himself irrelevant in the new imperial dispensation.

Hostages and Political Prisoners

Both Mulla Akmal Tashkandi and Beg Quli-Beg fled adverse circumstances, "pushed" from their homelands against their will. But "pull" mechanisms stood as an equally common catalyst for unwilling dislocation, and with similarly diverging consequences across the gradual dissolution of the Persian cosmopolis. Hostage-taking as a form of governance had deep roots in Eurasia.[33] In the Mongol Empire, for instance, tributary rulers were forced to send hostages to the Mongol imperial court as an insurance policy to ensure loyalty.[34] Before modern governments began disciplining entire populations,[35] the more limited reach of the state focused on controlling specific individuals of interest. The easiest way to monitor a potential rival was to physically move that individual. This practice continued into the colonial period, but with dramatically different implications.

A showdown between Bukhara and Kabul[36] over control of what is now northern Afghanistan (the same aforementioned *Chahar Wilayat* nearly entrusted to Beg Quli-Beg) illustrates the dynamics of hostage exchange. In the wake of Nadir Shah's collapsed empire, during the late eighteenth century this territory was the site of a contest between nascent successor states: the Manghit dynasty of Bukhara to the north of the Oxus, and the Durrani Afghan Empire to the south. In 1789 Timur Shah Durrani marched northward to assert control over the territories surrounding Balkh, which were then semiautonomous, and disputed between Bukhara and Kabul.[37] Bukharan and Afghan chronicles disagree over the outcome of the confrontation. Perhaps not shockingly, Bukharan chronicles insist on a Bukharan victory, and Afghan ones assert the opposite (Fayż Muḥammad Kātib Hazārah 2013, 53; Lee 1996, 94–97). Probably it was something of a draw.

Nevertheless, one Bukharan chronicle reveals an interesting detail: after the ambassador *(elchi)* came and left, the two sides secured a peace. "Then Amir [Shah-Murad of Bukhara] sent one of his own brothers, Fazil Bey, as well as Kichkina Mirza, the daughter of [the former Bukharan ruler] Rahim Khan, into the service [of Timur Shah Durrani] to honor *(ikram)* the monarch."[38] Even if Timur-Shah failed to subdue the Balkh region to his own satisfaction (and that territory would indeed remain quasi-independent through the latter half of the nineteenth century), noble hostages from Bukhara would offer him leverage during moments of ambiguity with regard to sovereignty over that territory. Despite the fact that the quote above comes from a Bukharan chronicle, any reference to Bukhara reciprocally securing Afghan hostages is conspicuously absent. In other words, even though the monarch of Kabul could not decisively integrate the northern territory into his burgeoning state, he did manage to acquire human leverage over his Bukharan rival.

Kabul was merely one of many political formations with which Bukhara dueled across the eighteenth and nineteenth centuries,[39] and hostage-taking was a governance strategy pursued in relation to peer competitors such as Kabul, as well as a tool for integrating semiautonomous principalities of all stripes. Over the course of the nineteenth century, Bukhara won periodic victories over other rivals such as Khoqand and relocated parts of those populations—sometimes entire communities—to Bukhara against their will.[40] The relinquishment of noble hostages to Timur-Shah was actually the second act in a longer confrontation between Bukhara and Kabul over the territories of Khurasan (i.e., what is now northeastern Iran and northwestern Afghanistan). Previously, the Bukharan ruler had forcibly resettled approximately 30,000 people from the formerly Kabul-controlled Marv to Bukhara, and filled those empty houses in Marv with Bukharan subjects.[41]

One more showdown in Khurasan brings together the stories of noble hostages and hostage populations. It seems that Fazil Bey—the brother Shah-Murad had relinquished as collateral to Timur—managed to integrate himself into the shared Persianate courtly culture of Kabul fairly successfully, and in short order. A year or so later, in approximately 1790, Fazil Bey marched from Kabul with an army to threaten Marv. Apparently being handed over to Timur-Shah had eroded his loyalty to Bukhara. Fazil Bey conquered several fortresses in the Marv region, kicked out the governor installed by his brother, and abducted Shah-Murad's daughter.[42] In retaliation, Shah-Murad marched on Marv, defeated his brother, and (presumably) reclaimed his offspring. Then Shah-Murad *once again* dealt with the Marv population by relocating them to Bukhara.[43] Thus, forced relocation of populations was a governance strategy pursued in tandem with hostage-taking and exile of elites. A later chronicler wrote: "Whoever they [the rulers of Bukhara] wish to exile is sent to Marv, where they are imprisoned under surveillance. There are around 500 such elite individuals *(buzurgan)* there right now" (Shams Bukharayi, 128).

While the ultimate fate of the noble hostages Bukhara sent to Kabul is murky, other cases shed further light on the interaction between Perso-Islamic high culture (or its absence) and involuntary movement. At first glance, Abdallah Beg Yakkabaghi enters the historical record as a fairly typical member of the *ulama:* a multitalented scholar renowned in the fin de siècle for his calligraphy in particular. Abdallah Beg's homeland of Yakkabagh was located squarely within the Russian protectorate of Bukhara. Yet only decades earlier Yakkabagh stood as a quasi-autonomous city-state. Conventional wisdom grafts a "three khanates" model onto nineteenth-century Central Asian history before the Russian conquest.[44] Yet far from "three khanates," Eurasia was made up of a tapestry of overlapping city-states, semiautonomous provinces, and aspiring empires (Perdue 2005, xiv).[45]

Yakkabagh was one of those quasi-autonomous city-states, located not far from the more fully autonomous city-state of Shahrisabz (both now located in Uzbekistan) and periodically under its control. Abdallah Beg was twelve years old when the Bukharan ruler Amir Muzaffar (r. 1860–1885) conquered his home city-state of Yakkabagh in the mid-1870s. Ironically, Bukhara's annexation of Yakkabagh was possible only *because* of the Russian conquest, which guaranteed its borders as a protectorate of the Russian Empire and opened up resources for territorial expansion and integration. Abdallah Beg's forebears had ruled over the province as independent monarchs, and Amir Muzaffar could not countenance the competing royal claims of its princes. Following the territory's subjugation, Muzaffar executed Abdallah Beg's older brother and acting ruler of Yakkabagh, Abd al-Rahman Beg, but spared Abdallah Beg for his "youth and beauty."[46] And thus Abdallah Beg moved to Bukhara—involuntarily, as a political prisoner.

Abdallah Beg spent the next ten years languishing in prison, during which time he taught himself the art of calligraphy without the benefit of a formal teacher. Per established custom, Abd al-Ahad Khan freed prisoners who committed minor offenses as a royal boon upon taking the Bukharan throne in 1885—an exoneration that did not include political prisoners.[47] In fact, so great was Abdallah Beg's perceived threat to the Manghit dynasty of Bukhara that his life remained in jeopardy until his demise (ca. 1913). His biographer also remarked that if not for the danger of guilt by association, he would have written an even more detailed work devoted only to the life of Abdallah Beg (Ziya, ff. 72b–74a).

It is remarkable that—even while incarcerated—Abdallah was able to raise his station through Persianate learning. He capitalized on the knowledge base he would have had access to as a young noble in Yakkabagh and continued his education in Bukhara. That Abdallah Beg, much like Mulla Akmal Tashkandi, migrated under duress and across rival polities did not change the fact that a unitary high culture permeated that same territory.

Unusually, Abdallah Beg Yakkabaghi's legacy outlived both his own death (ca. 1913) and the displacement of the Persian cosmopolis. Like many *ulama*, Abdallah Beg passed on his knowledge to numerous students. Unlike the majority of them, however, a few of those students managed to continue their careers at the Mir-i Arab, one of the three madrasas allowed to reopen after

1943 (Tasar 2016). Today, the students of his students' students still remember Abdallah Beg. In an interview, one Uzbek Islamic scholar described the prince-cum-calligrapher as fastidious *(daqiq nazar),* sometimes spending more than two hours shaving the perfect writing instrument. Abdallah Beg is recalled as having turned many prospective students away, accepting only the very best into his study. Incredibly, and despite the profound breach with the past heralded by the Bolshevik Revolution, this particular prince's intellectual *silsila* (chain of transmission) lives on to the present day the students of his students continues to pass on that knowledge to new students.[48]

Yet the continuity over time illustrated by Abdallah Beg's story was far from ordinary. While numerous other princes-in-exile were also able to rehabilitate themselves within the Persianate space, that particular kind of mobility ended with the Bolshevik Revolution in 1920. Abdallah Beg's legacy lives on, against all odds, but that of the majority of his colleagues does not. The scaffolding of their cultural world was systematically dismantled in Soviet Central Asia during the 1930s, and similar processes played out more gradually elsewhere as nationalist governments embarked on modernizing reforms (Khalid 2011).

Nor was this Persianate safety net equally present across space, even contemporaneously with Abdallah Beg. Just as Mulla Akmal's experience contrasts sharply with that of Beg Quli-Beg, who was ultimately cast aside by the new Russian hegemons, the many other Turkic princes who were removed from power and forced into retirement in Russian Turkestan faded into obscurity. Jura Beg was one such Turkic noble originating from circumstances not so different from those of Abdallah Beg, but with a very different conclusion to his story. Jura Beg was one of the last autonomous rulers of the city-state of Shahrisabz, a constant thorn in the side of the rulers of Bukhara. It was not until 1870 that Shahrisabz was decisively brought under Bukharan control—but only as a result of the direct intervention of Russian troops. After Russia militarily subdued Shahrisabz, the imperial administration "returned" Shahrisabz to Bukhara (despite Bukhara never really having controlled it in the first place) (Pickett 2018).

After the fall of his city-state, Jura Beg fled to Khoqand, which by that point was a Russian protectorate just like Bukhara. Fearing Russian retribution, the ruler of Khoqand handed Jura Beg (along with companions and family members) over to Russian custody in Tashkent. Jura Beg was now as much a hostage as Abdallah Beg. Realizing the deposed princeling's capacity to cause trouble, the Russian administration provided Jura Beg with a stipend—very similar to the one Beg Quli-Beg secured for a time (RGIA F 400 O 1 D 352, f. 1a). As a member of the Turkic military elite, Jura Beg enjoyed access to the same Persianate high cultural background as Abdallah Beg Yakkabaghi, but those skills were far less applicable in Russian Turkestan. To make himself useful to the Russian Empire, Jura Beg converted to Christianity[49] and enjoyed some success as a major general in Russian military service—only to be ignominiously killed by bandits in 1906 (Beisembiev 1992, 22). Jura Beg's companions and kin were even less successful in rehabilitating themselves in the Russian imperial context. Ultimately, washed-up Turkic princelings like Jura Beg or Beg Quli-Beg were a nuisance within the colonial context, and little more. They had the potential to cause trouble, but even the highest mastery of Persian poetry or legal reasoning could not elevate an individual to the upper echelons of the Turkestan governor-generalship.

As hostages and exiles, both Mulla Akmal Tashkandi and Abdallah Beg Yakkabaghi moved to a territory where the Persianate safety net was still in place. The protectorate of Bukhara continued to patronize Persian high culture through 1920, and Abdallah Beg's students even managed to improbably find employment in one of the vanishingly rare Soviet contexts where discrete elements of that Persianate skill set were still employable.[50] Beg Quli-Beg and Jura Beg moved under duress for very similar reasons, and both tried their luck in a very different world. Neither princeling was entirely unsuccessful, but the transferability of their skill set and claims to authority was entirely reducible to services they could offer the Russian Empire.

The disparate historical episodes woven together in this chapter have sought to illustrate dynamics of human connectivity across the transition between the high cultural cosmopolis and distinctly modern forms of social-political organization. Before the twentieth century, educated individuals trained in the same Persian poetry, read from similar Islamic legal manuals, and formed worldviews based on a common corpus of morality literature *(akhlaq)* whether they were trained in Bukhara, Kashgar, or Delhi.[51] This cohesion meant that when rulers moved educated elites by force—an all too frequent strategy of governance—their skills and knowledge forms were legible in their new environment. Historiography has tended to focus on travel literature produced by roving cosmopolitans. What is missed, or at least underemphasized, is that movement over large distances was an undertaking frequently precipitated by the threat of violence. Premodern states lacked the means to discipline entire populations, but they did take a keen interest in specific individuals—and sometimes targeted communities as well.

As recent scholarship has stressed, colonial empires precipitated intensified connectivity through new technologies such as the steamship and printing press. However, I have argued that this trans-imperial cosmopolitan*ism* was something quite different from Sheldon Pollock's premodern cosmopolis: individuals moving *between* empires and emergent national cultures, rather than *within* a single high cultural cosmopolis. This meant that as the nineteenth century wore on, adversity might push exiles and refugees into new imperial contexts where their high cultural skill set was no longer fully applicable. Despite moving for similar reasons in similar geographical circumstances and at roughly the same time, Mulla Akmal Tashkandi and Beg Quli-Beg met dramatically different fates as the former migrated within the Persian cosmopolis and the latter moved into the imperial space. The same went for Abdallah Beg Yakkabaghi and Jura Beg, respectively.

The emphasis in the preceding analysis has focused on the "why" of mobility in Persianate Asia—especially the involuntary variety. Yet it is also worth lingering a moment on the "where" angle. This has not been a study of "Central Asia" as an area studies unit coterminous with the Soviet Socialist Republics of Uzbekistan, Tajikistan, Turkmenistan, Kyrgyzstan, and Kazakhstan. Mulla Akmal Tashkandi moved between what is now thought of as Chinese Central Asia and post-Soviet Central Asia, but for him those distinctions meant nothing at all. Beg Quli-Beg traveled much more broadly still throughout Asia, from Xinjiang to Russian Turkestan to the Ottoman Empire and Afghanistan—yet without the same ease of relocation as Mulla Akmal, and despite all of those spaces falling squarely within the Persianate ecumene. Fazil Bey was sent as a hostage from Bukhara to the Afghan capital of Kabul, thus moving from Central Asia to a territory now just as often categorized as "South" Asia. Yet he was quickly integrated into the same Turko-Persian nobility, to the extent that he eventually found his way northward again with an army mustered in Kabul.

As Nile Green has pointed out, "Geographical models are analytical categories designed to enable the tracing of commonality or connectivity. And like other analytical categories, geographical ones deserve no special treatment once they have outlived their usefulness" (2014, 556). The area studies categories that divide up Asia explain little with regard to the widely varying outcomes of the case studies in question. However, cultural logics organic to the time and place in question provide a means of thinking about *why* and *how* different individuals were differently mobile, and with what outcome. Trains and steamships collapsed distances that had previously been insurmountable for most, but cultural dynamics were changing just as rapidly. When upheavals thrust individuals into motion against their will, seemingly diversionary competencies such as poetry and theoretical jurisprudence determined who landed on their feet and who was marginalized. The same forces that facilitated new kinds of connectivity rendered the old ones irrelevant, and that paradigmatic transformation was all too real for cultured itinerants such as those considered in this chapter.

Notes

My sincere gratitude to Jeff Eden and Patryk Reid, as well as the other members of the Asia Inside Out working group, for constructive feedback. This chapter follows the *International Journal of Middle East Studies* conventions for transliterating Persian and Arabic. For the sake of readability, I have opted for a full diacritical apparatus in the notes, but not in the body text.

1. This model has been most actively theorized in the context of Sanskrit, but it is equally applicable to the case of Persian (Pollock 2006; Beecroft 2015). I use "Persianate," "Perso-Islamic," and "Persian cosmopolis" interchangeably and inherently inclusive of Islam (rather than a secular overlay on the Islamic). The region in which this cultural complex was historically dominant has also been referred to as "Turko-Persia" (Canfield 1991).

2. Recent literature on Persianate high culture has emphasized continuities into the twentieth century, thereby complicating the narrative of rupture posited in this chapter (Kia and Marashi 2016). Although I certainly agree that it is important and interesting to examine the legacy and afterlife of the Persian cosmopolis (Pickett 2015b), it no longer exists as an integrated whole (Messick 2016, 30). For instance, contrast the account of Islamic practices in China sponsored by Arab states in Biao Xiang's chapter with the picture offered in this one: despite the overlap in territory considered, the two are worlds apart.

3. This stands in contrast also to Tamara Loos's account of Prisdang Chumsai, who was directly reacting to imperial and national notions of belonging; the Persian cosmopolis was something performed and enacted by the *ulama,* rather than an imagined community.

4. As Paolo Sartori has argued, the emphasis on long-distance journeys in the literature has occasionally overshadowed the far more intensive, short-range connections

(2016, 134–135). Even during the heyday of the celebrated Silk Road, most merchants moved only a few hundred miles at a time (Hansen 2017, 9; Christian 2000).

5. Jeff Eden (2017) has recently examined slavery in Central Eurasia, an equally important kind of involuntary migration not covered in this chapter.

6. The fact that enemies were ready and waiting for him when Mulla Akmal returned to Tashkent stands as circumstantial evidence favoring the possibility that he left Tashkent against his will—see below.

7. The Russian administration of Turkestan officially followed a hands-off *(ignorirovanie)* approach to Islam, but in fact eliminated key positions such as the censor *(muḥtasib)* and chief judge *(qāżī-yi kalān)* (Morrison 2008, 56).

8. Yaʿqūb Beg portrayed himself as a defender of Islam against the infidel Chinese, and so positions such as that of *qāżī* were taken quite seriously in his domain (Millward 2007, 121).

9. Like most biographical dictionaries, the source detailing Mullā Akmal's biography selected for luminaries worthy of emulation and is therefore highly partisan in his favor: "Because of the enmity of the envious *(ʿadāwat-i ḥāsidān)* . . . and attacks by his adversaries who lacked manhood / generosity *(muruwwat),* he emigrated *(hijrat)* to Bukhara." As part of this justification, Mullā Akmal's biographer inserted a hadith to the effect that it is permissible to flee from those who do not accept the Sunnah of the Prophet *(al-firār mimmā lā yuṭāq min sunan al-mursalīn),* thereby likening Mullā Akmal's flight to that of Muḥammad from Mecca to Medina. The hadith is not accepted as "sound" by many Islamic scholars, because the tradition implies that the Prophet fled in the face of adversity (al-Qārī, 318).

10. The Indian princely state of Arcot stands as a parallel example of a late Persianate efflorescence (Schwartz 2016).

11. Specifically, he wrote *qaṣīdas* in the style of Shaykh ibn al-Fāriż, a thirteenth-century Arab poet who wrote mystical verse, and Persian *qaṣīdas* in the *nūniyya* style (i.e., ending each verse with the "n" sound) (Sharʿī, 61b).

12. "Permanent royal retinue": *zumra-i mustaqīmān-i rikāb-i ʿālī* (Sharʿī, 61b–62a).

13. The nature of those meetings and discussions *(majālis-i munāẓarāt wa maḥāfil-i mukālamāt)* is left vague (Sharʿī, 61b–62a).

14. It is worth noting that the province of Shahrisabz had only just been integrated into Bukhara around a decade before Mullā Akmal visited it. Previously, it had been an independent, rival city-state at constant loggerheads with Bukhara. The amir faced powerful, locally entrenched forces hostile to Bukharan rule (Pickett, 2018).

15. Mounia Chekhab-Abudaya's chapter in this volume discusses the manuscript evidence of pilgrimages spanning the Islamic world.

16. Of course, the specific array of skills and knowledge forms was not identical across the entire territory understood as "Persianate" or the "Persian cosmopolis" (terms that are here used interchangeably). For instance, Iranian *ulama* mastered the

same Persian poetry as scholars of Bukhara, but jurisprudence from an entirely separate school of law (Pickett 2015a, chap. 3).

17. Muslim elite were quick to embrace and capitalize on the new technologies available in the nineteenth century (Gelvin and Green 2014, 2, 12, passim). These processes have been documented in the voluminous "nationalism" literature (Khalid 1998; Brophy 2016). As Sheldon Pollock argues, the nationalization of culture was productive for the modern nation-state but inherently destructive for the cosmopolis (2006, 17).

18. Tamara Loos's chapter offers a vivid example of this kind of cosmopolitan mobility as well. Although just as interesting in its own right, I argue that the emergent cosmopolitan*ism* of the nineteenth and twentieth centuries is a fundamentally distinct phenomenon. Literature on cosmopolitan*ism* conflates studies of cosmopolitanism as a philosophical position (*a la* Kant, and as counterposed to currents of Romantic nationalism) with examinations of deracinated communities of elite actors moving *between* discrete empires and states (Pollock et al. 2000; Hanley 2008).

19. It is worth noting that a danger of the "Persian" cosmopolis paradigm is that, semantically, it would seem to privilege specifically Persian cultural elements over the Arabic or Islamic or Turkic (Ahmed 2015, 84). Such is certainly not my intent; the terminological challenge is capturing the dynamics of pre-national culture, in which (for instance) Turkic poetry might be considered both Persianate and Islamic as a vernacular (in Pollock's usage of the term) of those registers.

20. Beg Quli's siblings were less fortunate and ended up as Qing prisoners. Eric Schluessel quotes Liu Jintang from the First Historical Archive in Beijing in an unpublished research note: "In the winter of 1877, when we purged the Muslim borderland, we captured four of the children of the deceased Andijani leader Yaʿqūb Beg's son Yin-shang Hu-li, including Man-di Hu-li. We also captured two of his grandsons, Ai-san and Ākhūnd, and two of his granddaughters, as well as four of the criminal's wives. Each has been imprisoned." While it is difficult to say what became of them after that, Schluessel further concludes that "Yaʿqūb Beg's grandchildren were to be sent to the northern forests and mountains of Heilongjiang, where garrisons watched the Russian border along the Amur River."

21. "Taranchi" refers to Turkic-speaking farmers who were relocated to the Ili valley and eventually absorbed by the Uyghur national project (Brophy 2005).

22. My gratitude to Eric Schluessel for bringing this source to my attention and translating from Taranchi.

23. Beg Quli also mentioned several Russian explorers, such as Nikolay Przhevalsky, whom he had received with respect and hospitality (RGVIA F 400 O 1 D 2168, f. 43b).

24. Beg Quli elected to settle in Pskent, a town not far from Tashkent.

25. Beg Quli clarified, however, that in the end the matter was resolved without need of his services (RGVIA F 400 O 1 D 2168, ff. 3a–3b). James Millward has examined the diplomatic ramifications of these negotiations (2007, 133–139).

26. The sultan treated him as a VIP, designating a fifteen-man armed contingent to guard Beg Quli at all times, and granting him residence in a palace (RGVIA F 400 O 1 D 2168, f. 3b).

27. These original letters (bearing a red wax seal) from Kaufmann to Yaʿqūb Beg survive in the Russian archive: RGVIA F 400 O 1 D 2168, ff. 6a–10b. Kaufmann addresses Yaʿqūb Beg by his epithet *badaulet / ba-dawlat* (by good fortune), as does the aforementioned Taranchi poem (Pantusov 1901, 7).

28. Here one is reminded of Leo Tolstoy's novel *Hadji Murad,* in which the titular character was careful to always carry documentary evidence of his correspondence with Russian military officials to prove his usefulness to the empire in a pinch. Leo Tolstoy, *Hadji Murad* (New York: Modern Library, 2003), chap. 8.

29. The file concludes simply noting that the War Ministry refused to provide the requested sum, and that local discretionary funds in the Turkestan budget were "unavailable." It's not impossible that the Turkestan governor-generalship eventually managed to cough up the money, but as far as these sources reveal, that was the end of Beg Quli's status as a Russian pensioner (RGVIA F 400 O 1 D 2168, f. 52a).

30. In the sixteenth and early seventeenth centuries, an expanding Russian Empire had been willing to absorb Muslim Tatar nobility (who, after all, shared a memory of integration under the Golden Horde with the Rus) into the imperial framework. By the nineteenth century, however, whatever commensurability had existed previously dissipated (Crews 2006).

31. This is in marked contrast to the British Empire, which "was able to create aristocratic elites out of much less promising material than the Beks and Amlakdars the Russians had to work with" (Morrison 2008, 119).

32. Beg Quli would have had much in common with other trans-imperial, globetrotting intellectuals (Alavi 2015; Green 2015), a number of whom are depicted in Seema Alavi's and Tamara Loos's respective chapters.

33. Ancient sources are rife with references to hostage-taking as a strategy for political control (Frye 1983, 147–148).

34. The mortal threat to hostages at the Mongol court incentivized the obedience of vassalized rulers; and, after being indoctrinated into Mongol imperial culture, those same hostages served as potential replacement vassals (Allsen 1987, 74). Tamerlane employed the same strategy (Manz 1989, 94).

35. Michel Foucault (1991) traced the shift from a ruler's emphasis on managing the household to managing the population at large. Some scholars have argued for the emergence of a (early modern?) fiscal military apparatus before the onset of colonialism (Stein 1985). Despite debate over the *extent* to which modern colonial regimes of governance differed from what preceded them, at the very least, modern technologies of governance (e.g., the census, prison regimes, etc.) amounted to "subject-constituting" regimes entirely different in scale, if not kind, from that which preceded them (Scott 2005, 28).

36. Although the term "Afghanistan" was in use by this period, Kabul did not yet control all of the territory associated with that term; Kabul didn't successfully consolidate control over the territory until the reign of ʿAbd al-Raḥmān Khān (r. 1880–1901). Therefore, I refer to Timur Shah's emirate as "Kabul" in this context to safeguard against the seeming inevitability of the state's current boundaries.

37. This maneuver was part of a continued rivalry between Bukhara and Kabul (not to mention Qajar Iran) over territories now situated in northern and eastern Afghanistan, which is further discussed in the next section of this chapter (Lee 1996).

38. *Dar miyāna īlchī āmad ū raft karda, āshtī namūdand. Amīr yak barādar-i khūd-rā kih Fāżil Bey būd, wa Kīchkinna Mīrzā kih dukhtar-zāda-i Muḥammad Raḥīm Khān būd, har dū-rā barāyi ikrām-i shāh ba-khiẕmat-i ū firistād* (Yaʿqūb Bukhārī, f. 7a).

39. This period of fractious city-state following the collapse of Nadir Shah's short-lived empire in 1747 might be characterized as Eurasia's "even longer" nineteenth century (Pickett 2016).

40. Forced resettlement of peasants and other nonelites merits further study. Although frequently mentioned in passing, most sources do not shed much light on what these resettlements must have meant for the victims. One chronicle hints at the trauma, describing the sobbing and wailing of residents of the city of Khoqand who were forced from their homes during the Bukharan occupation of 1842 (ʿAważ Muḥammad, f. 231b).

41. In sources friendly to the Afghan side, this episode is described fairly matter-of-factly (Chishtī, f. 62a). In Bukharan sources, which also cite the figure of 30,000 (Yaʿqūb-i Bukhārī, f. 6b), the population transfer is characterized as a pious religious act of the Sunni ruler Bukhara against the Shi'a population in Marv, with forced conversion as the primary goal: *Bi-sabab-i saʿī-yi ū [i.e. Shāh-Murād] hama Muslimān shudand* (Yaʿqūb-i Bukhārī, f. 6b; Saʿādatallah, ff. 55a–55b). However, such population transfers were a tried-and-true form of governance, and the ascribed sectarian motivations probably have more to do with religious politics at the time the sources were written (McChesney 1996; Pickett 2016, 495–497) than Shāh-Murād's actual motivations at the time. After all, in 1806, when Qajar Iran briefly conquered the city, Fath Ali Shah Qajar's son Baba Khan (leader of the campaign) employed exactly the same measures, relocating what was left of Marv's population to Mashhad (Munis 1988, 327) (Yaʿqūb-i Bukhārī, f. 12b). Just as the Safavid monarch relocated the Armenian merchants of Julfa (Aslanian 2011), or the Junghars relocated the aforementioned Taranchis to the Ili Valley (Brophy 2016, 30), Shāh-Murād shifted loyal populations into unruly territories and vice versa.

42. The text mentions only that Fāżil Bey captured Shāh-Murād's daughter *(ʿājiza)*. Perhaps the daughter was married to the defeated governor.

43. This after laying siege and cutting off the water supply *(khushk karda)*. In this instance the text does not mention the exact number of people resettled, but seems to imply that it was most of the remaining population of Marv: *Marw-rā khushk karda mardum-i ān-rā kūchānīda bi-Bukhāra award* (Yaʿqūbi-i Bukhārī, f. 7a).

44. The notion is that before the Russian conquest, the political makeup of Central Asia was characterized by three discrete "khanates": Khoqand, Khiva, and Bukhara, all of which were conveniently adopted as protectorates after the Russian conquests of the 1860s–1880s. However, this model must be revised in favor of a more complex understanding of sovereignty and authority during the precolonial period (Pickett 2018).

45. Similar observations can be made about the Ottoman Empire and even early modern Europe—during the alleged rise of "absolute monarchy" (Kołodziejczyk 2013; Oresko, Gibbs, and Scott 1997).

46. The romantic allure of young men is an omnipresent theme in Persianate literature (Andrews and Kalpakli 2005; Najmabadi 2005).

47. Ṣadr Żiyā' lamented that many of these criminals were in fact not so harmless and that their exile in Chārjūy turned the town into a hive of scum and villainy (Żiyā', f. 73a).

48. Interview conducted by the author on 10 August 2014 in Bukhara, Uzbekistan. The scholar in question prefers to remain anonymous.

49. Conversion as a strategy of imperial integration was quite rare in Russian Turkestan, which was closed to missionaries, but more common in the directly ruled parts of the empire (Werth 2000; Kefeli 2014).

50. Again, although the Persian cosmopolis *as a synthetic whole* was displaced, its constituent parts did not disappear. Rather, they were objectified and repurposed for nationalist and modernizing projects of various stripes—from India to the Soviet Union to Iran itself (Jabbari 2016; Pickett 2015b).

51. A perfect illustration of this point is encapsulated in the encyclopedic work *Jawāhir al-ʿulūm-i humāyūnī* by Muḥammad Fāżil ibn ʿAlī ibn Muḥammad al-Miskīnī al-Qāżī al-Samarqandī (ms. Khuda Bakhsh Oriental Public Library [Patna, India] no. 884), an Islamic scholar from Central Asia who relocated to the sixteenth-century Mughal court. Though he was trained a thousand miles away, Muḥammad Fāżil's effort to encapsulate all knowledge in a single work was perfectly transferable to the Indian context.

References

Primary Sources

ʿAlī ibn Muḥammad and Nūr al-Dīn al-Mullā al-Harawī al-Qārī. 2010. *Al-Asrār al-Marfūʿa fī al-Akhbār al-Mawḍūʿa al-Maʿrūf bil-Mawḍūʿāt al-Kubrā.* Beirut, Dār al-'Amāna.

Fayż Muḥammad Kātib Hazārah. 2013. *The History of Afghanistan: Fayż Muḥammad Kātib Hazārah's Sirāj Al-Tawārīkh.* Edited by Robert D. McChesney and M. M. Khorrami. Translated by Robert D. McChesney. 6 vols. Leiden: Brill.

Ḥājjī ʿAbd al-ʿAẕīm Sharʿī. *Taẕkirat al-Shuʿarā-i ʿAbd al-ʿAẕīm Sharʿī.* Ms. Institut Vostokovedeniia imeni Abu Raikhana Beruni Akademii Nauk Respubliki Uzbekistana, 3396 / III.

Imām Ḥusaynī Chishtī. *Ḥusayn Shāhī.* Ms. Khuda Bakhsh Oriental Public Library (Patna, India), no. 530.

Mīr Saʿādatallah. *Lutf-i Buzūrg.* Ms. Sankt-Peterburgskii Filial Instituta Vostokovedenii, Rossiiskoi Akademii Nauk: Institut Vostochnykh Rukopisei, B 1932.

Muḥammad Fāżil ibn ʿAlī ibn Muḥammad al-Miskīnī al-Qāżī al-Samarqandī. *Jawāhir al-ʿUlūm-i Humāyūnī.* Ms. Khuda Bakhsh Oriental Public Library [Patna, India], no. 884.

Muḥammad Yaʿqūb Bukhārī. *Risāla-i Muḥammad Yaʿqūb-i Bukhārī.* Ms. Institut Vostokovedeniia imeni Abu Raikhana Beruni Akademii Nauk Respubliki Uzbekistana, 1934.

Mullā Ḥājjī ʿAważ Muḥammad. *Tuḥfat al-Tawārīkh-i Khānī.* Ms. Sankt-Peterburgskii Filial Instituta Vostokovedenii, Rossiiskoi Akademii Nauk: Institut Vostochnykh Rukopisei, C 440.

Munis, Shir Muhammad Mirab. 1988. *Firdaws al-Iqbāl: History of Khorezm.* Translated by Yuri Bregel. Leiden: Brill.

Pantusov, N. N. 1901. *Materialy k izucheniiu narechiia Taranchei Iliiskago Okruga.* Kazan: Tipo-litografiia Imperatorskago Universiteta.

"Po khodataistvu byvshego kashgarskogo pravitelia Bek Kuli Beka o vydache emu posobiia." Rossisskiyi Gosudarstvennyi Voennyi Istoricheskii Arkhiv (RGVIA): F 400 O 1 F 2168.

"Po khodataistvu Turkestanskogo General Gubernatora o vydache soderzhanii byvshim srednaziatskim bekam Dzhurabeku, Baba beku, Abdugafar beku, Seid Bek i Shadi Beku" (1874). Rossisskyi Gosudarstvennyi Istoricheskii Arkhiv (RGIA): F 400 O 1 D 352; F 400 O 1 D 2168.

Shams Bukhārāyī. 1998. *Tārīkh-i Bukhārā, Khūqand va Kāshghar,* ed. Muḥammad Akbar 'Ashīq. Tehran: Āyinah-ʾi Mīrāṣ.

Sharīf Jān Makhdūm Ṣadr Żiyāʾ. *Taẕkirat al-Khaṭṭāṭīn-i Mīrzā Muḥammad Sharīf al-Mutakhalliṣ bil-Żiyāʾ.* Ms. Institut Vostokovedeniia imeni Abu Raikhana Beruni Akademii Nauk Respubliki Uzbekistana, 1304 / III.

Secondary Works

Ahmed, Shahab. 2015. *What Is Islam? The Importance of Being Islamic.* Princeton, NJ: Princeton University Press.

Alam, Muzaffar, and Sanjay Subrahmanyam. 2007. *Indo-Persian Travels in the Age of Discoveries, 1400–1800.* Cambridge: Cambridge University Press.

Alavi, Seema. 2015. *Muslim Cosmopolitanism in the Age of Empire.* Cambridge, MA: Harvard University Press.

Allsen, Thomas. 1987. *Mongol Imperialism: The Policies of the Grand Qan Möngke in China, Russia, and the Islamic Lands, 1251–1259*. Berkeley: University of California Press.

Andrews, Walter, and Mehmet Kalpakli. 2005. *The Age of Beloveds: Love and the Beloved in Early-Modern Ottoman and European Society and Culture*. Durham, NC: Duke University Press.

Aslanian, Sebouh David. 2011. *From the Indian Ocean to the Mediterranean: The Global Trade Networks of Armenian Merchants from New Julfa*. Berkeley: University of California Press.

Bayly, C. A. 1996. *Empire and Information: Intelligence Gathering and Social Communication in India, 1780–1870*. Cambridge: Cambridge University Press.

Beecroft, Alexander. 2015. *An Ecology of World Literature: From Antiquity to the Present Day*. New York: Verso.

Beisembiev, T. K. 1992. "Unknown Dynasty: The Rulers of Shahrisabz in the 18th and 19th Centuries." *Journal of Central Asia* 15(1): 20–22.

Brophy, David. 2005. "Taranchis, Kashgaris, and the 'Uyghur Question' in Soviet Central Asia." *Inner Asia* 7(2): 163–184.

———. 2016. *Uyghur Nation: Reform and Revolution on the Russia-China Frontier*. Cambridge, MA: Harvard University Press.

Brower, Daniel R. 1996. "Russian Roads to Mecca: Religious Tolerance and Muslim Pilgrimage in the Russian Empire." *Slavic Review* 53(3): 567–584.

Can, Lale. 2014. "Connecting People: A Central Asian Sufi Network in Turn-of-the-Century Istanbul." In *Sites of Asian Interaction: Ideas, Networks and Mobility*, edited by Tim Harper and Sunil Amrith, 144–170. Cambridge: Cambridge University Press.

Canfield, Robert L. 1991. "Introduction: The Turko-Persian Tradition." In *Turko-Persia in Historical Perspective*, edited by Robert L. Canfield, 1–34. Cambridge: Cambridge University Press.

Christian, David. 2000. "Silk Roads or Steppe Roads? The Silk Roads in World History." In *Realms of the Silk Roads: Ancient and Modern*, edited by David Christian and Craig Benjamin, 67–94. Silk Roads Studies, IV. Turnhout, Belgium: Brepolis . . .

Crews, Robert D. 2006. *For Prophet and Tsar: Islam and Empire in Russia and Central Asia*. Cambridge, MA: Harvard University Press.

Eden, Jeff. 2017. "Beyond the Bazaars: Geographies of the Slave Trade in Central Asia." *Modern Asian Studies*: 1–37.

Foucault, Michel. 1991. "Governmentality." In *The Foucault Effect: Studies in Governmentality*, edited by Graham Burchell, Colin Gordon, and Peter Miller, translated by Rosi Braidotti and Colin Gordon, 87–104. Chicago: University of Chicago Press.

Frye, Richard N. 1983. "The Political History of Iran under the Sasanians." In *The Cambridge History of Iran: The Seleucid, Parthian and Sasanian Periods*, edited by Ehsan Yarshater, 116–180. Cambridge: Cambridge University Press.

Gelvin, James, and Nile Green. 2014. *Global Muslims in the Age of Steam and Print.* Berkeley: University of California Press.

Green, Nile. 2014. "Rethinking the 'Middle East' after the Oceanic Turn." *Comparative Studies of South Asia, Africa and the Middle East* 34(3): 556–564.

———. 2015. *Terrains of Exchange: Religious Economies of Global Islam.* Oxford: Oxford University Press.

Gvosdev, Nikolas K. 2000. *Imperial Policies and Perspectives towards Georgia, 1760–1819.* Gordonsville: Palgrave Macmillan.

Hanley, Will. 2008. "Grieving Cosmopolitanism in Middle East Studies." *History Compass* 6(5): 1346–1367.

Hansen, Valerie. 2017. *The Silk Road: A New History with Documents.* New York: Oxford University Press.

Jabbari, Alexander. 2016. "The Making of Modernity in Persianate Literary History." *Comparative Studies of South Asia, Africa and the Middle East* 36(3): 418–434.

Kefeli, Agnès Nilüfer. 2014. *Becoming Muslim in Imperial Russia: Conversion, Apostasy, and Literacy.* Ithaca, NY: Cornell University Press.

Khalid, Adeeb. 1998. *The Politics of Muslim Cultural Reform: Jadidism in Central Asia.* Berkeley: University of California Press.

———. 2011. "Central Asia between the Ottoman and the Soviet Worlds." *Kritika: Explorations in Russian and Eurasian History* 12(2): 451–476.

Kia, Mana, and Afshin Marashi. 2016. "Introduction: After the Persianate." *Comparative Studies of South Asia, Africa and the Middle East* 36(3): 379–383.

Kim, Ho-dong. 2004. *Holy War in China: The Muslim Rebellion and State in Chinese Central Asia.* Stanford, CA: Stanford University Press.

Kołodziejczyk, Dariusz. 2013. "What Is Inside and What Is Outside? Tributary States in Ottoman Politics." In *The European Tributary States of the Ottoman Empire in the Sixteenth and Seventeenth Centuries,* edited by Gábor Kármán and Lovro Kuncevic, 421–432. The Ottoman Empire and Its Heritage, v. 53. Leiden: Brill.

Lee, Jonathan L. 1996. *The "Ancient Supremacy": Bukhara, Afghanistan and the Battle for Balkh, 1731–1901.* Leiden: Brill Academic Publishers.

Manz, Beatrice Forbes. 1989. *The Rise and Rule of Tamerlane.* Cambridge Studies in Islamic Civilization. Cambridge: Cambridge University Press.

McChesney, Robert D. 1996. "'Barrier of Heterodoxy'?: Rethinking the Ties between Iran and Central Asia in the 17th Century." *Pembroke Papers* 4: 231–267.

Messick, Brinkley Morris. 2016. "Islamic Texts: The Anthropologist as Reader." In *Islamic Studies in the Twenty-First Century,* edited by L. Buskens and A. van Sandwijk, 29–46. Amsterdam: Amsterdam University Press.

Millward, James A. 2007. *Eurasian Crossroads: A History of Xinjiang.* New York: Columbia University Press.

Morrison, Alexander. 2008. *Russian Rule in Samarkand, 1868–1910: A Comparison with British India.* Oxford: Oxford University Press.

Najmabadi, Afsaneh. 2005. *Women with Mustaches and Men without Beards: Gender and Sexual Anxieties of Iranian Modernity.* Berkeley: University of California Press.

Oresko, Robert, G. C. Gibbs, and H. M. Scott, eds. 1997. "Introduction." In *Royal and Republican Sovereignty in Early Modern Europe: Essays in Memory of Ragnhild Hatton,* 1–42. New York: Cambridge University Press.

Perdue, Peter. 2005. *China Marches West: The Qing Conquest of Central Eurasia.* Cambridge, MA: Belknap Press of Harvard University Press.

Pickett, James. 2018. "Written into Submission: Reassessing Sovereignty through a Forgotten Eurasian Dynasty." *The American Historical Review* 123(3): 817–845.

———. 2015a. "The Persianate Sphere during the Age of Empires: Islamic Scholars and Networks of Exchange in Central Asia, 1747–1917." PhD diss., Princeton University.

———. 2015b. "Soviet Civilization through a Persian Lens: Iranian Intellectuals, Cultural Diplomacy and Socialist Modernity, 1941–55." *Iranian Studies* 48(5): 805–826.

———. 2016. "Nadir Shah's Peculiar Central Asian Legacy: Empire, Conversion Narratives, and the Rise of New Scholarly Dynasties." *International Journal of Middle East Studies,* no. 48 (July): 491–510.

Pollock, Sheldon. 2006. *The Language of the Gods in the World of Men: Sanskrit, Culture, and Power in Premodern India.* Berkeley: University of California Press.

Pollock, Sheldon, Homi K. Bhabha, Carol Breckenridge, and Dipesh Chakrabarty. 2000. "Cosmopolitanisms." *Public Culture* 12(3): 577–589.

Sartori, Paolo. 2016. "Introduction: On Khvārazmian Connectivity: Two or Three Things That I Know about It." *Journal of Persianate Studies* 9(2): 133–157.

Schluessel, Eric. "The Fate of Yaʿqūb Beg's Family." Unpublished research note.

Schwartz, Kevin L. 2016. "The Curious Case of Carnatic: The Last Nawab of Arcot (D. 1855) and Persian Literary Culture." *Indian Economic and Social History Review* 53(4): 533–560.

Scott, David. 2005. "Colonial Governmentality." In *Anthropologies of Modernity: Foucault, Governmentality, and Life Politics,* edited by Jonathan Xavier Inda, 23–49. Malden, MA: Blackwell.

Stein, Burton. 1985. "State Formation and Economy Reconsidered: Part One." *Modern Asian Studies* 19(3): 387–413.

Tasar, Eren. 2016. "The Official Madrasas of Soviet Uzbekistan." *Journal of the Economic and Social History of the Orient* 59(1–2): 265–302.

Werth, Paul W. 2000. "From 'Pagan' Muslims to 'Baptized' Communists: Religious Conversion and Ethnic Particularity in Russia's Eastern Provinces." *Comparative Studies in Society and History* 42(3): 497–523.

9

Deploying Theravada Buddhist Geographies in the Age of Imperialism

TAMARA LOOS

Thailand is not the first country that comes to mind when one imagines themes central to the *Asia Inside Out* project—the "connected places," "changing times," or "mobile peoples" that have helped reveal a revised and renewed understanding of Asia. If it is remembered for anything at all, Thailand is known for having been the sole country in Southeast Asia that avoided colonization by European imperial powers. In fact, scholarship on Thailand plays up this very distinctiveness such that the nation often is seen as exceptional rather than representative of or comparable to other places (see Anderson 1978). Even scholars who are critical of the royal nationalist narrative tend to reify the nation when we compare Thailand with other colonized or imperial powers. More often than not, the comparisons serve to reinforce a conservative strain of national history rather than to integrate the location or its peoples into a broader historical narrative, whether that is based on geographic, environmental, religious, imperial, commercial, or other transnational themes. This trend has disconnected much of the history of Thailand (Siam) from regional, transnational, and imperial histories, which, for better or ill, linked colonies to metropoles through trade, surveillance, and other imperial technologies.

Yet Siam, at the edge of multiple European empires whose flags stabbed the lands east, west, and south of it, offered imperial and colonial subjects alike an anchoring refuge amid the vertiginous transformation known as colonial modernity: Buddhism. By the late nineteenth century, a trickle of Western men came to British colonial Asia to be ordained as Buddhist monks, while Asian political elites headed west for educational "enlightenment." Individuals such as Colonel Henry Steele Olcott (American Theosophist), Aleister Crowley (English occultist), Reginald Farrer (English Buddhist), U Dhammaloka (Irish Buddhist), and others came to Buddhist Asia to escape various forms of perceived repression at home and to explore non-Christian forms of spiritual emancipation abroad. Simultaneously, elite men born in colonial Asia sought emancipation of a more political and educational sort in European metropoles. They often returned to Asia to begin spiritual-political movements. They include individuals such as Ceylon's Anagarika Dharmapala (1864–1933), who revived Sinhala pride in Buddhism in the face of several hundred years of colonial domination and Christian missionizing (Kemper 2015, 3), and Ananda Coomaraswamy (1877–1947), born to a Ceylonese father and an English mother, who also studied the "ancient cultures" of the East as a form of critique of the modern West (Lipsey 1977, xiii).

Siam's Prisdang Chumsai numbers among these bilingual educated elite men who were political, spiritual, and educational activists in their local communities and abroad. Like Alavi's (this volume) enterprising Omani princes living at the interstices of empire and Pickett's (this volume) pious Islamic rulers in Eurasia, Prince Prisdang found opportunity for advancement under imperial auspices that he may not otherwise have been offered given his position as a lower-ranking prince. Educated in London at the Siamese monarch's expense, he became indispensable to Siam's foreign affairs in the late 1800s. But once he fell out of favor with the king and ruling elites, Prisdang fled Siam in a form of involuntary exile. Education, fluency in English, and royal status made Prisdang a cosmopolitan who felt relatively at home in Europe, but poverty and religion shaped his decision to live as a monk in a Buddhist country: British Ceylon, or Lanka as the Siamese called it.

Long-standing linkages between Siam (and Ayutthaya before it) and Lanka reveal themselves in monastic histories, shared sect lineages, Buddhist pilgrimages, and monastic disputes. Prisdang drew on this shared history to unify Buddhist brethren across Theravada Asia in a way that defied national histories. A brilliant and ambitious man, he energized a transnational Buddhist movement. His Buddhist activism constructed an "Asia" based on a combination of extensive Buddhist, Theosophist, and imperial networks that he mobilized against imperialism, Christianity, and the alleged superiority of Western civilizational norms grounded in social Darwinism. Many from Asia and the Western world considered this heady mix of Buddhist-led spiritualism as the one way in which Asia could claim superiority over the imperial West (Snodgrass 2003, 2009). Prisdang's Buddhist world was governed by norms distinct from and critical of notions of Western civilization. He sought to unify Buddhists under the sole remaining sovereign Buddhist king of Siam, who would rule like a pope over Theravada Asia, and who alone was worthy of distributing the sacred relics of the Buddha to the geobody of Buddhist countries—Burma, Ceylon, Cambodia—regardless of their rule by colonial, non-Buddhist imperial overlords. He did not rely exclusively on long-standing networks among Theravada monarchical states, but summoned several different networks including foreign diplomatic, Theosophist, and transnational royal circles to support his cause.

Thai National History and Prisdang

Prince Prisdang's birth in 1852 and death in 1935 encompass a period in which all territories in Southeast Asia except Siam were formally colonized. His fame in Thai history stems from a couple of "firsts" he accomplished. He was the first royal family member to graduate from a foreign university when he collected his certificate in civil engineering in 1876 from King's College London. Fluency in English and cultural competence in elite European society translated into a position as Siam's first national representative in a dozen European metropoles. As such, Prisdang stood at the center of the most important imperial maelstroms confronting Siam's leadership in the era of high imperialism. He navigated the diplomatic relationship between Siam and its new imperial neighbors in Southeast Asia from London, Paris, Vienna, the Vatican, and elsewhere in Europe.

The timing of his diplomatic venture was vital. Great Britain fought a series of wars against the Kingdom of Burma that resulted in the conquest of the coastal areas of Arakan and Tenasserim in 1826 and the rest of lower Burma by 1855. In the third Anglo-Burmese war, conducted in the mid-1880s, Britain finalized its conquest over all the territory once ruled by Burma's Buddhist monarch, King Thibaw, who lived the remainder of his life in exile in British India. On Siam's eastern borders, France's Napoléon III ordered the invasion

Jinawarawansa (Prisdang Chumsai), Waskaduwa Temple, Sri Lanka, November 5, 1896. Courtesy of the National Archives, Thailand.

of Vietnam in 1857. Gradually, French troops claimed all of what became French Indochina, starting in Tourane (Da Nang) in 1858, shifting west to Cambodia in 1863, and moving north to conquer the rest of Vietnam at the end of the Sino-French War in 1885. Siamese leaders feared, for good reason, that Britain and France eyed Siam as the next target for conquest.

As Siam's formal regional rivals collapsed around him, an anxious King Chulalongkorn (r. 1868–1910) consulted Prisdang, who by then had developed a cultural literacy that made him a skilled interpreter of the subtleties of European diplomacy. Prisdang interpreted for King Chulalongkorn the colonizing intent behind imperial descriptions of Asian kingdoms as politically backward. He shrewdly exposed the discourse of civilization as a strategy for territorial and cultural domination—a critique of Western imperial hierarchies that he continued to hone over time. He translated for Siam's ruler the challenges confronting the kingdom as it groped for its new place in the global hierarchy of nations. He outlined what the king must do to avoid colonization. However, his advice to King Chulalongkorn was not limited to Siam's international relations. Instead, he led a group of Siamese princes and officials residing in Europe to draft a comprehensive blueprint to reform Siam's domestic system of governance. The reforms included a recommendation to replace absolutism with a constitutional monarchy. The king did not decide to share power, but instead used the modernizing governmental reforms to strengthen the institution of the monarchy.

Regardless, through such efforts, Prisdang served as a perceptive and cunning interlocutor between imperialist notions of what makes a "modern" state and how Siam might reform its administration in ways palatable to its ruling elite. As such, he was also midwife to Siam's emergence as a modern state. His prominence makes his disappearance from Siamese statecraft and history even more mysterious. Most scholars point to the 1885 proposal as the cause for Prisdang's demise—they surmise that it incurred the king's wrath for suggesting a form of rule other than absolutism. Moreover, the majority of extant scholarship on Prisdang focuses on the domestic impact of the proposal at the time and various interpretations of Prisdang as a treasonous and fiscally corrupt official, or alternately as a loyal royalist and patriot. Regardless of one's interpretation of the reasons behind his departure, we know for certain that Prisdang fled into exile in 1890, five years *after* he submitted the proposal and had returned to Bangkok to assume the directorship of the Post and Telegraph Department. The complicated five-year period that led to his denouement within Thai national history is controversial because it reveals the dark underbelly of Siam's modern monarchy. He challenged Siam's social hierarchy in behavior and word, and paid the price for this by being shunned by elite society and the monarch. Rumors found him guilty of malfeasance, adultery, indebtedness, and treason, but no legal proceedings were filed against him or official explanations given for the disappearance of Siam's most well known, high-profile diplomat. While national historians focus on Prisdang's relationship to the monarch, they neglect to consider his actions outside the kingdom's boundaries, in exile.

Expatriate Patriot

From 1890 until his return to Bangkok in 1911, Prisdang took refuge in Japan, China, Hong Kong, French Indochina, British Malaya, and British Ceylon. He voluntarily exiled himself to various European colonies rather than Europe, where he had spent his twenties and early thirties. He believed it impossible to cleanse his reputation from within Siam, but hoped he could from abroad. Thai national histories of Prisdang stop here. Even Prisdang, who wrote an autobiography to set the record straight about his loyalty to Siam and King Chulalongkorn, totally omitted treatment of his first six years in exile, and downplayed the breadth of his activity in the fifteen years he spent in British Ceylon. To the extent he mentions Ceylon, it is to highlight his nationalistic efforts on behalf of King Chulalongkorn and his homeland. However, a bit of archival digging in Bangkok, Colombo, London, and Aix-en-Provence reveals that Prisdang's experiences in exile were at least as controversial and consequential as his life within Siam.

The telegraph—the very technological infrastructure his civil engineering degree and skills in diplomacy had helped Siam build—enabled foreign powers to share information about Prisdang's journey from Hong Kong, where he absconded from the Siamese diplomatic entourage, to Saigon in late 1890. The French colonial authorities tracked him in coded telegrams as he moved from Hong Kong through Indochina. They followed Prisdang as he boarded a ship to Saigon under the pseudonym Monsieur Giovanni (VNA 1890). He spent several months in Indochina and five years in British Malaya before he moved to Lanka. In each of these places, Prisdang attempted (among other endeavors) to enrobe as a monk but was thwarted for political and financial reasons until he reached Colombo in 1896. His motivations to become a monk were complex, involving political, psychological, and financial rationales. But each exilic space presented distinct obstacles and opportunities.

For example, in French Indochina, tensions between Siam and French colonial authorities arose over their competition for territory and influence, which complicated Prisdang's attempts to make a living. For all his clamoring about leading an anonymous life, Prisdang relied on his renown as a diplomat and royal family member. He used these credentials when pleading for assistance from colonial officials and famous monks in the region, but he also found it impossible to lead a quiet existence because of them. A dejected Prisdang resided at the Hôtel de l'Univers in Saigon until he could arrange for employment. Prisdang said, "[I] disguised myself as a commoner, but I got caught. People still knew I was a member of the royal family" (VNA 1890).

Prisdang sent desperate feelers to Buddhist monks and temples in French Cambodia to see if he would be allowed to be ordained as a monk, a status that would provide for his livelihood as well as protect him from legal prosecution—monks could not be imprisoned while enrobed. However, the French were wary of this for a couple of reasons. First, they strongly encouraged the nationalization of Buddhism in Cambodia as a way to sever links between the Thammayut sect in Thailand and that in Cambodia (Edwards 2007). Their efforts to "Khmerize" Buddhism hampered transregional and historical continuities with Buddhist institutions outside Cambodia while simultaneously furthering French colonial control. Second, French authorities worried that if Prisdang were ordained at an insignificant temple, it would offend the Siamese royal family. At the same time, as a royal family member out of favor with Siam's king, Prisdang could hardly be welcomed by Cambodia's royally sponsored temple without offending Siam's monarchy. The French negotiated with the Siamese government, which agreed to permit Prisdang's ordination in Battambang, then still loosely under Siamese suzerainty. From there, they could disrobe and arrest Prisdang—or assassinate him, according to Prisdang—without contravening French authority.

Sensing that his ordination plans in Cambodia would be thwarted, Prisdang sought assistance from a Ceylonese Buddhist monk, the Venerable Vaskaduve Subhuti, whom he had encountered as early as 1880 in Lanka. In a letter written from his hotel in Saigon in December 1890, Prisdang begged Subhuti to ordain him so that he could devote his life to the priesthood in another Theravada Buddhist country. As such, Prisdang could "make merit and denounce the world which has been so unprofitable and cruel to me. . . . Can you assist me without making it known in the first instant to get into the Order of Priesthood [in Lanka]" (SLNA 1890). He explained in correspondence with a colleague his reasons for ordaining:

> I will be willing to [be enrobed] because I am so tired of human beings, and tired of my work and everything. Nothing is real. . . . The brownnosers are rewarded like this. I can't stand it and would rather become a monk to get some peace in my life so I will at least have some peace when I die. . . . If I can't be ordained, then I don't know what to do because I do not have

> enough money to just sit around. No one wants to hire me for I belong to the royal family. Wherever I run I guess I still cannot escape from being royalty, and might be caught anywhere. So either I am ordained or I die. (TNA KT 1890)

With the long-term goal of enrobing in Lanka, Prisdang needed a short-term survival plan in the meantime, so he left French Indochina for British Malaya and Singapore in 1891. In need of a means of subsistence, he used his reputation as a former high-ranking diplomat to arrange for employment with the British colonial government so that he could fulfill some personal obligations before heading to Lanka. He spent several years managing the construction of roads that edged Siam's borders, almost as a taunt to his former countrymen. The Siamese government sent spies to track his movements, waiting for the opportunity to arrest him should he cross the border into Siamese territory. While in the British colony, he married a woman, presumably from a wealthy Chinese family. All that is known about her is that she was related to the last autonomous governor of Phuket, an island rich in tin located on the west coast of the Malay Peninsula (Loos 2016, 83). Phuket was soon thereafter incorporated into Siam's new *monthon* administrative system. Presumably the monies Prisdang accessed as a consequence of his marriage enabled him at last to dispense with certain obligations and to fund travel to British Ceylon in late 1896.

British Lanka

In anticipation of being ordained, Prisdang wrote to the Ven. Subhuti, "My sole aim and great desire is to devote my whole life to Religious object . . . in order to make merit and denounce [*sic*] the world which has been so unprofitable and cruel to me" (SNLA 1890). Despite his stated desire to lead a life of quiet contemplation, Prisdang led an exceptionally public life as a monk in Lanka. Whereas Prisdang repeatedly mentioned disavowing his royal blood and his diplomat career during the first six years of his exile, once he enrobed as a Buddhist monk in Lanka, he embraced and exploited the transnational aspects of his identity and past public life. The political context behooved him to play up his regal status. The British effectively abolished the Kandyan monarchy when they sent the last king into exile in 1815, after completing their colonization of Lanka. As a consequence, the traditional interdependence between one Buddhist sect, the Siyam Nikaya, and the Kandyan kings broke down. This contributed to disputes and the disestablishment of Buddhist orders that had already begun before the British arrived (Malalgoda 1976; Blackburn 2010). Lankan monks looked to royal surrogates such as the kings in Buddhist Siam and Burma (before 1885) rather than alien British authorities to help them settle disputes and establish legitimacy (Loos 2016, 104).

Prisdang's regal and Siamese identity mattered a great deal in Lanka, where Buddhism was factionalized, bereft of a Buddhist king, and in need of someone who could unify the various sects and harness their collective strengths to resist the influences of the British presence. Given the intractability of these conflicts within Lankan society, Prisdang benefited from being seen as a non-Lankan *and* non-Western outsider who could rise above the fray but still be seen as a member of the broader Buddhist community. An Asian Buddhist of regal blood filled the void perfectly. Lankan Buddhists, both laypeople and monks, saw in Prince Prisdang an opportunity to sidestep the British authorities and utilize instead a Buddhist royal figure to help settle lineage disputes and reestablish the legitimacy of the Buddhist orders, among other concerns.

The Amarapura Nikaya leader, Vaskaduve Subhuti, who (like other leading Lankan monks) had long-term personal connections with Siamese royalty, ordained Prisdang, who took the name Jinavaravansa. He was often thereafter referred to as the Prince Priest, a title that references his regal and religious status. For his part, Subhuti noted, "The Buddhists were overjoyed as this was the first time when a Prince was enrobed in Ceylon after the extinction of the Royal Family, and this, I suppose, is a great honor to Buddhism itself" (TNA R5 B 3/8, 1896). Prisdang's status as a blue-blooded monk facilitated his quick rise to prominence in a cultural context that prized Buddhist royalty.

International Buddhist Politics

Within months of his ordination in Lanka, Prisdang parlayed his former experience as an ambassador into a position of veritable international Buddhist diplomacy in Lanka. He quickly gained renown as an outspoken leader and international emissary for Asia's Theravada Buddhist communities in their relations with the British Empire. He did not simply fill a gaping void in Lankan Buddhist politics; he saw an opportunity to build a unified transregional Buddhist community that would offer an alternative moral hierarchy to British imperial rule and its buttressing notions of civilization. He worked with Theosophists, Buddhist leaders, foreign (Asian and European) royalty, and politicians to create educational opportunities for poor Lankans and to create a sacred Buddhist geography that was not isomorphic with imperial or national boundaries.[1] His impeccable English, royal blood, former career as a diplomat in Europe, and maverick political tendencies aligned him with individuals from all races who shared an elite yet anti-imperial perspective.

Prisdang's first attempt to unify Buddhists across the region occurred in 1897, just as Siam's King Chulalongkorn planned to stop in Lanka on his way to Europe. In Colombo, Prisdang spearheaded an effort to unify all Theravada Buddhists, including Lanka's factionalized Buddhist fraternities as well as those in British Burma and Siam, under King Chulalongkorn, who was touted as the sole remaining independent Asian Buddhist king. In Lanka, the desire of leading monks to unify and gain the patronage of an Asian Buddhist monarch dovetailed with Prisdang's personal aspiration to regain an intimate connection with King Chulalongkorn and return to Siam with the king's blessing.

In all these ways, Lanka's political and religious context proved a fertile ground for Prisdang to nurture his unique talents. Although Prisdang claimed credit for the idea, the desire for monastic unity had long been brewing. He drafted a letter in English to the king and asked Lanka's leading monks from the three main sects to sign it. Internal factionalism proved hard to overcome, however, so Prisdang began to build a network of supporters outside the Lankan Buddhist community to pressure the monks to unify. This included American Theosophist Colonel Henry Steele Olcott, whom Prisdang asked to intercede. Olcott had been visiting Lanka since 1880, when he converted to Buddhism, and was closely affiliated with the Buddhist Theosophical Society there. Olcott saw a kindred spirit in Prisdang, who, like him, had come to Lanka "in the hope of finding brotherly unity and religious calm, the very things to soothe his world-beaten spirit. . . . But the Prince-priest, like myself, found himself in an atmosphere of personal bickerings, childish sectarian squabbles, ignorance of the world about them, and incapacity to fit themselves to the ideals which the Lord Buddha had depicted for the government of his Sangha [monkhood]" (Olcott 1935, 155–156).

Olcott continues, "With his [Prisdang's] natural impetuosity he threw himself into the business with zeal and enthusiasm; wrote to the leading priests of Ceylon and their chief lay supporters, got pledges from many, but soon ran against the awful inertia which pervades all Asiatic countries (Japan now excepted) and bars progress. The personal factor everywhere obtruded itself, and the poor fellow, finding himself at a standstill with the King's visit near at hand, despairingly appealed to me as 'the only man who could awaken the slumbering Sinhalese'" (1935, 156). Both men viewed Lankan Buddhism through the lens of imperialism's patronizing contempt. The Prince Priest's words and actions, not all of which are repeated here, reveal that he considered himself superior to his Lankan Buddhist brethren. The cultural space conceded to him as Buddhist royalty and a former diplomat abetted his occasional condescension. Prisdang was a reformer with bold, transnational designs, but not immune from the discourse of civilization used against the colonized. And although one could focus on his imperfect delivery, one cannot deny he had an intrepid vision for a unified Buddhist Asia.

By late March, he had accomplished his goal of unifying the major lineages behind his idea. Prisdang (1897) wrote an open letter, published in early April in the *Ceylon Observer,* entitled "A Religious Manifesto." "We the undersigned for ourselves and on behalf of the rest of the Buddhist Priesthood in Ceylon beg to tender our deep regard and sincere love to Your Majesty as the only Buddhist Sovereign of the World," it began. In addition to inviting Siam's king to visit the various pilgrimage sites on Lanka, the priests also "look forward to the day when all Buddhist Priests and laymen here will recognize, acknowledge and yield implicit obedience to the laws and decisions of your enlightened ecclesiastical Government and Sovereignty" (TNA R5 B 3/9, 1897; Blackburn 2010, 169). He included British Burma in his vision of this unity, but curiously not Cambodia. Likely Prisdang's inability to speak French and his negative experiences with French authorities in Cambodia while in exile there shaped membership in his "map" of Buddhist Asia.

Prisdang's utopic vision required Buddhists to overlook their own cultural differences, and demanded that King Chulalongkorn treat all Buddhists equally. The monarch "must become one with the Buddhist public opinion of the world, and be the very foundation and part of Buddhism itself and be recognized and accepted as the fountain-head of all that is religious and the temporal head of Buddhist power and *the* Buddhist spiritual authority" (Prisdang 1897). One can almost feel the commanding reverberation of his voice coming through the printed page as well as the shame induced by his rebukes. He spoke in the timbre and deployed the discourse of a Buddhist imperialist-cum-revivalist preacher.

On the day of the king's arrival at the pier in Colombo, Prisdang arranged for a massive Buddhist reception of the king. According to the *Overland Ceylon*

Observer, record numbers of visitors poured into Colombo for the opportunity to see an Asian Buddhist king ("Paras from Our Contemporaries," 1897). Their welcome upstaged that of the British colonial government, which was denied the chance to exclusively receive the monarch. At 10:00 A.M. on April 21, 1897, a cheering crowd of thousands and a twenty-one-gun salute greeted the monarch at Colombo's jetty, decorated with flags and greenery ("Arrival of the King of Siam at Colombo," 1897). Upon disembarking, King Chulalongkorn was presented with Prisdang's petition, inviting the king to unite the divided sects and "assume the control of our church and its priesthood" ("Address of the Buddhist Priests to the King of Siam," 1897). King Chulalongkorn was likened to the pope, but for Buddhists rather than Catholics spread across the world ("Buddhism in Ceylon," 1897).

Prisdang's initial effort to unify all Buddhists under King Chulalongkorn failed for reasons having to do with Buddhist institutional complexities, Siamese authorities' fear of the potential damage to Siam's Buddhist reputation that could be done by the fractious Lankan Buddhists, and King Chulalongkorn's negative experience with officials in charge of managing the Tooth Relic in Kandy. After the king's enthusiastic reception at the pier, he and his entourage boarded a train to Kandy, where the renowned relic could be seen under a glass cover. In front of 500 chanting monks and crowds of locals, the king was denied his request to touch the relic, a privilege reserved for monks. Insulted and indignant, the king burst out of the temple and left Lanka as soon as he could. This soured King Chulalongkorn and may have influenced his decision to decline the offer to become the Buddhist pope. Regardless, Prisdang took an enormous risk in proposing and orchestrating such a scheme. The idea of uniting Asians under a single Buddhist ecclesiastical court was conceptually bold and not for the faint of heart. It also stemmed from a genuine desire to lionize King Chulalongkorn as Asian, as sovereign, and as a king, all in contradistinction to British colonial authority. Despite the failure, it did not stop Prisdang from trying one more time to boost the king as a global Buddhist monarch.

A few months after King Chulalongkorn left Lanka in pique, Prisdang took a Buddhist pilgrimage through British India where the birthplace of the Buddha had recently been discovered. He wanted to collect some relics for the king and Lankan Buddhists, as well as to write a Buddhist pilgrimage book for Thai tourists. Anagarika Dharmapala, by then a Buddhist activist who sought to reclaim from Hindus important Buddhist heritage sites in India, helped fund Prisdang's travel. Because Prisdang had failed to secure the necessary documents and funds from his own government, Dharmapala wrote letters of introduction, paid Prisdang's steamer fare to India in December 1897, and sent him additional funds in early 1898 (SLNA, Diaries of Anagarika Dharmapala, entries for December 14, 17, and 18, 1897, and February 1, 1898). In addition, Prisdang relied once again on Olcott's Theosophical Society connections. Prisdang used their international headquarters in Adyar, Madras, as his base from December 1897 until March 1898. It is unclear the extent to which he agreed with the principles espoused by the early Theosophists, but this did not stop him from using their networks to travel and connect with Buddhists in the region. Prisdang journeyed to Rangoon and Mandalay in British Burma with Olcott and Annie Besant to try to convince the monks there to unite under the ecclesiastical authority of King Chulalongkorn (Kemper 2015, 98). We know very little about the outcome of this trip to Burma or the reactions of monks who had witnessed the decimation of their Buddhist monarchy by the British in 1885.

For more than a year, Prisdang traveled to key Buddhist pilgrimage sites in South Asia, including the newly discovered (1896) birthplace of the Buddha in Nepal and to Bodh Gaya, where the Buddha obtained enlightenment. He traveled north, where he had heard about the discovery of authentic relics of the Buddha—jewels, pots, and the Buddha's bones and ashes (Allen 2008). With stunning speed and ingenuity, he then campaigned to have the British imperial government in India place the relics under the guardianship of the world's only remaining sovereign Buddhist monarch, King Chulalongkorn. Prisdang wrote a lengthy memorandum to British authorities in India in which he argued that since Europeans attached little importance to bones and ash relics, they might keep the vessels and jewels but pass on the contents to the king of Siam, who, for all the reasons rehearsed earlier in Lanka, was the rightful and legitimate custodian of such sacred items (Loos 2016; Peleggi 2002, 39, 180n89).[2] His proposal that King Chulalongkorn should receive the relics and distribute portions to Buddhists in other countries was a success. In early 1900, King Chulalongkorn hosted a grand public ceremony at which he ostentatiously presented portions of the Piprahwa relics to representatives from Burma and Lanka and enshrined the Siamese portion in the Golden Mount (Wat Saket) Temple in Bangkok (Allen 2008, 212–213). Prisdang's role in this has been omitted from British, Lankan, and Siamese historical accounts, which instead credit the British for their unilateral diplomatic generosity.

Prisdang returned to Lanka in about 1900, where he enjoyed a vibrant social and political life, established schools for indigent children, and entertained literary, political, and royal figures from around the world. Westerners were drawn to him and likened his life to that of the Buddha: a prince who had discarded his wealth and royal status to lead the life of an ascetic. Olcott summed this up in his description of Prisdang as someone who had "thrown up all the luxury, pomp and influence of his worldly position" to commit to the life of a monastic in Lanka (1935, 314–315). Nearly every European seeking enlightenment in the fabled East found him, including Alistair Crowley, who dedicated a play to Prisdang. Crowley's cutting critiques of Christian hypocrisy applied to the entire Christianized West may have found a sympathetic ear in the Prince Priest, who also found Christianity inferior to Buddhism. Olcott landed at the more erudite end of the spectrum of Westerners who disavowed Christianity in their admittedly Orientalist search for the metaphysical and spiritual in the ancient cultures and religions of the East. A German, a Dutchman, and an Austrian were ordained with Prisdang in 1905, the same year that he was appointed to the position of abbot of Dipaduttamarama Temple in Kotahena, Colombo. Reginald Farrer, the disaffected son of a British politician, sought out the Prince Priest at the Kotahena temple in 1907, where he too experienced a form of ordination (Aldrich 2015, 41–42; Charlesworth 2018). Members of the Rothschild family met him briefly and immediately donated funds for one of his causes. For all others, Prisdang and his temple were must-sees in early twentieth-century British guidebooks. He was disavowed by Siam but claimed by the world, especially the English-speaking world, as its "native" window into Asian Buddhism.

From Kotahena, Prisdang entertained visitors every year, and sometimes every month. The list is catholic and includes Buddhist royalty as well as European blue bloods. For example, Prince Arisugawa of Japan, Siamese royalty, Cambodia's Prince Suttarassa, Queen Victoria's granddaughter Her Highness Princess Louise of Schleswig-Holstein, and the crown prince of Germany sought him out ("The Approaching Visit of the Japanese Prince and Princess," 1905; "H.I.H. Prince Arisugawa in Colombo," 1905; "The King of Cambodia in Colombo," 1906; "The Kotahena Girls' Free School," 1906; "Local News," 1905; "Outstation News: Kurunegala," 1905; "The Visit of the German Crown Prince," 1910). As noted earlier, Prisdang was also close to notable local elites such as Sinhalese Anagarika Dharmapala and

Ananda K. Coomaraswamy, who also found the modernity that accompanied British imperial rule spiritually and culturally lacking (Lipsey 1977).

But Prisdang did not simply entertain guests. He used his political savvy to gain support for various causes, including educational ones. He had a particular take on the education of local Lankans under the British, best exemplified by a photograph he had attached to the door of his room. It showed "a young [Lankan] man, apparently well dressed and smoking a cigar, walking stick in hand and bottle of liquor by the side," underneath which the Prince Priest had written "the result of modern education of young Ceylon" ("The Governor at Matara," 1897). He held strong opinions about everything, including modern, Western education—the very education he had received in King's College London long ago. He spoke about civilization and enlightenment, principles allegedly propagated by a modern Western education. But instead of improvement of the human condition, he saw "the apparent increase of evils observed throughout the world, as education, civilisation and 'enlightenment' (so called) spread. . . . I see the increase of crimes and cruelties and no spiritual advancement made anywhere!" (Jinawarawansa [Prisdang] 1898, 292).

To rectify this, he worked closely with the governor of British Ceylon, Sir Henry Blake, and his wife, Lady Blake, to open a free and nonsectarian school for indigent boys (1905) and girls (1906) in Colombo. He spoke at both grand openings (Prisdang 1930, appendixes 15 and 16; *Independent,* March 22, 1905; *Morning Times,* August 17, 1906). In his speech at the public opening of the girls' school, he ranted about the poor state of the so-called civilization engineered by Westerners, many of whom were in the audience. His concerns were part of a larger post-Darwinian crisis of faith, which he mocked: "A period of unrest and struggle for existence has come . . . giving birth to a new doctrine as its fruition, which the modern sage of a matter-of-fact world pronounces in these terrible words, '*survival of the fittest?*'" (Prisdang 1930, 120; emphasis in original). For Prisdang, the influence of the West threatened to homogenize the world along Western lines, eradicating cultural difference. "The Civilisation of a go-ahead-quick world demands for its rapid progress [that] . . . we should live as one man with one view and speak the same language which, in Ceylon, *should be English*" (Prisdang 1930, 120; emphasis in original). The best way to counter this "undue and indiscreet Western influence of a low order" and "moulding the future to *a world of monotony*" was to promote the education of girls, "who are the backbone and sinews of the nation[.] Begin education at home, *in the nursery,* in which character is formed, by educating the future mothers" (Prisdang 1930, 120; emphasis in original). The school would teach English, Sinhala, cooking, needlework, math, and agriculture ("kitchen gardening"), all of which would be imbued with an unspecified moral essence, one "*without* the aid of the *figment* of a particular dogma or creed" (Prisdang 1930, appendix 16, 125; emphasis in original). He advocated for a secular but moral education that would be delivered in Sinhala as well as in English, for the poor of both genders. In the context of Lanka, this was a significant and distinctive approach to education.

Lady Blake, the official representative of the new school for indigent girls, balked: "I must say that I totally disagree with the Prince Priest that the doctrine of 'The Survival of the Fittest' is a terrible one. It seems to me that the terrible thing would be if the unfittest were to survive. I trust that this school will prove itself 'the fittest' and will survive" ("The Kotahena Girls' Free School," 1906). Indeed, both schools thrived in Colombo into the twenty-first century. The girls' school was named after the Kotahena temple's famous abbot, Mohottivatte Gunananda, and the boys' school, which initially faltered but later was revived under Prisdang's pupil Jinananda, was named Prince's College, in honor of the Prince Priest.

Prisdang's efforts to influence the political direction of Buddhism and colonial education stemmed in part from his restless and critical approach to life, and in part from the possibilities open to a man with his particular experiences and background. His activism ceased only after he returned to Siam in 1911, when Siamese authorities finally contained his energies and muffled his voice. He was forced to give up his robe, was blacklisted from all but the lowest-paid government positions, and denied the opportunity to return to Lanka. He died, poor and alone, in 1935. His descendants hosted a funeral ceremony for him at Khuruhabodhi Temple in Thonburi, across the river from Bangkok. Even though Prisdang succeeded in elevating himself as an emissary of Buddhism who was representative of the East within royal, official, and Buddhist circles, he failed to obtain such recognition in his home country. He hovered at the borders of his nation, an expatriate patriot who made Siam's monarch King of Theravada Buddhist Asia.

Prince Prisdang and his unusual experiences initially seemed to offer an excellent vehicle for writing a national history of Siam during the tumultuous imperial and "modernizing" era in the late nineteenth and early twentieth centuries. However, the national framework constrained and truncated the meaning and impact of his life, which far exceeded national and regional boundaries. In part, this stemmed from my immersion in the Thai language scholarship about him and the imperial era, which suffers from a royalist nationalist myopia focused on King Chulalongkorn (r. 1868–1910). I, like my Thai colleagues, was so fixated with Prisdang's contentious domestic impact in Siam that I initially was unaware of his decades-long exile and participation in international and regional activism in British Ceylon. No one else wrote about his years in exile, and even Prisdang, who wrote an autobiography, downplayed the fifteen years he spent engaged in Lankan politics. He sharply distinguished between his life in Siam and his life in Lanka, claiming he had been "reborn" when he began life as a monk in Colombo. As a consequence, Prisdang's "Asia" falls outside the purview of Thai national history.

Ironically, his expulsion from Siam—the last noncolonized Theravada kingdom—catalyzed his vociferous advocacy of Buddhism as an antidote to problems associated with imperial expansion and the spiritual malaise many felt in its wake. Prisdang's efforts outside Siam reveal the power of Buddhist cosmopolitanism as an umbrella critique of Western imperialism, transform understandings of anti-imperial transnational Buddhist politics, and demonstrate the astounding degree to which spiritual activists mapped a very different political geography. Thus, his life offers a vehicle for more than the history of Siam. It also reveals one pivotal man's subjective experience of global imperialism, the activism roiling Asia's Buddhist ecumene, and the pitfalls of Siam's political culture. His international journey reveals the constraints and possibilities enabled by global imperialism. Telling his story offers a human-scale entry point that grounds the otherwise abstract processes of global imperialism.

Notes

I thank Eric Tagliacozzo, Helen Siu, and Peter Perdue for bringing us all together. For help with locating many key sources, thanks are due to Anne Blackburn, Chris Peppé, Natasha Pairaudeau, and Dr. Sumet Jumsai and his wife, Suthini. This chapter builds on ideas I first discussed in chapter 6 of my book *Bones around My Neck: The Life and Exile of a Prince Provocateur*, published by Cornell University Press in 2016.

1. Madame Blavatsky, a Russian aristocrat in dire financial straits, and Henry Steel Olcott, an American Civil War colonel, founded the Theosophical Society in 1875 in New York City. They left in 1878 for India and Ceylon, where Olcott took the five basic precepts that allowed him to declare himself Buddhist. The Buddhist Theosophical Society was born in India in 1879 and Ceylon in 1880. Its pro-Buddhist and anti-Christian stance had greater appeal and success in Asia than anywhere else. The Theosophical Society, for example, had 121 lodges by 1885, 106 of them in India, Burma, and Ceylon, where the society had the bulk of its membership and where its headquarters are still located (in Madras, India) (Washington 1993, 68). Local Sri Lankans saw in it a safe way to engage in anticolonialism (Loos 2016).

2. Relics associated with the Buddha have been venerated as powerful sacred objects for centuries. The most powerful relics are those associated with the Buddha himself—teeth, bones, ashes, hair—but secondary relics such as the Buddha's footprint, robe, bowl, and the Bodhi tree also are imbued with sacral authority and power. According to some, the possession of a relic, each of which obtains its own pedigree and myths, helped constitute a proper monastery in Theravada Asia (Strong 2004, xiv–xv). Indeed, nearly every monastery claims to have a Buddha relic enshrined in its stupa.

References

Archival Sources

SLNA (Sri Lankan National Archives). 1890. 5/63/17/708. Prisdang to Subhuti (4 December).

SLNA. Diaries of Anagarika Dharmapala. Microfilm 1944.

TNA (Thai National Archives) KT (Krasuang Tangprathet / Ministry of Foreign Affairs). 1890. Prisdang to Phra Satja (13 December).

TNA R5 (Rama 5) B (Betthalet / Miscellaneous) 3 / 8. 1896. "High Priest Subhuti to king of Siam" (8 December).

TNA R5 B 3 / 9. 1897. "Jinawarawansa [Prisdang] et al. to King Culalankarana [Chulalongkorn]" (16 March).

VNA (Vietnam National Archives—II). 1890. IA16 / 215 Vinh Long 1881 V.L. 31 / 10. Telegramme. "Prince Prisdang accompagné octave confortable, arrivera ce matin Saigon par chemin de fer Mytho."

Interviews

Interview with Venerable Mahindawansa, Dipaduttamarama Temple, Kotahena, Columbo, Sri Lanka, June 4, 2015.

Newspapers

Independent (Ceylon)
Morning Times (Ceylon)

Secondary Works

"Address of the Buddhist Priests to the King of Siam." 1897. *Overland Ceylon Observer*, April 21.

Aldrich, Robert. 2015. *Cultural Encounters and Homoeroticism in Sri Lanka: Sex and Serendipity.* London: Routledge.

Allen, Charles. 2008. *The Buddha and Dr. Führer: An Archaeological Scandal.* London: Haus Publishing.

Anderson, Benedict. 1978. "Studies of the Thai State: The State of Thai Studies." In *The Study of Thailand: Analyses of Knowledge, Approaches and Prospects in Anthropology, Art History, Economics, History and Political Science,* ed. Eliezer B. Ayal, 193–247. Papers in International Studies, Southeast Asia Series, 54. Athens: Ohio University, Center for International Studies.

"The Approaching Visit of the Japanese Prince and Princess." 1905. *Ceylon Observer* (weekly edition), July 31, 1905.

"Arrival of the King of Siam at Colombo." 1897. *Ceylon Observer,* April 21, 1897.

Blackburn, Anne. 2010. *Locations of Buddhism.* Chicago: University of Chicago Press.

"Buddhism in Ceylon." 1897. *Overland Ceylon Observer,* April 7, 1897.

Charlesworth, Michael. 2018. *The Modern Culture of Reginald Farrer: Landscape, Literature and Buddhism.* Oxford: Legenda.

Edwards, Penny. 2007. *Cambodge: The Cultivation of a Nation, 1860–1945.* Honolulu: University of Hawai'i Press.

"The Governor at Matara." 1897. *Overland Ceylon Observer,* March 1, 1897, 365.

"H.I.H. Prince Arisugawa in Colombo." 1905. *Overland Ceylon Observer,* April 25, 1905, 596.

Hecker, Helmuth, and Bhikku Nanatusita, comp. and ed. 2008. *The Life of Nyanatiloka Thera: The Biography of a Western Buddhist Pioneer.* Kandy, Sri Lanka: Buddhist Publication Society.

Jinawarawansa, Ven. [Prisdang]. 1898. "An Open Letter [28 Dec. 1897]." *The Theosophist* 19, no. 5 (February): 292.

Kemper, Steven. 2015. *Rescued from the Nation: Anagarika Dharmapala and the Buddhist World.* Chicago: University of Chicago Press.

"The King of Cambodia in Colombo." 1906. *Ceylon Observer* (weekly edition), August 10, 1906.

"The Kotahena Girls' Free School." 1906. *Ceylon Observer* (weekly edition), August 17, 1906.

Lipsey, Roger. 1977. *Coomaraswamy. 3: His Life and Work*. Bollingen Series LXXXIX. Princeton, NJ: Princeton University Press.

"Local News." 1905. *Ceylon Observer* (weekly edition), July 26, 1905.

Loos, Tamara. 2016. *Bones around My Neck: The Life and Exile of Prince Provocateur*. Ithaca, NY: Cornell University Press.

Malalgoda, Kitsiri. 1976. *Buddhism in Sinhalese Society, 1750–1900: A Study of Religious Revival and Change*. Berkeley: University of California Press.

Olcott, Henry Steel. 1935 [1896–1898]. *Old Diary Leaves: The Only Authentic History of the Theosophical Society*, 6th ser. repr. Adyar, India: Theosophical Publishing House.

"Outstation News: Kurunegala." 1905. *Ceylon Observer* (weekly edition), May 25, 1905.

"Paras from Our Contemporaries." 1897. *Overland Ceylon Observer*, December 30, 1897.

Peleggi, Maurizio. 2002. *Lords of Things: The Fashioning of the Siamese Monarchy's Modern Image*. Honolulu: University of Hawai'i Press.

Prisdang, Prince. 1897. "A Religious Manifesto." *Ceylon Observer*, March 25, 1897.

Prisdang, Prince. 1930. *Prawat yo naiphan ek phiset phra worawongthoe phra 'ong jao pritsdang tae prasut pho. so. 2392 thung 2472* [Abbreviated history of special colonel Prince Prisdang, from 1850–1930] (Bangkok 2472 / 1930). Reprinted in the cremation volume for Luang Aneknaiwathi (M. R. W. Narot Chumsai). Bangkok, 1970.

Snodgrass, Judith. 2003. *Presenting Japanese Buddhism to the West: Orientalism, Occidentalism, and the Columbian Exposition*. Chapel Hill: University of North Carolina Press.

———. 2009. "Publishing Eastern Buddhism: D. T. Suzuki's Journey to the West." In *Casting Faiths: Imperialism and the Transformation of Religion in East and Southeast Asia*, ed. Thomas David Dubois, 46–72. New York: Palgrave Macmillan.

Strong, John. 2004. *Relics of the Buddha*. Princeton, NJ: Princeton University Press.

"The Visit of the German Crown Prince." 1910. *Ceylon Observer* (Weekly Edition), December 12, 1910.

Washington, Peter. 1993. *Madame Blavatsky's Baboon: A History of Mystics, Mediums, and Misfits Who Brought Spiritualism to America*. New York: Schocken Books.

Itinerant Singers

Triangulating the Canton–Hong Kong–Macau Soundscape

MAY BO CHING

People move, by all means. Even those with meager resources might move if they want to or need to. Understandably the tracks of movement are often market driven, but markets alone fail to explain the logic of a road map. Patterns of movement have to be appreciated against the historical connections built among different hubs and places over time. Between the mid-nineteenth and the mid-twentieth centuries, there was a triangular alignment of networks among Canton, Hong Kong, and Macau.[1] Their proximity to one another allowed itinerant seekers to find opportunities. The rise of Shanghai and other Chinese port cities, including overseas diasporic communities, enhanced the "hubbing" synergy. A distinctive soundscape emerged in which a certain standard speech of Cantonese was spoken and an affiliated Cantonese song culture matured. What is remarkable is that this soundscape of language and song was infinitely expansive, constructed, and improvised as it intertwined with the movement of performers and their audiences. In the process, a characteristic Cantonese cultural identity also evolved. The chapter starts with the story of a blind singer and ends with that of a Cantonese opera superstar. Both were twentieth-century persons, but the roots of the language and music culture they shared can be traced back to at least two centuries earlier.

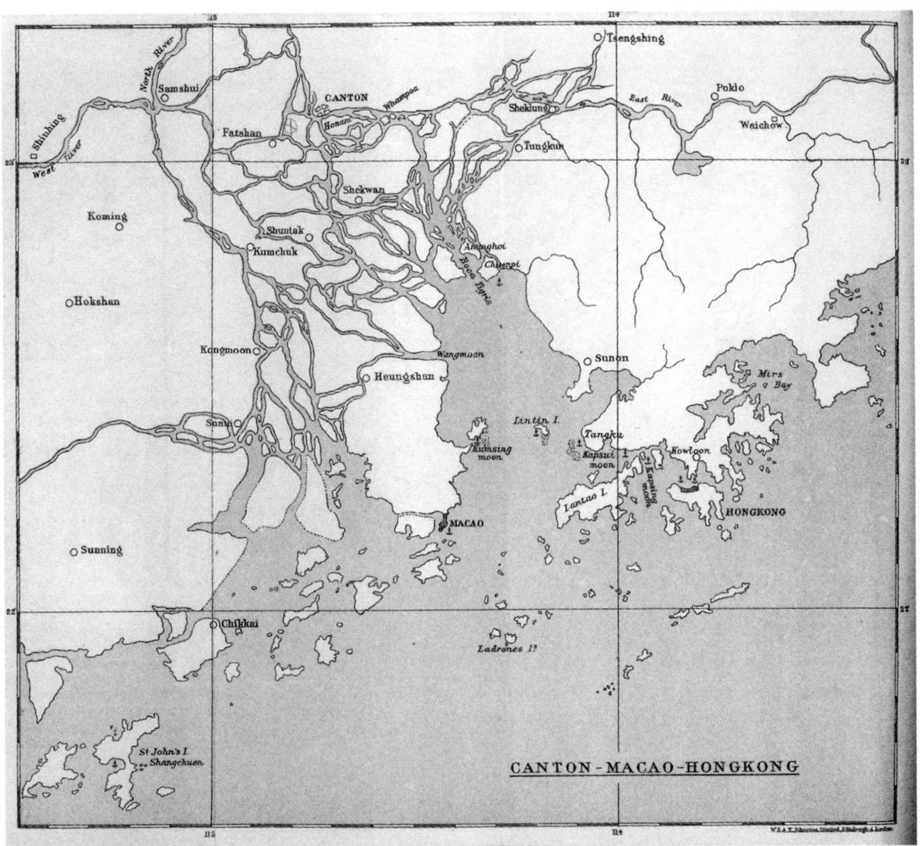

Map of "Canton-Macao-Hong Kong." From Hosea Ballou Morse, *International Relations of the Chinese Empire,* vol. 1 (London: Longmans, Green, 1910).

A Blind Singer in 1970s Hong Kong

Dou Wun (杜煥, 1910–1979), a blind male singer active in Hong Kong between the 1920s and the 1970s, had little but his voice to rely on in his youth. He moved from one place to another in the Pearl River delta in the first half of the twentieth century, and ended up spending the latter part of his life in colonial Hong Kong. A few years before his death, at a teahouse in the historical district of Sheung Wan 上環, he narrated his life story before performing a piece of dragon-boat song (short, crude Cantonese vernacular pieces performed by beggars carrying a small wooden dragon boat). It runs as follows:

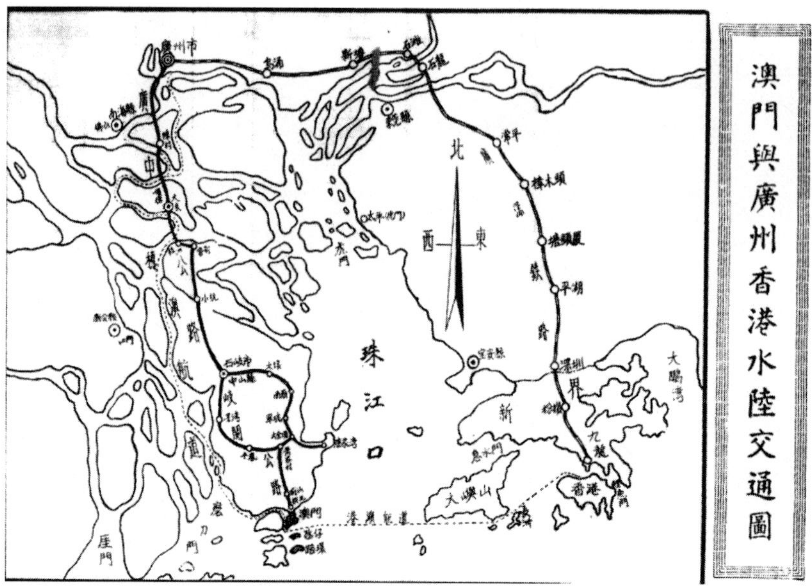

Map of water and land transports between Macau, Canton, and Hong Kong. From Aomen Gongshang Nianjian Bianjibu 澳門工商年鑑編輯部, *Aomen Gongshang Nianjian* 澳門工商年鑑 (Annual of Macau industry and commerce), vol. 3 (1958–1959) (Macau: Tai Chung Pou, 1959).

> Well, when I began to earn my living in every corner of the world [*jianghu* 江湖], I sang dragon-boat [*longzhou* 龍舟] songs. At that time I worked in the rural quarter [*sixiang* 四鄉] singing dragon-boat songs. Then I went to Honam Island [Henan Island in Guangzhou 河南島] singing Southern Tone [*nanyin*南音, long Cantonese vernacular lyrical pieces with more elegiac melodies] and from then on I shifted to performing Southern Tone. Well, I have been singing dragon-boat songs in teahouses for a long time. I once sang in Jianyuan 建苑 Teahouse in the Western District with my colleague [*hangjia* 行家] Blind Hua. Since then I have been singing dragon-boat songs in teahouses. (Du 2012)

This is the world (*jianghu* 江湖) of Dou Wun. Dou was born in 1910 into a poor family in the country of Zhaoqing 肇慶 in western Guangdong. His sight was accidentally damaged at the age of three months, and he became increasingly blind. The outbreak of flooding along the West River in 1914 and the death of his father had left the family destitute. Soon he went to Canton and acquired his skills of singing Southern Tone from a blind singer in Honam

Island in Guangzhou. But the city was embroiled in political turmoil in the 1920s, and they found it difficult to make a living. Dou Wun and his workmates went south to Macau via Shiqi 石岐, the county capital of Zhongshan 中山 in the Pearl River delta, and arrived in Hong Kong in 1926. At seventeen Dou started singing in Yaumatei 油麻地 and Mongkok 旺角 in Kowloon, working in neighborhoods where second-rate brothels[2] stood. He became addicted to opium. Nonetheless, he married a sing-song girl who worked in Yaumatei. They had four children, who unfortunately did not survive. In 1935, prostitution was made illegal in Hong Kong.[3] Sing-song business declined as a result, and the couple could hardly make ends meet. On Christmas Day 1941 the Japanese military occupied Hong Kong. Dou's wife died during the occupation period, and he was left on his own. After the war, he was able to sing for a living for a short while. In the 1950s, radio broadcasts, particularly the cable radio Rediffusion,[4] became popular in Hong Kong. Dou could no longer support himself by singing old-fashioned Southern Tone songs. Luckily, in 1955 he was invited to sing live, and his performances were broadcast at the Radio Television Hong Kong (RTHK). Sadly for him, the program was cancelled in 1970 because the listening public started to abandon traditional Cantonese music for Western popular songs. Dou ended up performing on the streets with his colleagues. As a street singer, he "lowered his head and felt great shame." He found it difficult to adjust to the circumstances. If he had not had the support of one of his former radio fans, he would have become even more desperate. Nonetheless, Dou Wun and his music left a trace. Before Dou died in 1979, Bell Yung, a professor of music at Pittsburgh University, recorded Dou's work and personal stories in 1975 (Du 2004). The audio records were later published in the 2000s.

In spite of his visual impairment, Dou Wun managed to move from Zhaoqing to the "Four Quarters," the hinterland of the provincial city of Guangzhou, then to Honam Island south of the city across the Pearl River. He passed by Macau and at last settled in Hong Kong. All these places, whether rural or urban, were simply part of his *jianghu*. But his choice of places was not arbitrary, nor was his choice of genres. As mentioned above, whereas dragon-boat songs are short, crude pieces performed by itinerant beggars in rural and urban communities, Southern Tone songs are in most cases long lyrical pieces with elegiac melodies addressing a literati audience in an urban setting of old Canton. The master whom Dou met on Honam Island told him that he should stick with Southern Tone. Moreover, he was advised not to be too skilled at playing musical instruments, as he might end up accompanying blind female singers. Singing Southern Tone songs, on the other hand, would make him look more refined (*siwen* 斯文) and earn him professional status. Dou Wun recalled that while singing Southern Tone in the residences of the well-to-do, the moment he put down his clappers, attendants would immediately pour him a cup of tea and serve him fruit as a gesture of respect. In his memory, singing Southern Tone was once a profession with dignity.

Dou Wun began his singing career in Canton expecting Southern Tone to bring him a respectable living. Never did he expect to end up a lowly street performer. In teahouses and brothels in Yaumatei and Mongkok, Dou Wun was no longer addressing a class of self-proclaimed literati, as it became more and more difficult to apply the category "literati" to anyone in twentieth-century Chinese society since the abolition of the civil service examinations in 1905 and the collapse of the imperial order in 1911. The crumbling of the literati world led Dou Wun to choose earthier pieces to perform. In the 1920s and 1930s, one of his most popular pieces must have been "Two brothel clients quarreling with each other" (*Liang laoqi aijiao* 两老契嗌交). He sang it again in the teahouse in Sheung Wan in 1975 when Bell Yung recorded him. Sung in the form of *banyan* 板眼, a format closer to rapping than singing, the lyrics depict the scene of Qing Canton rather than that of twentieth-century Hong Kong.

Acting as a client trying to show off his social network, Dou Wun sang with two different voices, A and B, to achieve an ironic effect of ridicule:

> A: Going to court, I am in a more advantageous position;
> Telling you who my backers are, you will be scared to death;
> The Provincial Governor is the man whom I call papa
> B: what he actually does is [following the high officials and] collecting the shit left by his horse!
> A: My younger uncle is the Provincial Administration Commissioner
> B: what he actually does is holding the peacock feather of the official cap!
> A: My elder uncle is not as high-ranking, and yet he is at least the Tartar-General
> B: he is actually responsible for keeping the time and tidying the *yamen*.
> A: My elder brother is the Nanhai County Magistrate
> B: well, he may take care of the wooden staves [at the magistrate court]
> A: My younger brother is the River Police Inspector

B: that is why he is always holding the Blue Dragon Flag [while sailing on the river]! . . .

B: Who are you? You are in fact a ruffian pretending to be a *hong* merchant! (Du 2011)

Singing the above lyrics in Hong Kong in the 1970s must have sounded anachronistic, as the song mentions only Qing official titles, but we can understand why Dou Wun used such terms. A singer like Dou Wun would bring to Hong Kong the songs he learned in Guangzhou from his teacher, who might in turn have learned them from his predecessors. The melodies and lyrics remained frozen in time, representing a scenario of late imperial Canton. Moreover, the choice of characters narrated in the lyrics, especially the *hong* merchants, is worth highlighting. As licensed merchants who specialized in foreign trade in Canton from the eighteenth to the nineteenth century, they were patrons who helped create *the* Cantonese culture in the course of becoming Cantonese themselves. Their history dates back to the eighteenth century or even earlier, with the arrival of *hong* merchants in Canton, or more precisely, the "West End."

The Merchants in the West End, Canton, 1700s–1800s

Beginning in the eighteenth century, the West End (西關 Xiguan, "Saí Kwan" in Cantonese) of Canton was an affluent district. Located in the suburbs outside the western city gate of Canton, the West End evolved from marshlands to a commercial-residential district between the 1700s and 1800s. The marshy area had in fact been vividly named "Bantang" (半塘 / 泮塘, lit., half of the place covered by ponds) since the Ming period. Natural sedimentation and reclamation efforts pushed the area's coastline toward the Pearl River and expanded the amount of usable land. Reclamation must have accelerated from around the early eighteenth century and intensified after Canton was designated the sole port for foreign trade in 1757. Because foreigners were not allowed to enter the walled city, the West End became the only district where they could find lodging. Studies of the China Trade paintings and related textual descriptions show that rows of hongs and factories[5] were built one after another between the eighteenth and nineteenth centuries. They were associated with particular European nations from the 1730s on, and became more and more Westernized in style after extensive renovations and rebuilding. Much of this real estate was owned by Chinese merchants, who usually resided on Honam Island on the south of the Pearl River but often worked in their firms in the West End, dealing with foreign traders. At the rear of these buildings was Thirteen-Factory Street, which ran perpendicular to the Old and New China Streets. These streets were lined with wholesale and retail stores run by Chinese traders catering largely to the daily needs of the foreign trading community (Conner 2009; Van Dyke and Mok 2015; Farris 2016). In other words, the West End would never have been *the* West End without the arrival of Chinese merchants and their foreign counterparts.

Among the first generation of Chinese merchants involved in the Canton trade, many came from Fujian. By the time they arrived in Canton in the late seventeenth and early eighteenth centuries, the districts within the city walls were already densely populated. The new immigrants could purchase estates only in the West End and on Honam Island. Ye Zhende 葉振德 (1646–1734), originating from Tongan 同安 county of Quanzhou 泉州 Prefecture in southwestern Fujian province, arrived in Canton in 1687 and resided in Shangjiu pu 上九甫 in the West End. He opened a candle shop there, making the front of the building his shop and the rear his residence. The Ye family later registered its household in Nanhai 南海 county, and Ye Zhende was remembered as "the first ancestor who moved to Guangdong" (*ruyue shizu* 入粵始祖; see *Yeshi Jiapu* 1924, 34).

The renowned hong merchant Puankhequa I (also spelled Poankeequa, Chinese name Pan Qi 潘啟, alias Zhencheng 振承, 1714–1788) also originated from Tongan and was initially involved in the trade with Manila (Van Dyke 2016, chapter 3). Upon settling in Canton, he probably found it easier to purchase land on Honam Island and hence built his residence and ancestral hall there. He named the place "Longxi Xiang" 龍溪鄉, making it his "village." He registered his household in Panyu 番禺 county as a merchant (*fuhu* 富户) and was considered "the first ancestor who moved to Guangdong" (*ruyue shizu* 入粵始祖). His biography in Pan's Genealogy states that "coming from a poor family, he had an upright character. Arriving at Guangdong from Fujian, he went back and forth three times doing trade in the Philippines. Well versed in the barbarian language (i.e., Spanish), he stayed with a Chinese merchant, Chen, in Canton, who dealt with foreign trade, and later became his business manager" (*Heyang Shixi Pan Nengjing Tang Zupu,* 30–31). After Chen retired, Pan established his own hong and named it "Tongwen" (同文) after the names of his native places, "Tongan" (同安) and "Wenpu" (文圃).

The walled city of Canton was located in the territories belonging to Nanhai and Panyu counties. Having registered their household in Nanhai or Panyu counties, these hong merchant families would have been entitled to local residency and to the rights of participating in civil service examinations. But these migrant merchants would never have been considered Nanhai or Panyu natives because they were not members of any local lineage or village community. It is perhaps more accurate to say that by not being able to become Nanhai and Panyu natives, they practically underwent a process of becoming "Cantonese," an identity with a distinctively "city" character.

One might assume that by working and residing in the West End, which fell within the area of Nanhai county, the migrant merchants and their descendants would at least have picked up Cantonese with a Nanhai accent in the course of becoming Cantonese. But accent is value-laden. By the nineteenth century, the accent spoken by people in the West End, no matter how it sounded, was named "the Saí Kwán wá 西關話" (West End speech) and not Nanhai dialect. It was considered "the correct pronunciation of pure Cantonese." In the introduction to *Cantonese Made Easy,* published in 1883, James Dyer Ball (1847–1919), the first interpreter at the Supreme Court in Hong Kong, asserted that "so far is this minute sub-division carried that even in the city of Canton itself, the seat and the center of pure Cantonese, more than one pronunciation of words is used; the standard, however, being the Saí Kwán wá, or West End speech, to which the learner should endeavor to assimilate his talk" (Ball 1883, xv). In the early twentieth century, the West End speech was established as the "standard" in philological terms. Some decades later, Chinese philologists made the same assertion. In a book entitled *Yuedong Pinyin Zipu* (粵東拼音字譜, List of Cantonese pronunciation), published in 1934, the author argued that the intonation of the character listed in his book was "tuned" according to the "standard speech" of the West End of Guangzhou (*yizhao* Guangzhou Xiguan *zhengyin tiaosheng* 依照廣州西關正音調聲) (Tan 1934, 2).

Paradoxically, the West End was initially part of the suburbs outside the walled city, and yet the "West End speech" was, and still is, considered the sound of urbanity. "Cantonese" (when referring to the population) was therefore not an equivalent to "Guangdongren" 廣東人; it comes closer to "Londoner" or "New Yorker." Whereas neither London nor New York reproduced a new London or a new New York inheriting the same accent of London urbanity (although there were many "Londons" elsewhere and New York was presumably a *new* York), the West End did. As I argue in the following paragraphs, the Chinese society of early colonial Hong Kong was a clone of the West End. The West End speech flowed with the movement of its speakers and became the accent of urbanity shared by different social strata and sectors of various Cantonese communities in many parts of the world.

The Sing-Song Girls and Their Literati Patrons on the Flower Boats, 1800s

Urban accent is a social marker, but its uses are not necessarily confined to one particular class. In the case of Cantonese, it was the joint efforts of the humblest female singers and respectable literati men in the mid-Qing period that vitalized the language with music. Because Cantonese is a tonal language, singing in Cantonese is closely related to how the language is spoken. The interaction of linguistic tone with the music of Cantonese is dealt with in such a way that tones sung in Cantonese are realized in accordance with its phonetics. When singing words with rising tones, singers are expected to sing in a rising contour, and likewise, falling tones in a falling contour (Chen and Chen 2010; Schellenbeg 2013). In other words, to address an urban audience, Cantonese singers are expected to realize their songs according to the urban accent of Cantonese and not to their own native village accent. Such a practice does not come naturally. It takes several generations of vocalists to perfect the art.

Among various genres of Cantonese songs sung in the Qing period, by the early nineteenth century, it was Southern Tone and *yueou* 粵謳 that became most popular among the sing-song girls and their literati patrons. The development of these two genres played a vital role in the perfection of Cantonese musical realizations. The diary of Xie Lansheng 謝蘭生 (1769–1831, extant diaries dated 1819–1829), the director of Yuexiu and two other academies of Canton and an in-law of Puankhequa II (his daughter was married to the second son of Puankhequa II), records in detail his participation in such sing-song activities. He spent much time on the flower boats (where sing-song girls and courtesans were stationed) anchoring at Litchi (Lizhi Wan荔枝灣) Bay on the waterways off the West End.[6] Xie and his friends, notably Zhao Ziyong 招子庸 (1793–1847), a degree holder from Nanhai, were particularly fond of Southern Tone and *yueou,* both of which were sung in accordance with West End speech with elaborate melodies.

To these literati men, singing in Cantonese was not only a matter of entertainment but also a means of expressing their cultural identity. In Qing times, it was fashionable among officials, merchants, and literati men in Canton to appreciate the Qinqiang 秦腔 theater and the Kunqu 昆曲, usually in the private gardens of the residences of high-ranking officials and merchants. Originating in Shaanxi and Gansu, the vocal style of Qinqiang is typified by its open and robust tones. Evolved from the Kunshan melody in the Suzhou region, Kunqu is considered the most refined style of Chinese opera. Despite their regional affiliation, both Qinqiang and Kunqu are performed in Zhongzhou 中州 speech-tones alienated from local speeches. Therefore, compared with Qinqiang and Kunqu, songs sung in Cantonese seemed crude and underdeveloped.

Nonetheless, by the early nineteenth century, some Cantonese literati men decided to uphold the musical tradition developed from their own language. They achieved this by means of the male-dominated literary efforts and corroborated by the sing-song courtesans who orally perfected their singing practices. In 1828, Zhao Ziyong collected more than a hundred pieces of Cantonese song lyrics and published a booklet entitled *Yueou* (Cantonese songs). Vocalized in most cases by flower-boat sing-song girls, the lyrics tell stories of rejected love, unquenchable desires, parting and abandoning, sorrow and suffering, of which the sentiment could well be shared, but not easily uttered, by men. Zhao enlisted a number of renowned local scholars to write prefaces for the book, and together they made a declaration defending the value of their own language. One of them lamented in his preface that "the Qin-voice sounds heroic and yet it is not what I am willing to listen to," "the Wu-songs sound gorgeous and yet it is not what I can commit myself to," and "only the southern tones can describe my lonely mood." Other preface writers also expressed similar sentiments and spoke highly of their "country speech" (*tuyin* 土音), as it was the speech of their own native place (*guxiang yin* 故鄉音), no matter how "barbarian" (*man* 蠻) it sounded to others (Zhao 1828).

Ironically, the "country speech" or the "barbarian voice" was in fact the sound of urbanity. The refinement of both *yueou* and *nanyin* implied "Cantonization" of musical realization, which in turn paved the way for the rise of operatic singing tuned in the West End speech of Cantonese in the early twentieth century, and that of Hong Kong Cantonese popular songs (Cantopop) in the second half of the twentieth century. We may remember that the blind singer Dou Wun once said that singing Southern Tone would make him more refined in the eyes of his patrons and would earn him much respect. Revisiting Qing Canton allows us to understand that what Dou Wun inherited was the singing style that emerged in the late eighteenth and early nineteenth centuries on the flower boats. Dou Wun knew that he should speak and sing in an urban accent so as to address a city audience in Canton and Hong Kong. His sound recordings were an audio proof of his efforts.

Cloning the West End in Hong Kong and Macau, Mid-1800s to early 1900s

There was nothing parochial about the West End speech and the Cantonese songs. They traveled in the following decades with their users to various port cities populated by Cantonese. Between the 1840s and the 1860s, Canton fell on hard times owing to casualties and losses caused by two Opium Wars, the Taipings, and the Red Turbans. The foreign factories along the quays were burned to ashes by the Great Fire in 1856, though they were soon rebuilt in the newly reclaimed British-French Concession on Shameen off the West End. The Canton trade system came to an end with China's failure in the First Opium War, but the vitality of the West End carried on.

Around the 1860s and 1870s the West End resumed its role as a regional wholesale market circulating commodities of the Asian and European-American trades. Walking in the West End in the 1870s, one would find, just to name a few, on Hing-Lung-Kai 興隆街, for sale by wholesale and retail, bales of Bombay cotton and hardware goods from England; on Hiu-Chue-Li 曉珠里, shops well stocked with Manchester goods; on Pan-Long-Kai (檳郎街 Betel-nut Street), cocoa-nuts and betel nuts from Hainan Island and the Straits of Malacca; on Pak-Mi-Kai 白米街, the Pohing's Chinaware shop, which sold a variety of porcelain vessels intended for European purchasers; and on Ch'eung-Hing-Kai 長興街, stone ornaments of various kinds and bracelets of glass made to resemble bracelets of jade, which were purchased by Chinese women as well as by Parsee and Mohammedan merchants who resided at Canton for forwarding to Bombay and Calcutta (Gray 1875). In short, one could find in the late nineteenth-century West End all kinds of commodities imported into China via the Indian and Atlantic maritime trades.

With the presence of a large number of merchants, traders, and laborers, the entertainment business prospered in the West End. In addition to the flower boats stationed along Litchi Bay, brothels appeared on a piece of newly

Map of "Canton with Suburbs and Honam," 1907, showing that the West End had become densely populated and urbanized by the 1900s. "CANTON with Suburbs and Honam," surveyed by Mr. F. Schnock, Engineer, 1907, reprinted in Guangzhou shi Guihua Ju, Guangzhou shi Chengshi Jianshe Dang'anguan, eds., *Tushuo Chengshi Wenmai: Guangzhou Gujin Dituji* (Guangzhou: Guangdongsheng Ditu chubanshe, 2010), p. 28.

reclaimed land located to the north of Shameen 沙面. The riverbank off the eastern suburbs was also developed to accommodate the expanding entertainment business. Around 1890 and 1891, several opera houses were erected in the West End and elsewhere outside the walled city (Ching 2010). By the late 1890s, real estate in the West End had become so well developed that residents there allied themselves in the form of *yue* 約 (alliances) and *fang* 坊 (quarters), probably for mutual aid and defense purposes. By 1910, when the Xuantong edition of *Nanhai County Gazetteer* was compiled, the number of recorded streets and roads in the West End district amounted to more than 1,700, and registered street numbers amounted to more than 4,000. These numbers indicate how urbanized the West End had become. A number of new markets were also founded (*Nanhai Xianzhi* [Xuantong edition], *juan* 6). Equally noteworthy is that the West End in the late Qing was where a number of philanthropic (*shantang* 善堂) and self-government associations (*zizhi hui* 自治會) were located, and thus became the center of protests in the circumstances of reform and revolution (Tsin 1999; Ching 2012).

What is more significant about the West End is that its landscape became a model that, together with the soundscape it bore, was duplicated in various Cantonese communities in different parts of the world. The first and most central of such cloning is Victoria City of colonial Hong Kong, or in Chinese terms, the "Four Wans" district—that is, Wan Chai 灣仔 and Causeway Bay 銅鑼灣, Central (Chung Wan 中環), Sheung Wan 上環, and Western District (Sai Wan 西環). While the colonial establishment (military and naval headquarters, churches, government offices, European residences) was located up on the hill in Central, the Chinese commercial and residential communities were situated on the reclaimed land along the "Four Wans." Like the West End, this area boasted retail and wholesale shops exchanging commodities from mainland China, Southeast Asia, Europe, and North America. One also found temples, charity halls, and hospitals, the most famous being the Man Mo Temple and its associated merchant charity, the Tung Wah Hospital, which were the de facto center of power of the Chinese communities (Sinn 2003). Although no Chinese opera houses were allowed to be built in the West End until the early 1890s, owing to the opposition of the Nanhai county magistrate (Ching 2010), three theaters had been erected in Sheung Wan by the 1870s (Ng Suet-kwan 2015). The Hong Kong version of the West End expanded westward on the island in the early twentieth century. Between 1890 and 1904, the Hong Kong government launched a large-scale reclamation project extending from the Central district to Sai Ying Pun 西營盤 to its west, which could be reached by tram service. Later, the government ordered all brothels and teahouses moved from Possession Point in Sheung Wan to Shek Tong Tsui 石塘咀 in Sai Ying Pun. Shek Tong Tsui thus became known as a neighborhood where high-class brothels stood, comparable to that of Chen Tang 陳塘 in the West End. The booming entertainment business in Shek Tong Tsui also led to the erection of a new theater, the Tai Ping 太平, in 1906.

Around the same time, one saw another version of the West End in Macau. It was located in the "Ha Wan" 下環 (Lower Bay) district along today's Rua Do Dr. Lourenco Pereira Marques on the western side of the peninsula. In the 1850s, large-scale reclamation of the area was initiated at a time when the Portuguese were attempting to strengthen their control of Macau, which formally become a Portuguese colony in 1887. Lined with brothels, teahouses, and gambling and opium dens, the Rua da Felicidade 福隆新街 was considered the red-light district of Macau. With the prosperity brought about by the indentured coolie trade,[7] the Chinese commercial community in Macau thrived. Between the 1860s and 1870s three Chinese opera houses (Auto China, Pou-heng, and Ch'eng-p'eng) operated in the "Ha Wan" district. Parallel to the Nine Charity Halls of Canton and the Tung Wah of Hong Kong, the Tongshan Tang 同善堂 Charity Hall in Macau was established near Rua da Felicidade. Although the ban on the coolie trade in 1873 halted the short-term economic expansion in the peninsula, resulting in the closure of two Chinese opera houses (Zeng 2017), Rua da Felicidade continued to be a center of entertainment comparable to Shek Tong Tsui and the West End until the end of the Second World War.

The West End speech also migrated with its users to Hong Kong, Macau, and elsewhere. Although Chinese migrants moving to Hong Kong came from different parts of Guangdong and spoke different dialects or accents, the "standard" Cantonese accent spoken in Victoria City in Hong Kong and soon within the entire colony was, and still is, the West End speech. Moreover, the thriving of entertainment businesses in the West End, Hong Kong, and Macau discussed above is no less significant to our discussion of soundscape. In the pre-gramophone and radio broadcast days, live singing performance was the only means by which the Qing tradition of Cantonese songs could still be presented and realized. Until the late 1920s, blind singers and sing-song girls sang Southern Tone and other Cantonese songs in brothels and teahouses, before operatic singing became fully tuned in the West End speech of Cantonese.

Human Agency: Maximizing Comparative Advantages

Hong Kong and Macau, with their colonial legal systems and proximity, became a haven where people from the Pearl River delta could diversify their investments and spread the risks. Zhang Zhidong 張之洞, the Guangdong-Guangxi governor-general from 1884 to 1889, reported in his 1887 memorial that thousands of people from Nanhai, Panyu, Xiangshan 香山, and Shunde 順德 traversed between Macau and Guangdong, investing in business and real estate at both ends. He also noted that it was easier to acquire a Portuguese nationality in Macau than in British colonial Hong Kong, as the government in Macau was more easily compromised (Yuan, Sun, and Li 1998, 539–544). In 1905, an officer working in the maritime customs in Canton was charged with corruption by the current Guangdong-Guangxi governor-general. He fled with his wife to Shanghai and then to Hong Kong, where they had purchased estates, with the hope of seeking protection under a different legal system (*Shishi huabao* 1905, No. 7). Such cases were not unusual. Since the founding of the two colonies, people from Guangdong were skilled in maneuvering between different political and legal systems.

Considering the comparative advantages of the three cities, serious entrepreneurs and political activists would find Canton and Hong Kong more complementary than Macau. The Portuguese colony did not have a sizable hinterland or market and could assume only a supplementary role. The term *Shenggang* in the *Shenggang da bagong* (省港大罷工 Canton–Hong Kong strike 1925–1926) was a case in point as far as political economic movements were concerned. Such a relationship extended to the operatic scene. The term *shenggang ban* (省港班 Canton–Hong Kong opera troupes) demonstrated the movement of the artists and the expansion of the Cantonese soundscape across the two cities. Cantonese opera troupes mainly targeted their substantial markets, investing heavily in hiring celebrated actors, composing new scripts, purchasing attractive costumes, and erecting elaborate stage settings in order to appeal to an urbane audience who shared a repertoire of audiovisual aesthetics. The coexistence of the two markets allowed these troupes to maximize profits and spread risks or losses. One of the strategies was to coordinate the scheduling of performances. In the 1920s, when the Peking Opera superstar Mei Lanfang 梅蘭芳 performed in Canton, the two most popular Canton–Hong Kong troupes would perform in Hong Kong instead. In turn, they would also "go up" to Canton (*shangsheng* 上省) when Mei performed in Hong

Kong (Aimei 1928). Here, the use of the preposition "up" is worth noting. The 1828 *Vocabulary of the Canton Dialect* instructs its readers to use such Cantonese phrases as *sheong shang sheng* 上省城 (to go up to Canton) and *lok ow moon*" 落澳門 (to go down to Macau) to describe traveling between the two cities (Morrison 1828, s.v. "Go"). The politically and culturally superior position of Canton in relation to Macau and later to Hong Kong was clearly articulated in the terms "going up and down." They expressed hierarchical connotations rather than a mere geographical orientation of "heading north and south."

Other pre-1940s developments also show how Canton and Hong Kong might have worked with each other to achieve a larger goal. Hong Kong was a preferred location for many small-scale manufacturers coming from the Pearl River delta to set up their factories, yet many of these factory owners would also register their businesses with the Nationalist government and have their products labeled "national" for marketing purposes (Ching 2008, 47). In the 1930s and 1940s, when light industries were being developed in both cities, a considerable number of manufacturers established factories in suburban areas in both Guangzhou and Hong Kong. Some manufacturers located their headquarters and main factory in the city center of Guangzhou, branch firms and factories in Hong Kong, and an additional branch in such cities as Singapore, so as to oversee businesses in mainland China, Hong Kong, and Southeast Asia (*Xianggang Gongchang Diaocha* 1948). By contrast, Canton–Hong Kong entrepreneurs seldom considered Macau a suitable site for factories, although branch firms or agents would be set up there for retail.

To the working masses, Macau has always been a second choice or transit stop, as its population and territory are too small to sustain significant production and consumption. The multisited strategies of businesses and manufacturers applied to musicians and performers as well. The blind singer Dou Wun passed by and did not stay in Macau on his way to Hong Kong around 1926 as he probably knew that Macau offered little opportunity. Other kinds of singers followed slightly different trajectories. In the late 1920s, blind men and women singers were gradually replaced by women operatic singers stationing at teahouses. These singers also preferred Hong Kong and Canton to Macau. But unlike their blind counterparts, they had a third choice. They would go to Shanghai to look for alternative performance opportunities, as the Cantonese population in Shanghai was large and affluent enough to sustain a Cantonese opera and song market (Zhou Xiuhua 1928).

Shanghai as an Amplifier and Macau the Last Haven before the 1950s

Unlike Hong Kong and Macau, Shanghai was not a duplication of the West End landscape; yet its centrality in cultural production helped amplify an intercity soundscape. This was well illustrated by the cases of the New Moon Records Company and the Cantonese broadcasts in Shanghai. Founded in Hong Kong in 1926 by a Cantonese man, Qian Guangren 錢廣仁, the New Moon Records Company was a typical example of how the three cities—Canton, Hong Kong, and Shanghai—worked together to spread the sound of urbanity. Graduated from St. Paul's College, an English missionary school in Hong Kong, Qian went to Shanghai and worked in a bank for three years. After spending six months in an English bookstore, he moved to a new job in the accounting department of a foreign company. He did not return to Hong Kong until his father asked him to help manage their family metal-ware business. He soon established his own Liquan Metal-ware Company in Hong Kong, which had branches set up in Guangzhou and Shanghai. It was on the basis of Liquan that New Moon Records was able to distribute its products (discs, gramophones, magazines, and other accessories) in various cities in China. In 1929 Qian registered the trademark of New Moon Records Company with the Nationalist government and promoted his gramophone as a "one-hundred-percent national product," concentrating on the recording of Cantonese music and songs and occasionally some Mandarin songs (Ching 2008).

Although most Cantonese operatic singers were based in Canton and Hong Kong, the first four series of New Moon gramophone records were done in Shanghai, as studios there were better equipped. There were also plenty of chances to meet superstars like Xue Juexian 薛覺先 and Ma Shizeng 馬師曾 in Shanghai, as they traveled back and forth among the three cultural hubs to start their careers in sound film. Other Cantonese singers, such as Lifang 麗芳, who was well known for being a "Gang-Hu *kunjue*" (港滬坤角 Hong Kong–Shanghai operatic actress), were also easily accessible in Shanghai. As seen from the booklet issued by the New Moon Records Company, it seems that Qian Guangren simply recruited singers he chanced to meet in the three cities who were happy to record with his label (*Xinyue ji* 1930). Gramophone recordings in those days could be relatively unstructured and at times coincidental, but the tracks of these Cantonese singers were not. Canton, Hong

Kong, and Shanghai would be the three cities among which the more renowned singers and performers traveled back and forth to a good living and a name.

Apart from recording newly composed Cantonese operatic pieces and more traditional ones, Qian Guangren invited composers to write new lyrics that came closer to the style of modern Mandarin popular songs. These new-style Cantonese songs displayed modern subject matter, and their lyrics occasionally mixed Cantonese vernacular with a few English words. They continued the Qing tradition of Cantonese singing, juxtaposed with attempts to explore the potential of a hybrid vernacular genre.[8] They could well be considered the pioneers of Hong Kong Cantopop, which emerged several decades later to fuel the music sensibilities of a consuming public in the latter part of the twentieth century.

The gramophone industry and radio broadcasts were mutually supportive. Qian's gramophone business must have benefited from the popularity of radio broadcasts in Shanghai. In the 1930s, the number of radio stations in Shanghai that broadcast Cantonese programs was striking. By 1939, sixteen radio stations in Shanghai broadcast news, drama, religious, business, and music programs in Cantonese, amounting to almost half of the radio stations running in Shanghai in those days. By the early 1940s, Shanghai even had one or two radio stations, notably Anhua 安華, that broadcast exclusively in Cantonese from 8:00 A.M. till midnight on a daily basis (Song 2017).

These sounds of entertainment shared by Shanghai, Canton, and Hong Kong became more or less silent when the three cities fell to the Japanese military one after another in November 1937, October 1938, and December 1941. Because Portugal stayed officially neutral, Macau rose to become the last wartime haven in South China and somehow benefited from the adversity suffered by the rest of the region. An overwhelmingly huge number of refugees fled from Canton, Hong Kong, and its vicinity to Macau. The population of Macau increased from 150,000 in 1927 to 250,000 in 1939, and to 370,000 in 1940 (Gu and Dai 1998). Entertainment businesses boomed. Between 1942 and the early 1950s, almost all Cantonese opera troupes that had previously been active in Canton and Hong Kong moved to Macau. To compete with each other in this small city, sojourning opera troupes composed thousands of new scripts between 1942 and 1945. Such wartime fortune was ephemeral. When peace returned, the population of Macau dropped abruptly from 400,000 to 188,000 in 1950. By 1955, almost all opera troupes

(1) 有个女子。	瓜子口面。
佢喺東方。	我喺西便。
大家分離。	眞是可憐。
吽佢番嚟。	見吓我面。
(2) SOME LIKES SWEETIE.	SOME LIKES MONEY
你要蜜糖。	我要仙士。
BLOW THE WHISTLE.	吹吓嗶嗶。
兩家 TALKEE.	揀个日子。
(3) SHE WILL LOVE ME.	佢好愛我。
嗎介東西。	吽造 WHAT FOR.
四月廿四。	APRIL 24TH.
去渡密月。	眞是冇錯。
(4) GO TO PAREE.	去到巴黎。
COM, PAN, LI VU,	你好喇喂。
BEAUFITUL DOLL	好靚公仔。
買个番嚟。	比你一睇。
(5) WHO'S YOUR FATHER.	問我老子。
我个老豆。	吽造 BILLIE.
你吽老爺。	我吽爹爹。
滿面 WHISKER.	好似羊咩。
(6) 佢好孤寒。	STINGY FELLOW.
POCKET EMPTY.	个袋冇貨。
THIRTY CENTS.	買的燒鵝。
同埋食飯。	唔使肚餓。
(7) TOO MUCH CHOW CHOW.	食飯大多。
胃口太窄。	點能收科。
但望天公。	來保祐我。
賜个 BABY.	當作 KAM SHAW.
(8) GET ONE AMAH.	請个使婆。
來 臭 BABY.	快的太个。
洗牛奶樽。	切勿打破。
順手掩門。	CLOSE THE DOOR.
(9) 若然唱錯。	請你諒我。
才疏學淺。	見識無多。
大家聽過。	笑口呵呵。
HAPPY NEW YEAR.	恭喜多賀。

New-style popular songs in Cantonese vernacular mixed with a few English words, composed and produced by the New Moon Records Company in the 1930s. The music was played on piano and trumpet. From *Xinyue Ji,* Vol. 1, 1930.

and individual opera actors and singers had left Macau for either Hong Kong or Canton.[9]

During the turbulent 1940s, Cantonese opera troupes continued to seek short-term opportunities in the Cantonese diasporic networks overseas, performing in San Francisco, Saigon, Singapore, and other cities. In fact, the circulation of Cantonese operatic activities had been transregional and transnational from the start. Around the time that a number of theaters started in Sheung Wan on Hong Kong Island, San Francisco's Chinatown also witnessed a similar process of theater construction. Early in 1868, the first permanent theater for performing Chinese operas supported by Chinese merchants in San Francisco was inaugurated on Jackson Street (Ching 2010). From the mid-nineteenth century through the 1940s, Cantonese opera performances thrived in various Chinese communities all over the world. This twentieth-century transnationality of Cantonese opera in North America, Singapore, and Southeast Asia, partly driven by the market, and partly structured by political circumstances, is well demonstrated in a recent work by Ng Wing Chung (2015).

The Downfall of *Jianghu*

The Canton–Hong Kong–Macau triangular alignment and its dynamic connections with other Cantonese communities inside and outside China began to collapse in the 1950s for obvious political reasons. The case of Mr. Luo Jiabao 羅家寶 (1930–2016), a celebrated Cantonese opera actor, illustrates vividly how people's transnational and transregional movements were disrupted after the 1950s. Born in Shunde county in Guangdong in 1930, Luo started his career in Shanghai at the age of nine in a troupe led by his uncle Luo Jiaquan 羅家權, who moved to Shanghai in 1939 to perform Cantonese opera. At that time Shanghai had already fallen into Japanese hands. It was said that Luo Jiaquan moved there to dodge scandals in which he was involved in Canton and Hong Kong. In 1940, Luo Jiabao moved to Hong Kong with his father, Luo Jiashu 羅家樹, a famous percussionist. His uncle also joined. When Hong Kong fell in December 1941, the three moved to Macau, where Luo Jiabao continued to develop his opera career. After the war, he spent some time in Canton and Wuzhou along the West River. Between 1949 and 1953, he had become a rising star and was able to lead his own troupe to perform in Singapore, Phnom Penh, Haiphong, Saigon, and Hanoi. It was during those years, Luo recalled, that he broke away from his father and uncle and explored opportunities and challenges on his own.

After the war, many Cantonese opera performers realized that they could no longer move as freely as before. The question was where to put down career roots. Luo said that it was common knowledge among the Cantonese opera performers that sojourning in Southeast Asia and America would not help them secure lasting professional recognition. Opera performers therefore chose between Canton and Hong Kong when establishing a base. In view of the fierce competition from his peers and the postwar economic recession in Hong Kong, Luo Jiabao chose to settle in Canton in January 1954. Like many other artists, he gained much satisfaction in his professional development between 1954 and 1957. The newly founded People's Republic of China pursued relatively liberal policies to attract overseas returnees. In January 1954, at the age of twenty-four, Luo performed for the first time the Cantonese opera's adaptation of the Tang dynasty story *Liu Yi Chuanshu* 柳毅傳書 (Liu Yi sending the letter on behalf of the Sea Dragon Princess), which became one of his most popular pieces. In 1957, Luo recorded his first album, which included *Liu Yi Chuanshu* and a few other pieces. His records were brought to Hong Kong by connoisseurs. They were broadcast in Macau as well. His voice was therefore heard in the music circles outside mainland China.

Nonetheless, by mid-1957, Luo, along with some of his opera pieces, was denounced as being culturally "feudal" and "superstitious." He suffered in various political campaigns between 1957 and 1968 and could perform only highly stylized "modern" revolutionary Cantonese operas. In 1969, during the Cultural Revolution, he was sent down to labor at a farm in northeastern Guangdong. He was allowed to return to Guangzhou after nine years of detention. Unbroken, he performed again in 1979. He gradually resumed his professional practice and recovered his reputation by engaging in serious traditional Cantonese opera performances. In August 1983, he led the state-run Guangdong No. 2 Opera Troupe to Hong Kong and acted his famous pieces with Hong Kong performers. Reunions with friends, colleagues, and relatives from whom he had parted in 1954 were heartwarming occasions. Most of the Hong Kong audience appreciated the professional foundation Luo had built for himself before and after the 1950s. But reviews also highlighted the differences between "Hong Kong" and "Mainland" performance styles. They suggested that singers long separated by the political divide not only displayed different stage acting styles but also *sounded* different. The intervening impact of the revolutionary plays was acutely felt. Furthermore, various discourses began to emerge in the early 1980s over the economic, social, and cultural gaps between the two cities. In 1984, the Sino-British negotiations on the future of Hong Kong were formally launched (Ching 2011).[10]

Luo was no doubt projected "back" to Hong Kong. Fans welcomed him, but he could stay in Hong Kong for only limited periods. The era for artists to travel freely from one port city to another to deliver performances (*zoubu* 走埠) had ended decades ago due to Maoist and Cold War politics. When he was given another chance to move on, he was already in his fifties. Whereas the blind singer Dou Wun was one of the unfortunate singers who had no resources to reach far beyond Hong Kong, Luo Jiabao attempted to decide his own fate but found himself grounded in Guangzhou for decades.

Individuals' movements, like those of Luo Jiabao, were restrained not only because of immediate political causes but also because of the long-standing consequences of political turmoil. Hong Kong as part of a triangulating cultural hub lost a great deal of its vitality and mentality. After the war, Hong Kong, consciously and unconsciously, continued to be a clone of Canton and a follower of Shanghai, until a separate urban identity emerged in the 1970s with the coming of age of a local born, postwar generation. Hong Kong has since been branded as Asia's world city with its own distinct cultural identity, but it has lost Canton as an indispensable part of the triangular alignment. The aura of old Shanghai as its model of modernity[11] has somewhat faded. The city's transregional and transnational ties with diasporic Cantonese communities have been shaped by different generations and classes of immigrants. The previous *jianghu*, constituted of "Three plus One Cities" (Canton–Hong Kong–Macau plus Shanghai) and "Two Oceans plus Two Gold Mountains" (South Ocean, i.e., Southeast Asia; East Ocean, i.e., Japan and Korea; Old Gold Mountains, i.e., America, in particular California; New Gold Mountains, i.e., Australia), used to be a "Superhub"—much bigger and more dynamic than the "Greater Bay Area" currently proposed by the Chinese government. What is left of this *jianghu*—a world with its unique landscape and soundscape that itinerant artists, performers, and an appreciating public have collectively forged for more than three centuries? In view of the rise of a wealthy, nationalistic, and culturally assertive China in the twenty-first century, what are the components of a new urban network and soundscape in the making? Who are the major players? We might not have an immediate answer. But what is almost certain is that the sound of the West End is fading out and will never return.

Notes

1. Both maps show the Canton–Hong Kong–Macau triangular alignment. The 1959 one shows that the three cities were well connected by the 1950s with the running of the Kowloon-Canton Railway (since 1911) and the Qi-Guan Motorway (connecting

Shiqi, the county capital of Zhongshan, with Guanzha, Macau-Zhuhai border, since 1933), alongside the long-established waterways.

2. In the 1920s and 1930s, brothels in Yaumatei / Mongkok in Kowloon were considered inferior to their counterparts in Shek Tong Tsui on Hong Kong Island. The sex workers in Kowloon were called "Ma (Yaumatei) -Flower" and were believed to be Tanka (*danjia* 疍家) boatwomen residing in Yaumatei, which was then a beach, a bay, and later a typhoon shelter. Tanka were treated by land residents as mean and inferior. The first issue (August 1928) of *Xianghua Huabao* 香花畫報 (Fragrant Flowers Pictorial), an entertainment magazine published in Guangzhou and distributed in Hong Kong and other towns and cities, has elaborate descriptions of "Ma-Flower."

3. From 1931 on, the Hong Kong government launched a series of measures to ban prostitution despite resistance from brothel and restaurant owners. Licensed prostitution was put to an end by June 1935. See the news reports in *Gongshang Wanbao* (dated December 14, 1931, and November 5, 1933), *Hong Kong Sunday Herald* (December 16, 1934), and *Tianguang Bao* (July 1, 1935).

4. Radio Rediffusion was established in Hong Kong in 1949 and featured the wired distribution of its radio channels. See the website of Rediffusion (Hong Kong) Limited (http://www.rediffusion.info/hk.html), accessed October 4, 2017.

5. The Cantonese word *hong* could refer to a licensed firm and to the buildings in which the firm was located or the merchants who owned them. The buildings in which foreign merchants resided were referred to as "factories," a common eighteenth-century word for godown, trading station, or warehouse. In Canton, *hong* and "factories" were interchangeable. See Van Dyke and Mok (2015, xv). The Chinese also called factories *yiguan* 夷館, which means "barbarian houses."

6. Entries describing his involvement in sing-song and opera activities, in particular *nanyin* and *yueou*, can be found throughout his diary. See Xie 2014.

7. In the 1840s, China became the major source of indentured labor supply for newly established sugar estates in the West Indies. Macau had been one of the embarkation ports for Chinese coolies since 1851. The Portuguese Macau government tried to regulate the coolie trade by legislation. Nonetheless, with more and more cases of mistreatment and cruelty by captains and crews, coolie trade was considered a slave trade and was an embarrassment to the Macau government. Under the pressure of both the Hong Kong and the Qing governments, the governor of Macau proclaimed in December 1873 that in obedience to the orders of the Portuguese government, the Chinese emigration carried on in Macau was to be prohibited. See Asome 2014.

8. Andrew Jones finds in these lyrics some colonial flavor underneath the nationalistic articulation of the brand name. See Jones 1999.

9. This paragraph on Chinese opera in Macau in the 1940s and 1950s is written according to the summary of *Zhongguo Xiquzhi (Aomen juan)* (Chronicle of Chinese Opera [Macau]) drawn by myself (manuscript, forthcoming).

10. My colleagues and I have produced a lengthy biography of Luo based on a series of interviews with Luo, archives, and other textual and visual materials. See Ching May Bo 2011.

11. Comparing the old Shanghai presented in Lee 1999 with the post-1949 one in Zhang 2015, one can tell how "revolutionarized" Shanghai became and how its connection with Hong Kong transformed in the second half of the twentieth century.

References

Aimei 愛梅 (pseudonym). 1928. "Guangzhouren ying Mei mang" 廣州人迎梅忙 [Guangzhou people are busy at receiving Mei Lanfang]. *Fei Fei Huabao* 非非畫報 [Fei Fei Pictorial], No. 5, November 1928.

Asome, John. 2014. "The Indentured Coolie Trade from Macao." *Journal of the Royal Asiatic Society Hong Kong Branch,* Vol. 54, 157–179.

Ball, James Dyer. 1883. *Cantonese Made Easy: A Book of Simple Sentences in the Cantonese Dialect, with Free and Literal Translations, and Directions for the Rendering of English Grammatical Forms in Chinese.* 4th ed., revised and enlarged, by A. Dyer Ball. Hong Kong: Kelly and Walsh, 1924 (1st edition prefaced 1883).

Chen Zhuoying陳卓瑩 and Chen Zhongyan 陳仲琰. 2010. *Chen Zhuoying Yuequ Xiechang Yanjiu* 陳卓瑩粵曲寫唱研究 [A study of the composition and singing of Cantonese operatic songs by Chen Zhuoying]. Hong Kong: Yijin chuban qihua youxian gongsi.

Ching May Bo. 2008. "Where Guangdong Meets Shanghai: Hong Kong Culture in a Trans-regional Context." In *Hong Kong Mobile: Making a Global Population,* eds. Helen F. Siu and Agnes S. Ku, 45–62. Hong Kong: Hong Kong University Press.

———. 2010. "A Preliminary Study of the Theatres Built by Cantonese Merchants in the Late Qing." *Frontiers of History in China,* Vol. 5, No. 2, 253–278.

———, ed. 2011. *Pingmin Laoguan Luo Jiabao*平民老倌羅家寶 [Luo Jiabao: A Cantonese opera actor and his time]. Hong Kong: Joint Publishing (H.K.).

———. 2012. "Poqiang er chu: Qingmo Minchu Guangzhou Xiguan diqu jingguan de yanxu yu bianqian" 破墻而出：清末民初廣州西關地區景觀的延續與變遷 [Breaking the walls: Continuity and changes in the landscapes of the West End district in Guangzhou from late Qing to early Republic]. In *Zhongguo Jindai Chengshi Wenhua de Dongtai Fazhan: Renwen Kongjian de Xin shiye* (中國近代城市文化的動態發展：人文空間的新視野 [The dynamic development of cities in Modern China: New perspectives on human spaces], ed. Billy Kee-long So 蘇基朗, 180–201. Hangzhou: Zhejiang Daxue chubanshe.

Ching May Bo 程美寶and Huang Sujuan 黃素娟, eds. 2017. *Sheng Gang Ao Dazhong wenhua yu dushi bianqian* 省港澳大眾文化與都市變遷 [The popular culture and urban transformation of Canton, Hong Kong, and Macao]. Beijing: Shehui Kexue Wenxian Chubanshe.

Conner, Patrick. 2009. *The Hongs of Canton: Western Merchants in South China 1700–1900, as seen in Chinese Export Paintings*. London: English Art Books.

Du, Huan (Dou Wun) 杜煥. 2004. *Piaobo hongchen hua Xiangjiang: Shiming ren Du Huan yi wang* 飄泊紅塵話香江：失明人杜煥憶往 [A blind singer's story: 50 years of life and work in Hong Kong (DVD and booklet). Hong Kong: Hong Kong Museum of History.

———. 2011. *Jueshi yiyin: Liang laoqi aijiao* 絕世遺音：兩老契嗌交 [Two brothel clients quarreling with each other] (sound disc and booklet). Hong Kong: Chinese Music Archive, the Chinese University of Hong Kong.

———. 2012. *Yukui baoshan: Gushi Du Huan yanchang longzhou banben* 玉葵寶扇：瞽師杜煥演唱龍舟版本 [Jade palm-leaf fan, sung by blind master Dou Wun in dragon-boat style] (sound disc and booklet). Hong Kong: Chinese Music Archive, the Chinese University of Hong Kong.

Farris, Johnathan Andrew. 2016. *Enclave to Urbanity: Canton, Foreigners, and Architecture from the Late Eighteenth to the Early Twentieth Centuries*. Hong Kong: Hong Kong University Press.

Gongshang Wanbao 工商晚報. 1931. "Gangfu juexin jinchang, jiulou laoban renren ziwei" 港府決心禁娼，酒樓老板人人自危 [The Hong Kong government is determined to ban prostitution. Restaurant owners are threatened]. December 14, 1931.

Gongshan Wanbao 工商晚報. 1933. "Jinchang qixian jue bu zhanhuan" 禁娼期限決不展緩 [Ban on prostitution will be implemented without further delay]. November 5, 1933.

Gray, John Henry. 1875. *Walks in the City of Canton*. Hong Kong: De Souza & Co.

Gu Wannian 古萬年 (Custódio N.P.S. Cónim) and Dai Minli 戴敏麗 (Maria Fernanda Bragança Teixeira). 1998. *Aomen ji qi renkou yanbian wubainian* (1500–2000): *Renkou, shehui ji jingji tantao* 澳門及其人口演變五百年 (1500年至2000年)：人口、社會及經濟探討 [Macau and its population changes (1500–2000): Studies on Demography, Society and Economics]. Macao: Statistics and Census Service.

Heyang Shixi Pan Nengjing Tang Zupu 河陽世系潘能敬堂族譜 [Genealogy of Pan Nengjing Tang]. Collection of Guangdong Provincial Zhongshan Library.

Hong Kong Sunday Herald. 1934. "Prostitution Reform: Registered Women Give Six Months' Notice." December 16, 1934.

Jones, F. Andrew. 1999. "The Gramophone in China." In *Tokens of Exchange: The Problem of Translation in Global Circulations*, ed. Lydia H. Liu, 214–236. Durham, NC, and London: Duke University Press.

Lee, Leo Ou-fan. 1999. *Shanghai Modern: The Flowering of a New Urban Culture in China, 1930–1945*. Cambridge, MA: Harvard University Press.

Morrison, Robert. 1828. *Vocabulary of the Canton Dialect: Part I: English and Chinese*. Macao: Printed at the Honorable East India Company's Press.

Nanhai xianzhi 南海縣誌 [Xuantong edition of Nanhai County Gazetteer].

Ng, Wing Chung. 2015. *The Rise of Cantonese Opera.* Hong Kong: Hong Kong University Press.

Ng Suet-kwan 吴雪君. 2015. "The Development of Cantonese Opera Theatres in Hong Kong (1840–1940)" 香港粵劇戲園發展 （1840–1940 ）. In *Xiyuan • Hongchuan • Yinghua: Yuan Shi Zhencang "Taiping Xiyuan Wenwu" Yanjiu* 戲園 • 紅船 • 影畫：源氏珍藏"太平戲院文物"研究[A study of the Tai Ping theatre collection], ed. Sai-Shing Yung, 98–117. Hong Kong: Hong Kong Heritage Museum.

Schellenbeg, Murray Henry. 2013. "The Realization of Tone in Singing in Cantonese and Mandarin." PhD thesis, University of British Columbia.

Shishi Huabao 時事畫報 [Illustrated news]. 1905–1913 (Guangzhou and Hong Kong). Reprinted 2014. Compiled by Guangzhou Museum, Guangdong Provincial Zhongshan Library, Sun Yat-sen University Library. Guangzhou: Guangdong Renmin Chubanshe.

Sinn, Elizabeth. 2003. *Power and Charity: A Chinese Merchant Elite in Colonial Hong Kong* (with a new preface). Hong Kong: Hong Kong University Press.

Song Zuanyou 宋鑽友. 2017. "Boyin li de Guangdong shengyin: Jianlun diyu wenhua zai Shanghai chuanbo de yuanyin" 播音裡的廣東聲音 ： 兼論地域文化在上海傳播的原因 [The sound of Guangdong in radio broadcast: Why did regional culture disseminate in Shanghai]. In Ching and Huang, *Sheng-Gang-Ao Dazhong wenhua yu dushi bianqian*, 325–352.

Tan Rongguang 譚榮光. 1934. Yuedong Pinyin Zipu 粵東拼音字譜 [List of Cantonese pronunciation]. Hong Kong: Dongya yinwu youxian gongsi.

Tianguang Bao 天光報. 1935. "Jinchang hou de Tangxi" 禁娼後的塘西 [Tangxi after ban on prostitution]. July 1, 1935.

Tsin, Michael Tsang-Woon. 1999. *Nation, Governance, and Modernity in China: Canton, 1900–1927.* Stanford, CA: Stanford University Press.

Van Dyke, Paul. 2016. *Merchants of Canton and Macao: Success and Failure in Eighteenth-Century Chinese Trade.* Hong Kong: Hong Kong University Press.

Van Dyke, Paul, and Maria Kar-Wing Mok. 2015. *Images of the Canton Factories 1760–1822: Reading History in Art.* Hong Kong: Hong Kong University Press.

Xianggang Gongchang Diaocha 香港工廠調查 [A survey of factories in Hong Kong]. 1948. Hong Kong: Nanqiao Xinwen Qiye Gongsi.

Xianghua Huabao 香花畫報 [Fragrant flowers pictorial], No. 1, Guangzhou, August, 1928.

Xie Lansheng 謝蘭生. 2014. *Chang Xingxing Zhai Riji (Wai Sizhong)* 常惺惺齋日記（外四 種） [Diary of Chang Xingxing study, with four additional works]. Transcribed and compiled by Li Ruoqing 李若晴. Guangzhou: Guangdong Renmin Chubanshe.

Xinyue Ji 新月集. 1930. 2 vols. Hong Kong: New Moon Records Company.

*Yeshi jiapu*葉氏家譜 [Ye's genealogy]. 1924. Collection of Guangdong Provincial Zhongshan Library.

Yuan Shuyi 苑書義, Sun Huafeng 孫華峰, and Li Bingxin 李秉新. 1998. *Zhang Zhidong Quanji*張之洞全集 [Collections of works by Zhang Zhidong]. Shijiazhuang Shi: Hebei Renmin Chubanshe.

Zeng Jinlian 曾金蓮. 2017. "Wan Qing Aomen Zhongguo Xiyuan Chutan" 晚清澳門中國戲院初探 [A preliminary study of Chinese theatres in late Qing Macau]. In Ching and Huang, *Sheng-Gang-Ao Dazhong wenhua yu dushi bianqian*, 122–133.

Zhang Jishun 張濟順. 2015. *Yuanqu de Dushi*: *Yijiuwuling niandai de Shanghai* 遠去的都市: 1950年代的上海 [A City Displaced: Shanghai in the 1950s]. Beijing: Shehui Kexue Wenxian Chubanshe.

Zhao Ziyong 招子庸. 1828. *Yueou* 粵謳 [Cantonese songs]. Guangzhou: Chengtian ge.

Zhou Xiuhua 周脩花. 1928. "Baiyanzai fu Hu quexun" 白燕仔赴滬確訊 [That Baiyanzai is going to Shanghai is confirmed]. *Haizhu Xingqi Huabao*海珠星期畫報 [Haizhu Weekly Pictorial]. No. 5.

Roast Beef versus Pigs' Trotters

Knowledge in Transit in the Work of a Chinese Food Evangelist

EMMA J. TENG

In *My Country and My People,* first published by John Day in 1935, Lin Yutang (1895–1976) mused on the infamous aversion of Westerners to Chinese food, even as they urged Chinese to learn much—science, Christianity, English football, American efficiency, and the use of table napkins—from the West. Of this unevenness, he wrote:

> In the cooking of ordinary things like vegetables and chickens, the Chinese have a rich store to hand to the West, when the West is ready and humble enough to learn it. This seems unlikely until China has built a few good gun-boats and can punch the West in the jaw, when it will be admitted that we are unquestionably better cooks as a nation. But until that time comes, there is no use talking about it. There are thousands of Englishmen in the Shanghai Settlement who have never stepped inside a Chinese restaurant, and the Chinese are bad evangelists. (Lin 1936, 323)

Lin's remarks perceptively link culinary ethnocentrism with the complex interplay of hard and soft power that shaped Sino-Western interactions for much of the nineteenth and twentieth centuries. China was commonly perceived by Westerners as a vast market and missionary field, as well as a source of goods, labor, and natural resources, but rarely as a source of cultural knowledge, let alone culinary wisdom. Tales of "stags' pizzles," birds' nests, and other "oddities" of the Chinese table were staples among early Western travelers to China, and hardly served to whet appetites for this foreign cuisine (Coe 2009). The rise of pseudoscientific discourses of race and euthenics in the early twentieth century served only to legitimize this culinary ethnocentrism and disdain for Chinese food. Euthenics discourse frequently emphasized that different racialized groups had distinct "natural" diets, which were separate but far from equal. As Helen Zoe Veit writes, euthenics advocates "claimed that European and white Americans' penchant for rugged fare like beef made them uniquely strong, martial, and adventurous, in contrast to Asians, whose meek vegetable diets were thought to make them passive and philosophical" (2013, 104–105). Global imbalances of power could thus be seen to stem from the very fundamental matter of food consumption and dietary preference, which produced "martial races" and effete ones. Reinforcing the conviction in the superiority of the Anglo-American diet, with its emphasis on meat, wheat, and "plain fare," euthenics discourse became a form of "knowledge in transit," transported to Asia through the Western powers' "civilizational" mission: so powerful were such ideas that even the famed Confucian philosopher Kang Youwei (1858–1927) rejected Confucius's example of frugal meat consumption and advocated a euthenics program to raise Chinese racial fitness through the daily consumption of British-style roast beef or mutton (Kang 1935).

Despite the currency of such ideas, however, counter to Lin's prediction, China did not in fact have to wait to punch the West in the jaw for Americans to be ready to hear the lessons of Chinese cookery. In the middle of World War II, when the United States and China became steadfast military allies, Buwei Yang Chao (1889–1981), a physician turned émigré housewife, stepped onto the scene as a Chinese food evangelist of sorts, driven by a mission to teach Americans "how to cook and eat in Chinese." Adventurous urbanites, of course, had already been sampling Chinese restaurant cuisine since the "chop suey craze" of the early twentieth century (Lee, n.d.), and recipes for Chinese-sounding dishes could be found in the pages of ladies' magazines as early as the 1910s, even as nativists railed against Chinese immigration (Teng 2015). World War II, however, set the stage for a new kind of engagement with Chinese cuisine: with China a crucial ally and rationing a disruptive force in American kitchens, the time was ripe for a Chinese food evangelist to challenge the primacy of roast beef. Published by John Day in the last months of the war, Chao's masterful primer of Chinese cookery, *How to Cook and Eat in Chinese* (1945), introduced terms such as "stirfry" and "pot sticker" into the American vocabulary and helped shape twentieth-century American understandings of "Chinese cuisine" beyond chop suey (Chen 2014). The book furthermore performed a critical intervention at a time when American public attitudes toward China and its people were undergoing a profound shift. Alongside the hundreds of recipes that she shared, Chao used her cookbook to contest the negative American stereotypes of Chinese foodways perpetuated during the Chinese Exclusion era (1882–1943), while advocating a model of transculturation that ran counter to the social Darwinian framework embraced by Kang Youwei and other Chinese intellectuals of the late Qing. In other words, if Kang had urged his compatriots to eat more roast beef and grilled steaks in the cause of whitening the Chinese race, Chao conversely set out to teach Americans to "go Chinese" in their kitchens and dining rooms as a means of ameliorating some of the excesses of modern American society.

With Chinese food now ubiquitous in the United States and increasingly across the globe, it is estimated that the restaurant industry and related businesses provided employment for over half of all Chinese migrants worldwide in the first decade of this century (Zhao 2015, 153). Chinese food is extremely popular, but are Chinese migrants? The editors of this volume note that "Asian peoples, products, and concepts have always traveled across land and sea routes, but since the 1990s, the scale, speed, and intensity of global interactions have increased dramatically" (Tagliacozzo, Siu, and Perdue 2015, 3). This intensification of global flows across boundaries defined by national or cultural borders has created transnational popular cultures and media, multilingual literatures, and other hybridized forms of culture, including global food chains and cuisines. Yet, recent years have also seen the rise of xenophobia and anti-immigrant sentiment across Europe and the United States, with nativists demanding that we return to more "authentic," homogeneous cultures while closing our borders and building walls against foreign goods, peoples, and cultures. Sinophobia was once again leveraged as a political tool in the 2016 American election. This may be an apt time, therefore, to reconsider the uneven processes of transnational flows, human and cultural, and the circulations of knowledge that have produced hybrid cultural forms such as Chinese American cuisine.

Appadurai argued in his classic work on "how to make a national cuisine" that "we need to view cookbooks in the contemporary world as revealing artifacts of culture in the making" (1988, 22). Cookbooks, he noted, "reflect shifts in the boundaries of edibility, the proprieties of the culinary process, the logic of meals, the exigencies of the household budget, the vagaries of the market, and the structures of domestic ideologies" (3). Whereas the history of Chinese American cuisine has predominantly centered on male migrants and entrepreneurs (Chen 2014; Coe 2009; Liu 2015), a focus on the cookbook, a genre that has long provided a public platform for American women (Avakian and Haber 2005), enables us to examine the particular role played by a female Chinese migrant in the making of "Chinese cuisine" for an American audience. It also provides an opportunity to consider broader questions of "knowledge in transit" as it constituted the transnational meanings of "Chineseness" in the twentieth century. As other contributors to this volume demonstrate, "knowledge in transit" is a crucial feature of human mobility—for ideas and notions circulate in tandem with migrants, refugees, exiles, students, and traveling athletes. In keeping with our endeavor to understand the role of mobile peoples in producing imaginings of "Asia" from the "inside out," an examination of Chao's efforts as a culinary evangelist brings to the fore issues of voluntary versus involuntary migration, moments of crisis versus moments of stability, the tension between exoticization and normalization, and the connections between nationalism and global circulation that are addressed by other authors in this volume. This chapter highlights the centrality of gender ideology at the intersection of migration and war as both a constraining and enabling feature of transculturation. In addition, reading Chao's cookbook as a wartime cookbook, and not simply as an ethnic cookbook, I demonstrate that her work went beyond the representation of Chineseness and ethnic authenticity to address fundamental issues of sustainability and food ethics that are still relevant for our time.

Culinary Ethnocentrism and Nativist Exclusion

The intertwining of diet, race, and culture shaped Sino-Western interactions not only in Shanghai's foreign concessions during the Treaty Port era (1842–1943) but also in the reception of Chinese immigrants in the United States. The early immigrants, mostly male laborers or merchants from Guangdong, quickly found that food could be a flashpoint at the nexus between economic competition and xenophobia. From the mid-nineteenth century on, nativists seized on the purportedly "strange" or even "repulsive" foodways of the

Chinese—frequently reported in British and American accounts of China—as evidence of their unsuitability for American society. Demagogues accused the Chinese of eating "rats and puppies" (Seligman 2013, xi). In *Meat vs. Rice: American Manhood against Asiatic Coolieism, Which Shall Survive?*, published by the American Federation of Labor in 1902 and again by the Asiatic Exclusion League in 1908, Samuel Gompers and Herman Gutstadt used the symbolic battle between meat, signifying American manhood, and rice, signifying Chinese "coolie" labor, to stoke American fears concerning the economic, social, and gendered impacts of Chinese immigration. Warning of the degrading effects of "cheap" Chinese labor, they quoted Maine senator James Blaine's declaration that "you cannot work a man who must have beef and bread alongside of a man who can live on rice. In all such conflicts, and in all such struggles, the result is not to bring up the man who lives on rice to the beef-and-bread standard, but it is to bring down the beef-and-bread man to the rice standard" (quoted in American Federation of Labor 1908, 22). Hence, whereas Kang envisioned elevating the rice-eating Chinese to the beef-eaters' standard, anti-Chinese propagandists in the United States spread fears that Chinese racial and cultural differences threatened the decline and degeneration of Western civilization.

Buwei Yang Chao, Grandmother of Chinese American Culinary Writing

Hailing from a very different background than the majority of early Chinese immigrants, Yang Buwei was born in Nanjing in the twilight years of the Qing dynasty, the daughter of a prominent lineage of scholar officials. Trained in Japan as a physician, and a committed New Woman, she opened her own obstetrical hospital in Beijing before marrying the eminent Chinese intellectual Yuen Ren "YR" Chao (1892–1982) in 1921. One of the first Boxer Indemnity Scholars, YR earned degrees at Cornell and Harvard, first in math and physics, then later in philosophy, before returning to China to teach at Tsinghua University. Shortly after their marriage, which they celebrated with a famously simple modern ceremony, YR was offered a teaching post at Harvard, and the couple set off for Cambridge, Massachusetts. Unable to practice medicine in the United States, Buwei became a full-time homemaker and mother. She nonetheless enjoyed an active social life that included other Harvard faculty wives as well as prominent Chinese intellectuals such as Hu Shih, Hu

Zhengxiang, and Jiang Menglin and the community of overseas Chinese students that gathered around them. Over the years, as YR took various scholarly positions in the United States, China, and Europe, she followed her husband in his sojourns, enjoying the privilege of mobility though lamenting the loss of a professional career (Chao 1947, 1972).

Although famous in China as a doctor and birth-control pioneer, an expert in a traditional genre of song-verse, and as the wife of one of modern China's foremost intellectuals, Mrs. Chao is primarily known in the United States as a cookbook author. Initially published in 1945, Chao's first cookbook, *How to Cook and Eat in Chinese,* was reprinted dozens of times; revised and expanded versions were issued in 1949, 1963, and 1972. As one of the first English-language cookbooks to provide a thorough and authoritative introduction to "authentic" Chinese cookery, *Cook and Eat* has been called "the Bible in the field" (Newman 2001, 75). Chao's book, as a canonical text, thus played a vital role in constructing the idea of "Chinese cuisine," as a major national cuisine with significant regional variation, for American audiences. Following the success of this book, Chao published *Autobiography of a Chinese Woman: Buwei Yang Chao* in 1947 and numerous other works in English and Chinese. It is notable that Chao had already finished the draft of her autobiography before beginning to write her cookbook, but it was the cookbook that most interested publishers of the time, and thus provided her an entrée into the American publishing world (Chao 1947, 1972). Hence, whereas carpets (in this volume) provide Erami's Iranian craftspeople with a globally recognizable and marketable means for heritage promotion, for this Chinese émigré it was food.

"Nice Ladies Should Not Be in a Kitchen"

Ironically, Chao was a reluctant entrant into the field of culinary writing. As she famously wrote in the preface to *Cook and Eat:*

> I am ashamed to have written this book. First, because I am a doctor and ought to be practicing instead of cooking. Secondly, because I didn't write the book. The way I didn't was like this. You know I speak little English and write less. So I cooked my dishes in Chinese, my daughter Rulan put my Chinese into English, and my husband, finding the English dull, put much of it back into Chinese again. (Chao 1949, xii)[1]

With this witty spin on the "humble words" conventionally employed by Chinese literati to preface their works, *Cook and Eat* introduces readers to the persona of Mrs. Chao, a doctor turned culinary author who must certainly have defied the mainstream American audience's expectations of Chinese womanhood during the 1940s. Interestingly, Chao mostly set aside her identity as a physician in her cookbook, choosing for the most part not to write in the authoritative professional voice of a doctor, but instead in the voice of a housewife, with a shared connection to her presumed audience of American homemakers.

Chao's prejudice against cooking stemmed as much from her class status as from her feminist convictions. She informs readers that she was raised in an upper-class family and "grew up with the idea that nice ladies should not be in a kitchen" (Chao 1949, xii). As revealed in her autobiography, contributing to Chao's early ignorance of culinary matters was the unusual fact that she was raised as a proxy son for her childless uncle, dressing and behaving as a boy until the age of twelve, and being educated alongside the male children in her extended family. Both the class and gender aspects of her early childhood socialization therefore conspired to keep Chao out of the kitchen. Even after reassuming a female social identity after puberty, Chao retained her disdain for "women's work" like sewing. After marriage, Chao continued to spurn cooking as domestic labor inconsistent with her role as a New Woman (Chao 1947, 203). Compelled to give up medicine upon migrating to the United States, Chao lamented: "Now that I had traveled ten thousand miles to a New World, I found myself thinking more and more like the narrow-minded housewife that I had hitherto looked down upon" (1947, 203).

"The War Job on the Kitchen Front"

Cooking came to assume new meaning for Chao, however, during World War II when she sojourned for a second time in Cambridge. The Chao family had fled from the Japanese invasion of China to sit out the war in the United States, and YR once again took a job at Harvard. This move entailed giving up her medical career, and Chao was restless at home without a clear way to contribute to society. After Pearl Harbor, Chao jumped at the opportunity to participate in home-front activities, but to her disappointment found little opportunity to make use of her medical training. Instead, she wound up contributing to the war effort like "any housewife in [her] place" (Chao 1947, 312). As Chao recounted in a chapter of her autobiography titled "War and Cooking": "I thought at first that the war would take me farther away from the kitchen. But exactly the opposite happened. With all the difficulties of rationing, I had never had so much to do with cooking in my life" (1947, 312). Thus, like so many American women of the time, Chao became a foot soldier on the "kitchen front," a domestic space that U.S. wartime propaganda deemed central to home-front efforts to secure victory (Bentley 1998, 35).

In an era of total war, American women, like women in Britain and elsewhere, were mobilized for the war effort in numerous ways, with the majority serving on the home front (Pidgeon 1944). Although often overlooked in mainstream American histories, Chinese American women contributed to the war effort with especial zeal. As Judy Yung has written:

> Moved by both Chinese nationalism and American patriotism, Chinese American women responded with an outpouring of highly organized activities in the areas of fund-raising, propaganda, civil defense, and Red Cross work on the home front. While some enlisted in the armed services, many others went to work in the defense factories and private sector outside Chinatown for the first time. The war years thus provided Chinese American women with unprecedented opportunities to improve their socioeconomic status, broaden their public role, and fall in step with their men and fellow Americans during a time of national crisis. (1995, 223)

Even as women experienced an expansion of their public roles during the war, however, they found their domestic duties expanded, and even glorified (Cornell 2010). In *Eating for Victory: Food Rationing and the Politics of Domesticity*, Amy Bentley demonstrates that "in general, wartime messages aimed at women were decidedly mixed; they urged women to enter new and unfamiliar 'men's' work while magnifying their position of domestic helpmate" (1998, 30–31). This ambiguity disappeared when it came to the vital matter of food and its wartime production, distribution, and consumption: "Messages specifically regarding food were clear and uniform: women's real and most important battlefield was the kitchen. There women could—and should—fight the war and prove their patriotism by cooking and serving the right kinds of foods in the right kinds of ways. Every meal served was a political act" (31). Under the central slogan of "Food Will Win the War and Write the Peace," government propaganda trumpeted food as "vital war material" or even as "a weapon," while messages such as "Planning meals is the way *I* can fight" directly targeted women and transformed the private activity of preparing family meals into a public and patriotic act.

With the food supply being identified as central to the total war effort, in both material and symbolic terms, the Food Fights for Freedom campaign urged housewives to "Produce and Conserve, Share and Play Square": to plant Victory gardens, can produce, reduce household food consumption and cut waste, share food with the armed forces and with Allies, comply with rationing, and fight black marketeers (United States 1943). Although World War II remained a time of relative plenty for Americans compared with their European, Asian, and African counterparts, food shortages and rationing, including rationing of sugar, coffee, meat, dairy, cooking oil and fuel, among other items, presented many new challenges for homemakers. Wartime cookbooks were churned out to teach home cooks how to cope with rationing and supplement the food supply through Victory gardens. These cookbooks not only doled out practical advice but also exhorted women to regard homemaking as a service to the nation.

Stymied in her attempts to use her medical training on the home front, Chao turned to cooking as an opportunity to step beyond the domestic realm and broaden her public role. In keeping with the notion of parallel (but gendered) contributions, she supported her husband's work directing the U.S. Army Special Training Program in Chinese language at Harvard by preparing meals for his team as her contribution "to the common effort" (Chao 1947, 313). Beyond her home, Chao volunteered for United China Relief along with several other faculty wives. For months on end she cooked a weekly luncheon for the group, feeding one hundred people each time to raise funds for China. Through a Yale connection, she once took charge of preparing a fund-raising supper for over 400 people at a New Haven church, collecting funds for a Chinese college. In these fund-raisers, Chao leveraged a heightened American interest in Chinese food promoted by wartime sympathy for China. While the Food Fights for Freedom campaign touted reduced consumption as a means of sharing food with hungry Allies, at these public events, consuming Chinese food became a symbolic way for Americans to express their unity with China. In Boston, with its long-standing Orientalist tradition, the war years saw United China Relief fund-raisers frequently featured in the *Boston Globe* society pages. Hence, cooking for United China Relief provided an opportunity for Chao to interact with prominent Bostonians while showcasing her culinary skills (Chao 1947).

Whereas Chao had been raised on the notion that "nice ladies do not belong in the kitchen," American wartime propaganda elevated the importance of this domestic space and helped transform cooking from a detested domestic chore into meaningful affective and symbolic labor: a means of showing moral support, bridging cultural difference, materially contributing to relief efforts for China, and demonstrating a dual patriotism to the United States and China.

"Food Will Win the War and Write the Peace"

War also spurred Chao to produce her best-known published work, *How to Cook and Eat in Chinese,* released in Boston on April 24, 1945 (Zhao and Huang 2001, 277). The idea of publishing the cookbook originated with her friend Agnes Hocking, the wife of Harvard philosophy professor William Ernest Hocking. Pearl Buck and her husband, Richard Walsh, founder of John Day, also encouraged the project. Although Chao quipped in her autobiography that she wrote this cookbook for Americans "in order to have done with [cooking] once and for all" (1947, 313), she had a deep commitment to the project, spending three years writing this magnum opus, with translation provided by her daughter Rulan (later a Harvard professor) and final editing and creative embellishments by YR (Chao 1972; Zhao and Huang 2001, 273). After the book's release, she excitedly wrote a friend back in China that her "cookbook" had finally been published and was raising a good deal of excitement, promoted by both YR and Hu Shih (Yang 1945, 4).

Publishing a Chinese cookbook was still a relatively new undertaking in the United States at the time. A number of such works had been published at least as early as 1910 (Newman 2001, 73), and recipes for chop suey and chow mein had become common in American ladies' magazines by the 1920s, even being featured in the *All-American Cookbook* of 1922 and the Army Cookbook of 1942 (Veit 2013, 147). However, these cookbooks were mostly written by non-Chinese and presumed that cooking Chinese food (or Americanized versions of Chinese dishes) was an occasional affair, a means of dabbling in the exotic without fundamentally giving up one's own food habits—a practice that Veit (2013) demonstrates was becoming increasingly common among Americans in the 1920s and 1930s, ironically even as "Americanization" campaigns directed at immigrant foodways stepped up their efforts.

More direct precedents for Chao's wartime cookbook were Fred Wing's *New Chinese Recipes* (1941), which was reissued in 1942 as a fund-raiser for

United China Relief in New York, and the "Oriental" volume in the *What's Cooking in Your Neighbor's Pot* series, also produced with participation from United China Relief. The latter series grew out of a joint effort between the Office of Civilian Defense's Food Fights for Freedom campaign and the Common Council for American Unity (Bruscino 2010, 38). The council sponsored a series of "Friendship through Food" parties and recipe exchanges focusing on ethnic foods as a means to promote cross-cultural understanding and also demonstrate "some of the concrete contributions the foreign-born housewife can make to the solution of the problems of the general American housewife in wartime" (Slocum 1944, 1). Hence, like similar campaigns conducted during World War I, the series also sought to generate creative approaches to rationing based on ethnic cuisines, suggesting that Americans could learn from their immigrant (or minority) neighbors in coping with meat and wheat shortages (Common Council for American Unity 1944). Similarly, *United Nations Recipes for War-Rationed Cooking* (1943) sought to promote global unity, sympathy for women and children in "invaded countries," and a multicultural approach to dealing with rationing. Reminding readers of Roosevelt's exhortation that "food is a weapon in total war," the cookbook contained recipes from around the allied world (United Nations 1943).

United China Relief was quick to seize on Chinese food's potential to attract audience interest, especially among women. Like *New Chinese Recipes,* Chao's cookbook was used by United China Relief as a fund-raising tool. The Boston chapter planned a major event around the book's release, with a book signing and cooking demonstration at its headquarters on Boylston Street. As the *Boston Globe* promised readers: "Housewives who shopped unsuccessfully this week-end for meat will find the cooking demonstration being planned for tomorrow morning at China Relief headquarters an especially valuable one. Buwei Yang Chao (Mrs. Yuen Ren Chao) will show how to prepare five selected dishes planned especially for food-short days" ("Today in Society" 1945). Several prominent Bostonian ladies were subscribers to the event, and China Relief purchased 500 copies of the book, selling over 300 autographed editions on the first day ("Today in Society" 1945; Chao 1972, 141).

Although Chao was not the first Chinese émigré to publish a cookbook, hers was the first comprehensive English-language manual to Chinese cookery, and according to the culinary historian Jacqueline Newman, she further made a signal contribution to the genre by including a "plethora of background" information to complement the recipes (2001, 77). Indeed, attempting to articulate what Hu Shih would call a "philosophy of Chinese cooking," the first fifty pages of the book were devoted to a careful, almost ethnographic explanation of Chinese cooking techniques, foodstuffs, and beliefs and customs related to food and eating. The importance Chao and her publisher granted this aspect of her work is confirmed by the fact that the East and West Association, in collaboration with John Day, published a short pamphlet, *Food for Philosophy: Some Brief Extracts from How to Cook and Eat in Chinese,* in 1944, prefacing the final publication of the cookbook.

Culinary Writing as Cultural Ambassadorship

Chao's culinary writing can be regarded as an extension of her community work as a cultural ambassador on the home front. Indeed, both Sherrie Inness (2006) and Madeleine Hsu (2015) have noted the vital role played by Chao, through her cookbook, as a cultural ambassador during the Cold War era, promoting American understanding of China and countering the negative stereotypes of Chinese immigrants. Pearl Buck's preface to the cookbook also draws our attention to the political work performed by the cookbook, generally considered a "humble" genre (Appadurai 1988), declaring that she would like to nominate Mrs. Chao for the Nobel Peace Prize for her "contribution to international understanding." Americans, Buck writes, "have known, abstractly, that the Chinese people is one of the oldest and most civilized on earth. But this book proves it. Only the profoundly civilized can feed upon such food" (Chao 1949, xi).

Cook and Eat certainly helped elevate the status of Chinese cuisine and promote American interest in "authentic" Chinese cuisine, in all its regional variety (Inness 2006; Chen 2014; Hayford 2012). Chao furthermore convincingly contested long-standing Orientalist stereotypes of Chinese culinary deviance (the notion of Chinese as eaters of rats, mice, dogs, "stags' pizzles," and other "weird" foods), insistently focusing on home cooking and plain fare. She carefully explained, for example, that bear paw was an extremely rare banquet dish that most ordinary Chinese would never eat. Countering the "Chinese eat everything" notion of indiscriminate omnivorousness, Chao carefully explained the *how* and *why* of Chinese cookery. Her lengthy introduction provided a rationale for the Chinese diet, explaining the preference for pork over beef, for example, and demonstrated that Chinese cookery is a *system* with its own internal logic (nuts to soup, not soup to nuts). Chao thus effectively used the domestic sphere and the voice of the housewife as a platform from which to challenge Orientalist stereotypes while promoting American knowledge of Chinese food as wholesome, healthful, diet-friendly, and frugal family fare. As Madeleine Hsu has written, Chao's cookbook provided "beguiling examples of compatibilities and equivalencies between Chinese and American peoples" and "presented a persuasive case that not only are Chinese and Americans not so different, but Americans could acquire some Chinese ways and Chinese were socially adept and capable of becoming American with charmingly Chinese characteristics" (2015, 120).

Chinese Cooking as Victory Cooking

Yet, Chao's primary agenda in writing this cookbook, I argue, was not cultural ambassadorship but rather cultural critique. In her Chinese-language memoir, Chao recalled how she rather ironically—for a "nice lady" who was raised not to cook—came to be an internationally recognized culinary author:

> Speaking about writing the cookbook, there was an amusing impetus. . . . During the war when we were living in Cambridge, there was difficulty buying things, and then on top of that, I saw Americans throwing away useful stuff, and so I often discussed the situation with some American ladies: now in a time of war, there are food shortages, and isn't it a shame that a whole load of edible stuff is being thrown away? Those ladies then said, please teach us how to cook [these things], and Mrs. Ernest Hocking . . . told me to quickly write a cookbook to teach Americans how to conserve things. (Chao 1972, 139; my translation)

Thus, the impetus for Chao's cookbook was a moral conviction that grew out of her experiences with wartime rationing and her despair over the food waste that she saw around her. Coping with the meat shortage, Chao sought out deals at wholesale markets, and whereas she was pleased to purchase skin-on pigs' trotters for pennies and to obtain chicken wings and gizzards for free, she was at the same time distressed that other edible "things" were regularly discarded. Chinese friends also shared her disapproval, a sentiment undoubtedly magnified by their awareness of the acute food shortages faced in China. She recalled: "One time Jiang Menglin came to visit, and he went with me to the market and saw them throw stuff away. He shook his head and said that

Americans really "wantonly destroy natural resources" [暴殄天物 *baotian tianwu*]. We then started going around like evangelists telling them what actually could be eaten, and what really had to be discarded" (Chao 1972, 142; my translation). With these imperatives, Chao thus set out to write a book that would teach Americans not just Chinese recipes but, more importantly, how to "cook *in* Chinese"—that is, to understand and employ the principles behind Chinese cookery, as codified in her work.

Whereas American ladies' magazines and cookbooks of the prewar era had primarily presented Chinese cookery as an Orientalist diversion for middle-class housewives, Chao's work cast this activity in a new light as a practical (and tasty) measure for dealing with food shortages and cutting waste: in other words, a means of advancing the national effort to make "food fight for freedom." Yet, unlike wartime cookbooks that doled out advice on temporary measures "for the duration," *Cook and Eat* is definitively not a book of "victory substitutes" or "wartime meals." Rather, the concept of "cooking and eating *in* Chinese"—which Chao encouraged readers to step into gradually by first integrating Chinese dishes into an American meal and then trying to "go Chinese"—is presented as a means of household economy without sacrifice. Her book shows Chinese cookery to lend itself naturally to lean times: relatively little meat is used, whereas vegetables are emphasized; pork and chicken are used more commonly than beef; seafood is abundantly used; sugar minimally (desserts are not eaten as a regular part of meals) and dairy very rarely; stir-frying requires little oil and cooking fuel and preserves the vitamin content of foods; fats are used primarily as a cooking vehicle and not as "eating materials" in and of themselves; and the plentiful consumption of rice enables the stretching of other foodstuffs. As Chao informed readers in the chapter on "red-cooked meat": "Remember that these recipes will serve six people American style and ten people in the Chinese way" (1949, 51). Rice, she explained to her audience, plays the opposite role of bread in the "American eating system," with dishes accompanying rice instead of bread accompanying dishes.

Chao furthermore touted the benefits of soybeans, which wartime campaigns pushed as a protein substitute for meat. "Soy beans not only give starch, but are also the most important source of protein [for poor families]," Chao explained, and "can be regarded as the typical classless kind of eating material in China" (1949, 22), being widely consumed in soybean milk and curd. Thus, in sharp contrast to Kang Youwei's privileging of beef consumption as a means to racial fitness, Chao downplayed the centrality of meat in the meal and offered an array of options for wartime homemakers compelled to stretch their meat rations (though she stopped short of advocating vegetarianism in the fashion of Sun Yat-Sen and Wu Tingfang).

In highlighting throughout the relative portions of American-style and Chinese-style meals (as well as the portions of meat), Chao underscored that the notion of "shortage," which preoccupied American consumers of the time, was a relative concept even in the war years. Hence, whereas wartime cookbooks that promised "victory substitutes and economical recipes for delicious wartime meals" (Berolzheimer 1943) took a notional food shortage as their very raison d'être, Chao's work suggests that if Americans perceived World War II as a time of shortage, it was partly because they did not recognize the wealth of "eating materials" that lay around them. She wrote:

> In vegetables, as in some other things, the Chinese are both poorer and richer than Americans. Poorer, because a smaller part of the population can afford any great variety of vegetables, or anything else. . . . Richer, because there are on the whole a greater variety of things, and because we eat more of the things which Americans have but do not eat. We try everything, watermelon rind, radish top, pea vines, and what not. (Chao 1949, 141)

Similarly, in terms of animal foods, Chao noted that gizzards, tripe, intestines, tongue, lungs, kidneys, other offal, pork and mutton skin, beef tendons, chicken wings and feet, duck tail, and fish heads were all eaten and could be "very good indeed" when correctly prepared (1949, 16). Although various organ meats were traditionally used in European and American cookery, by the World War II era their use had declined in the United States, and despite the fact that they were not rationed, Americans remained largely reluctant to eat them. Faced with a serious shortage of the preferred cuts of meat, which were prioritized for military consumption (again reinforcing the association of prime beef with masculinity and military strength), government propaganda aimed to promote what were euphemistically known as "variety meats" as a substitute. Chao's cookbook likewise encouraged the consumption of offal but differed fundamentally in representing these animal parts not as inferior and temporary substitutes but as integral to the Chinese diet. "The entrails of animals are usually prized more than simple lean meat," she wrote (Chao 1949, 16). Presenting four basic methods for preparing "chicken livers, gizzards, etc.," Chao noted that "the Chinese often use many gizzards in a dish as the main material. Some like it better than meat and chicken" (1949, 99). In addition, she expanded the repertoire of animal parts to be eaten by including more exotic items such as beef tendon, fish tongue, and sharks' fin, challenging commonplace American assumptions regarding the divide between edible and inedible, foodstuff and trash. At the end of the day, however, Amy Bentley shows that "wartime campaigns urging Americans to increase consumption of organ meats and soybeans received a lukewarm reception," and it is likely that Chao did not enjoy much more success with her readers (1998, 99).

For some of her audience, Chao's descriptions of gizzards and pork skin would perhaps only have confirmed the age-old stereotype that the "Chinese eat everything," possessing an indiscriminate omnivorousness driven by poverty and bizarre tastes, but Chao turned this into a virtue. Indeed, Chao was so intent on evangelizing against food waste that she devoted an entire subsection of her cookbook to "picking," explaining: "By picking I mean the separating of parts to throw away from the parts to keep" (1949, 36). As she pointedly wrote, "The general principle seems to be that the Chinese eat everything that can be eaten while the Americans throw away everything that can be thrown away" (36–37).[2] With an ironic twist on Anglo-American disparagement of Chinese for "eating everything," Chao showed American readers an unflattering image of themselves as a people who "throw away everything," even in a time of war. For most Americans, she wrote, "picking" was of little concern when shopping for meat: "You just buy what you want to eat. The market will throw away beforehand what you do not want, but often also what you do want" (37). In sharp contrast, Chao represents Chinese practices of "picking" as responsible stewardship of natural resources. Hence, the Chinese way of picking was more involved. With good humor (and written with YR's characteristic wit), *Cook and Eat* explained Sino-American differences with an imagined scene at the fishmonger's:

> The cooking of a Chinese fish dish in America begins with an argument with your fishman. Get a nice fresh carp and tell him to keep his head. But by habit he does it the usual way, and when you open your package after you get home, you find that you have lost your head. Next time you go, you complain about last time, and he is so nice apologizing that you are encouraged to go Chinese once more. So when he cleans the fish, you tell him, twice, to keep its tongue in its cheek, because that is the best part of the fish. Since he has never heard of such a thing, he cannot locate the

> tongue and throws it away together with the gills. But he is a nice man. Keep your temper and you will soon be able to keep your tongue. (Chao 1949, 37)

A Chinese approach to picking appears in Chao's cookbook as a viable alternative to the more common wartime exhortations to reduce consumption and increase production. Rather, in tune with calls to reduce waste, Chao urges readers to expand their repertoire of edible "things" as they learn to "cook and eat *in* Chinese." Chao highlights the avoidance of waste as an ethical practice, informing readers that even children from well-to-do Chinese families are taught to finish every last grain of rice in their bowls: "That is the fruit of the sweat of your fellow men" (1949, 13). Against the backdrop of war, Chao urges readers to view the eating of fish tongues not as a sign of Chinese culinary deviance but rather as a positive ethics of "eating everything that can be eaten"—an ethics that goes beyond the injunction to "clear your plate" to start with the more fundamental practice of picking. Picking becomes a vital means of reclaiming as *edible* things that were commonly discarded as *inedible,* or at least unworthy of eating in the "land of plenty." Following the Chinese example, American readers are encouraged to become rich by eating those "things which Americans have but do not eat." Shortage is shown to be a matter of poverty of perception.

Pearl Buck also considered the educational value of Chao's book in reducing food and other resource waste to be as valuable as its promotion of Sino-American cultural understanding. As Buck wrote in the preface:

> It is worth this book's weight in gold and diamonds if American women will learn how to cook vegetables as the Chinese cook them, quickly and lightly, without water and waste. It is worth jade and rubies if they will abandon the horrid American custom of putting cooked rice under the cold water faucet and washing out all its flavor. It is of inestimable value to the war effort and also to the economy of peace if they will learn to use meat for its taste in addition to something else, instead of using it chiefly for its substance. (Chao 1949, x–xi)

Reviewer Jane Holt, writing for the *New York Times* just after the surrender of Japan, similarly praised the book's valuable lessons in a time of food shortage:

> Rationing has made most of us conscious that any excellence our cooking had before the war was not due so much to our own skill as to the wonderful materials we had in the way of fine roasts, thick cream and so on. Deprived

> of these things . . . we have been rather at a loss as to where to find flavor to put into our one-pound-of-meat-stretched-for-eight-people main courses and our half-as-much-sugar-as-formerly-desserts. All of which is why the Chinese . . . are just the ones to teach us a thing or two. (Holt 1945, SM14)

For readers wondering how they could learn, Holt suggested Chao's book, which promised to "open minds" and "open mouths."

This chapter has considered "knowledge in transit" as a crucial feature of human mobility and a dynamic force in shaping ideas about "Asia," focusing on the individual agency of a Chinese woman émigré in this process. Seema Alavi (in this volume) argues that moments of crisis, in some ways more than moments of stability, can open up possibilities for mobile peoples pushed out of their homelands by invasion, war, or imperialism to find new avenues of agency or subjectivity. In Buwei Yang Chao's case, war and conflict compelled her to flee China and give up her medical career, compromising her feminist ideology to adopt the American wartime gender ideology of the "kitchen warrior," but yet also opened other opportunities. The context of World War II was vital in providing Chao with a public platform from which to serve as a "Chinese food evangelist." First, China's new position as a key ally to the United States in the war against Japan necessitated a reconfiguration of American attitudes toward China and prompted curious Americans to learn about Chinese culture. Second, the enhanced importance given to "food as a weapon" in an era of total war gave prominence to Chao's activities beyond the domain of "women's work." Third, rationing forced American home cooks to look for alternative dishes, ingredients, and methods of cooking, including those from non-Western cuisines. With encouragement from her American friends, Chao took up Chinese culinary evangelism, propounding a bilateral model of transculturation that recognized immigrants not only as targets of assimilation but also as agents of cultural change.

A reassessment of Chao's work furthermore reveals that contrary to the dismissal of culinary writing as a genre of self-Orientalism, or "food pornography," to use Frank Chin's provocative term, the cookbook can in fact serve as a site of resistance against hegemonic notions of race and culture as embedded in the old hierarchy of meat above vegetables, wheat above rice (Chin 1974; Pang 2002). I argue that Chao's text was not simply a work of cultural ambassadorship but also on a profound level a work of cultural critique, unsparing in its condemnation of American wastefulness and overconsumption, which the author found especially galling in a time of war. Leveraging the cookbook, one of the few avenues of publication open to Chinese American women of the time, as a vehicle for disseminating her message, Chao challenged American readers to take a hard look at their own food habits, issuing a strident, if humorous, commentary on the wastefulness of American foodways. Whereas the popularity of "slightly foreign, just for fun" foods in the 1920s and 1930s enabled American consumers, as Veit argues, to transgress social conventions "in small doses, meal by meal, without truly challenging their basic sense of order or of self" (2013, 150), Chao's text asks readers to consider foreign culinary practices precisely as a challenge to the basic sense of order embedded in habits such as "picking." Going beyond the simple measures of economy touted in most American wartime cookbooks, Chao presented an alternative vision of a food system that challenged conventional notions regarding the "edible" and "inedible." Chao's lengthy discussion of the Chinese "philosophy" of food highlighted the ethics of community and frugality that underlay this culinary tradition, and whereas she elaborated on the differences between China and America, she did so not in the interests of self-exoticism but rather in the spirit of a profound critique of American profligacy. Subtly, she undercut prevailing presumptions that America is "rich" and China "poor," viewed from a narrowly materialistic standpoint. Finally, the book contested derogatory American images of Chinese food prevalent during the Chinese Exclusion era, demonstrating that the cuisine was not strange and exotic but plain and wholesome fare suitable for the "war kitchen" and eminently adaptable for "the American way of life" (Chao 1949, 228).

Indeed, if food was to "win the war and write the peace," Chao's work helped ensure that Chinese food would be an integral part of the postwar American culinary story. Although it is very difficult to gauge the direct impact of Chao's cookbook on American food habits during the war—likely few Americans were persuaded to eat fish tongues, beef tendons, duck tails, or even kidneys and soybeans—the multiple reprintings of Chao's cookbook into the 1970s (twenty-two editions published between 1945 and 1972) suggest something of the text's reach as a form of "knowledge in transit." Chao's message may even have renewed relevance for us today, with mounting calls for food system sustainability and a vogue among foodies for the pleasures of eating "every last bit" (Bittman 2015, MM24).

Notes

I would like to thank the participants and organizers of the Asia Inside Out conference, held in Hanoi in January 2016, and participants in Radcliffe's Reading Historical Cookbooks seminar for stimulating discussions and feedback on this work. Earlier versions of this research were also presented at MIT, the Association for Asian Studies annual conference, and Pomona College. Thanks to Samuel Yamashita, Shuang Wen, Ted Bestor, Heather Lee, Barbara Haber, Barbara Wheaton, Tulasi Srinivas, Heather Paxson, Madeline Hsu, Allan Barr, and Anne McCants.

1. YR took over the editorial work on the cookbook in January 1945 (Zhao and Huang 2001, 273), leading to some spousal conflict (Chao 1972).

2. This aphorism also appeared very close to the front of *Food for Philosophy,* signaling its centrality to Chao's agenda.

References

American Federation of Labor, Samuel Gompers, and Herman Gutstadt. 1908. *Meat vs. Rice; American Manhood against Asiatic Coolieism, Which Shall Survive?* San Francisco: American Federation of Labor, printed as Senate document 137 (1902); reprinted with introduction and appendices by Asiatic Exclusion League.

Appadurai, Arjun. 1988. "How to Make a National Cuisine: Cookbooks in Contemporary India." *Comparative Studies in Society and History* 30(1): 3–24.

Avakian, Arlene Voski, and Barbara Haber. 2005. "Feminist Food Studies: A Brief History." In *From Betty Crocker to Feminist Food Studies: Critical Perspectives on Women and Food,* eds. Arlene Voski Avakian and Barbara Haber, 1–26. Boston: University of Massachusetts Press.

Bentley, Amy. 1998. *Eating for Victory: Food Rationing and the Politics of Domesticity.* Urbana: University of Illinois Press.

Berolzheimer, Ruth. 1943. *Victory Binding of the American Woman's Cook Book: With Victory Substitutes and Economical Recipes for Delicious Wartime Meals.* Chicago: Consolidated Book Publishers.

Bittman, Mark. 2015. "Every Last Bit." *New York Times Sunday Magazine,* May 24, 2015, p. MM24.

Bruscino, Thomas A. 2010. *A Nation Forged in War: How World War II Taught Americans to Get Along.* Knoxville: University of Tennessee Press.

Chao, Buwei Yang. 1944. *Food for Philosophy: Some Brief Extracts from How to Cook and Eat in Chinese.* New York: John Day.

———. (1945) 1949. *How to Cook and Eat in Chinese.* New York: John Day.

———. 1972. *Zaji Zhaojia.* Taibei: Zhuanji wenxue chubanshe.

Chao, Buwei Yang, and Yuen Ren Chao. 1947. *Autobiography of a Chinese Woman: Buwei Yang Chao.* New York: John Day.

Chao, Yuen Ren, Rosemary Levenson, Laurence A. Schneider, and Mary R. Haas. 1974. *Chinese Linguist, Phonologist, Composer and Author: and Related Material.* The Bancroft Library, University of California, Berkeley.

Chen, Yong. 2014. *Chop Suey, USA: The Story of Chinese Food in America.* New York: Columbia University Press.

Chin, Frank. 1974. *The Year of the Dragon.* N.p.: n.p.

Coe, Andrew. 2009. *Chop Suey: A Cultural History of Chinese Food in the United States.* New York: Oxford University Press.

Common Council for American Unity. 1944. *What's Cooking in Your Oriental Neighbor's Pot Party, March 6, 1944.* New York: Common Council for American Unity.

Cornell, Caroline. 2010. "The Housewife's Battle on the Home Front: Women in World War II Advertisements." *Forum: Journal of History* 2(1): 8.

Hayford, Charles W. 2012. "'Open Recipes, Openly Arrived At': *How to Cook and Eat in Chinese* (1945) and the Translation of Chinese Food." *Journal of Oriental Studies* 45(1 / 2): 67–87.

Holt, Jane. 1945. "FOOD: Chinese Food and Flavour." *New York Times,* August 26, 1945, p. SM14.

Hsu, Madeline Yuan-yin. 2015. *The Good Immigrants: How the Yellow Peril Became the Model Minority.* Princeton, NJ: Princeton University Press.

Inness, Sherrie A. 2006. *Secret Ingredients: Race, Gender, and Class at the Dinner Table.* New York: Palgrave Macmillan.

Kang, Youwei. 1935. *Datong shu.* Shanghai: Zhonghua shuju.

Lee, Heather. *Acquired Tastes.* Book manuscript. nd.

Lin, Yutang. 1936. *My Country and My People.* New York: John Day.

Liu, Haiming. 2015. *From Canton Restaurant to Panda Express: A History of Chinese Food in the United States.* New Brunswick, NJ: Rutgers University Press.

Newman, Jacqueline M. 2001. "Chinese Food: Perceptions and Publications in the United States." *Chinese Studies in History* 34(3): 66–81.

Pang, Ching Lin. 2002. "Business Opportunity or Food Pornography?" *International Journal of Entrepreneurial Behavior & Research* 8(1–2): 148–161.

Pidgeon, Mary Elizabeth. 1944. *Changes in Women's Employment during the War.* Washington, DC: U.S. Department of Labor, Women's Bureau.

Seligman, Scott D. 2013. *The First Chinese American: The Remarkable Life of Wong Chin Foo.* Hong Kong: Hong Kong University Press.

Slocum, Rosalie. 1944. "What's Cooking in Your Neighbor's Pot." Introduction to Common Council for American Unity, *What's Cooking in Your Neighbor's Pot.* New York: Common Council for American Unity.

Tagliacozzo, Eric, Helen F. Siu, and Peter C. Perdue, eds. 2015. *Asia Inside Out: Changing Times.* Cambridge, MA: Harvard University Press.

Teng, Emma J. 2015. "The Eaton Sisters and the Figure of the Eurasian." In *The Cambridge History of Asian American Literature,* eds. Rajini Srikanth and Min Hyoung Song, 88–103. Cambridge, MA: Cambridge University Press.

"Today IN SOCIETY: China Relief Feature Cooking Demonstration." 1945. *Boston Globe,* April 23, 1945, p. 4.

United Nations Recipes for War-Rationed Cooking. 1943. N.p.: n.p.

United States. 1943. *How to Mobilize Your Community to Make Food Fight for Freedom: Produce and Conserve, Share and Play Square: Food Fights for Freedom.* Washington, DC: GPO.

Veit, Helen Zoe. 2013. *Modern Food, Moral Food: Self-Control, Science, and the Rise of Modern American Eating in the Early Twentieth Century.* Chapel Hill: University of North Carolina Press.

Yang, Buwei. 1945. 楊「生」偉致傅先生函 (sic) [Letter to Fu Ssu-nien]. 傅斯年檔案 [Fu Ssu-nien archive] III-156. *Fu Ssu-nien Library* of the Institute of History and Philology, Academia Sinica.

Yung, Judy. 1995. *Unbound Feet: A Social History of Chinese Women in San Francisco.* Berkeley: University of California Press.

Zhao, Xinna, and Huang Peiyun. 2001. *Zhao Yuanren nianpu.* Beijing: Shangwu yinshuguan.

Zhao, Rongguang. 2015. *A History of Food Culture in China.* Translated by Gangliu Wang and Aimee Yiran Wang. Singapore: World Scientific Publishing.

12

The Asian Sportscape

Hubs of Play and Flows of Contention

WILLIAM W. KELLY

Asia—at least Soccer Asia—now stretches expansively from Brisbane to Beirut and from Melbourne to Mongolia. The Asian Football Confederation (AFC) is one of six world regional bodies that constitute FIFA, the global organization of the world's most ubiquitous sport, and the forty-seven current members of the AFC extend from Lebanon in the west to Australia in the east and north to Mongolia.

Asian soccer, like the rest of the world, intersperses local club competitions (organized in national leagues) with national team competitions (proceeding through several levels of regional tournaments to the FIFA World Cup final championship itself). Teams travel across the sporting continent, players move, investment capital flows, media and broadcast rights are fluid, and an industry of sporting goods is constituted by global commodity chains of production and lines of distribution (Weinberg 2015). Asia, from the perspective of sports, is all hubs and flows.

And this is not new. The history of the AFC itself goes back to 1954, when it was organized in Manila, the site of the second Asian Games that year. Before the Asian Games there were the Far Eastern Games (FEG), and before the FEG, Japan was invited into the nascent Olympic movement as the first

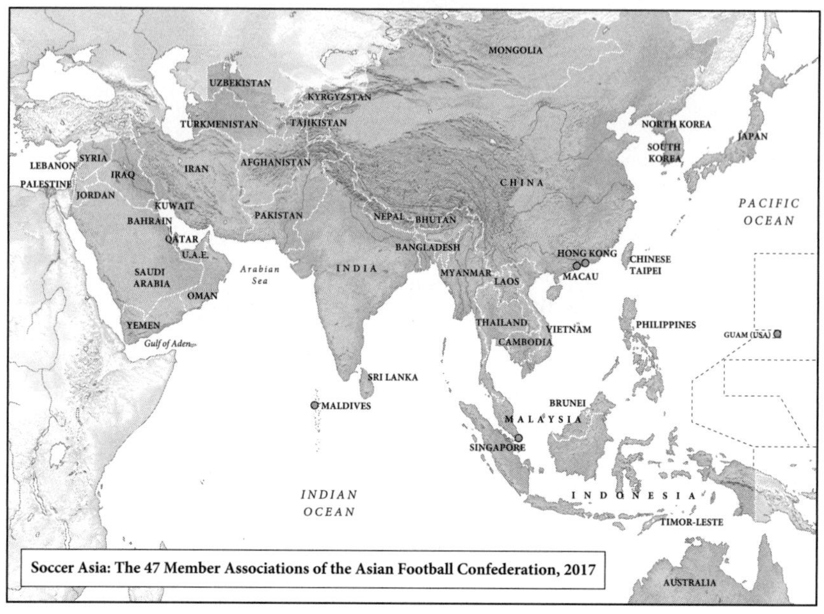

Soccer Asia: The 47 Member Associations of the Asian Football Confederation, 2017

Asian member, back in 1908. Sports—as participation and pedagogy, as spectatorship and rivalry, as media event and commercial profit, as national prestige and individual aspiration—have had deep roots in and dense connections across Asia for over a century.

It is thus odd that sports have been neglected in mapping Asia as a "space of flows" by "mobile peoples," the ambitious project conceived by the editor-architects of this multivolume project. A great many scholars have recognized the significance of popular and mass cultures as channels of connection across the continent, and they have traced the flows of film, music, fashion, cuisine, graphic arts like manga and anime, and others. By contrast, research and writing on Asian sport and its role as a plane of institutional connectivity and interpersonal mobility have only recently developed a critical mass.[1]

Yet I would submit that even more than these other cultural sectors, sports in Asia have been both historically deeper and far more embedded in local worlds, national agendas, and regional geopolitics. The distinctive force of sports is due to three features that set them apart from other cultural sectors. First, sports combine fixed, universal, formal codifications of a game with local expressions. The rules of soccer are everywhere the same, and this gives it a binding force; but the game is everywhere played by local teams, which develop distinct practices and followings.

Second, unlike concerts, plays, and fashion shows, sports events are agonistic competitions—they are intended explicitly to produce a winner and a loser. This has the doubled effect of creating enduring solidarities and strong rivalries that bind neighborhoods, regions, and nations as they pit them against one another. Sports are connectivity through contestation. They encourage multiple tactical elaborations to the universal formal rules as well as outright deception and cheating. The stakes are much higher when people are connected by sports than by other cultural modalities.

And finally, more thoroughly than film, music, fashion, or cuisine, sports combine education and entertainment. Of course, film and fashion can instruct us even as they delight us, but sports have made far more portentous claims to mold personal character, express local identity, and embody national pride, even as they constitute one of the most profitable sectors of the world economy. They have been inserted into national educational systems and military training, but at the same time they are of such mass entertainment value that sports stadiums across Asia attract far more spectators—and sports media far more viewers and readers—than concert halls and galleries.

The next three sections sketch the dimensions of sports' emplotment over the long duration of Asian modernity by characterizing each of three chronological eras thematically. Almost all of the sports that the world plays and watches had their origins or took their modern form in a few locations in the nineteenth century—predominantly the United States and Great Britain. However, they almost immediately spread rapidly to parts of Asia, where they were quickly domesticated to local purposes and frameworks. At the same time, the sports framework of physical competition had a transformative effect on existing Asian body practices, so what was striking about this first era of modern Asian sports is what the next section formulates as a dialectic of indigenizing and sportifying.[2]

Sports at various levels from youthful play to elite athletics were routinized in the early twentieth century, and they were soon appreciated by national elites for their potential to embody and convey nationalist campaigns, on the one hand, and visions of pan-Asianism, on the other. This is the theme that is developed in the second section. By the late twentieth century, sports had become so institutionally embedded and so commercially attractive across a wide sweep of Asia that they entangled the societies, polities, and economies of the continent in webs of continental sports governance, geopolitical rivalry, commodity chains of manufacturing and marketing, and the movement of athletes across multiple paths of sports migration. These are the themes developed in the third section. Finally, in concluding, I return to the distinctive features of sports as cultural performance and production to assess how they contribute to making contemporary Asia into a connected and mobile assemblage of people, places, and practices.

Indigenizing Anglo-American Sports and Sportifying Asian Physical Practices

Western sports entered Asia through imperial and mercantile circuits in the late nineteenth century. Through schools, merchants, administrators, and missionaries, the British introduced cricket, soccer, tennis, polo, and other recently formalized sports into the Indian subcontinent and to their colonies in Southeast Asia (Guha 2002; Malcolm, Gemmell, and Mehta 2009; Mills 2001). American teachers and missionaries brought baseball, volleyball, basketball, and other American sports to Japan, the Philippines, the Korean peninsula, and the Chinese mainland in the same decades (Reaves 2002).

While the Western teachers and promoters of these sports intended them as vehicles of a Western civilizing mission, more commonly sports were adapted into local frames of meaning and power and even turned against the foreigners. Japan enthusiastically took to American baseball in the 1880s, but in the 1890s when a schoolboy team soundly beat a veteran team of American sailors and merchants—on multiple occasions—baseball was indigenized with a nationalist samurai spirit.[3] And in India, the spread of cricket through the schools and across the countryside through administrators and dispatched military garrisons provoked a similar subaltern appropriation. This was vividly rendered in the 2001 Indian movie *Lagaan,* set in the countryside in 1893 during the British Raj period and featuring a challenge match between British soldiers of the local cantonment and the villagers of Champaner. The stakes were the annual taxes (the Lagaan) that the British sought to extract.

But this was only one aspect of the emerging sportscape. Westerners may have brought such sports as volleyball and swimming to Asia, but Asian societies had hardly lacked for long traditions of physical practices, including Kabbadi (Alter 2000) and Kalarippayattu (Zarrilli 1998) in South Asia; Sepak takraw in Southeast Asia (Jonsson 2003); buzkashi and other variants of horse polo in Central and Western Asia (Azoy 2011); wushu, karate, judo, and other martial arts schools of East Asia (Hong and Hua 2002; Inoue 1998); Japanese sumo, Khalkha bökh (Mongolian wrestling), Yağlı güreş (Turkish "oil wrestling" [Stokes 1996]), and other styles of wrestling; and Muay Thai and other traditions of boxing (Vail 1998). These were often embedded in rituals and festivals, imbued with religious significance, quite local in form, and lacking the rational record keeping and permanent organized competitions of the new Western sports; but one of the significant trends of the century, which drew these indigenous Asian practices into wider connections across the region, was the adoption of such qualities of sport into the indigenous pursuits. Thus, as Western sports were being adapted to local forms and interests, long-standing physical practices found across Asia were being reformed and repurposed to fit a sports mold. The Asianization of Western sports went hand in hand with the "sportification" of indigenous physical pursuits and gave a hybrid quality to the Asian sportscape. In the case of Japan, for instance, as noted above, the American sport of baseball was rendered by some participants and educators in a nationalistic samurai warrior idiom at the same time as the indigenous religious entertainment of sumo wrestling was restructured as a competitive sport, with fixed groups of wrestlers, an administrative body, rankings, and a tournament structure.[4]

Sports Nationalism and Pan-Asianism in the First Half of the Twentieth Century

One of the most consequential political tensions in modern Asia has been that between the nationalist movements throughout the continent and the century that created a nation-state order from an imperial epoch and, simultaneously, projects of pan-Asianism that proposed and proclaimed visions of common cause among the peoples of the continent. These twin processes were the central political dynamics of the century, and sports played a role, especially through the series of regional mega-events that began in the second decade of the twentieth century, surprisingly instigated by the American Young Men's Christian Association (YMCA), and continue today.

The YMCA was one of the main conduits in the American sphere of influence in East and Southeast Asia (Gems 2006). It was a Protestant lay organization that began in England but quickly flourished in nineteenth-century America, promoting faith, sobriety, and social commitment among young men. Its trinity of mind, spirit, and body was a "muscular Christianity" that built Christian ideals through physical education and sports competition; indeed, basketball and volleyball were invented at its training college in Springfield, Massachusetts. When its educators went abroad, they introduced these and other sports not only for Christian education but also as an American civilizing mission for Asian youth and their countries (Huebner 2016).[5]

The introduction of Western sports to mold Asian character depended crucially on the figure of the American Elwood Stanley Brown, a lifelong YMCA educator with close ties to the new Olympic movement, who took up a position in the Philippines in 1910. He established the Philippine Amateur Athletic Federation, and, in 1913, he organized the first of what were to become the Far Eastern Championship Games (FECG), a multievent amateur sports tournament that drew contingents from seven nations and colonies (the Philippines, the Republic of China, Malay and the Straits Settlements, Thailand, and the British crown colony of Hong Kong [Abe 2007]).

Brown was quite fervent in his belief that such international regional games of amateur teams could spread a gospel of internationalism, egalitarianism, and economic progress. However, Brown and the YMCA quickly lost the initiative in organizing the FECG to local Asian elites (including physical education directors, sports officials, politicians, and government officials). As the historian Stefan Huebner (2016) has shown in illuminating detail, these elites turned the Games into a platform for anticolonial nationalism. Significantly, however, they did not in fact reject the YMCA ideals but rather usurped them and converted them into their own projects of modern nationalism defined by anticolonialism. In so doing, they recovered and indigenized notions of the "Asia" projected from the West, and they used as additional leverage images of a "spiritual" Asia as opposed to the "materialist" West, which neatly trumped the YMCA ideal of the spiritual-physical.

At the same time, as the list of initial contingents suggests, there were wide variations in the nationalist ambitions and strategies and in the vision of what Asia should be among the participants. The Japanese intellectual Okakura Tenshin proclaimed as early as 1903 that "Asia is One," but one what? Certainly the Japanese formulated a devastatingly partisan vision—the Greater East Asia Co-Prosperity Sphere—and indeed, it was Japan's incursions into China that fractured the 1934 Games and led to their suspension. The widening war and Japan's imperialist reach put an end to any chance for regional sports events; there was no appetite for Japan's version of pan-Asianism.

But in 1951, India's prime minister Nehru took the initiative in creating the Asian Games Federation, which drew a wider membership than the earlier FEG, in order to further his postcolonial foreign policy of an Asianism that would be nonaligned to the two superpowers and would support nationalist movements in the remaining colonies. This too drew limited support across Asian countries, so the story of the postwar Asian Games is a fascinating one in which each subsequent host country attempts to showcase its own state agenda and its own notion of pan-Asianism.

Southeast Asia is often neglected in Asian sports history, which is much more centered on South Asia and East Asia, but it was key to the early years of the Asian Games (Hong 2006).[6] After Delhi, four of the next five Asian Games were held in the region, and the historian Stefan Huebner (2016) has provided a fascinating comparative account of the contrasting ambitions of the sponsoring nations and their leaders. By the time of the second Games in Manila in 1954, Filipino "Cold Warriors" insisted the amateur spirit of the Games could be realized only through democracy and was incompatible with Communism, on which basis they excluded Communist-ruled nations from participating. Japan's agenda in hosting the third Games in Tokyo in 1958 was to demonstrate its economic recovery and political rehabilitation from the Second World War and set the stage for the 1964 Olympic Games. Indonesian president Sukarno presided over the fourth Asian Games in Jakarta in 1962, but his vision of Asia nonalignment was pro-socialist, and thus Israel and Taiwan were excluded. At the same time, Huebner showed, Sukarno mounted the Games as a massive capital city construction program intended to bolster his claims of uniting the diverse ethnicities of the nation. The fifth and sixth Games were held in Bangkok in 1966 and 1970, and the country's military shifted the political tone toward a strident anti-Communism. At the same time, they joined with supporters of the king, and the Games contributed to "the personality cult of the king as the semi-sacral figurehead of the Thai nation" (Huebner 2016: 14).

Taken together across the decades, the Asian Games, Huebner shows, were useful platforms for state high modernism, a concept he draws from James C. Scott (1998). The fascinating irony of these thirty years of mega-events is that despite the radically different political motivations and unique geopolitics, what kept the Games going was a continuing commitment to the original ideals that animated Elwood Brown and the first FEG.

Paralleling the growing importance of the Asian Games was Asian nations' increasing involvement in the International Olympic Movement. The Games themselves were reorganized in 1981 under a new governing body, the Olympic Council of Asia, which was recognized by the International Olympic Committee (IOC). Long before then, Asian nations had participated ever more deeply in the Olympic movement. An early significant watershed was the first Asian hosting of the Games—the 1964 Summer Olympics in Tokyo. These Games were of extraordinary consequence not only for Japan (as a powerful domestic stimulus and also as the venue for regaining acceptance into the Western circle of advanced economies) but also for its Asian rivals. Tokyo's hosting demonstrated the political and economic uses of sports (Abel 2015, especially chapter 5; Collins 2011; Niehaus and Seinsch 2007). Another effect of the Asian enthusiasm for this global sports platform was to inject heated Asian geopolitics into the Olympic movement, from the cancellation of the 1940 Summer Games, which were to have been held in Tokyo, to the bitter "Two China" dispute that divided the IOC in the 1950s and 1960s, inter-Asian differences over the boycott of the 1980 Moscow Olympics, and the turbulent politics of the Korean peninsula in the lead-up to the 1988 Seoul Olympics (Kelly 2011).

In sum, the difficulties of reconciling projects of nationalism and visions of pan-Asianism that emerged in the FEG continued to be sources of friction through the longer history of the Asian Games and Asia's embrace of the Olympic movement. Despite the platitudes of sports as embodying the ethos of fair play and friendly competition, sports in Asia forged connectivity through contestation as much as through cooperation.

Globalizing and Commercializing the Asian Sports World

By the late twentieth century, not only had sports inserted themselves across Asia into school pedagogies, mass culture, and nationalist sentiments, but Asian nations were moving into prominence in the global sportscape. Contemporary sports significantly connect the economies, societies, and nations across Asia and between Asia and the rest of the world through participation in the two most global sports structures in the world, the Olympic movement and FIFA; through Asia-centered commodity chains of sporting goods; through the movement of sports players; and through the geopolitical rivalries that are expressed through, and often enflamed by, sports competitions.

These themes are taken up in this section to illustrate how the Asian sports world has matured from the previous century to the present.

Asia Comes to the Center of the International Olympic Movement

Tokyo 1964, Sapporo 1972, Seoul 1988, Nagano 1998, Beijing 2008, Pyeongchang 2018, Tokyo 2020, and Beijing 2022—this is the impressive litany of Asian locations for the Summer and Winter Olympic (and Paralympic) Games. The chronology demonstrates how quickly Asia, especially East Asia, has moved to the center of the Olympic movement in the early twenty-first century. Since its beginnings in the 1890s, the Olympic movement (headed by the IOC) has been global in its ambitions and lofty rhetoric, but in fact through much of the twentieth century, it was firmly Euro-American-centric in its governance, Games hosting, media connections, and corporate sponsorship. In recent decades, however, there has been a fundamental reorientation. The IOC recognizes that Asian markets, Asian media, Asian audiences, and Asian nations themselves are growing disproportionately in resources and determination, and Asian nations see that Olympic sponsorship is an effective means by which they can engage globally. To be sure, each of the eight Games hosted in Asia, from Tokyo 1964 through Beijing 2022, is motivated by a separate set of local circumstances and national interests (Horton 2011; Kelly 2010, 2011). Nonetheless, it is equally clear that this Asianizing of the Olympic Games has been and is being driven by regional rivalries; each of these Games has been crafted with an eye to geopolitical competition with its neighbors. China wanted the 2008 Games in part because it was trying to catch up with (and exceed) the Games of its regional rivals Japan and South Korea. Anxious about the success of Beijing 2008, Japan bid hard for 2016 and then, successfully, for the 2020 Games. South Korea staged the 2018 Winter Games in the mountains near the demilitarized zone, and Beijing jumped into the bidding for the 2022 Winter Games to keep up the pressure—Olympic sponsorship for these Asian rivals looks like a high-stakes poker game!

It is important to recognize that especially with the East Asian region, Olympic geopolitics are much more complex and continuous than merely these periodic competitions to host the Games themselves. An Olympics / Paralympics Games is an intense but brief four weeks, but the lead-up and the legacy of each Games stretches across several decades. This produces a continual and contentious Olympic "regionalism" of organizational streams and rhetorical rivalries that inflect all stages of producing the Games, from the infrastructural design in the years of preparation to the handling of the Games themselves (especially orchestration of the Torch Relay and the Opening Ceremony and the tensions between security and hospitality) to the struggles to define and determine the legacy of the Games in the years following. Intellectual property rights (including disputes between the IOC and Asian host cities), broadcast strategies, and even academic scholarship about the Olympics all become focal points in this new Asian field of the Olympics movement.

Soccer Gains in Asia

As indicated at the outset, of all the sports that gained popularity in participation and spectatorship, perhaps most consequential has been the spread of soccer across the continent. There are thousands of elite amateur and professional soccer clubs across the continent, with professional or semiprofessional leagues in a majority of Asian countries. Asian national teams have not done well in the FIFA World Cup final stages, but by most other measures—including league developments, national team investments, broadcast, print, and online media, introduction into youth and school sports, and soccer goods merchandising—soccer is now the preeminent Asian sport, in prestige and popularity (Manzenreiter and Horne 2004; Weinberg 2015).

There are several reasons for this rise in soccer. It is frequently argued that soccer's unusually global reach can be explained by the simplicity of the game and its minimal requirements: a ball and a field (shoes and net optional). Others note that speed and finesse are much more important than physical bulk or height, so the pathway to excellence is wider. These factors are no doubt consequential, but sociopolitical elements have proven critical as well. Unlike baseball and cricket, soccer governance is not associated with a former colonial power; indeed, neither the English nor the U.S. soccer federations are particularly powerful in FIFA. Soccer connects Asian nations not only to one another but also to Europe, Africa, and South America more than any other sport. Soccer is also the team sport that offers the most level playing field across Asia. Japan is powerful in baseball, India in cricket, China in basketball, and so on. Although there are still gross disparities, soccer is the only major team sport that provides parallel men's and women's competitive structures to the highest (World Cup and Olympic) levels. Soccer connects Asian women as well as Asian men through the same FIFA / AFC organization.

Moreover, AFC soccer, among professional spectator sports, has a dual structure of local clubs that are organized into domestic leagues and that often recruit mobile foreign players, and national teams whose roster citizenship requirements are determined by AFC governance and not by nation-state laws. The AFC now controls a staggering calendar of competitions. It runs seventeen All-Asia competitions among national teams, both men's and women's. It also sponsors three separate all-Asia multilevel competitions for clubs. Each of the five constituent regional federations within the AFC runs its own multistage championships for men's and women's national teams of several levels.[7] The sum effect is an extensive and dense web of sports mobility. Clubs are traveling, national teams are traveling, individual players are migrating, soccer citizenship status is fungible, and capital (club team ownership and national team sponsorship) is motile. Soccer's permutations of cross-cutting club and national competitions have created complex situational allegiances, affiliations, and rivalries.

Sporting Goods Commodity Chains across Asia

In April 2013, a garment factory in a Dhaka industrial park collapsed with horrific loss of life; over 1,000 workers were killed and twice as many were buried but rescued. It was a brutal reminder of the sweatshop labor conditions under which many Asian workers suffer to supply the pipelines of commodities to the Global North. Asia's growing centrality to global manufacturing and trade is well documented (Manzenreiter 2014a; Sage 2010). It now accounts for up to one-quarter of total global economic output and one-third of world trade (Manzenreiter 2014b: 230). Less appreciated is the degree to which Asian corporations and entrepreneurial capital are assuming control of this manufacturing and the level to which this output and trade now remain within Asia itself, binding its economies and not just flowing out to other world regions. Roughly half of all manufactured exports are to other Asian nations, and two-thirds of these are intermediate and semifinished goods (Ibid.).

One of the most important sectors of this global manufacturing and distribution is sporting goods (primarily equipment, sportswear, and shoes), and for this, Asian economies are dominant. In 2010, Asia was responsible for over

60 percent of all exports in this sector. As Manzenreiter (2014b: 235) notes, 90 percent of all athletic shoes are manufactured in four Asian nations: China, Vietnam, Indonesia, and Thailand. There are several corollaries of these Asian sports commodity chains. The first is that they are indeed chains of product production; the components of a single pair of sports shoes can be sourced from up to five Asian countries, and assembly itself can be distributed across several locations. Second, while European and American corporations like Asics and Nike predominated markets in the late twentieth century, Asian transnationals like Esquel, Mizuno, and Yue Yuen have assumed control of these production and marketing chains in recent decades.[8] In this feverishly competitive drive to supply world markets for sports shoes, clothing, and equipment (which have become ubiquitous items of everyday life and wear, far beyond the sports field itself), all of these chains of capital and contracts and locations of factories and production are highly transitory. As a political economy of material goods, sports have brought to the workers of Asia instability and insecurity along with unrelenting downward pressures on wages and working conditions.

Migrating Players, Mutable Ethnicities, and Flexible Sports Citizenship

Professional sports were formerly marked by fairly stable team memberships, rigid national barriers to leagues, and tight adherence to nation-state legal definitions of citizenship. None of this is the case now; elite athletes move freely, team rosters and league entry are permeable, the coding of ethnicity is situational, and even the determination of athletes' citizenship has been usurped by national and international sports federations from nation-states. The sports world has become a parallel global structure of governance to the international order of states.

Consider the conditions of mobile athletes in Japan, an instructive case because in the second half of the twentieth century it developed such an exclusionary mono-ethnic cultural nationalism. Even here, sports are having a noticeably solvent effect. About 10 percent of the 800 players in its professional baseball league are non-Japanese from Taiwan, Korea, and Australia and from the United States, Canada, and Central America (Kelly 2017). There is a smaller, reciprocal outflow of Japanese professional players to the US, Mexican, Caribbean, Taiwan, and Korean professional leagues. In the "national sport" of sumo, about 10 percent of the 750 registered wrestlers are non-Japanese, and they dominate the upper ranks, occupying fully 27 of the 42 wrestlers in the top Makunouchi Division (Schreiber 2016). Similar inflows and outflows can be traced for many of the minor sports as well. In distance running, almost all of the world marathon champions from Ethiopia and Kenya over the past two decades have trained and run in Japan with university and corporate clubs (Havens 2015). To date, there have been over 325 foreign rugby union players in university, corporate, and Top League teams; in the 2015 Rugby World Cup, 10 members of the Japanese national team were not Japanese citizens (see Besnier 2012 more generally for rugby ethnicities in Japan). Japan's professional basketball organization, the B.League, has 45 teams in three tiers. Each team can have three foreign players and one naturalized citizen on its roster, for up to 180 foreign players; additionally, any foreign-born player who was educated in Japanese schools is considered to be a Japanese player. "Mobile people" are at the center of almost every sport in Japan in the twenty-first century.

Not surprisingly, we find mobility in multiple forms to be most advanced in soccer (in Japan, the J.League is the top-level professional organization). Some of this connects Japan to soccer centers beyond Asia. Dozens of well-known players from Europe and South America have played for J.League teams, and the Japan national team has had a succession of coaches from Germany, France, Brazil, Bosnia, and Italy as well as a Japanese ex-player. Equally important, though, the J.League and the Japan national team have been platforms for Japan's engagement with South Korean players, with Nikkeijin and others from Brazil and with its own Zainichi Korean players, who often come out of Korean-language high schools in Japan that have long faced significant barriers in sports participation (Manzenreiter and Horne 2004; Kelly 2013).

Over 450 non-Japanese have played in the J.League since 1993, and the largest contingent (about one-quarter) have come from South Korea, Japan's arch regional soccer rival during those years. They often circulate among J.League and (South Korean) K-League contracts and appearances on the South Korean national team, garnering followings for their play with local J.League teams that is suspended when they turn up on the opposite side in international team matches. Fewer in number but equally significant for its ramifications for citizenship and nationality has been the dozen Japan-resident (Zainichi) Korean players.[9]

Their roots and their backgrounds in Japan vary widely. Some have come through the regular Japanese school system, while others went through the special schools operated by Chongryon, the North Korean resident association. Most well known of the latter players is Jong Tae-se, a star in Japan and a star for North Korea. Jong was born in Nagoya, Japan, to second-generation Japan-resident Koreans. His father retained South Korean citizenship, though his mother affiliated herself with the North Korean resident association, Chongryon. She sent her son to a Chongryon-affiliated school and then to Korea University, the private Chongryon university in Tokyo, where he was a soccer standout. Jong was signed to the J.League club Kawasaki Frontale upon graduating in 2005. He had an immediate impact in the league as a striker, and his stylish play and exuberant persona off the field made him a fan favorite, especially among Japanese and Korean youth. As the 2010 World Cup qualifying rounds approached, he was courted by Japan, South Korea, and North Korea. Through his father, he held South Korean citizenship (and Japan residency), but he eventually decided to play for North Korea. Because South Korea does not allow dual citizenship, North Korea issued him a travel passport, which satisfied FIFA rules for soccer citizenship, so he was simultaneously a South Korean citizen, a North Korean passport holder, and a Japan permanent resident permittee. After the 2010 World Cup, he signed with a German club, and in 2012 he was playing with a second German club. In 2013 he joined a South Korean K-League club, and FIFA designated him as a South Korean soccer citizen. Then in 2015, he was bought by Shimizu S-pulse, a J.League club, and returned to Japan, where he continued to play in 2017.

Lee Tadanari is another popular Zainichi player, but he followed a very different trajectory. Born as Lee Chung-sung in 1985 in Tokyo to third-generation Japan-resident parents (his father had played in the Japan corporate soccer league), Lee went to regular Japanese schools and joined a J.League team in 2004 after high school. That year, he also trained with South Korean junior U-10 national teams, but he was shocked at being teased by teammates with racist slurs about being half-Japanese. The Japan Football Association assisted in his becoming a Japanese citizen in 2007, and he adopted the Japanese form of his name, Lee Tadanari. He was immediately selected for the U-23 national team, and then in 2011, playing for Japan's main national team, Lee scored the dramatic overtime goal against Australia to win the Asian Cup for Japan. Lee told a South Korean newspaper in 2011, "I am a Korean person who was born and raised in Japan. Jong Tae-se mentioned this to the media before, but Korean-Japanese can be classified in three ways: Korean, Japanese and Korean-Japanese. Good or bad, we have two to three different identities" (Kim 2011). Despite giving up his South Korean nationality, Lee continued using his full Korean name on his jersey in J-League competition and used his surname on the back of his Japanese national team jersey at the Beijing Summer Olympics. In 2012 he moved to the English club Southampton, which had just gained promotion to the Premier League. In 2014 he signed with the Urawa Red Diamonds in the Japan J.League, for whom he was still playing in 2017.

These two cases and many others like them are instructive examples of at least three consequences of mobile persons in the realm of Asian sports. Even more than in sumo, rugby, and basketball, soccer's flexible sports citizenship is upending the earlier notion that wherever one plays as a club player, he returns "home" to play for his country. As the sociologist Hiroki Ogasawara put it, "The significance of being a member of a nation is now replaced by the possibility of becoming a member [of a nation]" (2004: 33). I would add to his claim that determining just where that floating "home" is located is no longer adjudicated by nation-states and their citizenship laws but by a parallel sports governance structure, in this case FIFA and its eligibility rules.

Third, and most consequential, flexible sports citizenship can have a powerful demonstration effect on national frames and regional geopolitics. The nationality status of ethnic Korean residents in Japan has been a political issue for much of the twentieth century, domestically and regionally, and the discriminations against this significant minority have drawn repeated attention to Japan's nationality and naturalization laws. As the 2010 World Cup approached, Jong Tae-se's choice of which of three national teams to play for was followed and debated by populations of all three countries. In August of that year, the media captured him crying openly as the North Korean anthem was played before the team's qualifying game with Brazil, and during the World Cup games, there were vivid photos of hundreds of Zainichi Korean-Japan residents gathering around television sets in different parts of Japan to watch and cheer Jong and the North Korean team. But after the World Cup, when Jong returned to Japan and to his Japanese club team, he was greeted equally enthusiastically by the throngs of club supporters.

It is critical not only for Japan but also for the emerging shape of northeast Asia in the twenty-first century to gauge how Japan will move in acknowledging and addressing its changing cultural and ethnic composition and how it will rethink its place in a rapidly changing Asia. Since the Pacific War, sports have been part of the problem for Japan because they have embodied dominant and essentializing images of nationalized ethnicity. Now in the new century, sports—at least soccer—may also be part of the way forward in demonstrating a more flexible sports citizenship. Soccer has the potential for broadening the realm of the possible and extending the horizon of expectations. In Japan, it is providing an arena for a more inclusive and creatively expressed multiethnicity evident in team life, in stadium behavior, in supporter association organization, and in league promotion (Kelly 2013). Regionally, it is proving to be, for better or worse, the sports medium that most intensely and most equally engages Japan and its East Asia rivals (and perhaps expanding to a larger notion of Asia) in highly public international competition. The mobility of players and the competitive and flexible sports citizenship of national teams in the Asian arena are decoupling the governance of citizenship from the nation-state.

The aim of this chapter has been to demonstrate how sports contribute to a modeling of Asia as a space of hubs and flows, interconnected across time and place on material, social, and ideological planes. As I have sketched above, the Asian sportscape took initial shape in the late nineteenth century as a conjunction of Asianizing newly introduced Western sports and sportifying indigenous leisure, festive, religious, and military physical regimes. A sportscape spread across the continent through the twentieth century because it was instrumental in expressing both nationalist agendas and competing pan-Asian visions. Asian teams, Asian countries, and Asian capital are now central forces in the most global sports venues—the Olympics and FIFA soccer—as well as multiple other sports. Sports Asia is now a reticulated web of mobile players, commodity chains, multilevel and crosscutting organizations, flexible identities, capital flows, and mega-events.

Of course, we must recognize that the penetrations and forms of modern sports have not been uniform across Asia. This is partly because of the distinct colonial histories and uneven economic development, and partly because of distinctly different nationalist movements and educational pedagogies and the differential tenacity of local sporting practices. The Commonwealth Games define one sphere of Asian sports competition (Baviskar 2010), the Southeast Asian Games another (Creak 2014); the strength of Australian Rules Football inhibits Australian integration into Asian soccer and other sports; and the violent political conditions in southwest Asia have greatly retarded sports at both national and international levels in that region. The long-term trajectory is toward a continental sporting "space of flows," but it is still a decidedly mixed social hydrology at present.

In its inter-Asian reach and multiple mobilities, sports share much with film, music, fashion, cuisines, and other sectors of mass cultural practice. In closing, however, I want to return to the three features of sports that I noted at the outset and that give a distinctiveness to the Asian matrix of sporting hubs and mobilities.First, far more than other sectors of cultural practice, sports combine fixed, universal, and formal codifications of a game with local expressions. The rules of soccer are everywhere exactly the same, and this gives it a binding force; but the game is everywhere played by local teams with distinct strategies and styles and followings. There may be conventions of filmmaking shared by production in Tokyo, Seoul, Hong Kong, and Bollywood, but there is nothing that approaches the "standardization of differences" that sports produce.

Second, sports are preeminently agonistic competitions. They are about winning and, more often, losing, and for that reason simultaneously create enduring solidarities and strong rivalries that bind neighborhoods, regions, and nations as they pit them against one another. Of course, fashion designers and fashion capitals compete for aesthetic recognition and economic success, but this is indirect, secondary, and figurative to the flows of fashion. Sports remind us that connectivity is often about contention. Flows are fractious as well as fluid.

And finally, more thoroughly than film, music, fashion, or cuisine, sports are an uneasy combination of education and entertainment. I have suggested some of the ways by which sports, over the modern decades in Asia, have come to mold personal character, express local identity, and embody national pride, even as they have become immensely profitable. Sports extend from schools to stadiums, from newsrooms to boardrooms, from morning Tai-Chi in the park to drug cheating at Olympic mega-events. They enliven participants and entertain spectators and fill media with content, but the passions of the Asian sportscape are as political as they are playful.

Notes

1. We do not yet have a comprehensive review of Asian sport studies. Some of this scholarship, which is strongest in history and sociology, is cited in the References. Among academic journals, the *International Journal of the History of Sport, Sport in Society, Asia Pacific Journal of Sport and Social Science,* and *Soccer and Society* have been particularly encouraging of Asian sport studies. Because this volume is directed broadly to scholars of Asia, I have avoided Japanese-language references.

2. The body and biopolitics in Asian societies have been subject to much study, for instance, the contributors to Kasulis 1993 and Zito and Barlow 1994. Three of the foundational studies of the sporting body are Alter 1992 for India, Brownell 1995 for China, and Spielvogel 2003 for Japan.

3. See Kelly 2009 for a fuller account of the ways in which a tradition of the Way of the Warrior was selectively fabricated from earlier martial codes in late nineteenth-century Japan and deployed as exhortation, discipline, and nationalist pride in many realms, including sports.

4. Horton 2012 and Pan 2012 are especially useful in formulating this reciprocal relationship. For further cases, see Mangan and Hong 2003; Bromber, Krawietz, and Maguire 2013; and Guttmann and Thompson 2001.

5. Eric Tagliacozzo drew my attention to the Young Men's Buddhist Association, a Buddhist lay movement that began in Ceylon in 1898; similar organizations appeared in Burma in 1908 (Swearer 1970). It was modeled on the YMCA but sought a regeneration of Buddhist initiatives to counter the Christianizing effects of the YMCA. Unlike the latter, though, it was not involved in sports and physical education.

6. I am not sure of the reasons for this comparative neglect, but it is true that the local education systems of the French and Dutch colonial administrations in Southeast Asia did not emphasize sports and physical education in their pedagogies.

7. In fact, it was the rapid growth and rising quality of play in the AFC that prompted Australia and New Zealand to withdraw from FIFA's Oceania Region and join the AFC. Another inspiration, especially for Australia, was the growing economic ties of these nations to the People's Republic of China. Their membership was an emphatic symbol of a shift in their national orientations from the Pacific to Asia.

8. And these Asian transnational corporations, especially Mizuno, have expanded their operations to include significant direct marketing and retailing in Europe and the Americas.

9. The third major category of migrant soccer players are from Brazil, usually Brazilians of Japanese descent. Indeed, I am focusing here on the multiple ways that soccer is connecting Asian nations in complex and overlapping networks, but it is equally significant to note the role that soccer (and the Olympics and other sports federations) plays to situate Asia within a truly global network.

References

Abe, Ikuo. 2007. "Historical Significance of the Far Eastern Championship Games: An International Political Arena." In *Olympic Japan: Ideals and Realities of (Inter) nationalism,* edited by Andreas Niehaus and Max Seinsch, 67–88. Wurzburg: Ergon Verlag.

Abel, Jessamyn R. 2015. *The International Minimum: Creativity and Contradiction in Japan's Global Engagement, 1933–1964.* Honolulu: University of Hawai'i Press.

Alter, Joseph S. 1992. *The Wrestler's Body: Identity and Ideology in North India.* Berkeley and Los Angeles: University of California Press.

———. 2000. "Kabaddi: A National Sport of India: The Internationalism of Nationalism and the Foreignness of Indianness." In *Games, Sports and Cultures,* edited by Noel Dyck, 81–116. Oxford and New York: Berg.

Azoy, G. Whitney. 2011. *Buzkashi: Game and Power in Afghanistan.* Prospect Heights, IL: Waveland Press.

Baviskar, Amita. 2010. "Spectacular Events, City Spaces and Citizenship: The Commonwealth Games in Delhi." In *Urban Navigations: Politics, Space and the City in South Asia,* edited by Jonathan Shapiro Anjaria and Colin McFarlane, 138–161. New Delhi: Routledge.

Besnier, Niko. 2012. "The Athlete's Body and the Global Condition: Tongan Rugby Players in Japan." *American Ethnologist* 31(3): 491–510.

Bromber, Katrin, Birgit Krawietz, and Joseph Maguire, eds. 2013. *Sport across Asia: Politics, Cultures and Identities.* London: Routledge.

Brownell, Susan 1995. *Training the Body for China: Sports in the Moral Order of the People's Republic.* Chicago and London: University of Chicago Press.

Collins, Sandra. 2011. "East Asian Olympic Desires: Identity on the Global Stage in the 1964 Tokyo, 1988 Seoul and 2008 Beijing Games." *International Journal of the History of Sport* 28(16): 2240–2260.

Creak, Simon. 2014. "National Restoration, Regional Prestige: The Southeast Asian Games in Myanmar, 2013." *Journal of Asian Studies* 73(4): 853–877.

Gems, Gerald R. 2006. *The Athletic Crusade: Sport and American Cultural Imperialism.* Lincoln: University of Nebraska Press.

Guha, Ramachandra. 2002. *A Corner of a Foreign Field: The Indian History of a British Sport.* London: Macmillan.

Guttmann, Allen, and Lee Thompson. 2001. *Japanese Sport: A History.* Honolulu: University of Hawai'i Press.

Havens, Thomas R. H. 2015. *Marathon Japan: Distance Racing and Civic Culture.* Honolulu: University of Hawai'i Press.

Hong, Fan, ed. 2006. *Sport, Nationalism and Orientalism: The Asian Games.* London and New York: Routledge.

Hong, Fan, and Hua Tan. 2002. "Sport in China: Conflict between Tradition and Modernity, 1840s to 1930s." *International Journal of the History of Sport* 19(2–3): 189–212.

Horton, Peter. 2011. "Sport in Asia: Globalization, Glocalization, Asianization." In *New Knowledge in a New Era of Globalization,* edited by Piotr Pachura, 119–146. Rijeka: Intech Open-Access Publisher.

———. 2012. "The Asian Impact on the Sportization Process." *International Journal of the History of Sport* 29(4): 511–534.

Huebner, Stefan. 2016. *Pan-Asian Sports and the Emergence of Modern Asia, 1913–1974.* Singapore: National University of Singapore Press.

Inoue, Shun. 1998. "The Invention of the Martial Arts: Kano Jigorō and Kōdōkan judō." In *Mirror of Modernity: Invented Traditions of Modern Japan,* edited by Stephen Vlastos, 163–173. Berkeley and Los Angeles: University of California Press.

Jönsson, Hjorleifur. 2003. "Mien through Sports and Culture: Mobilizing Minority Identity in Thailand." *Ethnos* 68(3): 317–340.

Kasulis, Thomas P., ed. 1993. *Self as Body in Asian Theory and Practice.* Albany: State Univrsity of New York Press.

Kelly, William W. 2009. "Samurai Baseball: The Vicissitudes of a National Sporting Style." *International Journal of the History of Sport* 26(3): 429–441.

———. 2010. "Asia Pride, China Fear, Tokyo Anxiety: Japan Looks Back at Beijing 2008 and Forward to London 2012 and Tokyo 2016." *International Journal of the History of Sport* 27(14): 2428–2439.

———. 2011. "East Asian Olympics, Beijing 2008, and the Globalisation of Sport." *International Journal of the History of Sport* 28(16): 2261–2270.

———. 2013. "Japan's Embrace of Soccer: Mutable Ethnic Players and Flexible Soccer Citizenship in the New East Asian Sports Order." *International Journal of the History of Sport* 30(11): 1235–1246.

———. 2017. "Japan: Professional Baseball in 21st-Century Japan." In *Baseball without Borders: The International Pastime,* edited by George Gmelch and Daniel A. Nathan, 183–201. Lincoln: University of Nebraska Press.

Kim, Jong-ryok. 2011. "Lee Wants a Crack at Korea in AFC Asian Cup Qatar." *Korea JoongAng Daily.* January 10.

Malcolm, Dominic, Jon Gemmell, and Nalin Mehta. 2009. "Cricket and Modernity: International and Interdisciplinary Perspectives on the Study of the Imperial Game." *Sport in Society* 12(4): 431–446.

Mangan, J. A., and Hong Fan, eds. 2003. *Sport in Asian Society: Past and Present* (Sport in the Global Society). London: Frank Cass.

Manzenreiter, Wolfram. 2014a. "Playing by Unfair Rules? Asia's Positioning within Global Sports Production Networks." *Journal of Asian Studies* 73(2): 313–326.

———. 2014b. *Sport and Body Politics in Japan.* New York: Routledge.

Manzenreiter, Wolfram, and John Horne, eds. 2004. *Football Goes East: Business, Culture and the People's Game in China, Japan and South Korea.* London and New York: Routledge.

Mills, James. 2001. "A Historiography of South Asian Sport." *Contemporary South Asia* 10(2): 207–222.

Niehaus, Andreas, and Max Seinsch, eds. 2007. *Olympic Japan: Ideals and Realities of (Inter)nationalism.* Wurzburg: Ergon Verlag.

Ogasawara, Hiroki. 2004. "'Back to the Pitch, Reclaim the Game' Is That Only What Matters? An Outer-National Reading of the World Cup." *Inter-Asia Cultural Studies* 5(1): 28–41.

Pan, Hua. 2012. "Asian Sport: Its Athletic Progress and Social Integration." *International Journal of the History of Sport* 29(4): 553–561.

Reaves, Joseph A. 2002. *Taking in a Game: A History of Baseball in Asia.* Lincoln: University of Nebraska Press.

Sage, George H. 2010. "The Global Sports Industry: Production and Promotion." In *Globalizing Sport: How Organizations, Corporations, Media, and Politics Are Changing Sports,* edited by George H. Sage, 100–139. Boulder, CO: Paradigm Publishers.

Schreiber, Mark. 2016. "Does Sumo Commentary Need to Stress the Foreignness of the Wrestlers?" *Japan Times,* February 6.

Scott, James C. 1998. *Seeing Like a State: How Certain Schemes to Improve the Human Condition Have Failed.* New Haven, CT, and London: Yale University Press.

Spielvogel, Laura. 2003. *Working Out in Japan: Shaping the Female Body in Tokyo Fitness Clubs.* Durham and London: Duke University Press.

Stokes, Martin. 1996. "'Strong as a Turk': Power, Performance and Representation in Turkish Wrestling." In *Sport, Identity, and Ethnicity,* edited by Jeremy MacClancy, 21–42. Oxford and Herndon, VA: Berg Publishers.

Swearer, Donald K. 1970. "Lay Buddhism and the Buddhist Revival in Ceylon." *Journal of the American Academy of Religion* 38(3): 255–275.

Vail, Peter Thomas. 1998. "Violence and Control: Social and Cultural Dimensions of Boxing in Thailand." PhD diss., Cornell University.

Weinberg, Ben. 2015. *Asia and the Future of Football: The Role of the Asian Football Confederation.* Abingdon, Oxon: Routledge.

Zarrilli, Phillip B. 1998. *When the Body Becomes All Eyes: Paradigms, Discourses, and Practices of Power in Kalarippayattu, a South Indian Martial Art.* Delhi and New York: Oxford University Press.

Zito, Angela, and Tani E. Barlow, eds. 1994. *Body, Subject and Power in China.* Chicago and London: University of Chicago Press.

Contributors

Seema Alavi is professor of history at Delhi University. She specializes in early modern and modern South Asia, with interest in the transformation of the region's legacy from Indo-Persian to one heavily affected by British colonial rule. She has written about the military, religious, and medical cultures of South Asia. Her most recent book is *Muslim Cosmopolitanism in the Age of Empire* (Harvard, 2015).

Mounia Chekhab-Abudaya is the curator for North Africa and Iberia at the Museum of Islamic Art in Doha. She completed her PhD in Islamic art history and archaeology at the Pantheon Sorbonne University and specializes in the Western Mediterranean, Islamic manuscripts, and pilgrimage-related devotional materials.

May Bo Ching is professor in the Department of Chinese and History, City University of Hong Kong. Her major research area is the social and cultural history of modern China, focusing in particular on South China and its connection with other parts of the world.

Narges Erami is assistant professor of anthropology and international and area studies at Yale University. She primarily works on the relationship between economy and religion and how it is played out in rituals of everyday life. Her work centers on the holy city of Qum in Iran and focuses on the world of Persian carpets.

Her forthcoming book, *Suspended between Heaven and Earth: Undertaking the Serious Business of Persian Carpets,* is a historical and ethnographic study of carpet merchants and their self-fashioning through the acquisition of specialized knowledge.

Erik Harms is associate professor of anthropology at Yale University, specializing in Southeast Asia, Vietnam, and urban anthropology. He is the author of *Luxury and Rubble: Civility and Dispossession in the New Saigon* (California, 2016) and *Saigon's Edge: On the Margins of Ho Chi Minh City* (Minnesota, 2011).

William W. Kelly is professor emeritus of anthropology and Sumitomo Professor Emeritus of Japanese Studies at Yale University. His research focuses on class and regional society in Japan and on sports and body culture in East Asia. He is the author of *The Sportsworld of the Hanshin Tigers* (California, 2018).

Angela Ki Che Leung is chair professor of history and director of the Hong Kong Institute for the Humanities and Social Sciences at the University of Hong Kong. Her research interests include the history of medicine, food, and health in China in the contexts of Asia and the world.

Tamara Loos is professor of history at Cornell University. Her books include *Bones around My Neck: The Life and Exile of a Prince Provocateur* and *Subject Siam: Family, Law, and Colonial Modernity in Thailand.* Her scholarship explores sex and politics, subversion and foreign policy, sexology, transnational sexualities, sodomy, the family, and citizenship in Asia.

David Ludden is professor and chair in the Department of History at New York University. His research has focused on very long-term histories of globalization in South Asia, particularly as they concern trajectories of capitalist economic development, spatial inequity, natural environments, and changing material conditions in everyday life.

Peter C. Perdue is professor of history at Yale University. His research interests lie in modern Chinese social, economic, and environmental history, the history of frontiers, and world history.

James Pickett is assistant professor in the history department at the University of Pittsburgh. His research focuses on religious networks in central Eurasia from the eighteenth through early twentieth centuries, with particular emphasis on empire and Islam as entangled sources of authority.

Qiang Ma (Ramadan) is professor at the Institute for Western Frontier Region of China, Shaanxi Normal University, and specializes in Islam and Muslim migration in China.

Helen F. Siu is professor of anthropology at Yale University. Since the 1970s she has conducted fieldwork in Southern China, exploring agrarian change, the nature of the state, and the refashioning of identities through community rituals and commerce. Most recently she has explored rural-urban interface in China, historical and contemporary Asian connections, and China-Africa encounters.

Eric Tagliacozzo is professor of history at Cornell University, where he also directs the Comparative Muslim Societies Program and the Cornell Modern Indonesia Project. He is the author of monographs on the history of smuggling and of the Hajj, in and around Southeast Asia.

Emma J. Teng is the T. T. and Wei Fong Chao Professor of Asian Civilizations and a MacVicar Faculty Fellow at MIT. With interests in both Chinese studies and Asian American studies, Teng has worked on issues of race and ethnicity, gender, Chinese frontiers, colonialism, travel writing, migration, and transculturation.

Biao Xiang is professor of social anthropology at the University of Oxford, specializing in migration and social changes in Asia.

Acknowledgments

This volume—the third in a series of three—represents the completion of an idea that has taken a number of us all over Asia in the past decade. We think about Asia "inside out" as a set of processes rather than having any proscribed geography. Toward this end, some three-dozen researchers across a range of disciplines and area-specific expertise were marshaled at three meetings in Hong Kong, Doha, and Hanoi. The workshops were followed by short trips to South India, Oman, and northern Vietnam to experience the themes we had identified together. Funding and logistical support for this multiyear, multisited project came from a number of sources, the Hong Kong Institute for the Humanities and Social Sciences (HKIHSS) being our primary benefactor. Cornell and the Council on East Asian Studies and the Inter-Asia Initiative at Yale have also been very supportive. We are grateful for their help in making this project possible financially and organizationally, over a long period of time, and over the diffuse and outstretched topography of the region.

We wish to acknowledge the many people who have made this last volume of the *Asia Inside Out* series possible over the past two years. First and foremost have been our chapter authors, who graciously lend us their vision of what "Asia" might be. Spending time to share and experience ideas intensely has been one of the salient pleasures of this series, as we have had to move outside our normal bailiwicks of academic exchange. We also wish to thank Angela Leung, director of the HKIHSS, who, in addition to her scholarly contributions, has made sure the organizational gears are oiled so that the project can indeed progress. Joan Cheng, Louise Mak, Yvonne Chan, and Roy Yiu of HKIHSS have been crucial in this regard. We are grateful to Erik Harms, who helped organize the Vietnam trip and has continued to supply scholarly ideas.

Finally, the publishing arm of our enterprise has ensured that the exciting ideas discussed would make it to print. We are very grateful to Kathleen McDermott, our editor at Harvard University Press, for believing in the project and for marshaling us through the publication process. Gershom Tse has intervened with good cheer, astute organizational skills, and artistic choices in readying the manuscript for publication. Rundong Ning provided us with a meticulous reference search and formatting for the introduction. As before, Isabelle Lewis came through with the thoughtfully illustrated maps in the frontmatter and Chapter 12, and Steve Moore with the index. We owe this debt toward Hong Kong, where we have experienced an enticing diversity of cuisines, ethnicities, cultural energies, and historical sensibilities, all contributing to unsettle the static East-West dichotomies. In a similar way, we appreciate Cambridge, Massachusetts, the birthplace of the series. Finally, we all wish to thank a variety of readers over the course of the series who have helped make the books better. *Asia Inside Out* is above all else a communal endeavor that—we hope—shows the power of bringing people together to explore creative ways of thinking. If it succeeds—even slightly—then all the efforts will be worth our while.

Index